Shakespeare, *Romeo and Juliet*, and Civic Life

This volume introduces 'civic Shakespeare' as a new and complex category entailing the dynamic relation between the individual and the community on issues of authority, liberty, and cultural production. It investigates civic Shakespeare through *Romeo and Juliet* as a case study for an interrogation of the limits and possibilities of theatre and the idea of the civic. The play's centres on civil strife, political challenge, and the rise of a new conception of the individual within society makes it an ideal site to examine how early modern civic topics were received and reconfigured on stage, and how the play has triggered ever new interpretations and civic performances over time. The essays focus on the way the play reflects civic life through the dramatization of issues of crisis and reconciliation when private and public spaces are brought to conflict, but also concentrate on the way the play has subsequently entered the public space of civic life. Set within the fertile context of performance studies and inspired by philosophical and sociological approaches, this book helps clarify the role of theatre within civic space while questioning the relation between citizens as spectators and the community. The wide-ranging chapters cover problems of civil interaction and their onstage representation, dealing with urban and household spaces; the boundaries of social relations and legal, economic, political, and religious regulation; and the public dimension of memory and celebration. This volume articulates civic *Romeo and Juliet* from the sources of genre to contemporary multicultural performances in political contact-zones and civic 'Shakespaces,' exploring the Bard and this play within the context of communal practices and their relations with institutions and civic interests.

Silvia Bigliazzi is professor of English literature at Verona University. She has worked on literature and the visual arts, textual and theatrical performance (co-ed, *Theatre Translation in Performance*, Routledge 2013), Shakespeare (*Oltre il genere*, Edizioni dell'Orso 2001; *Nel prisma del nulla,* Liguori 2005; *Romeo e Giulietta*, Einaudi 2012; co-ed, *Revisiting* The Tempest. Palgrave 2014), and Donne (co-ed., *Poesie*, Rizzoli 2009).

Lisanna Calvi is lecturer of English literature at Verona University. She is author of a book on Restoration tragedy (*Kingship and Tragedy*, QuiEdit 2005) and on James II (*La corona e la Croce*, ETS 2009) and she has edited *Memoria, maliconia e autobiografia dello spirito* (Pacini 2012) and co-edited *Revisiting* The Tempest (Palgrave 2014).

Routledge Studies in Shakespeare

1 **Shakespeare and Philosophy**
   Stanley Stewart

2 **Re-playing Shakespeare in Asia**
   Edited by Poonam Trivedi and Minami Ryuta

3 **Crossing Gender in Shakespeare**
   Feminist Psychoanalysis and the Difference Within
   James W. Stone

4 **Shakespeare, Trauma and Contemporary Performance**
   Catherine Silverstone

5 **Shakespeare, the Bible, and the Form of the Book**
   Contested Scriptures
   Travis DeCook and Alan Galey

6 **Radical Shakespeare**
   Politics and Stagecraft in the Early Career
   Christopher Fitter

7 **Retheorizing Shakespeare through Presentist Readings**
   James O'Rourke

8 **Memory in Shakespeare's Histories**
   Stages of Forgetting in Early Modern England
   Jonathan Baldo

9 **Reading Shakespeare through Philosophy**
   Peter Kishore Saval

10 **Embodied Cognition and Shakespeare's Theatre**
    The Early Modern Body-Mind
    Edited by Laurie Johnson, John Sutton, and Evelyn Tribble

11 **Mary Wroth and Shakespeare**
    Edited by Paul Salzman and Marion Wynne-Davies

12 **Disability, Health, and Happiness in the Shakespearean Body**
    Edited by Sujata Iyengar

13 **Skepticism and Belonging in Shakespeare's Comedy**
    Derek Gottlieb

14 **Shakespeare, *Romeo and Juliet*, and Civic Life**
    The Boundaries of Civic Space
    Edited by Silvia Bigliazzi and Lisanna Calvi

Shakespeare, *Romeo and Juliet*, and Civic Life
The Boundaries of Civic Space

Edited by Silvia Bigliazzi and
Lisanna Calvi

LONDON AND NEW YORK

First published 2016
by Routledge

2 Park Square, Milton Park, Abingdon, Oxfordshire OX14 4RN
52 Vanderbilt Avenue, New York, NY 10017

Routledge is an imprint of the Taylor & Francis Group, an informa business

First issued in paperback 2019

Copyright © 2016 Taylor & Francis

The right of the editors to be identified as the authors of the editorial material, and of the authors for their individual chapters, has been asserted in accordance with sections 77 and 78 of the Copyright, Designs, and Patents Act 1988.

All rights reserved. No part of this book may be reprinted or reproduced or utilised in any form or by any electronic, mechanical, or other means, now known or hereafter invented, including photocopying and recording, or in any information storage or retrieval system, without permission in writing from the publishers.

otice
Product or corporate names may be trademarks or registered trademarks, and are used only for identification and explanation without intent to infringe.

Library of Congress Cataloging-in-Publication Data

Shakespeare, Romeo and Juliet, and civic life: the boundaries of civic space / edited by Silvia Bigliazzi and Lisanna Calvi.
   pages cm. — (Routledge studies in Shakespeare)
Includes bibliographical references and index.
   1. Shakespeare, William, 1564–1616. Romeo and Juliet. 2. Shakespeare, William,
   1564–1616—Criticism and interpretation. 3. Literature and society—England—
   History—16th century. 4. Literature and society—England—History—17th century.
   I. Bigliazzi, Silvia, 1968- editor. II. Calvi, Lisanna, editor.
PR2831.S35 2015
822.3'3—dc23   2015016544

ISBN: 978-1-138-83998-4 (hbk)
ISBN: 978-0-367-87194-9 (pbk)

Typeset in Sabon
by codeMantra

Contents

Introduction   1
SILVIA BIGLIAZZI AND LISANNA CALVI

Prologue: Shakespeare and Verona   35
STANLEY WELLS

PART I
Dialectics of Private and Public Spaces

1 Classical Paradigms of Tragic Choice in Civic Stories of Love and Death   45
GUIDO AVEZZÙ

2 Private and Public Spheres and the 'Civic Turn' in Da Porto, Bandello, and Shakespeare's *Romeo and Juliet*   66
ROBERT HENKE

3 Shakespeare as 'Chief Architect and Plotter': *Romeo and Juliet* and Civic Space   82
ROY ERIKSEN

4 Inside-Outside: Love, Household, and City in *Romeo and Juliet*   100
MERA J. FLAUMENHAFT

5 Defiance and Denial: Paradigms of Civic Transgression and Transcendence in *Romeo and Juliet*   115
SILVIA BIGLIAZZI

6 Tying the Knot in "fair Verona": The Private and Public Spaces of Marriage in *Romeo and Juliet*   147
LISANNA CALVI

7 Silencing the Natural Body: Notes on the Monumental
   Body in *Romeo and Juliet*   171
   SILVIA BIGLIAZZI AND LUCIA NIGRI

PART II
Civic Performances and R&Jspaces

8 "For these dead birds sigh a prayer"   187
   PAUL EDMONDSON

9 "Wherefore art thou Marius?": Otway's Adaptation of
   Romeo and Juliet   202
   LORETTA INNOCENTI

10 Brooke, Garrick, *Romeo and Juliet*, and the Public Sphere   213
   MICHAEL DOBSON

11 At Juliet's Tomb: Anglophone Travel-Writing and Shakespeare's
   Verona, 1814–1914   224
   NICOLA J. WATSON

12 Producing a (R&)Jspace: Discursive and
   Social Practices in Verona   238
   SILVIA BIGLIAZZI AND LISANNA CALVI

13 *Perché sei tu?*: Lindsay Kemp's "gift of memory"   260
   JACQUELYN BESSELL

14 Stage(d) Reconciliations: *Romeo and Juliet* and the Politics of
   Bilingual Shakespeare Productions in Germany   278
   BETTINA BOECKER

   Afterword: "What's past is prologue": Civic Shakespeare in
   Romeo and Juliet and Beyond   291
   EWAN FERNIE AND PAUL EDMONDSON

   Contributors   299
   Index   305

Introduction
Silvia Bigliazzi and Lisanna Calvi

TALKING CIVIC

Choosing to explore a play like *Romeo and Juliet,* famous for its original recasting of an age-old love-and-death theme in ways that have survived the centuries, superseding in the collective memory all other competing stories (its narrative progenitors included), suggests an urge to look at it with an awareness of its irreducibility to mono-dimensional issues. It means claiming that the play exceeds its romanticized readings and its own intrinsic potential for sentimentality; it also means vindicating textual, conceptual, and performative complexity while acknowledging the play's capacity to stretch beyond the boundaries of all hypertrophies of subjectivity in order to relocate it within a wider context of social, political, and cultural dynamics, underscoring dialectics as the unavoidable core of its signifying power. Following Hegel's notorious magnification of the subject's tragic inner experience through the excision of the character's implication in societal conflicts, both in the past, and very recently,[1] Shakespearean tragedies, and this play in particular, have often been removed from the proper site of the manifold conflicting stances from which an original conception of tragic subjectivity eventually emerged. Civic space provides precisely one of the components of that manifold site of production of meaning, if not a tensional site itself, at once belonging to, and transcending, the political, historical, and broadly speaking cultural dimension of its original springing. Yet civic space is also a potential locus of re-actualization of that tragic core (and more generally dramatic dimension). Nowadays, it often provides the setting for globalized practices of appropriation and construction of Shakespeare-related places as well as for the performance of what Hedrick and Reynolds more generally call "Shakespaces", or territories traversing "discourses, adaptations, and uses'" of Shakespeare (2000, 1). The civic sphere allows to test drama's capacity for communal performance, but may also display (as typically in the case of *Romeo and Juliet*) living vestiges and prompt social practices contributing to an ongoing production and reproduction of public areas lived in civically, often with implications of commodity marketization (Lanier 2002, 142–67).

Thus the notion of 'civic Shakespeare' is more specific than political, popular, historical, and cultural Shakespeare, while at the same time it shares some of those features. The term 'popular', in particular, rests on a very shaky terrain. It has entered a fluctuating critical jargon encompassing notions of popularity etymologically related to an idea of people that has changed over time. It has gradually come to signify low culture, as opposed to high culture, entertainment, as well as folk traditions (Gillespie and Rhodes 2006).[2] If, as Shaughnessy sums up, 'popular' "denotes community, shared values, democratic participation, accessibility, and fun", but also "the mass-production commodity, the lowest common denominator, the reductive or the simplified, or the shoddy, the coarse, and the meretricious" (2007, 2), the civic only partially overlaps with this notion. At the same time, the political too invades the sphere of civic Shakespeare, by spurring discussions of operations of power in civic contexts, in ways that stretch from classical materialist readings of political Shakespeare (as in Dollimore and Sinfield 1985), to possible investigations relying on critical discourse analysis (Fairclough 1989 and 2013), to the adoption of critical tools derived from urban explorations focused upon the social production of space (Lefebvre 1991; Kilian 1998). And yet, the political does not identify itself entirely with the civic either. Historically, this word was used as a primary qualification of distinction, designating "the crown or garland of oak leaves and acorns given in ancient Rome as a mark of distinction to a person who saved the life of a fellow citizen in war" (*OED*, 1). But more precisely it concerned the rights and duties of citizens (*OED*, 2), the administration of a city (*OED*, 3), and was opposed to military life (*OED*, 4), while the synonym 'civil' (and 'civility') evoked "absence of anarchy or disorder" (*OED*, *n*.2). The word 'civic', therefore, denotes the communal life of a city, or polis, as opposed to spaces lacking institutions, cultural codes (legal, moral, etc.) and customs, but also to subgroups of 'specialized' people (such as soldiers). Thus this category includes both public and private spaces, and yet, intriguingly enough, it is not identical with their sum, disclosing that 'public' and 'private' themselves are shifting categories, often mutually permeable depending on social practices and norms. Thus while, on the one hand, civic spaces are the social arenas of conflicts and reconciliations between the 'public' and the 'private', on the other hand, they may also be considered as alternative to both. It is precisely this double, challenging perspective that will be explored in this volume.

The choice of *Romeo and Juliet* among Shakespeare's plays depends on its offering peculiar instances of the interaction between the multifarious civil stances recalled above. The social dynamics underlying the tensional but also fluid dimension of civic spaces and practices is precisely what is dramatized in *Romeo and Juliet* and what continues to be experimented upon in its afterlife performances. In this light, *Romeo and Juliet* is especially revealing because it focuses very closely on the early modern shaping of this complex idea of the civic through civil strife, family relations, political challenge, and the rise of a new conception of the individual in the face of issues of liberty and constraint. Other Shakespearean plays, such as *Coriolanus*, have elicited interpretations of the civic dimension as constitutive of their dramatic texture.[3] Yet *Romeo and Juliet* is particularly flexible in this respect because it foregrounds several different civic issues and their interaction at sundry levels, showing that its own tragic core relies on a peculiar intersection between the governance of the city, household feuding, and the individual participation in, and transgression of, urban life. On the other hand, the play's prolific capacity to stimulate forms of cultural, economic, and civic creativity to an unparalleled degree, has favoured over time the peculiar formation of alternative civic spaces, stratified with several ideological and competing discourses and social practices. Experiments in 'R&J urban spaces' have been carried out so that the play has come to affect concretely the life of the community and of visitors alike. Verona is a brilliant example of how a city may be turned into a global Shakespearean icon and of how civic performance may enliven – and commodify – an urban space.

It is no surprise that *Romeo and Juliet* has triggered fresh responses and reinterpretations of its civic dimension across the centuries, iterating age-old communal transactions and cultural conflicts, but also offering variations and prompting reflection upon the "Bardification of culture" (Kennedy 1998, 175). How do theatre in general, and Shakespeare in particular, participate in civic dynamics questioning the mobility of the private and the public? How does drama participate in the re-shaping of both spaces, and how has *Romeo and Juliet* dramatized civic issues, while in turn being re-utilized and performed in civic contexts?

Study of pre-Shakespearean patterns of love and death conditioned and absorbed by civic conflict will inaugurate the exploration of this play's wide-ranging topics in an expansive time span, helping analyze their persistence in the play's after-life. This will show how similar questions linger on over time but also change diachronically, interrogating forms of civic violence and individual liberty. Going beyond the Renaissance, it will then be possible to look at the ways in which the play's civic appropriations, celebrations, and re-articulations through time shape new forms of civic transaction, posing those same civic questions for us today. But why theatre and the civic?

THEATRE, PERFORMANCE, AND CITY SPACE

"[D]rama, unlike poetry, is a territorial art. It is an art of space as well as words, and it requires a place of its own, in or around a community, in which to mount its telling fictions and its eloquent spectacle" (Mullaney 1995, 7). Intrinsically social, theatre first established itself as a response to the city. From its beginning down to our time, theatre's agency has been implicated with social life, which it reflects and tests precisely because social life itself, "even in its apparently quietest moments, is characteristically 'pregnant' with social dramas. The primordial and perennial agonistic mode is the social drama" (Turner 1982, 11). Theatre, "including puppetry and shadow theatre, dance drama, and professional story-telling ... probe[s] a community's weaknesses, call[s] its leaders to account, desacralize[s] its most cherished values and beliefs, portray[s] its characteristic conflicts and suggest[s] remedies for them, and generally take[s] stock of its current situation in the known 'world'" (ibid., 12). How complex the relation between theatre and the city is appears from a quick glance at its Greek origins. From antiquity, the idea of civic performance coincided with the political establishment of theatre as an institutional form of entertainment and active participation in the life of the polis. Plays were selected by the eponymous archon the summer preceding the calendared event and were scheduled throughout the year. Control was exerted over the management of spectacles and the Dionysia, as well as over the choice of topics for their ethical and political relevance. Thus theatre as a civic institution was from the start ideologically and politically engaged (see Vernant and Vidal-Naquet 1988; Longo 1990). A precise protocol regulated also other civic events belonging to that festival (Guettel Cole 1993), such as processions through the streets of Athens, award-giving ceremonies dedicated to orphans, the presentation of homages received from foreign countries, and so on, as if the city wished to represent itself publicly even before staging civic narratives. Famously, Richard Schechner described the space in which the theatrical event took place in fifth-century Athens as a replica of the societal structure of the city fostering a sense of belonging in the citizens:

> Nested at the center of the Athenian theater was the open eye of the Altar of Dionysus. Around it danced the Chorus, giving a core of solidarity for the agonistic actions of the actors. The audience nested both Chorus and actors. But the agon of the contest among poets and actors for the prizes surrounded the whole theatrical event. Yet the solidarity of Athens, the polis, provided the ultimate nest for the entire sequence of performances and contests. Each agon was literally held in a nest of solidarity. The outer nest – the polis – was not metaphorical: there were definite geographical, ideological, and social limits to Athens; and each person knew what it was to be a citizen. The shape of the theater was a version of the social system which alternated agon and solidarity; it was open to debate and interrogation, but closed about who was or was not a member, a citizen. (2003, 180)

Simplified though this description may be,[4] it however conveys a distinctive idea of the actual incorporation of the theatre into the polis. Besides the dramatic contests in the theatre, other pre-theatrical performances, expressions of social groups not yet established into the polis, were also called civic. These were revels, carousals, merry making, and festive processions including sung odes, and belonged to the κῶμος [kômos], which would later develop into comedy. The Dionysiac and amateurish performances of the dithyramb, originally sung by male groups representative of the polis, turned instead into tragedy. Thus, from antiquity the idea of a civic theatre has been linked precisely with institutional authorities, rather than with unprofessional and spontaneous events, as well as with the construction of an ethical and political ideology for the city.

Yet theatres have not always been the expression of the city. Mullaney (1995), for instance, has clearly elucidated the relation between fifth-century Athens and Elizabethan London theatres and theatrical practices pointing out similarities and differences. Located outside the city's jurisdiction, in the liberties, early modern London theatres were a significant, if controversial, example of a contrary conception of drama relying on the power of the extra-civic location, profiting from unruliness and relative freedom. Situated in this extraterritorial site, marked by being either outside of the walls or simply on the other side of the Thames as a natural socio-political, and semiotic, boundary, open-air theatres notoriously took advantage of their urban dislocation outside the jurisdiction of the City, while suffering from political ostracism. The opposition between the intramural area, comprising official institutions, and its outside spaces, which still belonged to the metropolis according to a complex geopolitical system, connoted the cultural dynamism of the same metropolis. While the "trade guilds were confined largely to the City itself", which points to their being "the defenders of traditional ideas of community in London", the immigrants, the vagrants as well as the actors gathered in the liberties, making them "the vanguard of a more modern society" (Ward 1997, 3; see also Barish 1981; Pugliatti 2003 and 2008). In this more fluid, marginal, and dynamic dimension, the open-air theatres established an articulated relation with the Crown and the City, negotiating modes and strategies of dialogue, as well as opposition.[5] As Mullaney points out, the stage in Elizabethan London, as in Athens in the fifth century BC,

> reflects the cultural and ideological situation of drama, but the map of Elizabethan culture thus provided reveals the configuration of a distinctly different social system: not a geographically and ideologically closed system, but one that was in the process of opening up, of becoming unbound and less tightly coherent. (1995, 8)[6]

London open-air theatres were an eccentric phenomenon, both territorially and because looked at with suspicion from the City's governors, if not with outright opposition, as famously happened in the antitheatricalists' attacks inspired by Tertullian's *De spectaculis* (23). Civilly immoral, because places of camouflage and identity falsification through impersonation and cross-dressing, they were also ambiguously attractive and seductive, loci of pleasure alluring flocks of citizens. As an alarmed and terrified Philip Stubbes famously wrote in his *Anatomy of Abuses* (1583), one could see

> the flocking and running to theatres and curtains, daily and hourly, night and day, time and tide, to see plays and interludes, where such

wanton gestures, such bawdy speeches, such laughing and fleering, such kissing and bussing, such clipping and culling, such winking and glancing of wanton eyes, and the like is used, as is wonderful to behold. Then these goodly pageants being done, every mate sorts to his mate, everyone brings another homeward of their way very friendly, and in their secret conclaves (covertly) they play the sodomites, or worse. (1877–79, 144–5)

In turn, Anthony Munday underscored the contagious corruption of theatre by suggesting an active participation of the spectators in the action played out on stage, since "only the filthiness of plays and spectacles is such as maketh both the actors and beholders guilty alike. For while they saw nought, but gladly look on, they all by sight and assent are actors" (*A Second and a Third Blast of Retreat from Plays and Theatre*, 1580; Pollard ed. 2004, 66). Theatres, in a word, were places of Satanic temptation and transgression, as William Rankins eloquently wrote in his *A Mirror of Monsters* (1587):

First, they [the actors] are sent from the great captain Satan ... to deceive the world, to lead the people with enticing shows to the devil to seduce them to sin, and well-tuned strings to sound pleasing melody when people in heaps dance to the devil. But rather seem they the limbs, proportion and member of Satan.

First, are they his head that study to deceive the people with enticing shows, which (if Hydras) the sword of justice might soon cut. They are his tongues, which roar out pleasing (but yet damnable) tales into the ears of the people, easily pulled out by justice. They are his arms that stretch out to catch the people within the compass of his chain, whose joints justice may break. They are his cloven feet that plod in damned paths, in whose steps spring up sundry seeds of deadly desires. (ibid., 126)

As Stephen Orgel has rightly remarked in his discussion of Renaissance catharsis, a play such as Massinger's *The Roman Actor* (1626) precisely staged "the charge that mimesis can only be pernicious, since we inevitably imitate the bad and ignore the good; it shows drama confirming us in our passions, not purging them, and far from providing moral exempla, turning us into monsters of lust" (2002, 141). In short, what this well-known polemics points out is the actual implication of theatre in society in ways that publicly reveal its mimicking potential and its capacity to involve actively in the performance actors and citizens alike, representing social relations precisely as they occur in, and are being performed by, society itself.[7] In Turner's words, everyday life is "intrinsically connected with acting and vice versa" (1982, 113), and this is something that theatre made apparent already at that time, when everything was felt to be akin to amoral acting and suggesting faking and counterfeiting. Thus, not differently from the theatrical polemics, critique of clothing too was especially intense. Apparels in town soon became objects of attention, and against them proclamations were emitted. In 1574 the so-called Statutes of Apparel were enforced not only to cut on expenditures, but also in order to maintain a class system relying upon rules for attire. In 1583 an edict condemned dress-disorder as cause of social confusion – a topic that also appeared in that *Anatomie of Abuses* where John Stubbes fiercely attacked the actors too: "There is such a confuse mingle mangle in apparel in Ailgna [i.e. England], and such preposterous excess thereof, as every one is permitted to flaunt it out, in what apparell he lust himselfe, or can get by anie kind of meanes. So that it is very hard to knowe, who is noble, who is worshipfull, who is gentleman, who is not" (1877–79, 34). In the same *Anatomy* Stubbes also cited Schoolmaster Richard Averell's *Merualous Combat of Contrarieties* (1588) for his attack on those women who "from the top to the toe, are so disguised, that though they be in sexe Women, yet in attire they appear to be men, and are like Androgini, who counterfayting the shape of either kind, are in deede neither, so while they are in condition women, and oulde seeme in apparrell men, they are neither men nor women, but plaine Monsters" (ibid., 254). In fact such attacks on the elemental dynamics of interpersonal appearances and relations through clothes and disguises unveiled an awareness of a theatrically grounded conception of subjectivity upon which society itself was (and is) based.[8] Thus magnified on stage, this elemental dynamics constituted only one of the basic aspects of a dialogue between stage and town that then traversed other and more articulated social practices concerning the same political governance of the State as well as the city.[9]

Theatres, though, were located also within London intramural territory of civic institutions, and this suggested closer control and forms of mutual compliance. These were the inns of court as well as indoor halls, sites of performances of companies of boys, especially, at least in the 1576–1608 period, which produced what Mullaney has termed an "interstitial form of drama representing a less incontinent breach of civic authority than the playhouses outside the city" (1995, 53). In accordance with a more centralized and less contestant cultural dimension of the inside area of the metropolis, they were "a contained form of social critic, one that relies, as pre-Elizabethan drama had always done, on a stable and circumscribing social structure" (ibid.). Lucy Munro has more recently contested this position, claiming that in fact they too threatened the stability of the early years of King James, and that they did not efface the actual multivocal dimension of audience response, by their active interaction with the audience, who participated in the quips and even seated on the stage increasing physical proximity with the actors (Munro 2005, 72ff).[10] However, the arenas in the liberties were certainly more flexible and ideologically subversive, and clearly contrasted with a number of other official types of performances which took place within the metropolitan confines, in the streets, as royal exhibitions and negotiations of power. As Mullaney again has pointed out, the unfolding of royal pageants "invited Elizabeth's response, making her both audience to and central actor in the ongoing dramaturgy of state, they also shaped and qualified that response, eliciting vows of a peaceful, harmonious, and above all Protestant rule from the incipient queen" (1995, 11).[11] As Richard Mulcaster put it in *The Queens' Majestie's Passage*, the city of London was being turned into a stage for the "dramatic setting of Elizabeth's passage" and was "converted ... into a series of quite literal stages and scaffolds, erected at significant junctures along the way" (ibid.). But then, of course, London was also the site of a whole series of other street performances upon which studies of popular early modern culture have long focused.[12] This is just to say that the rooting of theatrical practices in early modern London took different and competing forms. All of them contributed to shaping a constellation of practices and discourses that set up circulating ideologies regarding citizenry, governance, and social identity. The intertwining of theatrical, popular, and royal performances in urban as well as extra-urban spaces socially produced highly diversified discourses of power and contestation, becoming consubstantial with the life of the city itself.

This stratification of different political, ideological, and social drives in the early modern metropolitan context strangely anticipates the manifold forms of civic interaction that theatre has developed across time. Drama and its performance, in its manifold instances, took on a broader meaning than playing within an indoor theatre only, pointing to various forms of both localized and unlocalized urban practices (see, for example, Carlson 1989). Resuming a comparison with Greek theatre, Schechner has underlined the transformation that official theatre gradually underwent over the centuries by acquiring the proscenium-type of architecture we know today. Closure and concealment of "the wings, flies, dressing-rooms, offices, and storage bins" replaced openness and visible contact with "the city and the countryside behind and around the theatre" (2003, 182). The early modern open-air theatres too excluded close contact with the city while being physically and jurisdictionally cut out from it. As today, however, theatrical performance took also different guises, relying on itinerant and occasional open-area impromptu structures as well as street practices, thus reflecting for the community and in their own un-precinct spaces the sense of everyday social life's own theatricality. From antiquity until today theatrical performances in fact have intersected civic life at various levels, bringing back closer contact with the community. In the twentieth century, for instance, "the open-theater movement ... has once again made the playing space part of the viewing space", by resorting to "thrust stage, arena, environmental theatre" (ibid.), leading to more recent experimental forms of communal performance in alternative urban spaces, such as documentary theatre, public art, and post-dramatic theatre. Shannon Jackson has made an extensive study on how art may function precisely as social activity and infrastructural aesthetics, that is, an art that engages with society so as to prompt reflection upon the interlacing of human and civic infrastructures (Jackson 2011). Yet the notion of performance itself is wider than this, and it is from communal forms of appropriation and relocation to not pre-set theatrical spaces that a broader idea of theatre may draw nourishment. In 1996 Joseph Roach offered a lengthy discussion of the close connection between performance, city, and remembrance, identifying three main meanings of the word performance: "to furnish forth", "to complete" or "carry out thoroughly" (as suggested by Turner 1982, 13; see also Bigliazzi 2002); to actually execute "an action as opposed to its potential" (as claimed by Bauman 1981); "restored behaviour" or "twice behaved behaviour" (Schechner 1985, 36–7), meaning that the fleeting performance is always "subject to revision" because it "cannot happen exactly the same way twice".[13] Roach assumed that in these three cases this word "stands in for an elusive entity that it is not but that it must vainly aspire both to embody and to replace", which suggests an affinity "between performance and memory", as a "[n]ostalgia for authenticity and origin" (1996, 3–4). Environmental performance, and its varied urban locations, including spontaneous, artistic, institutional or semi-institutional celebrations, locate precisely this idea of performance as nostalgia within the urban setting as a way to produce public spaces of memory.

From the city's original incorporation of the theatre and its later gradual dislocation to marginal places of potential subversion, with consequent practices of ideological, discursive, and social boundary-crossing, to the relocation of theatrical practices in the wider and potentially unlocalized spaces of the city, theatre and drama performance show their deep implication with an idea of the civic as a complex category involving multifarious social and communal practices. Plays absorb and reflect the conflicts and dynamics of the city they inhabit, but also produce civic spaces through social performances that interrogate the interdependence between the aesthetic domain, the public infrastructures, and the communal life (see for instance Harvie 2009). To such an interrogation the following pages are devoted by selecting one particular play as testing ground for the potential and limits of this intersection between drama and the city through forms of participation in, reflection upon, or violation of circulating ideologies and social practices. By selecting one play, the volume will explore some of these issues, providing a first, tentative, but systematic attempt to probe how drama both absorbs civic stances and, in turn, contributes to reshaping communal spaces, discourses, and practices. In particular, the essays here collected will explore how *Romeo and Juliet* articulates the following issues:

1 The city's social dynamics and spatial boundaries are absorbed and reinvented by dramas in ways that become relevant to the construction and articulation of complex messages and genres.
2 The city becomes one major locus of reflection upon the ideas of private and public spaces stimulating the audiences' response and agency in theatrical performances of civically aware texts.
3 The city provides conceptually devised as well as unlocalized and fluid settings for artistic and social performances related to the play that

produce public spaces where the community sees itself reflected in a continuous exchange between socially constructed urban settings and civic-oriented performances (readings, celebrations, etc.).
4 The city is transformed into civic hyperreal or fictional settings related to overtly authorial or mythical dimensions (such as Shakespeare-related places), spurring practices of communal and national identification, as well as forms of artistic commodification and popular migrations.

These points may be further articulated as well as recast in order to promote other possible investigations of either specifically or non-specifically civically oriented drama.

But why *Romeo and Juliet*?

WHY ROMEO AND JULIET

The civil dimension of this play is exemplary of a wide range of critical and performative possibilities which can be drawn here only selectively by signalling still fresh areas of research, some of which will be discussed in the essays collected in this volume. Schematically following the four categories identified earlier, here are only a few indications about why *Romeo and Juliet* in line of principle may prove particularly fertile:

1 *The interplay between the off stage city's spatial and social boundaries and their representation onstage:* the play's original performance location in the liberties is not devoid of ideological consequences bearing upon the civic as a dialectic category concerning the modes of its production and those of its reception. As Andrew Gurr has pointed out, the play was mounted "at the Theatre and from 1597 at the Curtain" (1996, 15), which may also suggest why Shakespeare might have devised particular spatial artifices that increased the sense of how space could be socially produced in complex ways. He could avail himself of peculiar facilities, such as a balcony, a trap door, the discovery space, allowing for a subtle articulation of an ideology of stage space. It has also been contended that Shakespeare might instead have started working on it during the plague years when theatres were closed; this would explain experimentation with lyrical forms and foregrounded stylization more attuned to an indoor production by a company of children. With the re-opening of theatres, though, he might have forgotten about it all, including the Choruses in sonnet form, and, having in mind a different audience and location, he might have added comic pieces, such as the one that has as protagonist William Kemp, who in 1594 joined Shakespeare's Company, the Lord Chamberlain's Men (Melchiori 1983). Whether this entailed a change in the conception of the play depending on circumstances, prospective venue, and audience,

or not, *Romeo and Juliet* eventually portrayed a variegated civic populace stressing class difference and roles. It included servants, musicians, the Nurse, the Friar, citizens as a civil militia, gentlemen of different social status, the Prince. The play also needed portable properties signifying social diversity and practices as well as civic conflicts (Levenson 1995): from swords, rapiers, partisans, bucklers and clubs, to fans (for the Nurse in 2.3), rope climbing ladders, masks, torches, mattocks, spades, crowbars, and so on (Gurr 1989, 22). All this reproduced, and produced, different social spaces and actions providing a compelling representation of communal life in its articulate class shadings. Although the term "'class' may be somewhat anachronistic for the sixteenth century" (Gillespie and Rhodes 2006, 6),[14] *Romeo and Juliet* reflects class difference and antagonism and one wonders how social tensions as well as a questioning of city governance might have been received by an audience including 'people' as citizens. Amphitheatres' audiences were extremely variegated, including, especially among the groundlings, artisans, merchants, but also whores as well as coney-catchers, and it was precisely from "citizens who upheld the values of the City" that the companies and theatres found support (Gurr 1987, 72; see also 54–79). For sure, "Juliet's rebellion against the Capulets' insistence that she marry the man of her parents' choice was an act of disloyalty which few London citizens were ready to applaud (ibid., 149). As noted by Loehlin (2002, 5), however, their exact reaction to the play and to its representation of civic tensions can only remain open to speculation, while inviting questions on its reception then and now.

2 *The representation and interrogation of public and private spaces*: *Romeo and Juliet*'s precise demands on the venue relied especially on its multiple-stage resources. The arena could provide solutions for situating the action in often adjoining but visibly different spaces on multiple stage levels, thus representing not only sundry inside areas of the house, but also outside locations. Two scenes, in particular, have called attention for the complexity of their staging, interlacing inside and outside spaces, and subtly hinting at overlapping connotations: the balcony and the tomb scenes.[15] Relying on the flexible dramaturgical potential of the unlocalized stage, Shakespeare introduced smooth shifts from Juliet's balcony to her bedroom, to the orchard and the interior of Capulet's house, all in the course of slightly more than two hundred lines. Likewise he craftily played with movements and props in the cemetery scene, suggesting sudden changes between the private and the public dimensions of the monument and the cemetery. This must have stimulated the audience to reflect upon the effects of such overlap in a period when the public and the private were considered very ambivalent categories. On the one hand, the private sphere was undergoing a process of gradual reconsideration with a growing emphasis on the value of privacy (Cowen Orlin 2008; see also Richardson 2006). On the

other hand, household spaces retained 'semi-public' functions, as in the case of the bedroom which at once was an intimate place and "the site of important public rituals of birth, wedding, and death" (Neill 2000, 266). As regards the public dimension of the street, this area was perceived as a transitional place "never completely separate from other public spaces or from private spaces", so as to make it intrinsically liminal (Laitinen and Cohen 2009, 1).[16] In the early modern period, this "liminality" foregrounded the "ambiguity of 'public' and 'private'" (ibid.), and, like other social spaces, showed that it is social practices and norms that define their status, standardizing behavioural rules. This is how spaces came (and come) to be perceived by people. As Ted Kilian has put it, the public and the private "are expressions of power relations in space, and hence, both exist in every space" (1998, 116). Thus, a play like *Romeo and Juliet*, intimately based on a dramaturgy of space production (in Kilian terms), invites to raise questions on the different orders of spaces it represents, from the street to the household and other communal spaces.

The interaction between the social and ideological position of the theatre and the performance of civic ideologies, conflicts, etc., on the one hand, and on the other and the dramatization of civic spaces and public/private issues penetrate the afterlife of *Romeo and Juliet Juliet*. This has happened in famous and less famous reinventions, such as Broadway *West Side Story* (1957), with its glamorous Hollywood movie rendition (1961), and its more recent extravagant Italian offspring *Sud Side Stori* (2000) by Roberta Torre (on which see Calbi 2011). As remarked by Kottman, the Laurents-Robbins-Bernstein musical and film version (co-directed by Robert Wise) emphasize a New York-based "broader ethnical tribal struggle or gang war, in which the lovers are caught up and by which they are defeated", reshaping the concept itself of "tragic", turned into the catastrophic fate of Tony and Maria who find themselves "at the wrong time among wrong people" (2012, 6). The more recent Palermitan setting of Torre's film projects the story's civic dimension into an interracial space which offers also an exploration of the signifying potential of its Sicilian relocation. In both cases, the theatrical setting (Broadway), and the two intermedial movie translations, featuring radically different productions and distributions, spur questions on the relation between the civic dimension they rearticulate through appropriation and reinvention of the story, and the ideological import of their urban performances in theatres and cinemas.

3 *The city provides conceptually devised as well as unlocalized and fluid settings for various forms of performances related to the play*: theoretical reference is here to Henri Lefebvre's categories of representations of space and representational spaces (1991), which are produced through different types of civic performance (Schechner 2013). The first type of space is the one devised by urbanists and city managers, the

second one is the space lived in by its inhabitants, artists, philosophers, and moulded by them. Performing *Romeo and Juliet*, which is a play about a city, in cities means precisely exploiting its duplicating potential for community purposes in a subtle interplay between discourses and social practices linked to pre-set infrastructures or spontaneous urban settings. This point dislocates the performative questions related to the urban space for the performance of the play to other Romeo-and-Juliet-related types of performances: from celebrations to civic re-enactments, and the interdiscursive[17] and intercultural effects they engender upon the institutions, the community, as well as visitors and tourists, in a tensional dialogue with the play.

4 *The city is transformed into civic hyperreal or fictional Shakespeare-related settings*: as an extension of what has been suggested previously in this section, *Romeo and Juliet* is an extraordinary example of drama's flexibility and capacity to adjust to the city spaces and penetrate social and communal practices, reshaping the life of the town. A case in point here is Verona as a significant, if controversial, specimen of what has been termed "'Dysneyfication' of history in the twentieth century" (Lanier 2002, 152). The result is the production of an urban space through pre-constituted social practices, which at the same time call for, and resist, alternative practices of social installation and communal performances of the play.

Roughly following this four-point scheme within the two main sections of this volume, the essays will attempt to relocate the study of this play within this manifold civic dimension, against the backdrop of a critical panorama that only occasionally, and fairly recently, has devoted attention to the civic. To a brief overview of some aspects of this critical scenario the following pages are dedicated.

TOWARDS THE CIVIC: CRITICAL VARIATIONS ON *ROMEO AND JULIET*

While describing it as a "volatile mixture of adolescent passion, lyrical poetry and poignancy", R.S. White points out that "[o]ddly enough, the only people who have neglected … [*Romeo and Juliet*], at least relative to their attentiveness to other plays, are Shakespeare critics, who have never quite accepted it as a 'mature tragedy'" (2001, 1). In the play's centenary history, no one has ever been as radically dismissive as Samuel Pepys who, back in 1662, wrote that the play was "the worst that ever I heard in my life" (1970, 3.39). Yet one should not forget that *Romeo and Juliet* was radically altered by Restoration playwrights James Howard, who made it into a tragicomedy, and Thomas Otway, who transformed it into a Roman play. Later on, it was popularly appropriated by David Garrick who made of Romeo's role one of his *pièces de résistance*.[18] Garrick emphasized – also preserving and augmenting Otway's addition of a sorrowful exchange between the two lovers in the tomb – the emotional and pathetic dimension of the play and presented *Romeo and Juliet* as innocent and unwitting victims of violence and fate. In the nineteenth century Shakespeare enthusiasts multiplied and the play, although considered somehow 'immature', was greatly appreciated for its lyrical quality and for the apparent prominence of love and passion, or better, of pure love as not tainted by experience and therefore apt to 'speak to all ages'. As William Hazlitt put it: "Romeo is Hamlet in love ... Hamlet is abstracted from every thing; Romeo is abstracted from every thing but his love" (1817, 147). Indeed, at least until the first half of the twentieth century, the play was regarded as an early, juvenile tragedy whose importance was to be appreciated (only) because of its promising seminality of future dramatic greatness, thus implying a teleological view of the Shakespearean canon.[19] In later years, though, *Romeo and Juliet* was apparently rescued from its 'minority', and critical attention slowly set off its signifying and even subversive potential. In the past century, from the exploration of its uneven generic status,[20] to a close attention to its linguistic and formal complexity, as both a 'tragedy of names'[21] and for its use (and critique) of the conventions of Petrarchism,[22] to the carving out of its deeper structures dealing with a psychoanalytical exploration of desire and death,[23] *Romeo and Juliet* offered a widespread range of critical occasions.

In general terms, we may identify two main critical tendencies, moving, on the one hand, towards the reaffirmation of the play's iconic and transhistorical status, and, on the other hand, towards its insertion into a properly early modern milieu, agitated by the social as a well as ideological drives of a changing vision of the world.

Attuned to the first interpretative leaning we have just mentioned, Ryan Kiernan has sharply spoken of *Romeo and Juliet* as being sundered from any historical or cultural collusion and detected the play's "estrangement from its era" (2001, 126) through the lovers' jettisoning the orders that oppress them as well as "tossing aside the obsolete texts of the school of love in which they have been educated and finding fresh answers elsewhere" (ibid., 123). Similarly, Harold Bloom has lamented the fact that "the tragedy ... is surrendered to commissars of gender and power, who can thrash the patriarchy, including Shakespeare himself, for victimizing Juliet" (2000, 187). Dismissing any poststructuralist reading of the play, Bloom has successively hailed it as the "largest and most persuasive celebration of romantic love in Western literature" (ibid., 189), standing, in this position, close to Stanley Wells who has defined the play's closure as an "elegy for wedded love" (2010, 167). In their lack of engagement with the play's social concerns or implications, these readings seemingly respond to Gillian Woods' recent claim that the "[e]motional valence of the play's love story has sometimes overshadowed its social structures" (2013, 160). However, this is certainly not the case with a whole series of studies that, on the contrary, have reiterated the play's own ideological function. Disaster – as Marianne Novy wrote in 1984 – ensues exactly from the dramatization of an all-encompassing patriarchal dimension that imposes on the protagonists and society itself a violent and insuperable code of "gender polarization" (1984, 108). Following its rules, Romeo is forced to re-enter the 'masculine' logic of the feud by killing Tybalt while Juliet performs a 'feminine' act of submission to familial constraints when begging for her father's pardon in 4.2 (which is true, although one should not overlook that, at this point, she is cunningly circumventing Capulet's wishes). A decade afterward, both Lloyd Davis (1996) and Susan Snyder (1996) emphasized *Romeo and Juliet*'s foregrounding of social and political drives that operate on the protagonists' subjectivities by controlling and tragically restricting their scope. The pernicious influence of ideological constraints on the individual has been observed with regard to the feud which, according to Susan Snyder's Althusserian interpretation, "offers a model of how ideology works" and "like ideology, flattens out personal differences, slotting individuals into predetermined roles" (1996, 88–9). This has been also remarked with regard to the role of patriarchal statutes and imperatives whose rigidity and violence, but also shortcomings in front of historical and cultural changes, both structure and determine all kinds of relationships within Veronese society. Following this line of reasoning, Dympna Callaghan interrogated how the transition from feudal society to a centralized state and the ensuing crisis of patriarchy constitute the "overarching narrative" (2001, 92) of *Romeo and Juliet*. In her opinion, the cultural construction of desire dramatized in the play especially adheres to Protestant and Puritan ideology of marriage as "conducive to the emergent economic formation of capitalism" (ibid., 85). Accordingly, Callaghan critically accentuated how the play "does not stand above history, but rather within it, doing the work of culture, instigating and perpetuating the production of socially necessary formations of desire" (ibid., 107).

This kind of approach also favoured a discussion as to the functionalization of the play's spaces. Coppélia Kahn early foregrounded *Romeo and Juliet*'s inherent rift between domestic and external spaces which, again, helps define the patriarchal milieu of the play in which men are free to roam Verona's streets, bawdily bragging about their sexuality, while women are securely kept within doors as precious and primary instruments of patriarchal future itself. Thus, the final suicide of the two lovers in the tomb addresses the play's inbuilt subversive quality by overturning "the traditional passage of the female over to the male house in marriage" (Kahn 1977–78, 20). A similar issue of private *vs* public spaces was also discussed by Sasha Roberts. Pointing out how *Romeo and Juliet* is "marked by careful attention to contrasts and conflict between public and private", Roberts argues that "[d]ifferent characters have different access to ... spaces according to their gender and status" (1998, 35). As Kahn's before her, her interpretation makes no actual reference to the civic import of these "contrasts and conflict" but lingers on their predominantly sexual symbolism, which she aptly extends also to the liminal space of the orchard and of Juliet's balcony, or better, window. Obviously marking a threshold in the relation between the two lovers, the window signifies the symbolical breach of the social divide between them and, predictably, once Romeo "gains entry to ... [Juliet's] window with the rope ladder, he also gains entry to her body" (ibid., 39). Likewise, Roberts draws attention to both the Nurse, who "enjoys more freedom of movement ... than any other woman portrayed in the play" (ibid., 74), and the Friar, who "as a member of a religious community ... infiltrates secular social domains" (ibid., 70). The apparent flexibility of the Nurse's social mobility is also tackled by Dympna Callaghan in her informative 2003 collection on *Romeo and Juliet*'s texts and contexts. In a chapter devoted to the idea of Italy among Shakespeare's English audience, Callaghan discusses the place of gender and sexuality within Verona's urban setting. Capulet's orchard becomes associated with the Biblical and medieval *hortus conclusus*, the enclosed garden, as typologically representative of female virginity, and the city walls themselves (and Callaghan's allusion here is to London rather than to Verona) are likewise "professedly impregnable boundaries" (2003, 161). This figurative arrangement is once again directly linked to the idea that "with the exception of the Nurse, we see men rather than women 'abroad' in Verona" (ibid., 162); if penetrating the orchard could eventuate in death for Romeo, venturing the streets equally exposes women to the risk of violence: "Sex in this city is always, it seems, potentially if not actually deadly" (ibid., 163). This kind of reading brings forth the idea that both private and public spaces are traversed and disciplined by sexual power and potential sexual violence which especially inhabit male-gendered outdoor spaces, but whose oppressiveness penetrates and controls also the domestic sphere through the enactment of patriarchal rule. Linked to an idea of boundary-crossing, Mercutio too has been the object of close study, providing a significant example of an intrinsically liminal character. His eloquence (Porter 1988) stands out in the play as freewheeling between private and public spaces in his double social capacity as nobleman and kindred to the Prince, and in his keenness for bawdy fun and wordplay. Engaging in witty duels with whomever he meets – be they Romeo, Tybalt or the Nurse –, Mercutio roams the public spheres of the streets and *piazzas*, and crashes parties. He is careless of his noble stock that would have him mix only with the Prince and his kin, while his bawdiness constantly alludes to the invasion of private spaces (and parts) in his persistent demystifying of romantic love and (hetero)sexual order (see Goldberg 1994).

Attention to the play's political overtones, moving further away from a universalistic 'play for all times' motif, has also been the focus of Jerry Weinberger who evaluated *Romeo and Juliet* as pivoting on a conflict between secular (Escalus) and priestly (Laurence) authority. According to him, in the play "Shakespeare depicts a unique problem of modern life: the extraordinary resilience and power of Christian morality and its baleful effects on politics" (2003, 374). In particular, the Friar's meddling into public affairs in order to settle the household rift between Capulets and Montagues – which eventually generates the well-known catastrophe – is dictated by political ambition. "His goal", Weinberger writes, "is to Christianize political relations" (ibid., 362) in that he wishes to bend both the families' and the Prince's actions to a providential plan. His motivation tragically jars with Romeo's and Juliet's ostensible indifference to political matters or familial/clannish responsibility since, while the lovers' love "soars above politics and partisan interest" (ibid., 362–3), the Friar's heavenly love, "though universal, is bound to particular political goals from start to finish" (ibid.). Weinberger also interestingly devotes his critical attention to Verona's citizenry and their active role (a feature that has been hardly underscored if compared, for example, with Shakespeare's Roman plays). In *Romeo and Juliet*, "[h]owever brief their part the people's interest in civil peace ultimately frames the action of the play" (ibid., 363) and in taking "no sides in the quarrel between the houses", they ultimately achieve their goal: "[T]he people want peace and quiet, and they get it at no cost to themselves" (ibid., 370).

If these approaches move towards the reinstating of *Romeo and Juliet* within late sixteenth-century historical, cultural, and political reality and emphasize a political reading of the play as well as its dramatization of the clash of emerging individualistic calls against society's limiting and at times even deterring standards, some very recent critical ventures have actually highlighted a contrariwise tendency. Paul A. Kottman has recently placed the core of his critical analysis far from the exploration of the "conflict between individual desires and the reigning demands of family, civic, and social norms", arguing that "Shakespeare's play shows how Romeo and Juliet are formed as subjects through acts of mutual self-recognition that mute such conflicts" (Kottman 2012, 5). Although differently put, this 'muting' partially resounds in Simon Palfrey's Connell Guide to *Romeo and Juliet* too, in which the author identifies the play's crucial feature in "the fierce separateness of Juliet, and Romeo in her wake, from the adult social world" which brings forth the idea that "any attempt to socialize the lovers is false" (Palfrey 2012, 20). Romeo and Juliet, Palfrey argues, stand as paradigms of a universal awareness of human powerlessness in front of love's all-devouring force and "embody the black cosmic comedy of our unfreedom" (ibid., 115).

Nevertheless – as Ewan Fernie also points out in the afterword to this volume – the political, social, and community-valuing aspects of the play may not be ignored and indeed current criticism presents us with a fine range of studies that move towards a reading of *Romeo and Juliet* as not separated from its social milieu, but as actively and dialectically involved in it.

If, as early as in 1970, Susan Snyder had foregrounded the play's communal tenets as functional to its apparent gesturing towards comedy, in more recent times, Hugh Grady, although engaging with a different set of critical problems, ranging from a renewed discussion of the play's generic status to its dealing with the *Liebestod* concept, reasserted the thought-provoking density of *Romeo and Juliet's* civic space and underlined that:

> It is within this carefully sketched civic space – a representation of early modern European urban life that is capable of constant updating – that the legendary love of Romeo and Juliet is kindled, and it is precisely love that challenges the power of the social.
> (Grady 2009, 208–9)

This same power is, according to Stephen Zelnick, the root cause of all evil in a city that "fails to marshal its own cultural stability, where the Prince 'wink[s] at ... discords' (5.3.293), where the heads of great families behave like boys, and where churchmen fail the test of honor and of truth", and "what fails in the state to achieve civic order fails also in the family to bring trust and stability" (2011, 245–6, 249). A similar concept has been perceptively further delved into by Lynette Hunter and Peter Lichtenfels who have ascribed Verona's civil unrest, signified by persistently violent and uncivil demeanours, to a generalized social and domestic frailty and ineffectuality:

> [T]he street-fighting and duels into which the sword-fighting in the play breaks down result not only from weak civic leadership but also from the lack of familial guidance in civil behaviour. They signify a failure of public responsibility and an indulgence of private perspective (2009, 92).

In a context of strained relations between "capital and the law and between the domestic, the civic and the state" (ibid., 60), even peace is disturbingly associated with sickness – the citizens' partisans are "cankered with peace" (1.1.91) – and acts indeed as a central paradox of the play's civic politics which the Prince tries to unriddle "at first through personal authority and only gradually by turning to the authority of the law" (ibid., 185). This movement dramatizes the emerging of a modern conception of state, which slowly liberates itself from the feudal burdens of private self-defence and personal revenge and sets up a system of civic, national protection guaranteed by the enforcement of the law.

The wriggling notion of early modern civility has also been examined with closer regard to civic issues especially by Glenn Clark, who pointed out how civility ambiguously comprised both "mannered and potentially violent aristocratic courtesy" and "cultivated refinement and productive sociability" (2011, 288). This equivocality, he claims, brings forth a possibly unsuspected disaffection and maybe even hostility between members of the same 'clan' but also between the "masters" and "their men". During the Capulets' feast Tybalt would assail intruder Romeo even inside his uncle's house ("To strike him dead I hold it not a sin", 1.4.172) but his intentions are swiftly rebuked by Capulet who calls to his authority as both Tybalt's elder and lord of the house ("Am I the master here or you?", 1.4.191). The scene testifies to "Tybalt's frightening lack of devotion to his elder" (Clark 2011, 282) and to his *un*civility's potential for subversiveness and treason. The same kind of expectancy is attributed to the opening exchange between Sampson and Gregory. "The scene", according to Clark, "purports to demonstrate the intensity of household loyalties, but in fact serves to acknowledge the depth of subordinate disaffection and aspiration" (ibid.). Sampson's prospective 'civility' towards the Montague maids makes him act (and feel) like a would-be tyrant, which exposes his "frustration with and contempt for service" and seemingly alludes to a "intra-domestic conflict between masters and servants, rather than as a claim to honorific inter-household conflict between Montagues and Capulets" (ibid., 283).

As these latest approaches illustrate, the exploration of civic issues unveils stimulating analytical gears which, while exposing critically unbeaten tracks, lead readers and viewers alike to ask whose tragedy *Romeo Juliet* is: is it "the tragedy ... of Juliet and Romeo, or of the young people who die, or of the families, or of the society led by the Prince?" (Hunter and Lichtenfels 2009, 127). Indeed, far from overshadowing or flattening out its emotional import, this perspective advances and deepens the comprehension of *Romeo and Juliet* and of its multifarious and ever-blooming tragicality.

THE VOLUME

Wishing to look at *Romeo and Juliet* then and now and from a double perspective foregrounding its own forms of civic dramatization and its propensity for civic performance, as described earlier, the volume is divided into two main parts. The first section ("Dialectics of Private and Public Spaces") concentrates on the way the play presents the relation between the individual and the community calling into question the private and the public as two ambiguous civil dimensions in an age of social transformation and reconfiguration of the ideas of individual, family, and civic space. After detecting classical paradigms of civic crisis and Renaissance narrative filiations, the volume explores the urban representation of the city of Verona and its dramatic function. Through an identification of different symbolic dimensions, from the private space of the individual to the public space of the community via private-public places such as the family household and the tomb, and their urban contexts (open and indoor places, the *piazza*, the house, etc.), the discussion progresses to an interrogation of how the individual and the community are brought to interact, questioning the very idea of civic belonging through transgression and final, if critical, reconciliation.

The second section of the volume – "Civic Performances and R&Jspaces" – moves the discussion to a particular type of Shakespeare-related civic uses of *Romeo and Juliet* over the centuries, bringing in questions of official cultural appropriations as opposed to spontaneous and socially dynamic forms of the play's re-articulation. Revitalizing plays over time in a range of diverse civic ways, from celebrations, to theatrical reconfigurations and appropriations, to touristic translations into marketable goods poses a whole series of cultural issues that claim to be raised. When theatre becomes civic in this way the fluctuation of values grows even more apparent in that it involves the mutable overlapping of cultural, artistic, political intentions and their more or less covert manipulation. The second part of the volume thus brings examples of different responses to *Romeo and Juliet* through the centuries, focusing upon problems of cultural identity and the public sphere, as well as of memory and civic space. It also interrogates the civic as a label for highly connoted discourses and social practices such as celebrations, marketing strategies of Bardification, and 'unofficial forms' of cultural articulation.

The volume opens with a "Prologue" by Stanley Wells on the relation between Shakespeare and Verona and the Bard's relationship with Italy in general, which lays the ground for further discussion. By pointing out that Verona is mentioned in four Shakespearean plays, and two of them, *The Two Gentlemen of Verona* and *Romeo and Juliet*, are partly set there, Wells notices that critics usually read them in edited versions in which geographical vaguenesses or inaccuracies have to some extent been tidied up. Attempts to demonstrate that Shakespeare must have had personal knowledge of Verona, emanating often from doubters of his authorship, often appear misguided, because in *Romeo and Juliet* he derived its local colour mostly from Arthur Brooke's poem *Romeus and Juliet* which provided him with massive 'indigenous' details in terms of narrative, characterization, moralization, as well as topography. Wells's contention is that the Shakespearean representation of space here is worth being analysed from an imaginative rather than geographical point of view. None of Verona's most remarkable landmarks is present in the play, although we know that the city is ancient and walled, it has orchards, boasting a variety of trees, groves, churches, and the houses of wealthy families, among whom, of course, the "great rich Capulet" (1.2.81). All these details, Wells claims, deliver "a local habitation for a traditional story" stimulating the contemporary audiences' as well as our own imagination.

The first section ("Dialectics of Private and Public Spaces") is introduced by Guido Avezzù's "Classical Paradigms of Tragic Choice in Civic Stories of Love and Death", which offers a full discussion of ancient Greek and Roman models of the intersection between private and civic spaces on the one hand, and on the other and social practices. In particular, among narrative patterns and stories circulating in Renaissance England, which are here examined in their basic structures and motifs, Ovid's *Pyramus and Thisbe* epyllion provides the primary focus. Avezzù identifies (with John J. Munro) two main archetypical plots: the separation- and the potion-plot. While the former is increasingly influenced by family and civic conditionings, the latter is dominated by the *peripeteia* of Thisbe's (and Juliet's) apparent death which eventually pushes

Pyramus (and Romeo) to commit suicide. Avezzù explores both Greek and Roman sources in order to verify the presence of both plots and appreciate not only the great variety of treatments they underwent in the antiquity, but also the multiple hints that could direct their successive re-enactments. As suggested by Kenneth Muir (1954), Avezzù hypothesizes that Shakespeare could have relied on "multiple sources" mediated even by unsuspected or overlooked texts. This allows to clarify the critical equivocation at the basis of all interpretation of 'source' foregrounding exclusivity. Indeed, classicists and Shakespearean scholars alike have mainly concentrated on the potion(-and-error)-plot, neglecting the fact that *Romeo and Juliet*'s conclusive action – indirectly inspired by Ovid – "does not exhaust the entire plot nor represents the unravelling of the play's early announced contradictions" which more deeply involve the civic and political context of the story.

These ancient paradigms of love and death were much later adopted also by Italian sixteenth-century novella authors. In his essay ("Private and Public Spheres and the 'Civic Turn' in Da Porto, Bandello, and Shakespeare's *Romeo and Juliet*"), Robert Henke concentrates on the early versions of the story of Romeo and Juliet as provided by Luigi Da Porto, who situated it in Verona, and soon afterwards by Matteo Bandello. Published in 1535 and 1554, respectively, the two texts are deeply affected by the chosen location, which entails a great emphasis on the function and nature of different spaces in town as the "lovers continually find places that ambiguously negotiate the private and the public". In both Da Porto and Bandello, the garden, the street, the church, the Friar's cell, and even the confessional box are traversed by social tensions that transform them into "contact zones" between the private and public spheres. In particular, the confessional-box, a closed, restricted and utterly private space devoted to "auricular confession", as Brooke had it, hosts the celebration of a ceremony that places Romeo and Juliet into the public sphere as man and wife, thus conjoining the two dimensions. Indeed, Friar Lorenzo, a cosmopolitan figure especially keen on his function of would-be mediator between the two warring families, foregrounds the civic resonances of the novellas, which may account for, and draw into relief, the civic component of Shakespeare's own play, and possibly trace a direct influence on it of the Italian stories of 'Giulietta e Romeo'.

Moving on to a discussion of Shakespeare's own drama, the following essay, Roy Eriksen's "Shakespeare as 'Chief Architect and Plotter': *Romeo and Juliet* and Civic Space", also deals with the play's clash between the private and the public which is tackled through the perspective of Shakespeare's enplotment of the "civic and urban arena" in the play. Shakespeare, Eriksen argues, manages a dramatic embedding of the civic component by means of a double process of ruralization and abstraction. In *Romeo and Juliet*, the most nasty and maze-like aspects of the city are avoided and Verona's civic space is full of different kinds of trees and graced by walled orchards, presenting us with the "open structure of a village rather than … [the]

congested streets of an Early Modern city". Conversely, large prominence is devoted to the "abstract entity of the polis" and to the gradual exposure of its frailties. The power balance within the city between the nobility and the merchant class – which Eriksen identifies with the Capulets and the Montagues, respectively – is ill-managed by the play's figures of authority: the feuding patriarchs, the Friar, and the Prince. Escalus, in particular, fails, also in rhetoric, to "exploit the space for peaceful interaction and reconciliation existing in the city", that is, "Freetown", which, although misused, positively emerges as civic space of order and settlement.

Considerations on *Romeo and Juliet*'s civic setting are furthered by Mera J. Flaumenhaft who in "Inside-Outside: Love, Household, and City in *Romeo and Juliet*" focuses on what she identifies as a recurrent 'inside-outside' paradigm that elicits a meditation on place and time in divided Verona. In a city ruled by the feud mentality realignments, shifting alliances, as well as civic life are made impossible and have distorted the private lives of its citizens too. The Capulet balcony, the most famous place in the play, Flaumenhaft argues, becomes the perfect symbol for the disordered relations of inside and outside in "fair Verona". It has no proper entrance or exit: one climbs in and one leaps – elopes – out. Even the erotic eruption of Romeo's and Juliet's beautiful and entirely private passion, the antithesis in itself of civic activity, is as violent as the outbreak of "civil brawls" in public and intriguingly participates in the characterization of the defective communal dimension that marks the play to its tragic ending and gloomy reconciliation.

With Silvia Bigliazzi's chapter ("Defiance and Denial: Paradigms of Civic Transgression and Transcendence in *Romeo and Juliet*") the focus is shifted onto the scapegoating pattern that the play claims to rely upon with the authority of the Prologue's voice and that of the Prince in the recapitulation scene. Through an investigation of the relational paradigms of behaviour elicited by an intrinsically conflictual community destabilized by household feuding and weak and self-contradicting governance, the essay discusses the ambiguities at the core of the civic system of Verona, providing the actual ground for a reshaping of the tragic experience. Civility turns into its opposite precisely as legality shows its illegal face, while patterns of defiance and denial, transgression and transcendence of the communal system trigger the tragic outcome, prompting an interrogation of the potential and limits of free will in the face of a civic bond donning the guise of coercion. These two paradigms, together with a recasting of the elemental pattern of violence and sacrifice in a new complex civic dimension, define the space of subversion and communal redress of crime, revealing an emerging crisis in the Renaissance conception of the individual and in the blind power of a social system of hierarchy that creaks under the push of bourgeois unrest. The argument foregrounds the social agonism widespread in fair Verona, where strife, tinged with tribal connotations of violence, sexual aggression, and legal repression, as well as household coercion, push the two lovers to re-define the scope of their freedom to go beyond household and communal rules. Thus, if a sacrifice is eventually enacted, it occurs in a post-sacrificial dimension of civic and 'commercial' transaction which seals a radical revision of the scapegoating scheme and its intrinsic relation with the community.

From the relevance of strife, coercion, and sacrifice and their problematically tragic implications, in Lisanna Calvi's essay ("Tying the knot in 'fair Verona': the Private and Public Spaces of Marriage in *Romeo and Juliet*") the attention is turned more specifically to the issue of marriage and family constraint. The analysis of this topic, central in the play as it was in Tudor society, reveals the presence of a grey area of interference denoting a challenging friction between individual consent and liberty of choice, on the one hand, and on the other familial as well as social conveniences. If the contemporaries regarded marriage as a farewell to youth and an alteration of status, attributing to it a function of preservation of social and civic harmony, they also debated the role of individual liking and generally showed some hostility towards arranged marriages, especially when conditioned by constraint and duress. In the play, the treatment of this issue exposes a complex intertwining of economic and civic reasons with personal and erotic drives that blur the boundaries between the private and the public. Indeed the two wedding contracts (the one scheduled by Capulet and the one secretly entered by Romeo and Juliet) trigger a dialectics of spaces, equally ambiguous in their duality of private-domestic and public-civic implications, opening up an interesting outlook not only on the (civic) function of marriage at the turn of the sixteenth century, but also on the role an individual might or might not play with respect to it.

In "Silencing the Natural Body: Notes on the Monumental Body in *Romeo and Juliet*" Silvia Bigliazzi and Lucia Nigri take up Calvi's final considerations on the conclusive monumentalization of the two lovers to unveil the discursive strategies inherent in the conception and representation of death as a site of conflict. Eventually assumed as glamorous civic icons of peace, the natural bodies of the two lovers are transfigured into monumental bodies that rewrite their story. Compared to the novella tradition, mention of their tomb is revelatory of a communal appropriation of their bodies that foregrounds separateness, rather than unity, and economic and political interest, rather than familial memory. The effacement of their individuality through their civic immortalization does not come unexpected once a discursive undercurrent pivoting on the grave/monument opposition and the bed-bier metonymy is related to the process of hybridization the bedroom and the tomb undergo. A peculiar use of stage properties contributes to pointing out the relevance of dramaturgy as a practice of space construction underlying the mutual permeability of the private and the public and the potentially tragic dimension of liminal spheres.

The second section of the volume – "Civic Performances and R&J spaces" – moves the discussion to a particular type of Shakespeare-related civic uses of

Romeo and Juliet over the centuries, bringing in questions of official cultural appropriations as opposed to spontaneous and socially dynamic forms of re-articulation of the play and its legacy.

The section is inaugurated by Paul Edmondson's "'For these dead birds sing a prayer'" which presents a fascinating reading of Shakespeare's poem *The Phoenix and the Turtle* (1601) pivoting upon the original assumption that "modern minds as well as early modern ones are troubled by the suicides of Romeo and Juliet". The poem, Edmondson argues, constitutes the Bard's own creative and civic response to *Romeo and Juliet*. Possibly occasioned as an homage to Sir John Salusbury's knighthood in 1601, this mysterious poem is regarded here as exquisitely civic in its allegorization of public pageantry and liturgy through which the two "dead birds" enter both a communal dimension of memorialization and symbolic celebration of a whole range of divided lovers that crowd the Shakespearean canon (Silvia and Valentine, Richard II and his Queen, Hamlet and Ophelia, Viola and Orsino, Desdemona and Othello, and of course Romeo and Juliet). Thus, the poem becomes the imaginary script of what Edmondson dubs as "the funeral rite for Romeo and Juliet", a masque-like piece of civic pageantry that, as he conceives it, reanimates the sculpted golden effigies in which the two unfortunate lovers are immortalized at the end of the play and sublimates their identities and their love into a transcendent unity in which "[n]either two nor one was called".

The concept of 'oneness' also informs Loretta Innocenti's essay "'Wherefore art thou Marius?': Otway's Adaptation of *Romeo and Juliet*". As the title announces, Innocenti concentrates on Thomas Otway's *The History and Fall of Caius Marius* (1680) offering a fresh critical outlook on this neoclassical adaptation of Shakespeare's play. Set in late Republican Rome during the civil wars between Marius and Sulla, the play's gist is primarily political, especially if one reads it in the light of the late 1670s religious and constitutional struggles. Although taking into account this scenario, Innocenti rather concentrates on Otway's reuse of the Shakespearean text of *Romeo and Juliet* which he adapts as a love subplot between Marius junior and Lavinia, the daughter of Marius senior's enemy, Metellus. Their love and subsequent marriage are of course opposed by their families but, far from voicing a challenge to patriarchy and civic rules their union becomes part of the civic story itself and their untimely death transforms into the outcome of "the inevitable tragedy of obedience" to political and communal values. The civic potential of the play is therefore reinforced through the intrusion of public issues of civil strife into the young protagonists' love story whose private dimension is imbued with public concerns. Marius junior and Lavinia are constantly torn between their mutual affection and their loyalty to their duties as Roman citizens: a polarity that cannot be solved but in death.

In 1680 Thomas Otway famously had Juliet wake up before Romeo's death and appended a lachrymose exchange between the two lovers to the play's finale. This addition was later adopted and expanded by eighteenth-century actor and theatrical manager David Garrick who, in 1748, adapted the play for Drury Lane theatre. Moving from a set of insightful considerations on how Shakespeare, unlike what happens in Arthur Brooke's poem, decidedly veered towards the civic by making Romeo and Juliet "first and foremost citizens of Verona", in "Brooke, Garrick, *Romeo and Juliet*, and the Public Sphere" Michael Dobson argues that Garrick's adaptation further moved the play into the public sphere by moulding its plot of forbidden marriage into the nascent discourse of national identity. Nevertheless, this public fashioning of the play was no trouble-free process and if, on the one hand, the contemporaries celebrated *Romeo and Juliet*'s political valence as the emblem of nationalistic, even pro-revolutionary instances, on the other hand, the doubtful morality of the young lovers' clandestine affair was called into question as potentially subversive and especially risky for well-educated city girls. At the same time appealing and taboo at times of nation-building, *Romeo and Juliet* was further appropriated by Garrick himself when, in 1769, he inaugurated the celebration of the Stratford Jubilee by delivering a celebratory ode that pictured Shakespeare as both Britain's Romeo and as the nation's own 'god of idolatry' and cunningly moving Romeo's and Juliet's love story into a context of civic (and national) devotion towards both the Bard and his "star-crossed lovers".

If Garrick's celebrations contributed to the construction of a civic-national identity through the 'canonization' of Shakespeare, English travellers of the nineteenth-century looked for the relics of the 'god of their idolatry' also outside Britain. Unsurprisingly Verona was one of their preferred destinations chosen in order to find out and pay homage to what local tradition had long identified with the tomb and house of Juliet Capulet. The changing dynamics that guided such pilgrimage during the nineteenth century and Verona's early civic responses to it are explored by the next essay: Nicola Watson's "At Juliet's Tomb: Anglophone Travel-Writing and Shakespeare's Verona, 1814–1914". After the English victory at Waterloo in 1814, the pioneers of what we nowadays call 'literary tourism' revered Verona's 'Shakespearean' sites with romantic effusion, collecting relic-like souvenirs and recording their experience with rapture. Later on Victorian historicism damped down previous enthusiasm, although it did not quench visitors' curiosity nor warded off their flow. Verona, as Watson points out, "was providing a place to understand Shakespeare as global" and to celebrate English superiority through the location of the Bard on the Continent. Later on, also in the wake of this interest, Verona's civic authorities slowly enfranchised the legend as part of the town heritage and progressively adjusted both the tomb and the house as sites to tourist expectations celebrating an ideal naturalization of the Shakespearean presence in the city, which had nevertheless "little to do with the dysfunctional civic represented in the play".

Modern Verona's problematic engagement with Romeo and Juliet is further discussed in Silvia Bigliazzi and Lisanna Calvi's "Producing a (R&)Jspace: Discursive and Social Practices in Verona" that deals with the city of Verona as a deeply Shakespeare-related urban setting for cultural and tourist industry. Taking Montague at his word, Verona has been turned into the city of Juliet and while Romeo has been somehow left behind, the Shakespearean heroine has slowly been implanted not only in the city's traditional spaces of the house and the tomb, which civic authorities subjected to a targeted makeover in the 1930s, but also in modern cultural practices and discourses. Disneyland-like and hyperreal, although not avowedly fake, these 'Juliet spaces' are "replete with signs of remains deprived of an original referent"; they signify her myth of sacrificed faithfulness, but controversially occult the power discourses that traversed her story. Juliet is not only the titular owner of a house and a tomb, but also presides over medieval festivals, marathons, and civic awards as the tutelary deity of a whole town. Besides, tons of letters are famously written to her from people all over the world who have turned her into the icon of starry-eyed passion. Nonetheless, Bigliazzi and Calvi suggest, this cultural and discursive arrangement ultimately seems to constrain Juliet and her story into a stilted, if golden, civic model of (feminine) love and sacrifice, producing discursive and social practices that encase a hyperreal (R&)Jspace within the larger city.

Developing this chapter's final mention of a very recent alternative R&Jpractice in Verona which took place at its Teatro Nuovo in April 2013, Jacquelyn Bessell's "*Perché sei tu?*: Lindsay Kemp's 'gift of memory'" offers a critical account of this civic experimental performance carried out as a workshop and a dance-theatre adaptation of *Romeo and Juliet* run and directed by Lindsay Kemp. Revolved around the idea of an open master class as the culmination of previous months of training, *Perché sei tu?* ("Wherefore art thou?") was deployed as a civic event by means of "an instance of 'inductive theatre' in which the action of the play happens to the audience". During the event, blurring the line between rehearsal and performance, Kemp constantly called the audience's attention, and *our* attention as "'we'" became "part of the experiential, kinaesthetic element of this event". Kemp's choreographic score is certainly remindful of both Testa's (realized for Franco Zeffirelli's 1968 film) and Kenneth MacMillan's (1965), yet, Bessell avows, it activated in her memory a comparison with Carlos Saura's 1981 film *Bodas de sangre*, "another danced response to the heightened language of another poetic tragedy of forbidden love". Indeed both Kemp and Sauras rely on the dramatic power of rehearsals and both of them also vary and transcend their sources at the climax. Kemp's finale can be valued in terms of "a prismatic sequence suggesting a shared experience of the lovers' ascension after death", which both transcends the crisis/es and the reconciliation dramatized in the original Shakespearean script, and, presented to the audience as a "gift of memory", transforms it into a valuable communal experience.

With Bettina Boecker's essay "Stage(d) Reconciliations: *Romeo and Juliet* and the Politics of Bilingual Shakespeare Productions in Germany", we move from Verona to German bilingual performances of *Romeo and Juliet* as yet another form of civic, or maybe civically transnational, event.

Starting from the consideration that the nature of the play, rooted in conflict and civil strife, is actually fertile ground for bilingual adaptations, Boecker's attention is particularly devoted to three German and one Swiss bilingual stagings of *Romeo and Juliet,* which especially thrive on the play's central civic *vs* personal issues conflict by reconfiguring it into a potentially didactic instrument whose scope goes beyond the intentions of the original drama. The four bilingual productions Boecker takes into account (a German-Polish one staged at Schwedt, Brandeburg, in 2000, a German-Russian presented at Tübingen in 2010, a German-Czech mounted by the travelling amateur Bavaria Youth Theatre, and a German-French that premiered at Fribourg in 1989) are cases in point for the exploration of the play's civic potential. Not only do they engage with public issues, placing them "in a contact zone and almost always in the context of a conflict between two opposing political and/or social groups", but are also concerned with the audience's duties and obligations in securing the welfare of the commonwealth, here imagined as the community of (two neighbouring) nations.

Borrowing Antonio's cue in *The Tempest*, "What's past is prologue" (2.1.249), in the volume's afterword Ewan Fernie turns his attention to *Romeo and Juliet*'s first Prologue. Discussing "the play's further potential for a more civic reading", Fernie points out how this Prologue's famously proleptic account of "ancient grudge" and "new mutiny" points to the idea, central in this volume but also in the play, that "civil strife … is much more than nicely contrasting scenery". Far from banalizing our reading of *Romeo and Juliet* by privileging social concerns over the love intrigue, the civic approach announced by the Prologue freshens our interpretation of it and even enhances the multi-faceted and at times disturbing complexity of the play and of its diversified civic re-enactments. By hinting at the "violence afflicting the world of the play in general", which will be dramatized not only in the death of the two lovers, but also of other youths, it anticipates the play's terrifying prospect of 'gerontocracy' after the entombment of the new, if conflicting, generations. A "discomfiting reading of the Prologue", this one however unveils "the kind of complex and relatively neglected life in this much studied play" through a "more deliberately civic approach". Yet this also requires "going beyond close reading". One such attempt is finally provided, and included in this volume, as a rounding-off creative conclusion penned by Paul Edmondson as a celebratory response to the play's more famous sonnets, carried out in the name of 'Civic *Romeo and Juliet*'.

NOTES

1. Reference is to G.W.F. Hegel, "Dramatic Poetry", in Kottman 2009; see also Kottman 2012.
2. For articulated discussions of the uses and implications of 'popular' and 'popular culture' with reference to Shakespeare today, see Lanier 2002, 1–20; Shaughnessy ed. 2007; Gillespie and Rhodes (2006, 1–17) concentrate instead

on a discussion of the notion of popular culture in the early modern period; see also Patterson 1989; Bristol 1997.

3. In has been noticed that "The term 'popular' itself appears only six times in Shakespeare, four of these references occurring in *Coriolanus*, a play which undoubtedly splices the 'old Romans' with contemporary English matter. It is significant that the popular voice in this play is represented by characters called 'citizens', who are eligible to vote, rather than by the inarticulate mob" (Gillespie and Rhodes 2006, 6). These remarks rely on Shrank 2003, which examines "Martius's uncivil language ... [as] a natural extension of his antipathy to the civic community" (408) and his "refusal to partake in civic life or to moderate his excessive individualism for the common good" (422). Implication with current political and civic history is here related to the "way in which far wider sections of the population experienced the kind of political participation that would have made *Coriolanus*'s Rome recognizable: namely, the civic politics of the 204 towns and cities throughout England that had been incorporated by the end of the first decade of the seventeenth century. These corporate towns and cities enjoyed a degree of legislative autonomy and civic jurisdiction, and many had the right to elect parliamentary representative" (407). Stress on the civic dimension of the play has also been laid by Marcus 1988, 202–3.

4. Schechner's position needs revision especially as regards the exclusive involvement of citizens. In the Spring festival (the Great Dionysia) spectators arrived from the whole Greek world and actively participated also in the most ostensibly political performances, accessory to the spectacles. Furthermore, also the foreign residents (the 'metics') could be called to contribute financially to the preparation of the spectacle (*khoregia*). For recent criticism see Csapo and Slater 1995; Gould 1996; Goldhill 1996; Silk ed. 1996; Wiles 1997; Wilson 2000; Billings et al. 2013.

5. To recall but few classical studies, see Greenblatt 1980 and 1988; Montrose 1996.

6. In passing, it should be noticed that the Athenian reality was in fact more complex. To the Athenian territory there belonged borough theatres (*demoi* = 'boroughs'), also in places like Piraeus, which certainly was "less tightly coherent" with the City (*asty*), seat of the central government, because inhabited also by non-Greek people.

7. On the kindred idea of theatre's power of reshaping a community of citizens-spectators engaged in watching a performance, see Flaumenhaft 1994.

8. Cf. Goffman 1959; Turner 1974; Wilshire 1982; for an interpretation of Shakespeare's theatre in this key, see McGinn 2006. Upon gender and cross-dressing on and off stage see Orgel 1996; on the paradoxes of cross-dressing see Platt 2009, 164ff.

9. See the seminal collection in cultural materialism Dollimore and Sinfield eds 1985.

10. For a comprehensive study of theatres and audiences see Gurr 1988.

11. On Royal progresses see also Bergeron 1998; Leahy 2010; Dillon 2010, esp. 18–48.

12. To name but few classical and more recent studies, cf. Burke 2009; Weimann 1978; Patterson 1989; Bristol 1997; Gillespie and Rhodes eds 2006; Pugliatti and Serpieri eds 2008.

13. Roach 1996, 3. For a discussion of the role of performance in translation studies and practices in the contemporary panorama, see Bigliazzi, Kofler, Ambrosi 2013.

14. Gillespie and Rhodes specify that "Elizabethan commentators do identify three, or perhaps, four social orders. William Harrison, writing in 1577, described hierarchy of gentleman (including nobility, knights and esquires), citizens and burgesses, yeomen, and finally those who had 'neither voice not authority in the commonwealth, but are to be ruled and not rule other.' This is very similar to the scheme outlined earlier by Sir Thomas Smith, who compared the English to the Roman social structure. He divides the rank of gentlemen into two, 'Nobilitas major' and 'Nobilitas minor': then describes citizens and burgesses who 'serve the common wealth' and may be elected to parliament 'to have voices in it': then treats yeomen 'whom our laws doe call *Legalem hominem*'; and finally 'those which the olde Romans called *capite censij proletarij* or *operae*, or day labourers, poore husbandmen, yea merchants or retailers which have no free lande; copy-holders, all artificers, as Taylers, Shoomakers, Carpenters, Brickmakers, Bricklayers, Masons, &c'"; they also suggest that it is less clear "what might be meant by 'people'" because "citizen and yeomen were frequently classed together as 'the middling sort of people'" (2006, 6).
15. A review of a debate on the use of the upper stage sparked by Hosley 1954 and Adams 1956 is offered by Foakes 1958, 146; for articulated comments on the stagecraft in the tomb scene, see Gurr 1996.
16. A street, as Laitinen and Cohen have remarked, "[p]rovides a passageway for the movement of goods, beasts, and people; it also structures the town by demarcating blocks and outlining houses; and it brings people together, when they step outside of their houses and move from place to place. Streets open out to market places and plazas, and also funnel in, to yards, gateways, paths, passages, and stairwells" (2009, 1).
17. Here 'interdiscursive' is used as in critical discourse analysis, on which see Fairclough 1989, 2013.
18. On Otway's and Garrick's renderings of the play see Innocenti and Dobson in this volume.
19. See, for example, A.C. Bradley 1904 and, although more appreciative of *Romeo and Juliet*'s experimental quality, H.B. Charlton 1948.
20. See, for instance, Brooke 1968; McCown 1976; Snyder 1970.
21. See Belsey 1993, but also Calderwood 1971; Levin 1960.
22. Among the others, Colie 1974; Slater 1988; Whittier 1989.
23. See Rabkin 1967, and more recently Kristeva 1993.

WORKS CITED

Adams, John Cranford. 1956. "Shakespeare's Use of the Upper Stage in *Romeo and Juliet*, III, V". *Shakespeare Quarterly* 7: 145–52.

Barish, Jonas. 1981. *The Antitheatrical Prejudice*. Berkeley and Los Angeles: University of California Press.

Bauman, Richard. 1989. "Performance". In *International Encyclopedia of Communications*, edited by Erick Barnouw, 3.262–6. New York: Oxford University Press.

Belsey, Catherine. 1993. "The Name of the Rose in *Romeo and Juliet*". *Yearbook of English Studies* 23: 126–42.

Bergeron, David M. 1988. "Representation in Renaissance English Civic Pageants". *Theatre Journal* 40 (3): 319–31.

Bigliazzi, Silvia. 2002. *Sull'esecuzione testuale. Dal testo letterario alla performance*. Pisa: Edizioni ETS.

Bigliazzi, Silvia, Peter Kofler, and Paola Ambrosi. 2013. *Theatre Translation in Performance*. London and New York: Routledge.
Billings, Joshua, Felix Budelmann, and Fiona MacIntosh eds. 2013. *Choruses, Ancient and Modern*. Oxford: Oxford University Press.
Bloom, Harold. (1998) 2000. "Romeo and Juliet". In *Modern Critical Interpretations. William Shakespeare's Romeo and Juliet*, edited by Harold Bloom, 187–200. Philadelphia: Chelsea House Publishers.
Bradley, Andrew Cecil. 1904. *Shakespearean Tragedy: Lectures on Hamlet, Othello, King Lear, Macbeth*. London: Macmillan.
Bristol, Michael. 1997. "Theatre and Popular Culture". In *A New History of Early English Drama*, edited by John D. Cox and David Scott Kastan, 231–48. New York: Columbia University Press.
Brooke, Nicholas. 1968. *Shakespeare's Early Tragedies*. London: Methuen.
Burke, Peter. (1978) 2009. *Popular Culture in Early Modern Europe*. Farnham: Ashgate.
Calbi, Maurizio. 2001. "'This Is My Home, Too': Migration, Spectrality and Hospitality in Roberta Torre's Sud Side Stori (2000)". *Shakespeare* 7 (1): 16–34.
Calderwood, James L. 1971. *Shakespearean Metadrama*. Minneapolis: University of Minnesota Press.
Callaghan, Dympna. (1994) 2001. "The Ideology of Romantic Love: The Case of *Romeo and Juliet*". In *Romeo and Juliet. Contemporary Critical Essays*, edited by R.S. White, 85–115. Houndmills Basingstoke: Palgrave.
Callaghan, Dympna, ed. 2003. *William Shakespeare: Romeo and Juliet. Texts and Contexts*. Boston and New York: St Martin's.
Carlson, Marvin. 1989. *Places of Performance: The Semiotics of Theatre Architecture*. Ithaca, NY: Cornell University Press.
Charlton, H.B. 1948. *Shakespearean Tragedy*. Cambridge: Cambridge University Press.
Clark, Glenn. 2011. "The Civil Mutinies of *Romeo and Juliet*". *English Literary Renaissance* 41 (2): 280–300.
Colie, Rosalie L. 1974. *Shakespeare's Living Art*. Princeton, NJ: Princeton University Press.
Cowen Orlin, Lena. 2008. *Locating Privacy in Tudor London*. Oxford: Oxford University Press.
Csapo, Eric, and William J. Slater. 1995. *The Context of Greek Ancient Drama*. Ann Arbor: University of Michigan Press.
Davis, Lloyd. 1996. "'Death-marked love': Desire and Presence in *Romeo and Juliet*". In *Shakespeare Survey, 49*: Romeo and Juliet *and its Afterlife*, edited by Stanley Wells, 57–67. Cambridge: Cambridge University Press.
Dillon, Janette. 2010. *The Language of Space in Court Performances 1400–1625*. Cambridge: Cambridge University Press.
Dollimore, Jonathan, and Alan Sinfield. (1985) 1994. *Political Shakespeare: Essays in Cultural Materialism*. Manchester: Manchester University Press.
Fairclough, Norman. 1989. *Language and Power*. New York: Longman.
Fairclough, Norman. (1992) 2013. *Discourse and Social Change*. Cambridge and Malden, MA: Polity.
Flaumenhaft, Mera J. 1994. *The Civic Spectacle. Essays on Drama and Community*. Boston: Rowman & Littlefield.
Foakes, R.A. 1958. "Shakespeare's Life, Time and Stage". In *Shakespeare Survey, 2: Shakesperian Production*, edited by Allardyce Nicoll, 142–8. Cambridge: Cambridge University Press.

Gillespie, Stuart, and Neil Rhodes, eds. 2006. *Shakespeare and Elizabethan Popular Culture*. London: Bloomsbury (The Arden Shakespeare).

Goffman, Erving. 1959. *The Presentation of Self in Everyday Life*. New York: Doubleday.

Goldberg, Jonathan. 1994. "Romeo and Juliet's Open Rs". In *Queering the Renaissance*, edited by Jonathan Golberg, 218–35. Durham, NC: Duke University Press.

Goldhill, Simon. 1996. "Collectivity and Otherness – The Authority of the Tragic Chorus: Response to Gould". In *Tragedy and the Tragic. Greek Theatre and Beyond*, edited by Michael Stephen Silk, 244–56. Oxford and New York: Oxford University Press.

Gould, John. 1996. "Tragedy and Collective Experience". In *Tragedy and the Tragic. Greek Theatre and Beyond*, edited by Michael Stephen Silk, 217–43. Oxford and New York: Oxford University Press.

Grady, Hugh. 2009. *Shakespeare and Impure Aesthetics*. Cambridge: Cambridge University Press.

Greenblatt, Stephen. 1980. *Renaissance Self-fashioning: From More to Shakespeare*. Chicago: The University of Chicago Press.

Greenblatt, Stephen. 1988. *Shakespearean Negotiations: the Circulation of Social Energy in Renaissance England*. Berkeley and Los Angeles: University of California Press.

Guettel Cole, Susan. 1993. "Procession and Celebration at the Dionysia". In *Theater and Society in the Classical World*, edited by Ruth Scodel, 25–38. Ann Arbor: University of Michigan Press.

Gurr, Andrew. 1988. *Playgoing in Shakespeare's London*. Cambridge: Cambridge University Press.

Gurr, Andrew. 1996. "The Date and the Expected Venue of *Romeo and Juliet*". In *Shakespeare Survey, 49: Romeo and Juliet and its Afterlife*, edited by Stanley Wells, 15–26. Cambridge: Cambridge University Press.

Harvie, Jen. 2009. *Theatre and the City*. Houndmills, Basinkstoke: Palgrave Macmillan.

Hazlitt, William. 1817. *Characters of Shakespear's Plays*. London: Hunter and Ollier.

Hedrick, Donald, and Bryan Reynolds. 2000. *Shakespeare Without Class. Misappropriations of Cultural Capital*. Houndmills, Basingstoke: Palgrave.

Hosley, Richard. 1954. "The Use of the Upper Stage in *Romeo and Juliet*". *Shakespeare Quarterly* 5 (4): 371–9.

Hunter, Lynette, and Peter Lichtenfels. 2009. *Negotiating Shakespeare's Language in Romeo and Juliet: Reading Strategies from Criticism, Editing and the Theatre*. Aldershot: Ashgate.

Jackson, Shannon. 2011. *Social Works: Performing Art, Supporting Publics*. New York and London: Routledge.

Kahn, Coppélia. 1977–78. "Coming of Age in Verona". *Modern Language Studies* 8 (1): 5–22.

Kiernan, Ryan. (1995) 2001. "'The Murdering Word'". In *Romeo and Juliet. Contemporary Critical Essays*, edited by R.S. White, 116–28. Houndmills, Basingstoke: Palgrave.

Kilian, Ted. 1998. "Public and Private, Power and Space". In *The Production of Public Space*, edited by Andrew Light and Jonathan Smith, 115–34. Lanham: Rowman and Littlefied.

Kottman, Paul A., ed. 2009. *Philosophers on Shakespeare*. Stanford: Stanford University Press.
Kottman, Paul A. 2012. "Defying the Stars: Tragic Love as the Struggle for Freedom in *Romeo and Juliet*". *Shakespeare Quarterly* 63 (1): 1–38.
Kristeva, Julia. 1993. *Histoires d'amour*. Paris: Denoël.
Laitinen, Riitta, and Thomas Vance Cohen, eds. 2009. *Cultural History of Early Modern European Streets*. Leiden: Brill.
Lanier, Douglas. 2002. *Shakespeare and Modern Popular Culture*. Oxford: Oxford University Press.
Leahy, William. 2005. *Elizabethan Triumphal Processions*. Aldershot: Ashgate.
Lefebvre, Henri. (1974) 1991. *The Production of Space*. Translated by Donald Nicholson-Smith. Oxford: Blackwell.
Levenson, Jill. 1995. "'Alla stoccado carries it away': Codes of Violence in *Romeo and Juliet*". In *Shakespeare's Romeo and Juliet: Texts, Contexts, and Interpretation*, edited by Jay L. Halio, 83–96. London: Associated University Presses.
Levin, Harry. 1960. "Form and Formality in *Romeo and Juliet*". *Shakespeare Quarterly* 11 (1): 3–11.
Loehlin, James N., ed. 2002. *Romeo and Juliet. (Shakespeare in Production)*. Cambridge: Cambridge University Press.
Longo, Oddone. 1990. "The Theatre of the Polis". In *Nothing to Do with Dyonisus? Athenian Drama and in Its Social Context*, edited by John J. Winkler & Froma I. Zeitlin, 12–19. Princeton, NJ: Princeton University Press.
Marcus, Leah S. 1988. *Puzzling Shakespeare: Local Reading and its Discontents*. Berkeley: University of California Press.
McCown, Gary M. 1976. "'Runnawayes eyes' and Juliet's Epithalamium". *Shakespeare Quarterly* 27 (2): 150–70.
McGinn, Colin. 2006. *Shakespeare's Philosophy*. Harper-Collins e-books.
Melchiori, Giorgio. 1983, "Peter, Balthasar, and Shakespeare's Art of Doubling". *The Modern Language Review* 78 (4): 777–92.
Montrose, Louis Adrian. 1996. *The Purpose of Playing: Shakespeare and the Cultural Politics of the Elizabethan Theater*. Chicago: The University of Chicago Press.
Mullaney, Steven. (1988) 1995. *The Place of the Stage: Licence, Play, and Power in Renaissance England*. Chicago: University of Chicago Press.
Munro, Lucy. 2005. *Children of the Queen's Revel. A Jacobean Theatre Repertory*. Cambridge: Cambridge University Press.
Neill, Michael. 2000. *Putting History to the Question: Power, Politics, and Society in English Renaissance Drama*. New York: Columbia University Press.
Novy, Marianne. 1984. *Love's Argument: Gender Relations in Shakespeare*. Chapel Hill: University of North Carolina Press.
Orgel, Stephen. 1996. *Impersonations: The Performance of Gender in Shakespeare's England*. Cambridge. Cambridge University Press.
Orgel, Stephen. 2002. "The Play of Conscience". In Stephen Orgel, *The Authentic Shakespeare and other Problems of the Early Modern Stage*, 129–42. London and New York: Routledge.
Palfrey, Simon. 2009. *The Connell Guide to Shakespeare: Romeo and Juliet*. Chippenham: Connell.
Patterson, Annabel. 1989. *Shakespeare and the Popular Voice*. Oxford: Blackwell.
Pepys, Samuel. 1970. *Diary*. Edited by Robert Latham and William Matthews, 10 vols. London: G. Bell.

Platt, George P. 2009. *Shakespeare and the Culture of Paradox*. Farnham: Ashgate.
Pollard, Tanya ed. 2004. *Shakespeare's Theater. A Sourcebook*. Malden, MA, Oxford and Victoria: Blackwell.
Porter, Joseph A. 1988. *Shakespeare's Mercutio. His History and Drama*. Chapel Hill, NC: University of North Carolina Press.
Pugliatti, Paola. 2003. *Beggary and Theatre in Early Modern England*. Aldershot: Ashgate.
Pugliatti, Paola. 2008. "A Lost Love: The Activity of Gipsies as Performers on the Stage of Elizabethan-Jacobean Street Theatre". In *English Renaissance Scenes: From Canon to Margins*, edited by Paola Pugliatti and Alessandro Serpieri, 259–310. Bern: Peter Lang.
Rabkin, Norman. 1967. *Shakespeare and the Common Understanding*. New York: Free Press / London: Collier-Macmillan.
Richardson, Catherine. 2006. *Domestic Life and Domestic Tragedy in Early Modern England: The Material Life of the Household*. Manchester: Manchester University Press.
Roach, Joseph. 1996. *Cities of the Dead: Circum-Atlantic Performance*. New York: Columbia University Press.
Roberts, Sasha. 1998. *William Shakespeare: Romeo and Juliet*. Plymouth: Northcote House.
Schechner, Richard. 1985. *Between Theater and Anthropology*. Philadelphia: University of Pennsylvania Press.
Schechner, Richard. (1988) 2003. *Performance Theory*. London and New York: Routledge.
Schechner, Richard. (2002) 2013. *Performance Studies: An Introduction*. London and New York: Routlegde.
Shakespeare, William. 2000. *Romeo and Juliet*. Edited by Jill L. Levenson. Oxford: Oxford University Press.
Shaughnessy, Robert, ed. 2007. *The Cambridge Companion to Shakespeare and Popular Culture*. Cambridge: Cambridge University Press.
Shrank, Cathy. 2003. "Civility and the City in *Coriolanus*". *Shakespeare Quarterly* 54: 406–23.
Silk, Michael Stephen, ed. 1996. *Tragedy and the Tragic. Greek Theatre and Beyond*. Oxford, New York: Oxford University Press.
Slater, Ann. 1988. "Petrarchanism Come True in *Romeo and Juliet*". In *Images of Shakespeare*, edited by Werner Habicht, D.J. Palmer, and Roger Pringle. Newark: University of Delaware Press.
Snyder, Susan. 1970. "*Romeo and Juliet*: Comedy into Tragedy". *Essays in Criticism* 20 (4): 391–402.
Snyder, Susan. 1996. "Ideology and the feud in *Romeo and Juliet*". In *Shakespeare Survey, 49: Romeo and Juliet and its Afterlife*, edited by Stanley Wells, 87–96. Cambridge: Cambridge University Press.
Stubbes, Philip. (1583–95) 1877–79. *Anatomy of the Abuses*, Part I. Edited by Frederick J. Furnivall. London: Traübner, The New Shakespeare Society.
Turner, Victor. 1974. *Dramas, Fields, and Metaphors*. Ithaca: Cornell University Press.
Turner, Victor. 1982. *From Ritual to Theatre: The Human Seriousness of Play*. New York: Performing Arts Journal Publications.
Vernant, Jean Pierre, and Pierre Vidal-Naquet. 1988. *Myth and Tragedy in Ancient Greece*. New York: Zone Books.

Ward, Joseph P. 1997. *Metropolitan Communities. Trade Guilds, Identity, and Change in Early Modern London*. Stanford, CA: Stanford University Press.

Weimann, Robert. 1978. *Shakespeare and the Popular Tradition: Studies in the Social Dimension of Dramatic Form and Function*. Baltimore: Johns Hopkins.

Weinberger, Jerry. 2003. "Pious Princes and Red-Hot Lovers: The Politics of Shakespeare's *Romeo and Juliet*". *The Journal of Politics* 65 (2): 350–75.

Wells, Stanley. 2010. *Shakespeare, Sex, & Love*. Oxford: Oxford University Press.

White, R.S., ed. 2001. *Romeo and Juliet. Contemporary Critical Essays*. Houndmills, Basingstoke: Palgrave.

Whittier, Gayle. 1989. "The Sonnet's Body and the Body Sonnetized in *Romeo and Juliet*". *Shakespeare Quarterly* 40 (1): 27–41.

Wiles, David. 1997. *Tragedy in Athens: Performance Space and Theatrical Meaning*. Cambridge: Cambridge University Press.

Wilshire, Bruce. 1982. *Role Playing and Identity: the Limits of Theatre as Metaphor*. Bloomington: Indiana University Press.

Wilson, Peter. 2000. *The Athenian Institution of the Khoregia: The Chorus, the City and the Stage*. Cambridge: Cambridge University Press.

Woods, Gillian. 2013. *Shakespeare* Romeo and Juliet. *A Reader's Guide to Essential Criticism*. Houndmills, Basingstoke: Palgrave Macmillan.

Zelnick, Stephen. 2011. "*Romeo and Juliet*: The 'True Ground of All These Piteous Woes'". In *William Shakespeare: Romeo and Juliet*, edited by Joseph Pearce, 245–57. San Francisco: Ignatius Press.

Prologue
Shakespeare and Verona

Stanley Wells

In this essay I want to write mainly about Shakespeare's portrayal of Verona, but it may be worth starting with a few thoughts about his relationship with Italy in general. It is remarkable that the action of about half of his thirty-seven or so plays takes place in this country, whether it is the Italy of classical times, as in the plays most commonly spoken of as the Roman plays, or Renaissance Italy. Though we Brits may like to think of him as a quintessentially English writer, it would be fairer to regard him – and indeed many of his contemporaries – more broadly as a European. And he was especially strongly influenced by Italian culture. It is clear that from his schooldays onwards he developed a deep fondness for classical literature, especially Ovid's *Metamorphoses*, both in the original and in Arthur Golding's translation, and that he knew and made use of such Roman writers as Virgil, Cicero, and the playwrights Plautus, Terence, and Seneca. Italy reached him too through writers of the Renaissance such as Petrarch, Boccaccio, Bandello, and Castiglione. In his own time Italian writers living and working in England – including John Florio, who was the Earl of Southampton's Italian tutor, and whom Shakespeare may well have known personally – influenced his work. Indeed Florio is one of the most recent – and most absurd – candidates put forward by the anti-Shakespearians as the author of his works. This is in a book by Lamberto Tassinari.

The first English book about the country, *The History of Italy*, published in 1549, was written by a Welsh civil servant, William Thomas, who lived here for at least three years and made a serious study of Italian language, history, and culture, which he greatly admired. He writes from personal knowledge of many Italian cities and city states, but does not have much to say about Verona. There is no reason to suppose that Shakespeare read Thomas's fascinating book, but the facts and opinions that it purveyed must have helped to form English opinions about the country in general. Some writers portrayed it as a sink of iniquity; an Italianate Englishman was proverbially spoken of as a 'diablo incarnato' ('the devil incarnate'). In *Piers Penniless*, published in 1592, Thomas Nashe slandered the country in lurid terms: "O Italy, the academy of manslaughter, the sporting place of murder, the apothecary shop of poison for all nations!" (Nashe 1964, 46). And in *The Unfortunate Traveller*, of 1594, he writes of Italy as a land from which a traveller may bring "the art of atheism, the art of epicurizing, the art of whoring, the art of poisoning, the art of sodomitry" (ibid., 259). This book is virtually a fictionalised guide book to the country. Nashe's traveller visits various Italian cities and writes of them with a particularity which gives at least the illusion of close familiarity. In Rome, for instance, he says "I was at Pontius Pilate's House, and pissed against it. The name of the place I remember not, but it is as one goes to St Paul's Church not far from the Jews' Piazza" (ibid., 244).

Though it is unlikely that Shakespeare would have learned Italian at school, he certainly appears to have been able to read the language. The story of Othello told by Giraldi Cinthio in the *Hecatommithi*, published in 1555, had not been translated into English when Shakespeare based his great tragedy on it, and although there was a French translation there is reason to believe that Shakespeare used the original. And a speech of Portia's in *The Merchant of Venice* shows that a command of Italian was regarded as a necessary accomplishment of an English gentleman. Speaking of her would-be suitor "Falconbridge, the young baron of England", she complains that he "hath neither Latin, French, nor Italian" (1.2.61–2, 64–5). I like to think that Shakespeare would not have written this if he himself did not have at least a reasonable fluency in all three languages.

Now for Verona, which he mentions in four plays (one of them indirectly), three of them written early in his career. The exception is *Othello*, which has only an indirect reference – we learn that Cassio has arrived in Cyprus on "A noble ship of Venice ... a Veronessa" (2.1.22–7), that is, a Veronese ship, or one equipped by the city. Verona was a principality of Venice, as was Cyprus from 1489 to 1570, when it came under Ottoman rule. So clearly by this point in his career Shakespeare had some knowledge of the city's history.

Earlier, he alludes to Verona directly in *The Taming of the Shrew*, where Petruccio appears at least figuratively to be shaking the soil of the city from his shoes when he first comes on stage. Within a few moments, however, he is in Padua:

> Verona, for a while I take my leave,
> To see my friends in Padua, but of all
> My best belovèd and approvèd friend
> Hortensio; and I trow this is his house. (1.2.1–4)

Hortensio asks "what happy *gale* / *Blows* you to Padua here, from old Verona?" (1.2.47–8). This might, especially in view of Shakespeare's notorious geographical unreliability, seem to imply that Petruccio has travelled the forty or so miles between the two inland cities by water – or by wind-bicycle –, but of course Hortensio may be speaking figuratively. Later Petruccio says that he was born there. And that is all so far as that play is concerned.

Two plays, however, are set partly, one of them largely, in Verona, and one of them even names the city in its title. *The Two Gentlemen of Verona*, loose in construction, slight of plot, though full of good humour and poetical charm, is, I believe, Shakespeare's first play. And none – except perhaps *The Winter's Tale* – has got him into more trouble for geographical vagueness and error. Usually, of course, we read the play in texts that have been tidied up by editors, who have quite a task in trying to sort out the puzzles posed by its original printing in the First Folio. William C. Carroll, the Arden editor, justly remarks that "were it not for the final word of the play's title, we might be hard-pressed to identify just which Italian city was home to Proteus, Valentine, and Julia" (Shakespeare 2004, 75). "Those in the audience", he says,

> who had read descriptions of Italy – by English travellers or in translated accounts – might have expected some reference to the two most remarkable landmarks of Verona, the Piazza Bra and the Arena, one of the largest surviving Roman amphitheatres in the world, but *Two Gentlemen* offers no such reference. The Verona of the play seems, instead, to be a fairly generic small town, from which the ambitious youths leave to go to the sophisticated court world of Milan. The sole distinguishing feature of Shakespeare's Verona in *Two Gentlemen* is that its river (the Adige, not named in the play) seems to have a tide, even though it is far inland. (ibid., 76).

And, noting that "The river [*sic*] Thames of course did have tidal effects", Carroll pertinently cites Andrew Gurr's remark that all Shakespeare's "cities are versions of London" (ibid.). One thing that Verona and London have in common is the fact that both of them were walled cities with a river standing in for one of the walls.

Not only is Verona depicted vaguely in this play, there are also a number of points in the Folio text – the only early one we have – at which the characters seem remarkably ill informed of their whereabouts. At the start of 2.5, Speed welcomes Lance (and his dog) to Padua when the story actually requires them to be in Milan. It is possible that "Padua" is a first thought, rejected but not cancelled in Shakespeare's manuscript; Padua, described in *The Taming of the Shrew* as a "nursery of arts" (1.1.2), had (and has) a famous university (the second oldest in the country) to which Valentine might appropriately have been sent, especially if he wanted to study medicine. On the other hand it is equally possible that Shakespeare was just playing around with the names of various Italian cities with no regard for geographical consistency.

A few scenes later the Duke of Milan seems to think he is in Verona when he is actually at home, in Milan. "There is a lady in Verona here / Whom I affect", he says in the Folio text. In the eighteenth century, Pope altered "Verona" to "Milan" in the interests of geographical consistency. Later Collier, with more concern for metre, read 'Milano' – "There is a lady in

Milano here" –, and this is followed by some later editors, including Evans in the Riverside edition. In the Oxford edition I prefer, like Halliwell in the middle of the nineteenth century, the simple change from "in Verona here" to "of Verona here" as a way of rescuing Shakespeare from error, though really this is textual tinkering rather than scholarly editing.

Still more difficult is a moment in the last act when, in the Folio, Valentine threatens Thurio: "Doe not name *Silvia* thine: if once againe, / *Verona* shall not hold thee". Actually Verona does not hold Thurio here, and so far as we know it never did. In fact at this point the action requires him to be in Milan. Shakespeare's early editor Lewis Theobald changed the line to read "Milan shall not behold thee", altering "hold" to "behold" presumably in order to rectify the metre. The Riverside edition reads "Milan" but retains "hold", which leaves the line unmetrical: "[Milan] shall not hold thee. Here she stands". It would have seemed more logical of the editor to follow Collier here, reading 'Milano'. In this case, perhaps illogically, I preferred not to make a change at all while noting the problem and suggesting that in performance "This Milan" or "Our Milan" might be substituted. For some reason, perhaps because an edition can be annotated, one is more willing to confront a reader than a playgoer with nonsense. Roger Warren, in his World's Classics edition, also retains the Folio reading, admitting that it is "perhaps another Shakespearian slip" while suggesting, rather desperately, that "perhaps Valentine in incoherent fury naturally refers to his home town" (Shakespeare 2008, 180). It would be quite a challenge for any actor to convey such fury, I should have thought. Carroll's Arden edition also lets "Verona" stand with the to-me-enigmatic note "it is just possible that *Verona* should be understood as fitting Valentine's frame of reference" (Shakespeare 2004, 281).

The most notorious of Shakespeare's errors in this play is the fact that, as Dr Johnson put it, he "conveys his heroes by sea from one inland town to another in the same country" (1968, 2.173). Valentine travels by water from Verona to Milan even though both cities lie inland. "My father at the road / Expects my coming, there to see me shipped", says Valentine (1.1.53–4). Later, too, Proteus makes the same journey by ship (2.2.13–15). This has generally been regarded as yet another of Shakespeare's geographical *bêtises*. In recent years however anti-Shakespearians – those who believe that Shakespeare did not write the works generally attributed to him – have exultantly claimed that, in fact, it was possible to travel between the two cities not by sea but by canal, and therefore that the lines are not nonsensical after all. This theory is documented at extraordinary length and with implausible, not to say verbose ingenuity by an American lawyer, Richard Paul Roe, in his book *The Shakespeare Guide to Italy*, subtitled *Retracing the Bard's Unknown Travels*, published posthumously in 2011. The level of this book's Shakespearian scholarship may be judged by its statement that *Romeo and Juliet* is "commonly said to be the first play the author wrote" (2011, 5). It is not. Mr Roe seems to have had great fun after retiring from the legal profession in driving round Italy and investigating archives in the attempt to demonstrate that the author of the plays had what he calls an "astonishing" "familiarity with Italy, its sites and sights, specific details, history, geography, unique cultural aspects, places and things, practices and propensities, etc." (ibid.). He refers to the authorship controversy while declaring that "this book shuns all existing arguments about the identity of the playwright, simply calling him 'the playwright' or 'the author'" (ibid.). Nevertheless, and predictably, his book has been seized upon by anti-Shakespearians as a significant contribution to their cause. It was hailed by Sir Derek Jacobi as "essential reading for all concerned with who really wrote the works of Shakespeare", by William Leahy, described as "Head of the School of Arts, Shakespeare Authorship Studies, Brunel University'" as "a hugely significant intervention in the study of Shakespeare and his dramatic works", and by Michael York – described inaccurately, one might even say fraudulently, as an associate artist of the Royal Shakespeare Company, with which he has never appeared (not in any case that that would qualify him to pronounce on scholarly matters) – as "a revolutionary and revelatory book". But the claim that it is possible to travel between Verona and Milan by canal, tortuously defended, solves nothing. The simple fact that Proteus says to Speed:

> Go, go, be gone, to save your ship from wreck,
> Which cannot perish, having thee aboard,
> Being destined to a drier death on shore (1.1.142–4)

is in itself enough to show that the playwright imagined a voyage by sea, not by canal, on which ships, shores, and wrecks are to say the least uncommon.

* * *

There is reason to believe that before writing *The Two Gentlemen of Verona* Shakespeare had already read Arthur Brooke's poem *The Tragicall Hystorye of Romeus and Juliet* (Bullough 1957, 1.209), published in 1562; both plays include a Friar Laurence and a rope ladder intended to enable a lover to ascend to his mistress's bedroom. Brooke's long poem is written in the old-fashioned poulter's measure (couplets made up of a line of twelve syllables followed by one of fourteen) most familiar to us, perhaps, from Arthur Golding's translation of Ovid's *Metamorphoses*. Brooke was drowned at sea, but there is no more reason to suppose that he, who based his poem on Boaistuau's French translation of Bandello, travelled to Italy than that Shakespeare did. There is incidentally an extraordinary article in the *Shakespeare Oxford Newsletter* declaring that "many Oxfordians consider this poem a youthful composition by de Vere who later expanded and revised the story for the stage" (Altrocchi 2007, 24). It is also proposed that de Vere, not Golding, is the translator of Ovid's *Metamorphoses*. Horrifyingly the author of an internet article, Michael Delahoyde, promulgating these absurdities teaches a Shakespeare course at Washington State University.

Anyhow, Brooke's poem gave Shakespeare masses of material for his play, in terms of narrative, characterization, moralization, and topographical detail. And of course *Romeo and Juliet* is the most Veronese of Shakespeare's plays. In writing briefly about it I want to concentrate rather on his imagination than on his geography, to look at the ways in which he characterizes the city of Verona. In this play, as in *The Two Gentlemen of Verona*, there is no reference to what Carroll refers to as the city's most remarkable landmarks, the Piazza Bra and the Arena. The scene of Mercutio's death takes place in what Benvolio calls "the public haunt of men" (3.1.49), which may imply a kind of *piazza*. Like the real Verona – and also like London – the Verona of the play is a walled city with gates patrolled by watchmen (3.3.166); it is close enough to Mantua for Romeo to be banished there but far enough for post horses (in the plural) to be needed to make the journey – in Brooke only one horse is needed so perhaps Shakespeare is imagining the distance between the cities to be rather greater than the roughly twenty miles it actually is.

The city is 'ancient' – Juliet speaks of "a vault, an ancient receptacle, / Where for this many hundred years the bones of all my buried ancestors are packed" (4.3.37–9). And of course it is now possible to visit the crypt of the beautiful Monastery of San Francesco al Corso where Juliet was allegedly buried. According to its website, soon after Shakespeare wrote the play the lid of Juliet's sarcophagus and her mortal remains were "taken to a secret location by the Venetian government because they did not want the two suicides to have too much public attention". We are told that "for a Hollywood film of 1937 the sarcophagus was taken into the convent vaults for filming the death scene, where it can be still be admired today". And (for a fee) you can get married beside the sarcophagus, if you wish.

Back to the play. Verona is ruled by a Prince named Escalus, as in both Brooke's and William Painter's versions of the story, Shakespeare's main sources. The city is characterized in the very first sentence of the prologue as "fair" Verona, and enjoys, it would seem plenty of sunshine. "The day is hot", says Benvolio at the start of the third act, in which Mercutio is to be killed, and "in these hot days is the mad blood stirring" (3.1.2–4); the Nurse can bask in sunshine under the dovehouse wall. The city has orchards, and (like Shakespeare's Stratford) a variety of trees, including yews, medlars – native to the Mediterranean but grown in England and well-known from the bawdy name for their fruit, the 'open-arse' – and, most notoriously, sycamores. I say notoriously because Richard Paul Roe, in the book I mentioned, exults over his discovery that sycamore trees grow outside one of Verona's western gates.

The cause of his excitement is Benvolio's statement that he has seen Romeo walking "underneath the grove of sycamore / That westward rooteth from the city's side" (1.1.118–19). The fact that there is such a grove, and that it may have been there in Shakespeare's time, is for Roe enough to demonstrate that the author of the play had actually visited Verona, and thus cannot have been Shakespeare (on the reasonable but unprovable assumption that he never visited the country); and this is often quoted by anti-Shakespearians. It says little for its proponents' belief in the power of the imagination.

Verona's population includes wealthy families – we hear of "great rich Capulet" (1.2.81) whose house has a "great chamber" (1.5.12) and who can employ as many as "twenty cunning cooks" (4.2.2–3) and a number of musicians. It has an abbey behind the walls of which Romeo's man will bring to the Nurse the rope ladder with which he plans to mount to Juliet's bedroom. One of its churches is dedicated to St Peter (3.5.114, 116, 154) – a change from Brooke, where it is "St Francis' church" (l. 2006) – though the Friar in the play twice refers to St Francis (2.2.65, 5.3.121). This seems not to be without interest since as well as the apostle Peter there was a St Peter of Verona, martyred in 1252, and Roe makes very heavy weather of finding that there are four medieval churches in Verona dedicated to one or other of the Peters. One of them is, he proclaims, not only "in Juliet's parish, but directly on the path between lovely Juliet's house and the monastic cell of her confessor" (2011, 33). But there were plenty of St Peter's churches in England, too, and in spite of the change from Brooke it is over-fanciful to imagine that Shakespeare had a specifically Veronese one in mind as he wrote.

Somewhere apparently outside Shakespeare's city of Verona is a place called "old Freetown", "the common judgement place" (1.1.99) where justice is dispatched. Escalus summons Montague to it after the play's opening brawl. This name too comes from Brooke, who refers to Freetown as a place where old Capulet intends to provide a "costly feast" (l. 2258) for Paris before his wedding day. The town Villafranca di Verona is now the location of Verona's airport, and it was a 'Freetown' because in the twelfth century it was granted freedom from paying taxes. Shakespeare may have thought of it in the same terms as "the melancholy vale, / The place of death and sorry execution, / Behind the ditches of the abbey here" (5.1.121–8) to which the Duke of *The Comedy of Errors* goes in the expectation of witnessing the beheading of Egeon.

In briefly sketching some of the principal features of the Verona *of Romeo and Juliet* I hope to have shown some of the ways in which Shakespeare provided a local habitation for the traditional story. In the theatres of his time, of course, the city's physical features would have been conjured up only in the audience's minds, but what he wrote has stimulated the imaginations of innumerable later artists, stage, film, and ballet designers to attempt to realize it in material terms, often of great beauty.

WORKS CITED

Altrocchi, Paul H. 2007. "Shakespeare, Not Arthur Brooke, Wrote Tragicall Historye of Romeus & Juliet". *Shakespeare Oxford Newsletter* 43 (1): 22–6.

Bullough, Geoffrey. 1957. *Narrative and Dramatic Sources of Shakespeare*, vol. 1. London: Routledge and Kegan Paul / New York: Columbia University Press.

Johnson, Samuel. 1968. *Johnson on Shakespeare*. Edited by Arthur Sherbo. 2 vols. New Haven and London: Yale University Press.

Nashe, Thomas. 1964. *Selected Works*. Edited by Stanley Wells. London: Edward Arnold.

Roe, Richard Paul. 2011. *The Shakespeare Guide to Italy. Retracing the Bard's Unknown Travels*. New York: Harper Collins.

William Shakespeare. 2004. *The Two Gentlemen of Verona*. Edited by William C. Carroll. London: Thomson Learning (The Arden Shakespeare Third Series).

Shakespeare, William. 2005. *The Oxford Shakespeare: the Complete Works*. Edited by Stanley Wells, Gary Taylor, with John Jowett and William Montgomery. Oxford: Clarendon Press.

Shakespeare, William. 2008. *The Two Gentlemen of Verona*. Edited by Roger Warren. Oxford: Oxford University Press.

Tassinari, Lamberto. 2009. *John Florio, The Man Who Was Shakespeare*. Montréal: Giano Books.

Part I
Dialectics of Private and Public Spaces

1 Classical Paradigms of Tragic Choice in Civic Stories of Love and Death

Guido Avezzù

Classical philologists are normally required to identify the precedents of the modern versions of an archetypal story along a diachronic line. In the case of *Romeo and Juliet*, they paradoxically tend to concentrate upon the less civic dimensions of the play, although its action starts off in the public space of the streets and its thematic core is rooted in civic feuding. This attitude is shared by Elizabethan theatre scholars such as John J. Munro who, in investigating the "tales of unhappy loves", pointed out "two main elements" as distinctive features of the 'separation-' and 'potion-romances': (*a*) the separation of two lovers by some obstacle, and (*b*) their ruin brought about by an error (1908, ix–x, xlviii–ix). Thus the 'potion-plot' and the subsequent *peripeteia* escape all dynamic confrontation with the primarily civic dimension of the 'separation-plot', represented by Sampson's and Gregory's early ruthless exhibition of both symptoms and effects of civic feuding. Conversely, concentrating on the "error" as the triggering element of the tragic dénouement and defining it as a sort of reversed tragic recognition entailed an emphasis on the novelistic components over the civic context, which is nonetheless clearly alluded to by some details of the 'potion-plot' (such as Friar John's mishap, 5.2.5–16) and stressed by the Prince's final intervention in 5.3. Indeed, this has led critics to focus mainly upon the last two acts, looking for the earliest literary attestations of stories pivoting on the apparent death of a character resulting in the death of her/his lover and in the final suicide of the former. It is well known that this plot closely follows the narrative pattern of Pyramus's and Thisbe's story narrated in Ovid's *Metamorphoses*. The search for antecedents – at least since Douce's *Illustrations of Shakspeare* (1807) – has invariably looked at Hellenistic tales and romances, whose dating and intertextual relations remain in the haze. The survival and the dissemination of these texts in the fifteenth and sixteenth centuries have not been fully elucidated (see, for instance, Xenophon Ephesius's *Ephesian tales*, which has been numbered among *Romeo and Juliet*'s indirect sources, or even Chariton's *Chaereas and Callirhoe*). These intertextual and derivational ramifications have been further complicated by the hypothesis of a direct descent of the Italian novellas (Da Porto, Bandello) from the *Ephesian tales*. On the one hand, this does not help clarify whether it is a matter of genetic descent or instead of inheritance of a narrative archetype;

on the other hand, it shows that other possible and verifiable ascendancies of the dramatic text have been neglected.

As Kenneth Muir pointed out, apart from the obvious reference to epics, other narrative genres should also be explored. Muir distinguished between ascertainable and ascertained "conscious" sources, but also underlined "numerous unconscious sources", and called for the "need for a full-length study of Shakespeare's use of *multiple sources*" (1954, 152–3; my emphasis). It is worth calling attention to yet another aspect – which I will also discuss below – of Muir's analysis of "Shakespeare's method". The same source, Muir argues, may have been available to Shakespeare through several narrative adaptations but also through the concomitant translation/s of the source that was the model for those same adaptations. With regard to the story of Pyramus and Thisbe, Ovid's epyllion (short epic poem) reached Shakespeare through the Italian novellas and Brooke's eventual poetic translation, but also – as Muir clearly showed – through other kinds of mediation, both 'high', such as Golding's translation of Ovid's *Metamorphoses*,[1] and 'low', such as some *Elizabethan Miscellanies*, which were probably addressed to a larger and less sophisticated audience (ibid., 142–3). This hypothesis brings forth the idea – to which I will also come back – that the latter sources interacted with the basic narrative paradigm stirring suggestions that found fertile ground in both the author's and the audience's expectations.

As regards other 'sources', we should especially look at Greek and Roman tragedy, in that not only did it contribute to the shaping of the Ovidian narrative – as has already been remarked – but also exercised this modelling function through other kinds of mediation. "Metamorphic" in itself (Barchiesi 2005, cxliv),[2] "of its nature anti-generic" and at the same time "an anthology of genres" (Kenney 1986, xviii), Ovid's poem, "following a dynamics already firmly established in the Hellenistic poetry ... offers itself as the final outcome of the entire tradition of Greek and Latin tragedy" in "a sort of global reading", prompting the reader "to compare the destinies that the single works keep somewhat separated" (Barchiesi 2005, cxliv-vi). Among the many lots narrated in the *Metamorphoses*, the reader finds those of incestuous pairs such as Byblis and her brother Caunus (Ovid 2004, 9.450–665) or Myrrha and her father Cinyras (ibid., 10.298–502).[3] The two stories are united by the precept that girls should love only those they are allowed to ("Byblis in exemplo est ut ament concessa puellae", 9.454; "Byblis ought / To bee a mirror unto Maydes in lawfull wyse to love", Golding 1567, 117^v) and by the observation that "nunc opus est leviore lyra ... canamus ... inconcessisque puellas / ignibus attonitas meruisse libidine poenam" (10.152) ("now I neede a meelder style to tell ... of unlawfull joyes / That burned in the brests of Girles, who for theyr wicked lust / According as they did deserve, receyved penance just", Golding 1567, 124^v). It is likely that the extremity of these stories, pivoting on a love that "res ipsa vetat" (Ovid 2004, 10.354: "the thing itself forbids it")[4] and on the subsequent repudiation of one's familial belonging[5] that we will find in *Romeo and Juliet* (2.1.75–8), did not prove suggestive only after a reading of Golding's version of Ovid's *Metamorphoses*. Besides, these stories are not merely about incest, but more generally entail an erotic investment so radical as to subvert not only the family institution, but also dynastic convenience, and end up by threatening the existence of the desiring subjects within the city itself. This predicament brings about a tragic finale and, in Ovid especially, a metamorphic sentence. In this regard, the role of Plutarch's *Moralia* should not be undervalued since in the sixteenth century their translations became available to the "ordinary cultivated reader" (Gillespie 2004, 426).[6] The whole corpus was translated into French by Jacques Amyot in 1572, but a few titles had been already individually printed in English from 1528 onwards (the same year in which Thomas Wyatt published his *Quiet of Mind*, taken from Plutarch's *De tranquillitate animi* – a work that would be translated by Queen Elizabeth too). Furthermore, both Plutarch's *Moralia* and his *Lives* (translated by Thomas North in 1579) granted the transmission of the textual fragments of both surviving and lost Greek tragedies, located in textual contexts that used them as witnesses and interpretative paradigms of both approved and disapproved behaviours. However, it is no exaggeration to affirm that the *Moralia* conveyed a tragic conception, as well as fabulistic patterns, in a more effective way than the still slow dissemination of the extant Greek dramatic texts would allow. In this scenario, the suggestions exercised not only by the contents, but also by the models, were assimilated and sometimes combined: the principle "omnia mutantur, nihil interit" (Ovid 2004, 15.165) ["all changes, nothing perishes"] applies also in this regard. A close analysis may not overlook other debts towards Greek tragedy – even though possibly mediated. The extent and pervasiveness of the dissemination of ancient Greek texts in Britain – even in the original – is also witnessed by the fortune of a fragment from Critias's *Sisyphus* (second half of the fifth century BC). This forty-line fragment, transmitted by Sextus Empiricus's *Adversus mathematicos*, 9.54,[7] deals with the 'invention of the gods', and was adapted by Robert Greene in his 1594 *First Part of the Most Tyrannicall Tragedie and Raigne of Selimus* (Greene 1898, ll. 312–43). The derivation from Sextus Empiricus is apparent and the fact that his *Adversus mathematicos* – available at the time only through a Latin translation published in Paris in 1569 – was well known is confirmed by the 'hellish verses' supposedly composed by Walter Raleigh.[8]

Some narrative subgenres, such as the condensed form of prose epyllia represented by Parthenius's *Love Romances*, also show affinities with the plot in question. I will start by introducing an overview of this kind of literature, and then move on to Greek tragedy. This will mean to look at the narrative and dramatic models of the 'less civic' dimension of *Romeo and Juliet* as a foil to help foreground what I suggest could be considered as a horizon of expectations regarding civic motifs and topoi of classical origin circulating in Renaissance England. While not providing direct sources, they may assist us in mapping out the cultural construction of an idea of the civic based on a widespread dissemination of classical texts and their unexpected oblique effect upon Shakespeare.

The story of Pyramus and Thisbe, narrated in Ovid's *Metamorphoses* (4.55–166), can be segmented into six phases:[9]

a   ll. 55–80: the love between the protagonists is hindered by their parents;
b   ll. 81–92: the lovers promise each other to meet at night under the mulberry tree next to Ninus's grave;
c   ll. 93–104: Thisbe temporarily remains alone, and an unforeseen event seems to produce evidence of her death;[10]
d   ll. 105–27: at his arrival, Pyramus gathers from this evidence that she is dead and kills himself;
e   ll. 128–63: she returns, discovers the body of her beloved, and commits suicide;
f   ll. 164–6: the gods and the parents are moved by the event; the gods will perpetuate the mulberry metamorphosis: the fruits, which had been white until then, have been turned blood red (ll. 125–7) and finally black (ll. 165–6); the parents will immortalize the memory of the two lovers, whose ashes will be indissolubly mingled together "una ... in urna" (l. 166, "in a single urn"): this will be a "monimentum" (l. 161, "memorial shrine") no less than the mulberries "gemini monimenta cruoris" (l. 161, "memorials of our twinned blood").[11]

We can identify here the emergence of the narrative pattern of the apparent death that, long before being valorized by the Hellenistic romance (Kerényi 1973, 24–43), was already well-known in classic Athens. It can be found in Sophocles's *Electra* ll. 62–3, in which Orestes, who is planning to fake his own death, says: "Yes, often in the past I have known clever men dead in fiction but not dead" (Lloyd-Jones 1994), thus alluding to renowned shamanic figures and/or to protagonists of myths (Finglass 2007, 111 and Wehrli 1965, 142–3). Yet, not differently from what will happen in *Romeo and Juliet*, in *Pyramus and Thisbe* this attitude is not conducive to the stigmatization of popular beliefs, but to the activation of a deductive process similar to the one that in Greek tragedy regulated the *anagnorisis* (exemplar in this regard is Electra's traditional recognition of her brother Orestes which Euripides fiercely criticizes in his *Electra*; see Boitani 2002 and 2014, 133–79). Keeping to the story of Pyramus and Thisbe, its linear unfolding encompasses: (a) conflict, (b) intrigue, (c) Pyramus's departure and Thisbe's apparent death, (d) his fallacious deduction and ensuing suicide, (e) her return, discovery of his dead body and suicide, (f) the perpetuation of their memory, entrusted to nature and to posthumous legitimation by their parents. This sequence can be applied to the analysis of the mythemic motifs and their several appropriations on their way to *Romeo and Juliet*.[12]

To date the search for the earliest precedents of the Shakespearean drama has led to the so-called *Story of Pamphilus and Eurydike*, preserved in a first-century BC Michigan papyrus.[13] In its scanty twenty-seven lines, this papyrus "presents a prose narrative closely related to the famous episode of Pyramus and Thisbe ... whose version appeared until then fairly isolated within the Greek-Latin literary tradition" (Stramaglia 2001, 82). If we compare *Pamphilus and Eurydike* with the segmentation of the Pyramus and Thisbe storyline presented above, we can detect some common elements (the letters correspond to the ones assigned to the *Pyramus and Thisbe* plot; literal quotations from the papyrus, essential to the reconstruction of the story, are in italics):

a the presence of *openings* – although unspecified at least in the readable portion of the papyrus – which are remindful of Ovid's "tenui[s] rima" (4.65, "little chink") that allowed the two lovers to communicate secretly;
b Pamphilus being late for the appointment, after *having left* his beloved *alone*;
c not finding her and seeing her *clothing* (which we may presume to be blood-stained) and a *circular* set of footprints as if she had been chased, Pamphilus presumes that Eurydike has been *eaten by a wild beast*.

Thanks to the new, more satisfactory dating of the papyrus fragment to the late first century BC,[14] the anonymous and fragmentary *Pamphylus and Eurydike* should be ascribed at the latest to the epoch in which Parthenius was active, that is, the second half of the first century (possibly between 52 and 26 BC).[15] His very short *Love romances* ('Ερωτικὰ παθήματα, literally 'love sufferings') present various stories that terminate in the suicide either of the male protagonist, who blames himself for having unwillingly caused the death of his beloved (or, in any case, of a girl), or of the female protagonist as a consequence of her lover's death – of which she is in no way responsible. In this regard it is essential to mention at least the cases of Leucone and Cyanippus, Clite and Cyzicus, Anthippe and Cichyrus, and Arganthone and Rhesus, which are representative of two distinct typologies of masculine and feminine suicide:[16]

I. 'EXPIATORY' SUICIDE (masculine):
10. *Leucone and Cyanippus*:[17] Cyanippus kills his jealous wife mistaking her for a wild beast and then kills himself.
32. *Anthippe and Cichyrus*: Anthippe hides in a bush with an unnamed young boy with whom she has fallen in love. Cichyrus, the king's son, mistaking her for a wild beast, kills her. As soon he realizes his error, Cychyrus faints, is unhorsed, and dies.[18] Nothing is known of Anthippe's anonymous lover's fate.

II. 'WIDOWED' SUICIDE (feminine):
28. *Clite and Cyzicus*: Cyzicus dies fighting the Argonauts and Clite commits suicide.
36. *Arganthone and Rhesus*: Rhesus dies in the Trojan war and Arganthone commits suicide.

The two mythemes variously combine under the common sign of love and death, and sometimes the tales they are actualized in can 'lend' some components to other narrative patterns, giving a more rounded connotation to the characters. This is why *Anthippe and Cichyrus*, even though its two protagonists are not lovers, is numbered among the Greek sources of the Ovidian Pyramus and Thisbe episode.[19] Other more recent tales can be traced back to the same cultural mood that had brought forth *Pamphilus and Eurydike* and, later on, Ovid's *Pyramus and Thisbe*.[20]

In short, we should remark that this pattern is not typical of romance and can at most provide the narrative backbone of short narratives probably belonging to collections of tales exemplifying the sublimation of various kinds of violence that may prove somehow tragic: unintentional violence (Cyanippus, Cichyrus), divine violence (Callirhoe of Patras), social or war violence (Pyramus and Thisbe, and Arghantone and Rhesus, respectively). On the contrary, the Hellenistic-Roman romances often make use of the apparent death narrative device in order to set off the action (as in Chariton), trigger meaningful turns (as in the romances by Xenophon of Ephesus and Antonius Diogenes), or simply enrich the plot through the insertion of unexpected events (as in Iamblichus's *Babylonian tales*):

> In the first book of *Chaereas and Callirhoe*, Chaereas believes the false accusations of a slanderer and becomes fiercely jealous of his wife Callirhoe. As a consequence, he kicks her and, when she faints, presumes her dead. Deposed in a "magnificent grave" (1.6.5), the woman wakes up in time to be kidnapped by the pirates (18.1–9.1). The first four chapters, culminating in the jealousy scene, take place entirely in an urban setting, among the religious ceremonies, assemblies and personal rivalries of the late fifth-century Syracuse – Hermocrates, Callirhoe's father, is the commander (*strategos*) who defeated the Athenians in the Peloponnesian War. From the fifth to the eighth chapter, the action unfolds in parallel lines: inside the city with the solemn funeral and the trial that will acquit Chaereas, and outside, in the tomb of Hermocrates's family erected by the sea.[21] The apparent death and ensuing awakening set off the adventures of the couple who will be reunited only at the end of the romance.
>
> In his *Ephesian tales*, Xenophon of Ephesus narrates how Anthia, the female protagonist, asks the physician Eudoxos for a poison in order to escape an unwanted marriage by committing suicide, but he provides her with a sleeping potion without her knowing. Believed to

be dead, she is buried with great pomp, and when she later wakes up in the crypt she is kidnapped by bandits (3.5.5–8.2). A kindred narrative can be found in Achilles Tatius's *Clitophon and Leucippe*.

In Iamblichus's *Babylonian tales*, the two lovers Rhodane and Sinonis try to poison themselves together, but again the poison is replaced by a sleeping draught. Rhodane has a nightmare that wakes them both and then Sinonis unsuccessfully tries to kill herself with a sword.[22]

In Chariton's and Xenophon's romances, whose dating has been recently ascribed to the years between 50 and 70 AD (Bowie 2002), the apparent death as well as the seemingly outrageous removal of the corpse (both heroines are kidnapped after their awakening in the tomb) do not lead the survivors to commit suicide, not even Chaereas who had kicked his wife to death. As for Xenophon, it has been observed that Anthia's apparent death could have inspired Masuccio Salernitano and consequently, following the well-known chain of intermediate steps, Shakespeare (see my appendix). In Greek and Roman romances the sequence 'apparent death-suicide' is adopted to get rid of minor characters or deployed in digressions from the main narrative:

In Antonius Diogenes's *The Unbelievable Things beyond Thule*, Thruscanos, the villain, after pestering Derkyllis with his advances, kills himself as soon as he believes her dead.[23]

In the already mentioned *Babylonian tales*, Rhodane's dog tears to pieces the dead bodies of a boy and a girl. The father of Sinonis, Rhodane's lover, recognizes the dog and presumes that the disfigured girl is his daughter. He, therefore, kills the dog, buries the girl and, with the blood of the animal, writes an epitaph on her grave saying, "Here lies beautiful Sinonis". Finally, he hangs himself. When Rhodane and Sorechos the Just (who is also in love with Sinonis) arrive, they see the carcass of the dog, the inscription, and the hanged man. The obvious conclusion is that Sorechos tries to hang himself too, while Rhodane, after adding the words "and the beautiful Rhodane" to the inscription, attempts to kill himself with a sword. However, both men are rescued by the intervention of a maid who tells them that Sinonis is alive (77a29-b9, Henry 1960, 44–5).[24] If Patriarch Photius's summary is to be trusted, the protagonist goes on to greater things, marrying Sinonis and becoming King of Babylon.

In order to conclude this survey of the motifs that circulated between the first century BC and the second century AD with special regard to the unexpected turns of the action triggered by cases of apparent death, we should not forget that in the *Babylonian tales* (or better, in Photius's possibly highly selective summary of this romance) these same motifs repeatedly brought about unhoped-for recoveries.[25] In conclusion, the motif of the apparent death, which will characterize first-century AD romances, is a key motif in both prose and verse short first century narratives, as *Pamphilus and Eurydike* and Ovid's *Pyramus and Thisbe*.

Given its fragmentariness, we do not known whether the motif of the tomb was already present in *Pamphilus and Eurydike*, but Ovid's *Metamorphoses* include it by referring – although without developing it in a narrative way – to Ninus's tomb as the designed meeting place of the two lovers, thus explicitly alluding to yet another love romance of the antiquity: *Ninus and Semiramis*. In *Romeo and Juliet*'s immediate antecedents, this detail will be made functional to the plot through the introduction of the "vault" as a funereal reduplication of Capulet's palace. This happens even more clearly in Shakespeare, for example through the repetition of the torch and light motifs (see for instance 1.4.11–2, 35, 5.3.1, 21). Unfortunately it is not possible to document the diffusion in Britain of Phlegon Trallianus's second-century tale, which was published in its original Greek version by Xylander in 1568 and later translated into French by Pierre le Loyer (1568, 380–91). Originally included in a *Book of Wonders*, the story of Philinnion, a girl who comes back from death for three nights, and her lover, Machates, ends with the definitive death of the girl and her final burial in the "chambre voustée où les corps morts de sa famille & parenté estoient ensepulturez" (ibid., 389) ["the vaulted chamber where the bodies of her family and relatives were buried"]. The English translation of the *Discourse des Spectres* (*Book of Spectres*, 1605) is not complete and does not include the Phillinion and Machates narrative; therefore, no connection, fascinating though it may be, can be traced between its impressive ending, with the mourning of the parents on their daughter's 'second' death and the citizens crowding near the house and then moving on to the sepulchre, and either Brooke (*Romeus and Juliet*, ll. 2809–14) or Shakespeare (*Romeo and Juliet* 4.3.45–51, 4.4.43–117, and 5.3.190–2).

***

This list of the ancient mythemic analogues of the intrigue that in *Romeo and Juliet* Friar Laurence styles as a "desperate ... execution" (4.1.69) does not wish to be exhaustive. I only meant to exemplify the great variety of treatments the basic scheme may have undergone and the multiple hints that may have directed the first author – or maybe the second, if we are to trust Arthur Brooke – to give this material a dramatic form. I have also put forward the hypothesis that these suggestions were not conveyed by the Italian novellas and Brooke's poem *Romeus and Juliet* only, but also by other possible versions of Ovid's *Metamorphoses*, in addition to the fabulistic paradigms derived from Greek tragedy included in Plutarch's works and/or in other direct or occasional sources. As we will see, one of the most peculiar traits of Shakespeare's treatment of the basic scheme of actions seems to consist in a different and wholly original combination of motifs associated with the relation between the civic dimension of the play and the 'wedding-and-potion-plot', which traditionally involved the two lovers only. A 'philologically correct' *scire per causas* would place the ancient narrative prototypes into a deterministic frame of stemmatic construction. Yet their analysis produces a far more complex framework, which suggests how each narrative pattern may be affected by several fabulistic solutions. These are sometimes borrowed from other adjacent motifs and prompted by different external stimuli, or even alternative to those privileged by traditional investigations of the sources.

A brief comparison between the diverse realizations of the narrative scheme FALSE DEATH / FIRST SUICIDE / SECOND SUICIDE allows to verify that this pattern intrinsically belongs to the novella rather than to the romance tradition. And it could not be otherwise, given the vocation of the romance towards happy endings in which the fantastic undergoes, in Hegelian terms, the "nötige Korrektion" (Hegel 1955, 2.2.3.2.c, "the necessary correction")[26] through the reunion of the lovers and their full social recognition on the community's part. Abandoned by the narrator at the finally reconquered city gates, we can only imagine this metamorphic correction that consists in the protagonists' individual adjustment to the communal values of the social environment which they have steadily and rightly re-entered. At best, we may appropriate the malice Hegel voiced in his considerations upon the *Bildungsroman*, and its protagonists' landing at the "philistine rationality of the subsisting relationships" (ibid.). Silently signifying to the reader the stability of their new condition, the romances suggest that the couple's new status may find its realization in time, virtually without limits. Indeed, Eros's dialectic ritual game, virtually endlessly prolonged by Lack (*Penia*) and Transition (*Poros*),[27] has been brought to a solution. Joint death may even be called for (as Callirhoe does in the last page of Chariton's romance), but only as the crowning achievement of a shared existence. It is no surprise that this kind of existence does not interest the reader, and that it may be just a consolation, or rather an occasion to be ironic, as Hegel was. Nevertheless, the protagonists' falling back into the norm is introduced by the narrator as if it were fully dependent on them: Rhodane becomes king of Babylon, Chaereas and Callirhoe triumphantly land at Syracuse, Habrocome and Anthia return to Ephesos, where they "array their parents' burial places, and live together as always celebrating" (Dalmeyda 1962, 5.15.3). The structural contrast with the story of Pyramus and Thisbe, and its successive derivations, could not be more evident, starting from the posthumous civic recognition carried out by the parents who include their children into a legally recognized space such as the burial one, after they have forced them to a deadly *peripeteia* in a suburban or extra-urban space. Indeed, in the novella, the same antagonistic drives we have in the romance – from the familial and communal conditionings, to the encounter with other desiring subjects, either noble or vile, to the adventures in a generally liminal territory – do not find a solution in the achievement or in the restoration of a mundane balance in which the protagonists may play an active role. In both Ovid, where it coincides with the metamorphosis which justifies the protagonists' inclusion into his own epic, and in *Romeo and Juliet*, where the *coup de théâtre* of the reconciliation between the two families is an expected and almost foregone conclusion following a proven narrative tradition, the burial of the lovers is a crucial moment and can offer significant variations. In the despotic context of an eastern city-state, the reconciliation between the two families was implicitly circumscribed to subjective mourning, while in Renaissance society it responded to the magnates' political will.

Similarly to what happens in the novella tradition, the *Pyramus and Thisbe* epyllion takes its leave of the lovers once the *Liebestod* motif has been accomplished. Yet, such turn is anti-tragic in that it presents a plot that is not inscribed in "a series of sequels that promise new directions" nor in "a variety of new beginnings" (Dunn 1996, 70).[28] At the same time it introduces a wholly mundane mythology, dominated by "casus" (Ovid 2004, 4.142, literally 'mis-fortune', or "chaunce", Golding 1567, 45^r), where the gods are nothing more than the personification of nature. Being the first story in the *Metamorphoses* recounted by a human being and also the first love story in which gods or demi-gods do not have a share, but whose protagonists are "human and 'bourgeois'" (Rosati 2007, 256), *Pyramus and Thisbe* introduces a peculiar trait that makes it the authentic antecedent of *Romeo and Juliet*, far beyond the separation-and-potion plot it contains. Once the protagonists are dead, *Pyramus and Thisbe* circularly closes on the initial perspective inaugurated in Babylonia (Ovid 2004, 4.57–8) with the parents' forbiddance. After the aetiological annotation on the different colours of the mulberry, that is seen as a durable concession from the gods, the parents, evoked by Thisbe's prayer, reappear to grant the pair's rest "in one Tumbe as Thisbe did desire" (Golding 1567, 45^v). Differently from other lovers, Pyramus and Thisbe did not meet in a temple or during a procession (as, for example, Habrocomes and Anthia in Xenophon's *Ephesian tales*), but are, very 'bourgeois-like', neighbours in a decidedly civic context (Ovid 2004, 4.57–8). In Golding's version, the focus is primarily set on the city rather than on the loving pair and the properly urban features of the city are greatly stressed – from the "huge walles so monstrous high and thicke" (Golding 1567, 43^v) to the houses leaning one on the other so as to look as one huge, single house:

> Pyramus et Thisbe …
> contiguas tenuere domos, ubi dicitur altam
> coctilibus muris cinxisse Semiramis urbem. (Ovid 2004, 4.55–8)

> Within the towne (of whose *huge walles* so *monstrous* high and *thicke*
> The fame is given Semyramis for making them of bricke)
> Dwelt hard together two yong folke in houses joynde so nere
> *That under all one roofe well nie both twaine conveyed were.*

> The name of him was Pyramus, and Thisbe calde was she. (Golding 1567, 43ᵛ; my emphasis)

This spatial intimacy fostered a sentiment that would have found its realization in marriage, had not the parents forbidden it (Ovid 2004, 4.59–61). Golding, who as usual expands and almost glosses Ovid's account, magnifies the description of the protagonists' falling in love, and particularly insists on their "neyghbrod":

> Notitiam primosque gradus vicinia fecit;
> tempore crevit amor. Taedae quoque iure coissent:
> sed vetuere patres. (Ovid 2004, 4.59–61)

> This neighbrod bred acquaintance first, *this neyghbrod* first did stirre
> *The secret sparkes, this neighbrod* first an entrance in did showe,
> For love to come to that to which it afterward did growe.
> And if that right had taken place they had bene man and wife,
> But still their Parents went about to let which (for their life)
> They could not let. (Golding 1567, 43ᵛ; my emphasis)

This proximity is obstructed by the presence of a wall that apparently repeats, although on a minor scale, the demarcation and separation intent that guided the building of the city walls. The microcosm inside those walls corresponds to the macrocosm in which Babylon itself is set. Within the city, we find familial spaces marked by a wall, impenetrable but for a "tenui[s] rima" (65; lit.: "a little chink" or "a cran[n]y" in Golding as well as in *A Midsummer Night's Dream*, 3.1.65 and 5.1.162)[29] and many "domus" (86, "houses") surveilled by parents who act like "custodes" (85, "custodians"). The escape from the two families will then coincide with an escape from the walled city:

> ... statuunt, ut nocte silenti
> fallere custodes foribusque excedere temptent,
> cumque domo exierint, urbis quoque tecta relinquant. (Ovid 2004, 4.84–6)

> ... they covenanted to get
> Away from such as watched them and in the Evening late
> To steale out of their fathers house and eke the Citie *gate*. (Golding 1567, 44ʳ)

The suburban space is initially only an indistinct realm located outside the city walls, yet it is soon depicted as a "latu[m] arvum" (87, "the fieldes", Golding 1567, 44ʳ) as opposed to the "urbis ... tecta" (86, "city houses"), and gets eventually crowded with different landmarks: Ninus's tomb (88), the mulberry tree (89–90), a cold spring (90), and a cave (100). This space is nevertheless exposed to the intrusion of "chaunce" (this is how Golding translated "casus", l. 142, as pointed out above) and is irreducibly far from an urban and civic dimension. Golding's "Ninus tomb ... without the towne" (ibid.) helps sketch the map figured out in Ovid (ll. 88–100), although it never fits into the urban topography. The tomb gives Ovid the chance to name Ninus, Semiramis's husband, perhaps – as already remarked – only in order to allude to their own romance. The monument's stateliness (as ancient tradition had it, this "bust[um]", 88, or "tumulus", 95, was nine stadia high and ten broad)[30] made it a landmark even in the dark. However, the tomb does not have any explicit narrative function nor does it host any cultic practice. We may easily assume, therefore, that no suggestion will come from it in later reprises of the story. In fact, even the exact location of the "tumulus idem" (157) and of the "una ... urna" (166), where Pyramus and Thisbe will be laid, is unspecified. In such a context the reappearance of the families at the end of the epyllion in order to unravel the separation plot provides only an indirect allusion to the urban and civic dimension that started off the action. Shakespeare did look at a variously mediated version of this ancient model (Muir 1954). Yet, in *Romeo and Juliet* – and even more in Brooke – the diverse components of the civic body (the Prince, Capulet, and Montague) eventually reassert their dominion not only upon the civic space, but also on memory and death through the potential eternizing power of the two statues made of "pure gold" (5.3.298).[31] This is not simply a matter of posthumous recognition, entailed in an epigraphic tribute and/or in the establishment of a cultic homage to the sepulchre. The dénouement does not involve the "desperate ... action" the protagonists have been forced to, but the very reasons of that constraint. In this regard, the investigation of the sources should become aware of its partiality and offer instead to clarify the different semiotic processes activated by the various interactions between the potion-plot and its frame, that is, the separation-plot. In *Romeo and Juliet*, the latter attains a particular importance also from a quantitative point of view, together with a marked civic and political connotation.

If attentively looked at, the proportions of the separation- and potion-plot in the Italian novellas, in Brooke's poem, and in Shakespeare actually denounce the inherently equivocal nature of our notion of 'source'. Ovid's 112 lines do not exhaust the entire plot and in the same way *Romeo and Juliet*'s conclusive action does not represent the unravelling of the play's early announced contradictions. This extrication is to be found in the coda, after the recapitulation. In the space of twenty lines, the situation we have experienced at 1.1.77ff. ("Rebellious subjects, enemies to peace ...") is once again repeated by the Prince himself: "Where be these enemies?" (5.3.290). Capulet gives Montague his hand performing a gesture that belongs to mercantile and political proxemics. Montague's response is a sort of compensation (the golden statue) to which Capulet reacts engaging in an analogous commitment ("As rich shall Romeo's by his lady lie",

5.3.302) and perfectly tying the score. The two families will testify to the (re)gained harmony through the two simulacra and will thus pay their debt to the city which has been for a long time plagued by their feud. The mutual donation anticipates the Prince's judgement, at least with regard to the political nature of the ancient rivalry, since criminal justice, much differently from what happened in Brooke (ll. 2985–3400), is almost discarded in Shakespeare ("Some shall be pardoned, and some punished", 307, is all the Prince eventually says). And it is precisely in this regard that the comparison with the 'source' appears particularly fruitful, showing a shared analogy in the reprises of the Pyramus and Thisbe motif, but also emphasizing *Romeo and Juliet*'s significant innovation. As happened in the epyllion, also in *Romeo and Juliet*, as well as in its immediate antecedents, the two lovers' suicide freezes their being in time and asserts the eternity of the perfectly symmetrical couple. Yet in *Romeo and Juliet* we find the averment of another kind of eternity, established in the name of the city and sealed by a contractual reciprocity that parodically repeats the lovers' mutual sacrifice. It is a closure that, in a radically different fashion from Ovid's choice of keeping them indistinct and undistinguishable – "una … in urna" – more or less consciously succeeds in the intent of keeping them separate.[32]

APPENDIX

Looking at the complex pedigree of *Romeo and Juliet*, Carol Gesner privileged the "separation-potion plot of [Xenophon's] *Ephesiaca*". Although she was aware that this romance, transmitted in a single codex previously belonging to the Badia Fiorentina,[33] was printed only in 1726, Gesner suggested at first "that Masuccio's contacts with the humanist circles may have led him to a reading of the La Badia codex, thus establishing the Greek romance potion plot firmly in the domain of Renaissance letters" (Gesner 1970, 62–4).[34] She also adds that "it is reasonable to conjecture that Masuccio and Bandello read the La Badia manuscript" (ibid., 152). This stance is a perfect example of a method which has been applied to other subjects too. Regarding *Othello*, for instance, Gesner wrote that "its story line [is] a modification of the slandered bride plot of Chariton" (ibid., 70). Still, it is too easily forgotten that, if Chariton recounts the slanderous scheme hatched by the tyrant of Akragas, it is our perspective that connects his subtleties with Iago's cunning. Even though we overlooked the fact that Chariton's *Chaereas and Callirhoe* will remain unknown to the general public of readers until 1750, and even if we discounted the differences between the two characters (Akragantinos's personality is far less complicated than Iago's, and he is spurred by much more straightforward motivations), we can but admit that narrative patterns do not obey to a teleological arrangement and are solely guided by paradigmatic choices that respond to a variety of influences.

As a source of *Romeo and Juliet*, Xenophon has already been correctly dealt with by Gerald Sandy (1979, 55). Yet, it is worth pointing out that Angelo Poliziano, the supposed *trait d'union* between the La Badia codex and Masuccio Salernitano (who died before 12 August 1475, while Poliziano's *Miscellanea* was published in 1489), made a partial translation of the *Ephesiaca* (from 1.2.2 Ἤγετο to 5 Ἀνθία and 3.1 from Ὡς to παρθένοι). Poliziano did not annotate any detail of the plot since this short passage was exactly what he needed in order to clarify an excerpt by Martial (*Miscellaneorum centuria* 1.51: "Cur in Ephesiae Dianae templo molles appellati honores a Martiale"). Among the romances contained within the La Badia codex, only *Clitophon and Leucippe* and *Daphnis and Chloe* will be printed in the original before the eighteenth century. Although they are the only ones attested also in other manuscripts, they will be both published more than one century after the *Miscellaneorum centuria*. Achilles Tatius will be translated into Latin and modern languages not earlier than 1546; Longus, never translated in Latin, will be published in Italian only in the seventeenth century (Manzini, 1643; Annibal Caro's sixteenth-century version will remain unpublished for two centuries and a half), while Amyot's French translation will be printed in 1559 and an English translation will appear in 1587. Chariton and Xenophon will not be circulated in the original nor in a modern language translation until the eighteenth century. Certainly the diffusion of these works in the "domain of Renaissance letters" (Gesner 1970, 64) has not been eased by Poliziano's scholarly attitude in glossing them nor by the likely difficulty of gaining access to the La Badia codex, nor above all by the fact that the romances passed almost unobserved among the many Byzantine works included in the same codex. The texts of the *erotici scriptores* will remain buried there at least until the spring of 1700, when Bernard de Montfaucon will rediscover the codex.

It may be useful to summarize in a table the print diffusion of a selection of tales and romances. As regards the romances, there are minimal differences with those listed by Wolff (1912, 8–10) and the most relevant one is the partial adaptation of Heliodorus by Sandford, not included in Hägg (1983).

| Author, work | Greek text | Latin | First translations | | English |
			Italian	French	
Parthenius's *Love romances*	1531			Fornier 1555	
Pseudo-Plutarch's *Love stories*	1509	1500	1598	Amyot 1572	Sandford 1567
Phlegon's *De mirabilibus*	1568				

Classical Paradigms of Tragic Choice in Civic Stories   59

Author, work	Greek text	Latin	First translations Italian	French	English
Heliodorus's *Aethiopica*	1534	Waschewiczki 1552	Ghini 1556	Amyot 1547	Underdowne 1569 Sandford 1567†
*Achilles Tatius's *Clitophon and Leucippe*	1601	Cruceius 1554†	Dolce 1546 Coccio 1551	Rochemaure 1556 Belleforest 1568 (from Cruceius)	B(urton) 1597
*Longus's *Daphnis and Chloe*	1598		Caro 1784¹	Amyot 1559	Day 1587 (from Amyot)
**Chariton's *Chaereas and Callirhoe*	1750		1752	1763	1764
**Xenophon Ephesius's *Ephesiaca*	1726		1723	1736	1727

LEGENDA:
† Adaptation of Book 4;
* Works transmitted by MS. Florence C.S. 627 and other MS(S);
** Works transmitted only by MS. C.S. 627.

¹Annibal Caro, who died in 1566, completed his translation before 1538 (see Henderson 2009, 10).

NOTES

1. The translation of the first four books was published in 1565, while the complete edition appeared in 1567.
2. All quotations from secondary texts are presented in my translation.
3. See on this Nagle 1983.
4. As Myrrha has it in Golding 1567, 128^v: "[Y]it even the very thing / Is such as will not suffer thee the same to end to bring".
5. "[Byblis] iam nomina sanguinis odit" (9.466-7); "now shee utter hateth all / The names of kin" (Golding 1567, 118^r).
6. See also Spencer 1957, 33 and Martindale and Martindale 1990, 128.
7. Bury 1936, 29-33.
8. See Greenblatt 1988, 21-65.
9. As regards Ovid and Shakespeare see Martindale and Martindale 1990 and Bate 1994. On Pyramus and Thisbe, see especially Schmitt-von Mühlenfels 1972; Rudd 1979; Holzberg 1988; Garrison 1994 and Hüls 2005.
10. On the motif of the apparent death and its religious antecedents, see Wehrli 1965, 142-6.
11. An antecedent of the common urn can be found in the Odyssean episode of Patroclus and Achilles (*Odyssea* 24.76-7). The colour of the mulberries is a particularly valid aetiological motif in poetry (see Aeschylus, *The Cretan Women*

frg. 116, Sophocles, *The Prophets* or *Polyidus* frg. 395: "First you will see a crop in flower, all white; then a round mulberry that has turned into red; lastly old age of Egyptian blackness takes it over", Lloyd-Jones 1996).

12. In *A Midsummer Night's Dream* the episode of Pyramus and Thisbe is functionally meta-theatrical. *Titus Andronicus* (yet another play written in the 1590s) is also indebted to Ovid, especially in 2.3. In this tragedy dead Bassianus's paleness is compared to the moon's pallid ray that illuminates Pyramus soaked in Thisbe's blood ("So pale did shine the moon on Pyramus / When he by night lay bathed in maiden blood", 231-2). This allows us to conjecture an intertextual relationship between the "blood-drinking pit" (224) and the "madefactaque sanguine radix" (4.126, "the root soaked up by blood"), while the "cruentum solum" (4.133-4, "the ground covered with blood") is echoed by the brutally violent atmosphere of the whole drama. As for *A Midsummer Night's Dream* see Rudd 1979; on *Titus Andronicus* see Valls-Russell 2010.
13. Papyrus Michigan Inv. 3793 (Accessed March 21, 2015. http://quod.lib.umich.edu/a/apis/x-2115/3793r___tif). See Renner's first edition (1981); Stephens and Winkler 1995, 470; López Martínez 1998, 391-8, as well as Stramaglia's recent analytical approach (2001).
14. The new dating of the papyrus has been suggested by Gabriella Messeri Savorelli (*apud* Stramaglia). Renner, instead, proposed a later chronology spanning from the third to the fourth century (1981, 93).
15. Parthenius dedicated his *Love romances* to Cornelius Gallus between 52 and 26 BC (see his dedicatory Preface). See also Gaselee 1916, 256-7 and Lightfoot 1999, 9-16.
16. See on this Gaselee 1916, 288-91, 332-3, 336-9, and 344-7 and Lightfoot 1999, 328-9, 354-5, 358-9, 362-5. The success of these narrative motifs is introduced and discussed by Stramaglia also with regard to 'entertainment narrative' (2001, 92-8). Unlike Stramaglia's opinion (ibid., 92), I believe that the story of Dimoetes and Euopis (epyllion 31) cannot be included among the ones mentioned here.
17. This tale is included also among the Pseudo-Plutarchean *Greek and Roman Parallel Stories*, 21 (310E-F), among which we can found another similar story (see Babbitt 1936, 286-8).
18. This tale and the preceding one belong to the same typology of the Herodotean tale of Adrastus who, during a boar hunt, kills Croesus's son by mistake and subsequently commits suicide (1.34-45).
19. See Lightfoot 1999, 537-42. Vandersmissen (2013) brings forth a new argument supporting Lightfoot's hypothesis.
20. This is probably not the case with the story of Coresos, although some consider it to be similar to those tales. After being rejected by Callirhoe of Patras, Coresos offers himself in sacrifice in order to save her from immolation. The girl, who had so firmly refused his love even to the point of preferring to die rather than being with him, is eventually moved by his courage and kills herself. The tale, which has been recorded in the Patras region by Pausanias (*Periegesis* 7.21.1-5), undoubtedly dates from an epoch earlier than the author's own (the second century) and is likely to have been produced in the milieu of the local shrine of Dionysus. The revelation of Coresos's extreme love seemingly prompts Callirhoe's 'posthumous' falling and leads her to commit suicide in reparation for his, finally conflating the 'expiatory' and 'widowed' suicide typologies.

Classical Paradigms of Tragic Choice in Civic Stories   61

21. Hermocrates's "splendid tomb" is so wide that the funeral offerings pile up inside it and become a "treasure", so that the tomb itself transforms into a sort of strongroom akin to the Delphian *thesauroi* built up by the Greek cities. We may picture it not as a sarcophagus but as a vault similar to the one in *Romeo and Juliet*.
22. The main witness of this 'action romance', whose earliest date is the mid-second century AD, is Patriarch Photius (*Bibliotheca*, cod. 94, Henry 1960, 34–48). See on this Habrich 1960 and Borgogno 1975. This part of the tale can be found in 75a22–36, Henry 1960, 38.
23. This romance, largely summarized by Photius (cod. 166, Henry 1960, 140–9), has been dated between the end of the first century and 130 AD (see Bowie 2002, 58–9).
24. Passages from the *Babylonian tales* are quoted by page, column, and line number of Immanuel Bekker's edition, Berlin 1824–25.
25. Rhodane and Sinonis lick some poisoned honey and faint, and this saves them from their pursuers (74b3–8, Henry 1960, 36). Soon afterwards, still pale and emaciated, they manage to escape the soldiers that stopped them by pretending to be ghosts (75b37–41, Henry 1960, 37). Later on, after a girl who was presumed dead is brought home, they take her place in the sepulchre and again elude their pursuers (74b41–75a16, Henry 1960, 37–8). No details of this burial place are provided but we know it contained clothing, food, and water offerings, even though it is unclear whether it was a sarcophagus or a vault.
26. "Wir sehen das Phantastische daran die nötige Korrektion erfahren muß" ["We see how the fantastic must therefore undergo the necessary correction"].
27. I am obviously referring to Eros's parents in Plato's *Symposium*. On the Platonic reading of Hellenistic romances, see, among the most recent contributions, Lev Kenaan (2008) and Dressler (2011).
28. Unlike what happens in Greek tragedy, in the novella the plot neither moves nor obeys the *mythos* because of genre conventions or explicit requirements. In Euripides's *Electra*, for example, Orestes's, Electra's, and Pylades's destinies are revealed at the end of the play. The same happens in all great mythical frescoes from which the theatre drew its inspiration: from Orestes's vengeance (except for the intriguing and hermeneutically still unsolved exclusion of Sophocles's *Electra*) to Oedipus's story.
29. "Fissus erat tenui rima, quam duxerat olim, / cum fieret, paries domui communis utrique. / Id vitium nulli per saecula longa notatum / (quid non sentit amor?) primi vidistis amantes, / et vocis fecistis iter, tutaeque per illud / murmure blanditiae minimo transire solebant" ["The wall that parted house from house had riven therein a crany / Which shronke at making of the wall. This fault not markt of any / Of many hundred yeares before (what doth not love espie) / These lovers first of all found out, and made a way whereby / To talke togither secretly, and through the same did goe / Their loving whisprings verie light and safely to and fro", Golding 1567, 43ᵛ].
30. That is, 1665 × 1850 mt, or 5625 × 6250 ft.
31. *Romeo and Juliet* is quoted from Shakespeare 1988.
32. On the significance of the tomb in *Romeo and Juliet* see Bigliazzi and Nigri in this volume.
33. Florence, Biblioteca Medicea Laurenziana, MS. Conventi Soppressi 627. Until 1809, the La Badia's was the *codex unicus* for Chariton's and Xenophon Ephesius's romances; it also contains Longus's and Achilles Tatius's 1–4.4.

34. Bullough (1957, 269ff.) agrees on this although Francis Douce had already suggested that Luigi da Porto "had met the manuscript of the Greek romance" (1807, 198–9). Later on, John J. Munro would hypothesize Shakespeare's debt to Xenophon as regards the "sleeping potion" (1908, xvii). However, his words sound rather cryptic: "Luckily there exists a Middle Greek romance of the fifth century, in the *Ephesiaka* ... which proves the existence of such a source" (ibid.). The peculiar dating he suggests may have been taken from Dunlop 1888, 63.

WORKS CITED

Albrecht, Michael von. 2011. "Ovid and the Novel". In *Fictional Traces: Receptions of the Ancient Novel*, vol. 1, edited by Marilla P. Futre Pinheiro, Stephen J. Harrison, 3–19. Groningen: Barkhuis Publishing.

Amyot, Jacques. 1547. *L'Histoire Æthiopique de Heliodorus, nouellement traduite de Graec en François*. Paris: Estienne Groulleau.

Amyot, Jacques. 1559. *Les amours pastorales de Daphnis et de Chloé*. Paris: Vincent Sertenas.

Amyot, Jacques. 1572. *Les oeuvres morales & meslees de Plutarque*. Paris: Vascosanus.

Babbitt, Frank Cole, ed. 1936. *Plutarch's Moralia*, vol. 4. Cambridge, MA: Harvard University Press / London: Heinemann.

Barchiesi, Alessandro. 2005. "Introduzione". In *Ovidio. Metamorfosi*, vol. 1: *Libri I-II*, edited by Alessandro Barchiesi, ciii–lix. Milano: Fondazione L. Valla – Mondadori.

Bate, Jonathan. 1994. *Shakespeare and Ovid*. Oxford: Clarendon Press.

Belleforest, François. 1568. *Les amours de Clitophon et de Leucippe*. Paris: Iean Borel.

Boitani, Piero. 2002. *The Genius to Improve an Invention: Literary Transitions*. Notre Dame: University of Notre Dame Press.

Boitani, Piero. 2014. *Riconoscere è un dio. Scene e temi del riconoscimento nella letteratura*. Torino: Einaudi.

Borgogno, Alberto. 1975. "Sui 'Babyloniaca' di Giamblico". *Hermes* 103: 101–26.

Bowie, Ewen L. 2002. "The Chronology of the Earlier Greek Novels since B.E. Perry: Revisions and Precisions". *Ancient Narrative* 2: 47–63.

Bullough, Geoffrey. 1957. *Narrative and Dramatic Sources of Shakespeare*, vol. 1. London: Routledge and Kegan Paul / New York: Columbia University Press.

Burton, William. 1597. *The most delectable and pleasaunt history of Clitiphon* (sic) *and Leucippe*. London: Thomas Creede, for William Mattes.

Bury, Robert Gregg, ed. 1936. *Sextus Empiricus*, vol. 3. Cambridge, MA: Harvard University Press / London: Heinemann.

Coccio, Francesco Angelo. 1551. *Achille Tatio Alessandrino Dell'amore di Leucippe et Clitophonte*. In Venetia: P. et Fratelli De Nicolini da Sabio.

Cruceio (Della Croce), L. Annibale. 1554. *Achillis Statii* (sic) *Alexandrini de Clitophontis & Leucippes amoribus Libri viii*. Basileae: Io. Heruagius.

Dalmeyda, Georges, ed. 1962. *Xénophon d'Éphèse. Les Éphèsiaques*. Paris: Les Belles Lettres.

Day, Angel. 1587. *Daphnis and Chloe*. London: Robert Walde-graue.

Dolce, Lodovico. 1546. *Amorosi ragionamenti. Dialogo, nel quale si racconta un compassionevole amore di due amanti*. In Vinegia: Gabriel Giolito de' Ferrari.

Douce, Francis. 1807. *Illustrations of Shakspeare, and of Ancient Manners*, vol. 2. London: Longman, Hurst, Rees, and Orme.

Dressler, Alex. 2011. "The Sophist and the Swarm: Feminism, Platonism and Ancient Philosophy in Achilles Tatius' *Leucippe and Clitophon*". *Ramus* 40: 33–72.
Dunlop, John Colin. 1888. *History of Prose Fiction*. Revised by H. Wilson, vol. 1. London: George Bell.
Dunn, Francis M. 1996. *Tragedy's End. Closure and Innovation in Euripidean Drama*. Oxford: Clarendon Press.
Finglass, Patrick J., ed. 2007. *Sophocles. Electra*. Cambridge: Cambridge University Press.
Fornier, Jean. 1555. *Les affections de divers amans*, faictes & rassemblées par Parthenius de Nicée. Paris: Gilles.
Garrison, David Lee. 1994. *Gongora and the Pyramus and Thisbe Myth from Ovid to Shakespeare*. Newark, DE: Juan de la Cuesta.
Gaselee, Stephen, ed. 1916. *The Love Romances of Parthenius and Other Fragments*. In *Daphnis and Chloe by Longus. The Love Romances of Parthenius*, edited by George Thornley, John Maxwell Edmunds, and S. Gaselee, 248ff. Cambridge, MA: Harvard University Press / London: Heinemann.
Gesner, Carol. 1970. *Shakespeare and the Greek Romance*. Lexington, KY: The University Press of Kentucky.
Ghini, Leonardo. 1556. *Historia di Heliodoro delle cose ethiopiche*. In Vinegia: Gabriel Giolito de' Ferrari.
Gillespie, Stuart, 2004. *Shakespeare's Books: A Dictionary of Shakespeare Sources*, (2nd ed.). London and New York: The Athlone Press.
Golding, Arthur. 1567. *The xv bookes of P. Ouidius Naso, entytuled Metamorphosis*. London: Willyam Seres.
Greenblatt, Stephen. 1988. *Shakespearean Negotiations*. Berkeley and Los Angeles: University of California Press.
Greene, Robert. (1594) 1898. *The Tragical Reign of Selimus, Sometime Emperor of the Turks: A Play Reclaimed for Robert Greene*. Edited by Alexander B. Grosart. London: Dent.
Habrich, Elmar, ed. 1960. *Iamblichi Babyloniacorum reliquiae*. Lipsiae: Teubner.
Hägg, Tomas. 1983. *The Novel in Antiquity*. Oxford: Blackwell.
Hegel, Georg W.F. 1955. *Ästhetik*. Berlin: Aufbau-Verlag.
Henderson, Jeffrey, ed. 2009. *Longus, Daphne and Chloe. Xenophon of Ephesus, Anthia and Habrocomes*. Cambridge, MA: Harvard University Press.
Henry, René, ed. 1960. *Photius. Bibliothèque*, vol. 2: *Codices 84–185*. Paris: Les Belles Lettres.
Holzberg, Niklas. 1988. "Ovids 'Babyloniaka' (*Met*. 4.55–166)". *Wiener Studien* 101: 265–77.
Hüls, Rudolf. 2005. *Pyramus und Thisbe. Inszenierungen einer 'verschleierten' Gefahr*. Heidelberg: Winter-Universitätsverlag.
Kenney, Edward John. 1986. "Introduction". In *Ovid. Metamorphoses*, translated by Alan David Melville, xiii–xxix. Oxford: Oxford University Press.
Kerényi, Karl. 1973. *Die griechisch-orientalische Romanliteratur in religionsgeschichtlicher Beleuchtung* (first ed. Tübingen 1927). Darmstadt: Wissenschaftliche Buchgesellschaft (with *addenda*).
Lev Kenaan, Vered. 2008. *Pandora's Senses: the Feminine Character of the Ancient Text*. Madison, WI: University of Wisconsin Press.
Lightfoot, Jane L., ed. 1999. *Parthenius of Nicaea: The Poetical Fragments and the Erotika Pathemata*. Oxford: Clarendon Press.

Lloyd-Jones, Hugh, ed. 1994. *Sophocles. Ajax, Electra, Oedypus tyrannus*. Cambridge, MA: Harvard University Press.
Lloyd-Jones, Hugh, ed. 1996. *Sophocles. Fragments*. Cambridge, MA: Harvard University Press.
López Martínez, María Paz. 1998. *Fragmentos papiráceos de novela griega*. Alicante: Universidad de Alicante, Servicio de Publicaciones.
Loyer, Pierre le. 1586. *IIII Livres des spectres*. Angers: Nepueu.
Martindale, Charles and Michelle Martindale. 1990. *Shakespeare and the Uses of Antiquity. An Introductory Essay*. London and New York: Routledge.
Muir, Kenneth. 1954. "Pyramus and Thisbe: A Study in Shakespeare's Method". *Shakespeare Quarterly* 5: 141–53.
Munro, John James. 1908. *Brooke's 'Romeus and Juliet' Being the Original of Shakespeare's 'Romeo and Juliet'*. New York: Duffield & Co. / London: Chatto & Windus.
Nagle, Betty Rose. 1983. "Byblis and Myrrha: Two Incest Narratives in the *Metamorphoses*". *The Classical Journal* 78: 301–15.
Ovid, Publius N. 2004. *Metamorphoses*. Edited by Richard J. Tarrant. Oxford: Clarendon Press.
Renner Theodor T. 1981. "A Composition Concerning Pamphilus and Eurydice". In *Proceedings of the 16th International Congress of Papyrology*, edited by Roger S. Bagnall [et alii], 93–101. Chico, CA: Scholars Press.
Rochemaure, Jacques de. 1556. *Les quatre derniers livres des propos amoureus contenans le discours des amours & mariage du Seigneur Clitophant* (sic) *& Damoiselle Leusippe*. Lyon: Claude Marchant.
Rosati, Gianpiero. 2007. "Commentary to *Metamorphoses*' book iv". In *Ovidio. Metamorfosi*, vol. 2: *Libri III–IV*, edited by Alessandro Barchiesi and Gianpiero Rosati. Milano: Fondazione L. Valla – Mondadori.
Rudd, Niall. 1979. "Pyramus and Thisbe in Shakespeare and Ovid. *A Midsummer Night's Dream* and *Metamorphosis* 4.1–166". In *Creative Imitation and Latin Literature*, edited by David West and Tony Woodman, 173–93. Cambridge: Cambridge University Press.
Sandford, James. 1567. *The Amorous and Tragicall Tales of Plutarch, whereunto is annexed the Hystorie of Cariclea & Theagenes, and the Sayings of the Greeke Philosophers*, translated by I. S. London: H. Bynneman for Leonard Mayland.
Sandy, Gerald N. 1979. "Ancient Prose Fiction and Minor Early English Novels". *Antike und Abendland* 25: 41–55.
Sandy, Gerald N. 1996. "The Heritage of the Ancient Greek Novel in France and Britain". In *The Novel in the Ancient World*, edited by Gareth Schmeling, 735–73. Leiden: Brill.
Schmitt-von Mühlenfels, Franz. 1972. *Pyramus und Thisbe. Rezeptionstypen eines Ovidischen Stoffes in Literatur, Kunst und Musik*. Heidelberg: Winter-Universitätsverlag.
Shakespeare, William. 1988. *The Complete Works*. Edited by Stanley Wells and Gary Taylor, with John Jowett and William Montgomery. Oxford: Oxford University Press.
Spencer, Terence John Bew. 1957, "Shakespeare and the Elizabethan Romans". In *Shakespeare Survey, 10: The Roman Plays*, edited by Allardyce Nicoll, 27–38. Cambridge: Cambridge University Press.
Stephens, Susan A. and John J. Winkler, eds. 1995. *Ancient Greek Novels: The Fragments*. Princeton, NJ: Princeton University Press.

Stramaglia, Antonio. 2001. "Piramo e Tisbe prima di Ovidio? PMich inv. 3793 e la narrativa d'intrattenimento alla fine dell'età tolemaica". *Zeitschrift für Papyrologie und Epigraphik* 134: 81–106.

Underdowne, Thomas. 1569?. *An Æthiopian Historie written in Greeke by Heliodorus*. London: Henry Wykes for Fraunces Coldcocke.

Valls-Russell, Janice. 2010. "'So pale did shine the moon on Pyramus': Biblical Resonances of an Ovidian Myth in *Titus Andronicus*". *Anagnórisis* 2. Accessed March 21, 2015. http://www.anagnorisis.es/pdfs/valls_russell.pdf.

Vandersmissen, Marc. 2013. "Ovid, *Metamorphoses* IV 94 – Parthenius, Ἐρωτικὰ Παθήματα 32.1–2. A Moral Interpretation". *Emerita* 81: 203–7.

Waschewiczki, Stanislaus, trans. 1552. *Heliodori Aethiopicae Historiae libri decem*. Basileae: Ioannem Oporinum.

Wehrli, Fritz. 1965. "Einheit und Vorgeschichte der griechisch-römischen Romanliteratur". *Museum Helveticum* 22: 133–54.

Wolff, Samuel Lee. 1912. *The Greek Romances in Elizabethan Prose Fiction*. New York: Columbia University Press.

Xylander, Guilelmus [Wilhelm Holtzmann], ed. 1568. *Antonini Liberalis Transformationum congeries, Phlegontis Tralliani De mirabilibus*. Basel: Thomas Guarinus.

2 Private and Public Spheres and the 'Civic Turn' in Da Porto, Bandello, and Shakespeare's *Romeo and Juliet*

Robert Henke

When Baz Luhrmann, in his 1996 film version of *Romeo and Juliet*, keeps the doomed Romeo alive for a final passionate scene with Juliet after she awakes from her false death, he revives the ending of the story as the early sixteenth-century novella authors Luigi Da Porto and Matteo Bandello conceived it. Take almost any moment in Shakespeare's play, which is a transnational feast of intertextuality, and alternative possibilities proliferate. If the play misses tragicomedy by the slim margin of an undelivered letter to Romeo, it was often performed on stage as an averted tragedy. In the commedia dell'arte scenario "Li tragici successi", the Romeo figure's despair suddenly converts to joy when he beholds the Juliet figure alive after she has woken from the potion (Scala 1976, 187–93).[1] The narrative can turn at any point, and the many intertextual links richly connect Shakespeare's text with European early modern storytelling on page and stage.

This essay explores the Da Porto and Bandello *novelle* with particular attention to their civic and political resonances, which in several respects are cast in even greater relief relative to Shakespeare's play. The story itself, as represented by folklore, the Italian novella authors, their French and English adaptors, Luigi Groto in his 1578 play *Adriana*, commedia dell'arte actors, Arthur Brooke, and Shakespeare, pointedly engages the intersection of the private and the public. First, the very notion of a feud invokes the problem of individual versus community authority, as what might appear a private dispute between families grows so in magnitude and violence that it erupts into the public forum, and individuals cede control to the authority of the state. Secondly, the Romeo and Juliet story pits two young lovers, with small power relative to their worlds (compare later Shakespearean lovers such as Antony and Cleopatra) against a public world that finally engulfs them. If, as Wallace Stevens says, "Death is the mother of beauty", the ever-present threat of death presses the lovers into staking out fragile, precarious, but all the more compelling private spaces etched in the interstices of public discord. More precisely – and here the alternative narratives of Da Porto and Bandello are extremely instructive – the lovers continually find places that ambiguously negotiate the private and public. What is merely a plot device in Shakespeare – Juliet uses the excuse of confession to go to Friar Lawrence's cell so that she can get married – is an ambiguously private and public space in the *novelle*. In Da Porto and Bandello, Giulietta and Romeo actually get married inside a confession box, with Giuletta's mother unsuspectingly standing just outside in the Bandello novella. Other liminal places, some of which do not appear in Shakespeare's play, abound in the *novelle*, as the lovers manage moments of privacy in gardens, churches, streets, and finally the tomb. The window or balcony itself, as Jane Tylus has shown in a study of its frequent use in commedia dell'arte performance, allows women cannily to negotiate private and public space in complex ways (Tylus 1997).

Preceding the Da Porto and Bandello versions, Masuccio Salernitano (Tommaso Guardati) produced the first novella version, published in 1476. Masuccio's tale casts the story in a circum-Mediterranean, romance mode noticeably lacking the public and civic dimensions that, in fact, Da Porto is the first to interject (Masuccio 1968). No interfamilial feud clouds the passionate love blossoming in Siena, not Verona, between the Romeo figure, named Mariotto, with Ganozza. No public festival is necessary to draw them together. In the Boccaccian tradition of anti-clerical satire, the lovers bribe the corrupt friar (Augustinian rather than Franciscan, as in the later versions) into secretly marrying them. In an entirely private dispute, Mariotto kills another citizen, for which he is punished with permanent banishment. After a tearful goodbye to Ganozza, having told his brother in Siena to keep him informed of all developments, Mariotto sails to Alexandria, where he joins the company of his merchant uncle. When forced by her father to marry against her will, Ganozza begs the Friar to help her, and appears to be the one to come up with the idea of the potion.[2] As with Da Porto and Bandello, the Juliet figure possesses more agency than Shakespeare's heroine, and takes it upon herself to send a letter to Mariotto via courier. When the potion takes its apparently deadly effect, Ganozza is buried in the church tomb. Since there is no thought that Mariotto can ever return to Siena, once awoken she disguises herself as a friar (the possibility of Juliet escaping in male disguise is proposed, although not executed, in the Da Porto and Bandello versions) and sails to Alexandria to join her lover. Meanwhile, the brother of Mariotto dutifully writes him that Ganozza has died; whereas this letter arrives promptly, the letter sent by Ganozza is doomed when her courier is captured by pirates and slain, and Ganozza's sea voyage itself is delayed. The distraught Mariotto returns to Siena, forcibly breaks into the tomb to mourn his supposedly dead lover, and just before he sees what would have been an empty tomb is apprehended by several friars, who think he is a thief intent on robbing dead bodies. Taken before the mayor, under torture he confesses the cause of his return and, while pitied by the ladies, is beheaded. Ganozza, learning that Mariotto has returned to Siena in the belief that she is dead, returns also to Siena (again disguised as a man) and, on learning the crushing news of Mariotto's fate, is convinced by the Friar to enter a convent – as the Friar advocates to the Juliet figure in Da Porto, Bandello, and Shakespeare. The historical basis of Masuccio's story hangs on a thin thread: a Sienese citizen has told the tale, which was supposed to have recently occurred in Siena, to three lovely women. This Boccaccian-style frame lends the story none of the historical context of Da Porto's and Bandello's versions, and Masuccio further invests it with generalizing romance motifs, such as the courier's capture by pirates. Siena, as a city and civic polity, plays no role in the story, functioning simply as a site for the action.

Luigi Da Porto, born in 1485 in Vicenza, decisively recast the Romeo and Juliet story in the civic and political dimensions that characterize almost all subsequent retellings. This, in fact, is just what one would expect from a man born to a noble and powerful family, who lived intensely through the League of Cambrai conflict, for which he provided detailed testimony in the *Lettere storiche*.[3] As control over their native Vicenza went back and forth between Venice and the allied powers of France, the Holy Roman Empire, and the Papacy, the Da Porto family was caught in the middle, declaring that they would obey whoever won. Da Porto is the first novella author to introduce the theme of the family feud, and it is tempting to think that he might have done so because his own Savorgnan family was caught in a bitter dispute with the family of Gregorio Amaseo. Amaseo accused Da Porto of helping his uncle Antonio Savorgnan kill two witnesses of an ambush that the Savorgnan family had organized against their enemies. As the war advanced, Da Porto gained the opportunity to fight on behalf of the Venetians, engaging in three battles. In the third encounter, in June 1511, he was seriously wounded, which rendered him disabled for the rest of his life.

In his *Istoria di due nobili amanti con la pietosa loro morte intervenuta gia nella città di Verona nel tempo del Sig. Bartolomeo Della Scala*, Da Porto reports that he first heard the story in Friuli during one of these military campaigns (Da Porto 1831, 19–20). An archer named Peregrino, both a courageous soldier and a man who "innamorato sempre si ritrova" ["always found himself in love"], tells him the story because he believes that Da Porto himself was suffering from love melancholy. Da Porto, in fact, wrote a sonnet in which he alludes to a young love occurring when he was about twenty-one years old, the very age of the Romeo character (Brognoligo 1904, 22). (It is not exactly clear why this story in particular would relieve Da Porto's supposed love melancholy, and it does not seem to have helped the continually amorous Peregrino either).

Da Porto is the first to place the story in a specific historical period, setting it in Verona under the rule of Bartolomeo Della Scala between 1301 and 1304, and he first introduces the feuding families of the Montecchi and the Cappelletti. Both the figure of Della Scala and the coupling of these particular families bear distinct roots in the person and poem of Dante Alighieri, whose *Commedia*, notwithstanding its primarily spiritual agenda, never strays far from civic and political themes. Historically, the Montecchi were a powerful Ghibelline family from Verona and the Cappelletti an equally notable Guelph family from Cremona; there is no historical evidence that these families from different northern cities directly fought against each other, although they were certainly divided along the lines of the great conflict that was tearing medieval Florence and northern Italy apart. Dante links the two families in the sixth canto of *Purgatorio*, which is set in ante-purgatory and regards those killed by violence, especially by factionalism. One of the more political *canti* of the *Purgatorio*, Dante takes this violent factionalism to be a sign of great Italian shame and to indicate the need of a strong imperial ruler peaceably working together with the papacy. The two families are invoked in an impassioned rebuke that Dante makes to the Emperor Albert of Austria (1248–1308), whom Dante castigates for never coming to strife-torn Italy. To Albert, scathingly described as provincially 'German' rather than civically 'Roman', Dante declaims:

Vieni a veder Montecchi e Cappelletti,
Monadi e Filippeschi, uom sanza cura:
Color già tristi, e questi con sospetti! (Dante, *Purgatorio* 6.106–08)[4]

For Dante, then, the interfamilial hostility practiced by families such as the Montecchi, Cappelletti, Monaldi, and Filippeschi was nothing if not a civic and political problem: a pernicious disease arising in the vacuum of strong imperial leadership. Furthermore, by setting the story during the Veronese rule of Della Scala, Da Porto adds a second Dantesque reference that is both personal and suggests some remedy for private-turned-public violence. Bartolomeo Della Scala, in fact, received the exile Dante in 1304 and was known for his efforts to promote peace during his rule. So Da Porto declares that his novella takes place "nel tempo che Bartolomeo Della Scala, Signore cortese e umanissimo, il freno alla mia bella patria a sua posta e strignea e rallentava" (1831, 20) ["in the time that Bartolomeo Della Scala, a humane and courteous Lord, closely held the reins of my beautiful country"]. In contrast to Dante's leaderless Italy, compared to "fiera ... fella / per non esser corretta da li sproni" (*Purgatorio* 6.94–5) ["a beast (made) wild being no more corrected by the spur"], Da Porto's Dalla Scala governs Verona with discipline. If he is not able to quell completely the enmity between the Montecchi and the Cappelletti (the latter, as if drawn by Dante's parataxis relocated in Verona), his strong threats do have the effect of pacifying the families enough that Messer Antonio Cappelletti "uomo festoso e giocondissimo" ["a festive and cheerful man"], decides to hold a public feast during the time of carnival. The very encounter between the two lovers, at Cappelletti's feast, is thus made possible by a strong ruler who both personally befriended Dante and could stand as the exemplar to derelict figures such as Albert of Austria. Relative to Masuccio, who simply says that the predominantly *mercantile* families were "notato e molto estimato" (Masuccio 1968, 242) ["noted and very esteemed"], Da Porto moves the story towards Shakespeare's "two households, both alike in dignity" (Shakespeare 2012, Prologue 1) and thus possible subjects of tragedic issue: "nobilissime famiglie, di valorosi uomini e di ricchezza ugualmente dal cielo, dalla natura, e dalla fortuna dotate" (Da Porto 1831, 20) ["extremely noble families, endowed equally from the heavens, nature, and fortune with valiant men and wealth"].

A close reading of both Da Porto's and Bandello's texts will clarify the Italians' negotiation of public and private in their tellings of the story. As in Shakespeare, a friend of Bandello's Romeo urges him, effectively, to repair from the private existence of love melancholy to the public haunts of the extended festival season beginning during Christmas, to which Romeo agrees. (Shakespeare's Montague declares that Romeo, while suffering the pangs of love for Rosaline, "private in his chamber pens himself, / Shuts up his windows, locks fair daylight out / And makes himself an artificial night", Shakespeare 2012, 1.1.136–8). In the public world of Cappelletti's feast in Da Porto's version, gender categories are particularly labile, with Giulietta assuming an agency and power beyond what she carries in Shakespeare's play. Hoping to see the young woman he was pursuing (Shakespeare's Rosaline), who actually is at the feast in Da Porto, Romeo Montecchi enters the hall disguised as a nymph, and when he removes his mask the women are overcome by his dazzling, hermaphroditic beauty, said to surpass that of any woman in attendance (a thought later seconded by Giulietta when she first encounters him). The virtue that Shakespeare has Romeo ascribe to Juliet – "O, she doth teach the torches to burn bright" (Shakespeare 2012, 1.5.43) – ironically derives from the conceit, clarified even further in Bandello and Brooke, that it is Romeo's beauty that is illuminated by the torches illuminating Cappelletti's grand hall. Da Porto's Romeo then suddenly beholds the "supernatural" ("sopranaturale") beauty of Giulietta, as she does him; as they fall in love with each other, Romeo withdraws from the crowded dancing. At midnight, just before the ball ends, the last dance, named the "Torchio", begins, which involves all the dancers forming a circle with the men and women successively changing partners. Romeo joins the dance – not explicitly required in Shakespeare's text – moving through the various ladies up to the Rosaline figure, and finally Giulietta. On the other side of Giulietta stands the embryonic version of Shakespeare's Mercutio, named "Marcuccio", who has the odd trait of having perpetually cold hands (this is carried through by Brooke, and dropped by Shakespeare). While the cold-handed Marcuccio takes Giulietta's right hand, Romeo takes her left. As in Shakespeare, the conceit of the lovers' initial exchange regards hands, but in Da Porto via a comic register as the forward Giulietta, who speaks the first line, thanks Romeo for having a warm hand, rather than the freezing one of Marcuccio. After the lovers exchange passionate words and vows, they part. Giulietta, who has known from the outset that her new love comes from the rival family, enters into protracted deliberation whether or not to pursue Romeo. She first wonders whether Romeo has been sent by the Montecchi to entrap and shame her, but finally decides in favour of the match in the *civic* hope – restricted by Shakespeare to the Friar – that it could heal the enmity between the two houses. Bandello gives Giulietta particular strength and agency:

> Io ho pure più volte udito dire che per gli sposalizii fatti, non solamente tra privati cittadini e gentiluomini si sono de le paci fatte, ma che molte volte tra grandissimi prencipi e regi tra i quali le crudelissime guerre regnavano, una vera pace ed amicizia con sodisfacimento di tutti è seguita. Io forse quella sarò che con questa occasione metterò tranquilla pace in queste due casate.
>
> (Bandello 1952, 734)[5]

Bandello's Giulietta, really an extension of Da Porto's, explicitly recognizes both the difference between private and public spheres and the possibility, with the grand gesture of a marriage across the feuding families, of those spheres being bridged.

Da Porto and Bandello next have the lovers negotiate a series of spaces that are liminally both private and public: either public places where the lovers attempt to exchange private glances, such as a church (explicitly mentioned in Da Porto 1831, 23) or the street (Bandello 1952, 734), or the more private space before Giulietta's window, where there is great danger of being publically discovered. In Bandello, Romeo passes before Giulietta's house both by night and day, each progressively inflaming the other with amorous glances. A striking detail in Da Porto, Bandello, and Shakespeare, but notably absent in Brooke,[6] suggests the possibility that Shakespeare may have encountered the Italian *novelle* directly, or seen a version on stage that used the highly theatrical idea that Romeo listens to Giulietta's voice before revealing himself or being discovered:

> ... quasi tutta la notte, con grandissimo periculo della sua vita, dinanzi alla casa dell'amata donna solo si stava; ed ora sopra la finestra della sua camera per forza tiratosi, ivi, senza ch'ella o altri il sapesse, ad udire il suo bel parlare si sedea ...
>
> (Da Porto 1831, 23–4)[7]

At one point the moon shines so brightly that the Da Porto Giulietta notices the lurking Romeo (the moment preserved in Brooke), beginning a series of passionate encounters on the balcony, until during one snowy evening the freezing Romeo requests entrance into her chamber. (Bandello's Romeo also entreats Giulietta to let him enter her room, but without the excuse of snowy weather). In both Da Porto and Bandello, Giulietta's sharp rebuke to Romeo prompts their mutual agreement to get married; it is the resourceful Giulietta who thinks of having "Fra Lorenzo", who has long been her confessor, secretly marry them.

In both the Da Porto and Bandello *novelle*, the Friar carries significantly more public and civic weight than he does in Brooke, who in his prefatory note inveighs against "superstitious friars" as the "naturally fitte instruments of unchastitie" (Bullough 1957, 284), while also providing in his own person a contact zone between private and public spheres. Da Porto lends him a certain heft beyond both Masuccio's corrupt Augustinian and Shakespeare's benign herbalist: "Era questo frate dell'ordine minore di osservanza, filosofo grande e sperimentore di molte cose, così naturali come magiche" (Da Porto 1831, 25) ["This friar belonged to the Minor Order of Osservanza and was a great philosopher and experimentalist in many matters, both natural and magical"]. Bandello's Friar remains every bit as weighty, and is further distinguished by his cosmopolitan travel:

> Era il frate un grandissimo esperimentatore che ai suoi dì aveva cercati assai paesi ed erasi dilettato di provare e saper cose diverse, e sopra il tutto conosceva la vertù de l'erbe e de le pietre ed era uno dei gran distillatori a quell tempi si trovassero.
>
> (Bandello 1952, 748)[8]

In addition to his prestige as a philosopher, scientist, and world traveller, the Friar plays a more central public role in the Verona of Da Porto and Bandello than does Shakespeare's Friar Laurence. In Bandello, Friar Lorenzo moves between Montecchi and Cappelletti, men and women, "ed in confessione udiva la più parte de la nobilità" (ibid., 736) ["and in confession listened to the greater part of the nobility"]. It is particularly as confessor that he negotiates the public and the private. On the one hand, he knows the hearts and minds of individuals – he is said to know "ogni segreto del cuor" (Da Porto 1831, 25) ["every heart's secret"] of Da Porto's Giulietta; on the other hand, following Giulietta's initial idea, he sanctions the lover's union with the plan of publically reconciling the two families. With his public ambitions complementing (or perhaps conflicting with) his more private philosophical and medical pursuits, he is sometimes cast in the novella as an opportunist. For example, in Da Porto's version, he has formed an alliance with Romeo for deliberate, even manipulative reasons. He must secure a close friendship with a gentlemen in the city "volendo il frate ad un tratto ed in buona opinione del suo volgo restare, e di qualche suo diletto godere" (ibid.) ["because the Friar both wished to remain in the good graces of the people and to pursue his own desires"] – and he chooses Romeo. The relationship between Romeo and the Friar, then, trades a private benefit relative to Romeo for a public benefit relative to the Friar: Romeo enjoys being able to fully disclose his heart to the Friar, also his confessor; the Friar is raised even more in the estimation of the city for his close relationship with the noble Romeo.

Unsurprisingly, the Catholic sacrament of confession plays a much greater role in the novella. In the moralistic prefatory note "To the Reader", Brooke sweepingly claims the lovers' use of "auricular confession ... for furtherance of thyr purpose" to be "the key of whoredom, and treason" (Bullough 1957, 284). Brooke and Shakespeare retain the trappings of confession, but retract the material details supplied by the Italians. In Brooke, Juliet arrives at the monastery first encumbered by her Nurse and a younger maid, then entering the Friar's 'cell' (not explicitly designated as a confessional box) where she meets Romeo, does confess with him, and then is married. In Shakespeare, Juliet comes alone to the monastery, meets Romeo and the Friar in what appears to be the nave of the church, and the two of them are led into a more closed space by the Friar: "Come, come with me, and we shall make short work" (2.6.35).

In the *novelle*, the confession-as-wedding cunningly conjoins the private and the public. In Da Porto, under the pretext of confessing herself Giulietta sets out alone for the Franciscan monastery, and enters one of the "confessori" (1831, 26) (confessional boxes) used by the monks. Hearing Giulietta call out for him from within the confessional, Friar Lorenzo enters the convent and then the confessional box with Romeo in tow, shuts the door separating the confessional from the outside but opens an iron grate – "lama di ferro tutta forata" (ibid.) – separating the two lovers from within the closed space. Once their desire to be married is confirmed, the Friar performs the frequent, if controversial *per verba dei presenti* marriage: "Allora in presenza del frate, che'l tutto in confessione diceva accettare, per parole dei presenti Romeo la bella giovane sposò" (ibid.) ["Then, in the presence of the Friar, who performed everything under the seal of confession, married Romeo and the beautiful girl *per verba dei presenti*"]. Because, in Bandello, Giulietta's mother Giovanna accompanies her daughter, along with several serving women, to the Saint Francis monastery for confession, the achievement of a secret public ceremony is even more vexed. In this case, Friar Lorenzo has already placed Romeo within his confessional box ("ne la cella del suo confessionario", Bandello 1952, 738) and locked him inside. Taking Giovanna, Giulietta and the other women into the monastery church, Friar Lorenzo first enters the confessional (with Romeo already inside), followed by Giulietta herself. Inside the confessional, she gives a sign to the Friar, and he lifts a grating ("graticola" ibid.) separating the lovers. As in Da Porto, once the lovers have confirmed their desire to be married, the Friar pronounces the divinely sanctioned wedding ceremony, and with Romeo bestowing the ring on Giulietta they become man and wife. Limited to one short kiss in Da Porto, Bandello's lovers (with Madonna Giovanna standing just outside) kiss freely through the opened "graticola" and, as in Da Porto, make arrangements for their wedding night. With Romeo able to make a secret escape (how exactly this occurs remains a mystery), and the "graticola" within the "confessionario" carefully reset, the Friar sequentially hears the happy Giulietta's confession, followed by those of her mother and the serving women. The Friar has masterfully negotiated private and public space.

Perhaps the most notable difference between Da Porto and Bandello, suggested by Bandello's lengthening of the lovers' kiss after they have been married inside the confessional box, is Bandello's considerably greater emphasis on sexual pleasure. Da Porto says little of Romeo and Giulietta's sexual enjoyment after their wedding, only that "più notti del loro amore felicemente goderono, aspettando di trovar modo, per lo quale il padre della donna, che agli loro desii essere contrario sapeano, si potesse placare" (1831, 26–7) ["for several nights they happily enjoyed their love, waiting to find a way that they could placate their father, who they know would be hostile to their love"]. Bandello places them not in the altogether private place of Giulietta's bedroom, but in the semi-public, semi-private place of the garden, under cover of darkness, and with a greater sense of sexual thrill than a completely private space would have afforded. In a tone that is simultaneously explicit and joyous, Bandello revels in their sexual pleasure:

> Come egli vide Giulietta, incontra l'andò con le braccia aperte. Il medesimo fece Giulietta a lui, ed avvinchiatogli il collo stette buona pezza da soverchia dolcezza ingombrata che nulla dir poteva. Era al medesimo segno l'infiammato amante, parendogli simil piacere non aver gustato già mai. Cominciarono poi a basciarsi l'un l'altro con infinito diletto ed indicibil gioia di tutte due le parti. Ritiratisi poi in uno dei canti del giardino, quivi sovra certa banca che ci era, amorosamente insieme giacendo consumarono il santo matrimonio. Ed essendo Romeo giovine di forte nerbo e molto innamorato, più e più volte a diletto con la sua bella sposa si ridusse.
> (Bandello 1952, 739)[9]

In the case of the street brawl between the two families that undoes the lovers' bliss, Bandello casts the episode in a more civic light than his predecessor. Whereas Da Porto emphasizes over specifically political causes the abstract and perverse power of Fortune, "d'ogni mondan diletto nemica" (1831, 27) ["enemy to every earthly pleasure"], and has Romeo kill Teobaldo (Tybalt) without much deliberation simply after seeing dead Montecchi kinsmen in the street, Bandello places the renewed hostilities at the very point when Fra Lorenzo was about to reveal the secret marriage to the lovers' parents, so successful had his mediation efforts between the two factions been up to that point (Bandello 1952, 739–40). Where Bandello's Fra Lorenzo leaves off in promoting peace between Montecchi and Cappelletti, Romeo picks up the civic mission in the public space of the street, which is exactly specified in Bandello: "su il Corso vicino a la porta dei Borsari verso Castelvecchio" (ibid., 740). (Shakespeare's Benvolio vainly attempts to talk Mercutio and Tybalt out of fighting "in the public haunt of men", 3.1.49, urging them either to "reason coldly of [their] grievances", 3.1.51, in the common space of the street, to "withdraw unto some private space", 3.1.50, in order to fight, or to withdraw from each other). Fully aware of the Friar's peacekeeping efforts, Bandello's Romeo is gravely disturbed by the renewed fighting; he manages, however, with an impassioned speech to get several Montecchi to lay down their arms, but Teobaldo ambushes him from behind and thrusts his sword at Romeo's flank. Saved by a protective "corazza", Romeo still attempts to assuage Teobaldo: "Teobaldo, tu se grandemente errato sei tu credi che io qui sia venuto per far questione né teco né con i tuoi. Io a caso mi ci sono abbattuto, e venni per levarne via i miei, bramando che ormai viviamo insieme da buoni *cittadini*" (Bandello 1952, 740; emphasis mine) ["Teobaldo, you are seriously wrong if you think that I have come to dispute you and your followers. I came here by accident, and then was beginning to take away my people, desiring that from now on we can live like *citizens*"].

Romeo's peacekeeping efforts, of course, bear no fruit in the Bandello version; when Teobaldo savagely attacks him the second time, he kills him in self-defense. In Bandello, the Cappelletti and the Montecchi each make a passionate but reasoned case before Della Scala in the public forum. Bandello represents Della Scala's decree of banishment for Romeo – a quintessentially civic punishment – as lenient: a response to the validity of the Montecchi's arguments that Romeo tried to establish peace and only killed Teobaldo in self-defense. Not only have the Montecchi apparently prevailed in Della Scala's judgement, but apparently the prince has assured Romeo's father that the ban will probably be lifted, so that Romeo later counsels the desperate Giulietta to be patient.

After Teobaldo's death and the decree of banishment, the more chaste Da Porto version reunites the lovers again in Fra Lorenzo's confessional box, where Giulietta introduces the theme, dear to the early modern Italian stage, of the heroine travelling in disguise as a man. Da Porto's Giulietta declares, "Io m'accorcierò queste chiome, e come servo vi verrò dietro" (1831, 28) ["I will cut my hair, and as servant I will follow you"]. Romeo cannot accept that Giulietta be with him in any other form than as a woman; in a neo-Platonic key common for the literary/academic circles in which Da Porto and Bandello moved, Romeo claims that while his body will be absent in his exiled destination of Mantua, his soul will remain in Verona (ibid.). Bandello adds one more garden scene: the lovers meet, Giulietta makes the same disguise proposal, Romeo gives the same response (in the strong belief that the banishment will be lifted), and the lovers have one more passionate, if tearful, scene that ends, as in Shakespeare, with the approaching dawn.

Bandello's Romeo, in fact, is the one to take up a disguise – that of a "mercadante straniero" (Bandello 1952, 743) ["foreign merchant"] as he takes up his exile in Mantua. In both Da Porto and Bandello, Giulietta quickly falls into a deep melancholy and is even said to lose her beauty. Bandello's Romeo vainly counsels her by letter to keep her spirits up, but so great is her depression (in both Da Porto and Bandello) that her parents decide that only an arranged marriage will revive her spirits. In Bandello, Giulietta's mother sees the problem in private-public terms: her daughter is wallowing in private grief because she has seen other girls her age publically becoming wives during carnival season. Giulietta, in both Da Porto and Bandello, reacts with fury and despair at the prospect of marrying the Paris figure, but she still plays a strong hand. In order to escape to the Friar to find some remedy for the situation, she delivers in Da Porto a consummate speech of Catholic contrition, reflecting the much greater prominence in the *novelle* of the confession theme. Her melancholy must derive from "qualche peccato commesso" (1831, 32) ["some sin that she has committed"]; her last confession cheered her up so much (as it certainly did!) that she wishes to return. In Bandello, where as in Da Porto the entire story is calibrated to the Catholic liturgical year, Giulietta explicitly invokes the pretext of the approaching Feast of the Virgin to make her 'confession'.

Once arrived at Fra Lorenzo's cell under cover of confession, Giulietta immediately asks him for poison to kill herself in the Da Porto version, threatening otherwise to stab herself with a dagger. Da Porto's relatively more opportunistic, and more political Friar protests that he cannot do this for fear of his own reputation and then proposes the potion plan. The more roundabout Bandello version has Giulietta despairing that Romeo will come to help her, even though she has written him about the forced marriage to Paris. (When Bandello's Romeo, after hearing the false news of Giulietta's death, blames himself for not coming earlier, we can perhaps agree with him). Then she proposes the plan of disguising herself as a boy and travelling to Mantua, to which the Friar responds in a patronizing manner, as if she could not take the path taken by so many female characters in romance and *commedia erudita*: "Tu sei troppo giovanetta, delicatamente nodrita, e non potresti sofferire la fatica del viaggio" (Bandello 1952, 747) ["You are too young, delicately nourished, and you could not bear the difficulties of the voyage"]. Feeling miserable and trapped, she demands mortal poison from the Friar, having heard from Romeo what a great "distiller of herbs and other things" he is, also threatening to kill herself if the Friar does not consent. Bandello's Friar talks Juliet out of suicide on two counts: the Catholic respect for the sanctity of life, and, more profanely, his own reputation, which would greatly suffer if he were implicated in Giulietta's death: "Tu puoi ben intendere che per l'ordinario poche cose d'importanza si fanno che io con la mia autorità non ci intravenga" (ibid., 749) ["You can well understand that ordinarily few things happen in this city without my authority"]. Explaining the scheme of the potion, Bandello's Friar takes pains to boast that the greatest doctors in the world will not be able to tell that Giulietta is not really dead – suggesting the superiority of this mountebank-friar relative to medical authority. In the Da Porto version, the Friar tells Giulietta that after she wakes up from the potion he will take her, disguised as a friar, to Mantua (in Bandello, the plan is for Romeo to return secretly to Verona, and with the Friar take the woken Giulietta out of the tomb). In general, the colloquy with Giulietta after Romeo's banishment reveals the larger civic and political role that the Friar carries in the *novelle*.

Ever resourceful, Da Porto's Giulietta deliberately frames her false death to look like a suicide provoked by her desire to escape the forced marriage. There is no nurse, but she makes sure that a servant and an aunt see her drinking a glass of water with powder mixed in, declaring to them "mio padre per certo contra mio volere non mi darà marito, s'io potrò" (Da Porto 1831, 35) ["My father certainly will not force me against my will into marriage, if I have anything to do about it"]. (The two women only realize after Giulietta's 'death' what this meant). Bandello's Giulietta drinks the potion in secret and introduces the theme (expressed by the Friar in Da Porto who worries how Giulietta will be when she wakes up in the tomb) of Giulietta's terror at the prospect of waking up before the rotting Teobaldo in a ghastly tomb – all of which is expressed in graphic detail. In Da Porto, it is just as important – and disastrous – that the Friar suddenly has to leave Verona during this period as it is that the letter (written in Da Porto by Giulietta and given to the Friar to deliver) does not arrive. It is taken as a given in Da Porto that Pietro, Romeo's servant, would have consulted him before delivering the fatal news to Romeo, but the Friar is not there. Improving upon Da Porto's rather tendentious explanation that Fra Lorenzo's fellow friar simply could not locate Romeo when he came to Mantua with the letter, Bandello introduces the theme of the plague-thwarted letter sustained in Brooke and Shakespeare (which, ironically, would have been natural for Da Porto since he frequently wrote about plagues infesting northern Italy in his *Lettere storiche*). Bandello's detail about agents of the Sanità intervening to quarantine the friar in the house where another friar was suspected of plague death would have resonated very topically for Bandello's readers.

When Pietro does deliver the terrible news, Romeo in Da Porto and Bandello blames his inaction. In the latter version Romeo's anguished self-rebuke is couched in the terms of an agonized confession to his 'saint': "Perdonami, perdonami, moglie mia carissima, ché io confesso il gravissimo mio peccato" (Bandello 1952, 757) ["Forgive me, forgive me, my dear wife, for I confess to you my terrible sin"], although he quickly follows this orthodox Catholic formula by the heretical attempt to kill himself, from which he is narrowly prevented by Pietro. In Bandello, although Romeo still intends to die – now in Giulietta's tomb – he has enough presence of mind to make Pietro think that his life is not in danger and to write a detailed letter to his father – a detail not present in Da Porto. In the letter, Romeo is remarkably public-minded for someone still resolved to take his life. First, he explains the entire story of his secret marriage to his father; this is the only aspect of the letter that Shakespeare mentions and it is this corroboration (notably absent in Da Porto) that exonerates the Friar. Next, he asks his father that a solemn mass of the dead be performed in perpetuity for Giulietta, and he takes care to endow it with an inheritance that he has just received from his aunt. Then, he asks his father that the first revenues that come from his aunt, who died just a few days before, be given "a' poveri per amor di Dio" (ibid., 759) ["to the poor for the love of God"]. Finally, Romeo tells his father that he has provided that his servant Pietro have enough money so that he will be freed from service in the future, asking that his father make sure that this be carried out.

In Da Porto, Romeo takes "una guastadetta di acqua di serpe" (Da Porto 1831, 38) ["a container of snake's venom"] that he somehow already had with him, disguises himself as a farmer and travels to Verona. As a young man of great strength ("gran nerbo", ibid., 39), Romeo is able to lift the cover off of the Capulet tomb, and then descends and beholds Giulietta among the bones and decaying remains of the deceased. After an anguished lament, he downs the poison, then embraces her. As in Bandello (and Luhrmann), Giulietta wakes before Romeo has died, but in her confused state she first thinks that it is the Friar who is embracing her. As the desperate and confused Romeo sees her begin to stir, the thought of Pygmalion comes into his mind (ibid., 40). Giulietta tearfully explains to Romeo the scheme of her false death, marvelling that her letter did not reach him. Romeo tells her how Pietro instead delivered the news that she was dead. After protracted lament, with Romeo still barely alive, Fra Lorenzo enters the tomb to encounter the tragic lovers, whereupon Romeo expires. Fra Lorenzo tells Giulietta that he will place her in a convent. Giulietta declares that she wishes nothing more than to stay forever in the tomb with Romeo, and dies by holding her breath!

Bandello points the way towards Brooke's and Shakespeare's apothecary by having Romeo declare to Pietro that he has received the poison in Mantua, presumably recently, from "quello Spoletino che aveva quegli aspidi vivi ed altri serpenti" (1952, 760) ["that fellow from Spoleto who had live snakes and serpents"]. Bandello takes further what was already implied in Da Porto: that Romeo has procured the poison from one of the legions of mountebanks selling non-authorized snake oil and other kinds of drugs and cures in Italian piazzas. Since many of these mountebanks travelled from city to city, and some were genuine medical experimentalists, the line between them and the "great distiller" Fra Lorenzo, who travelled from country to country in his youth, becomes thin. If these figures were often destitute, and were aligned with urban perfume-sellers and apothecaries, Brooke and then Shakespeare transform Bandello's "Spoletino" into an impoverished apothecary. In Shakespeare, Romeo talks the apothecary into selling him his illegal poisons because, according to Romeo, his desperate poverty puts him above the law. In Brooke, the full force of the law is directed precisely at the apothecary, who is hanged while Pietro/Peter and the Friar are pardoned.

Bandello follows much of Da Porto in narrating the lovers' final moments. But unlike Da Porto's Romeo, Bandello's drinks the vial of poison right before the eyes of Pietro, giving him at that point the letter he has written to his father and explaining that he has provided means to free Pietro from service. The tomb scene follows similar contours, except that Giulietta's dazed thought that the Friar is molesting her is made, as is typical for Bandello, more sexually explicit. So Giulietta "sentendosi basciare dubitò che il frate venuto per levarla e averla a portar in camera, la tenesse in braccio ed incitato dal concupiscibile appetito la basciasse" (Bandello 1952, 761) ["feeling herself being kissed, she feared that the Friar had come to take her away to his cell, and was holding her in his arms and driven by his sexual appetite was kissing her"]. As with Da Porto, much is made of the lovers' mutual lament made possible by Romeo's slow death, with Bandello particularly emphasizing the way the lovers instantaneously feel intense joy (the chance to see each other one last time) and the height of despair.

Whereas in Bandello, as in Brooke and Shakespeare, the Friar is quickly pardoned – in all of these texts the letter of Romeo to his father corroborates the Friar's testimony – Da Porto puts his somewhat more opportunistic and problematic Friar through his paces. The authorities rush into the tomb just after Giulietta has died, see the Friar weeping over Giulietta's dead body (they at first do not perceive the body of Romeo), and accuse the Friar of forcibly entering the tomb to steal dead bodies. Like a criminal, the Friar is apprehended and taken before the Prince. Having been evasive up to that point, he tells the Prince a flat-out lie, claiming that he has descended into the tomb because he had not been able to attend her funeral and had come to say prayers in order to liberate Giulietta's soul from the torments of purgatory. The Prince would have believed this, according to Da Porto, except that in the meantime Romeo's body has been discovered – a fact that the Friar's previous story does not explain. Only at this point does the Friar reveal the entire truth. The great Bartolomeo Della Scala, seeing the entire situation, is moved to compassion and orders a grand public funeral, and a grand public memorial. The reconciliation that is finally, and tragically achieved between the two families – which is suggested to be permanent – has much to do in Da Porto with the direction of Della Scala, the strong civic leader that he so highly praised at the beginning of the novella. Bandello, who provides the final dénouements taken up by Brooke and Shakespeare, and still represents Della Scala as a compassionate and strong figure, is less optimistic about the future: "tra i Montecchi e Capelletti si fece la pace, ben che non molto dopoi durasse" (Bandello 1952, 765) ["The Montecchi and the Capelletti made peace, but it did not last very long"].

Whether one sympathizes with Da Porto's optimism or Bandello's scepticism, the civic purchase of their stories is palpably clear. Shakespeare, who is continually attracted to romance plots, in some ways can be said to draw back to Masuccio, in the sense that his version has less overt civic particularity. But Shakespeare, largely through Brooke but possibly also directly, is deeply informed by Da Porto and Bandello. A close reading of Da Porto and Bandello, such as we have attempted here, can draw into relief the many and important traces of the civic idea, and the negotiation of private and public space, in Shakespeare's play. If these civic traces may occasionally be latent in Shakespeare, his somewhat less particularized text (relative to Da Porto and Bandello) provides a fine scaffold for the many and interesting civic and political 'translations' of the play that have been made, from *West Side Story* to Baz Luhrmann.

NOTES

1. For an excellent discussion of the relation of "Li tragici successi" and other commedia dell'arte scenarios to *Romeo and Juliet*, see Andrews 2014, 43–7. For the best English edition of Scala's scenarios, see Andrews 2008.
2. Masuccio's text leaves the issue implicit, but suggests that the idea is Ganozza's. As her father is forcing her into the unwanted marriage, "prepuose con un modo non che strano ma periculoso e crodele, e fuorsi mai udito recontare, ponendo lo onore e la vita in piriglio, a tanti mancamenti satisfare" (1968, 244) ["she resolved with a plan that was not only strange but dangerous and cruel, and perhaps never heard of before, placing her honour and her life in danger, to find a satisfying way out of her difficulties"]. She then is said to "reveal to the Friar what she wanted to do", which is followed by the Friar's procurement of the potion (All translations from the Italian are my own).
3. Not published until 1560–62, well after Da Porto's death in 1529.
4. "Come and behold, you irresponsible man, the Montecchi and the Cappelletti, the Monadi and the Filippeschi, those already sad, these under suspicion".
5. "I have often heard that by making marriages, peace can be achieved not only among private citizens and gentlemen, but many times, among great princes and kings wracked by terrible wars, a true peace and friendship satisfactory to everyone can follow".
6. In Brooke, Romeus repeatedly walks in the garden before Juliet's window in the hope that he may see her. The lovers keep missing each other, until one night "the Moone did shine so bright / That she espyde her love" (ll. 468–9).
7. "… almost the entire night, at great danger to his life, in front of his beloved lady's house he stood, and sometimes pulling himself up to the window of her chamber, without her or anyone else knowing, he sat and listened to her voice …".
8. "The Friar was a very great experimenter who in his days had explored many countries and had desired to understand and experiment with many different things, and above all else he understood the powers of herbs and stones and was one of the greatest distillers that you could find in those days".
9. "When he saw Giulietta, he went up to her and cast his arms open. Giulietta did the same, and winding her arms around his neck she just stood there, overwhelmed by a powerful, unspeakable sweetness. Romeo, who was on fire, felt the same way, sure that he had never before tasted such pleasure. They began to kiss each other with infinite delight and unspeakable joy on both their parts. Then they withdrew into a corner of the garden, and there on top of a bench that lay there, lying together, lovingly consummated their sacred marriage. And Romeo, being strong and stout and madly in love, joyfully came back to his beautiful wife time after time".

WORKS CITED

Alighieri, Dante. 1970–75. *The Divine Comedy*. Translated and edited by Charles S. Singleton. Princeton: Princeton University Press.

Andrews, Richard. 2008. *The Commedia dell'Arte of Flaminio Scala: A Translation and Analysis of 30 Scenarios*. Lanham, MD: The Scarecrow Press.

Andrews, Richard. 2014. "Resources in Common: Shakespeare and Flaminio Scala". In *Transnational Mobilities in Early Modern Theater*, edited by Robert Henke and Eric Nicholson, 37–52. Farnham: Ashgate.

Bandello, Matteo. (1554) 1952. *Tutte le opere di Matteo Bandello*. Edited by Francesco Flora. Verona: Mondadori.

Brognoligo, Gioachino. 1904. "La vita e le opera di Luigi Da Porto". In Gioachino Brognoligo, *Studi di storia letteraria*, 1–118. Roma: Società Dante Alighieri.

Bullough, Geoffrey, ed. 1957. *Narrative and Dramatic Sources of Shakespeare*, vol. 1. London: Routledge and Kegan Paul / New York: Columbia University Press.

Da Porto, Luigi. (1535) 1831. *Istoria di due nobili amanti con la pietosa loro morte intervenuta gia nella città di Verona nel tempo del Sig. Bartolomeo Della Scala*. Pisa: Tipi dei Fratelli Nistri.

Masuccio (Salernitano). 1968. *Il Novellino*. Edited by Roberto di Marco. Bologna: Sampietro Editore.

Scala, Flaminio. 1976. *Il teatro delle favole rappresentative*, 2 vols. Edited by Ferruccio Marotti. Milano: Il Polifilo.

Shakespeare, William. 2012. *Romeo and Juliet*. Edited by René Weis. London: Bloomsbury (The Arden Shakespeare Third Series).

Tylus, Jane. 1997. "Women at the Windows: Commedia dell'Arte and Theatrical Practice in Early Modern Italy". *Theatre Journal* 49: 323–42.

3 Shakespeare as 'Chief Architect and Plotter'
Romeo and Juliet and Civic Space

Roy Eriksen

This article does not focus on the famous love story of Romeo and Juliet, the most accomplished expression of the myth of *Liebestod* in world literature, but aims to investigate how the dramatist emplots the civic and urban arena in which the drama of their abortive love unfolds. Each of the novella sources "in the main line of descent reflects contemporary social, economic, and political realities with subtle difference", Jill Levenson reminds us (Shakespeare 2000, 6), but it is the particular changes Shakespeare makes in them that may tell us how he configured the society that produces the tragedy.

In William Painter's *The goodly Hystory of the true, and constant Loue between Rhomeo and Ivlietta* (1567), one of Shakespeare's sources for *Romeo and Juliet*, we learn that the Capulets have a castle called Villafranca outside the city walls (Shakespeare 2002, 87).[1] Arthur Brooke in 1562 gives it the name "Free town" in Shakespeare's main source for the play, *The Tragicall Historye of Romeus and Juliet* (1562),[2] where the Capulets and the Montagues both belong to the Veronese nobility. In Shakespeare's play we understand the families live in houses within Verona, and Brian Gibbons comments in his edition of the play that "Shakespeare visualizes Capulet as living in a merchant's house rather than a castle. This dignity he transfers to Escalus" (Shakespeare 2002, 87). This is not quite correct. Prince Escalus probably lives in a castle or palace, though this is not mentioned anywhere in the text, but it is not called "Freetown". In Brooke's novella "Free town", the Capulets castle, is where Juliet must swear before witnesses that she consents to marrying "Counte Paris", or else be rejected by her father:

> Onlesse by Wensday next, thou bende as I am bent,
> And at our castle cald Free towne, thou freely doe assent
> To Counte Paris sute, and promise to agree
> To whatsoever then shall passe, twixt him, my wife, and me.
> (Brooke 1562, ll. 1972–5)

Commenting on Shakespeare's reference to "Freetown" in the opening scene (1.1.100), Jill L. Levenson surprisingly explains that it "serves as a judgement place" (Shakespeare 2000, 151), whereas in the novella the family castle merely is the chosen site for the meeting and betrothal of Paris and

Giulietta. The passage in Brooke is placed much later in the action of the play, as a part of Friar Lawrence's stratagem (4.2.1–47) to allay the feud that threatens the commonwealth. In fact, the term "Freetown" itself probably is Painter's misinterpretation of "Villefranche", Pierre Boaistuau's name for the grand Capulet estate, Villa Franca.[3]

It nevertheless remains a fact that Shakespeare retains the name "Freetown", but intriguingly transfers it to a shared neutral ground of adjudication within the city itself, "old Freetown, our common judgement-place" (1.1.100), where he can conduct talks with Montague. This apparently insignificant shift, I would argue, provides a clue to the power relations in Shakespeare's Verona. It does in fact point to the existence of a civic space of law-regulated arbitration within the commonwealth, as it were a *Porto Franco*[4] in the townscape, where Escalus can conduct negotiations. This move and the reason for it may partially explain some of the substantial differences of structure and thematic emphasis existing between Brooke's sprawling, sometimes smutty, narrative, and Shakespeare's carefully designed drama of the clash between public and private life. For as Dympna C. Callaghan points out "in the play capitalism again becomes an active principle still identified with the consolidation of the state and prosperous families" (1994, 71).

In his innovative study of dramaturgy, *Shakespearean Design* (1972), Mark Rose explains the difference in terms of the new design that Shakespeare creates: "The narrative is Brooke's, but the shaping pattern is wholly Shakespeare's".[5] It is a fact that the dramatist abbreviates, restructures, and adds to his main source, for instance by adding episodes of violence in 1.1 and 5.3. Gibbons describes how Shakespeare reshapes Brooke's episodic narrative by strengthening

> the symmetrical pattern of the action, increasing the importance of a number of minor characters to provide parallels and interweave motives; he also greatly develops one or two in order to alter the balance of Brooke's poem ...
>
> (Shakespeare 2002, 38)

As Rose convincingly shows, *Romeo and Juliet* "bears witness to Shakespeare's growing architectonic powers" (1972, 145), exemplified by the use of compositional schemes that create connectedness and focus. These schemes are systematically deployed in the transformation of what at first promises to be an Italianate love comedy focused on the conflict between passionate young lovers and a traditionalist parent generation. Susan Snyder explains how "action and characters begin the familiar comic mould and are then transformed or discarded, to compose the shape of tragedy" (1979, 57). The deeply ingrained feud between the Capulets and the Montagues invited Shakespeare to develop the "correspondences between patriarchal state and patriarchal family, political and social order" (Shakespeare 2000, 31) into an exploration of civic space. The clash between the interests of the rivalling families with those of the Prince and the majority of citizens raises the question that according to Markku Peltonen was the main concern in John Barston's *The Safeguard of Societie* (1576), namely, "how was the government of a commonwealth to be organized?" (Peltonen 1995, 187).

To grasp the broader cultural context for Shakespeare's dramatization of the need for governance, Ben Jonson's revealing lines on the organization of poetry in *Discoveries* offer insight:

> As, for example, if a man would build a house, he would first appoint a place to build it in, which he would define within certain bounds; so, in the constitution of a poem, the action is aimed at by the poets, which answers place in a building, and that action hath his largeness, compass, and proportion. So the epic asks a magnitude, from other poems: since, what is place in the one is action in the other, the difference is in space.
>
> (Jonson 1976, 92–3)

The passage pinpoints how early modern writers perceived the close relationship between a poetry that was able to teach and delight and the civic art par excellence, architecture, an art of utility, beauty, and public display. At the level of disposition, then, both are arts of spatial organization and Jonson is far from the first to underline the shared poetics of building and drama. Various Elizabethan writers on poetics like Richard Wills,[6] George Gascoigne,[7] Sir Philip Sidney,[8] George Puttenham, and William Scott demonstrate how Italian conceptions of literature in terms of planning a building, or edification both moral and material, are essential to the Elizabethans, and poets like Edmund Spenser (Hieatt 1960), Christopher Marlowe (Eriksen 1985, 49–74), and Samuel Daniel provide examples of such use (Røstvig 1979, 22–37). Shakespeare is no exception (Rose 1972; Eriksen 2001; Cunin 2008). In *2 Henry IV* 1.3.35–62 he makes Lord Bardolph align the task of plotting a rebellion with that of building according to a design.[9] Shakespeare does not, however, appear to be interested in the material aspects of that larger building, the physical city, nor signals any curiosity for Renaissance "ideal cities",[10] whereas he on several occasions uses the image of the house to express the plight of individual characters.[11] Urbanism was invented in early modern Italy and although many of Shakespeare's plays are set in Italian towns, he conveys no more than a vague impression of town life in Italy.[12] Brian Gibbons thinks that Shakespeare "absorbs" "the impression of Italian summer", but admits that the rivalling families resemble English merchants rather than Italian nobility although there is absolutely nothing in *Romeo and Juliet* to suggest that we are in Verona (Shakespeare 2002, 38). Shakespeare's cities, frequently Italian ones and often set in Veneto, do not display the expected amount of Renaissance civic order and splendour.

Still the distance between the factional Verona of *Romeo and Juliet* and the inclusive world of *The Merry Wives of Windsor* is great. So just how does Shakespeare inscribe his play into the urban matrix in which it is set?

Addressing the clash between the public and private spheres in the play, I suggest that Shakespeare communicates his idea of civic space by means of a double process of "ruralisation" and "abstraction". "Ruralisation" is a tendency Gail Paster attributes to Shakespeare's city comedies (1985, 178), but the phenomenon is not limited to comedy. Although Verona in actual life was a famous Renaissance city, Shakespeare's textual version definitely does not communicate any particular urban "feel". In my view, this does not imply that he is not concerned about the issues at stake in a city or state.

This second process, "abstraction", represents a studied development towards ethics and ideology in Shakespeare's oeuvre,[13] a tendency that already emerges in the way he handles plot and dramatic dialogue in *Romeo and Juliet*. He teases out what Jon Snyder in an observation on Milton's method of indirection calls "an inter-subjective exchange not only of conversational phrases ... but of contrasting ideas and intellectual perspectives as well" (1989, 6). This is the very process that contributes to establishing civic space in the play, for Shakespeare's emphases differ from those of many of his contemporaries when he lets ethos approach ideology in the context of the *civitas*. The conspicuous paucity of intradiegetic pointers to places and buildings,[14] signals that Shakespeare's text is not fully embedded in the material city. We instead witness a greater focus on the abstract entity of the *polis*, based on socio-political relationships, to the exclusion of any detailed description of urban life, an emphasis that contributes to the formation of a third position between the opposite poles of the play.[15] His reliance on abstract design, on an architecture of actions, is at plot level underscored by the great attention paid to the crafting of speeches at important points in the play. Although Shakespeare at the outset underlines that factional strife is an exception in Verona, where quiet and decorum constitute the norm (1.1.87–9),[16] he also gradually and systematically exposes the fragility of that balance.

RURALIZING VERONA

For Shakespeare the city frequently appears either to be maze-like or confusing, a place of deception and entrapment. It never emerges as a place of reason and order, but one characterized by irrationality and violence, before order is established. Thus the labyrinthine world of Syracuse in *The Comedy of Errors* contrasts with that of *The Merry Wives of Windsor*, where the action is set in a few traditional, almost archetypal locations: the cottage, the tavern, the commons, and the forest. Such avoidance of city life may be grounded in the dramatist's scepticism about life in the metropolis, even though he and the theatres where he worked were deeply embedded in the urban fabric and thrived on its bustling multicultural life. The crowded city was also an oppressive, plague-ridden, and menacing environment compared to that of Stratford.[17] One response to this hostile ambience may have been what Paster points to in *The Idea of the City in the Age of Shakespeare*:

> Shakespeare tends to ruralize his city comedies: the Messina of *Much Ado*, the Padua of *Taming of the Shrew* and the Athens of *Midsummer Night's Dream* lack almost all the traces of an urban habitation but the name. (1985, 175)

This is a fine observation, but the tendency is not limited to these city comedies only, as it is equally evident in *Romeo and Juliet*. No clear sense of an urban space is conveyed, and we soon learn about groves, fields, individual houses with walled orchards, that is, we are instead introduced to the open structure of a village rather than to congested streets of an Early Modern city. Thus Benvolio tells Lady Montague that he saw Romeo wandering "underneath the grove of sycamore / That westward rooteth from this city side" (1.1.119–20). Later Romeo escapes from his mates and leaps over an "orchard wall" (2.1.5), and he is said to be in hiding under a "medlar tree" or "poperin pear" tree, when Juliet appears at the window above. Moreover, we first encounter Friar Lawrence in a field where he is filling an "osier cage ... / With baleful weeds and precious-juiced flowers" (2.3.3–4) while muttering to himself. In the play open spaces vie with interiors: we are inside the house of the Capulets, in Juliet's chamber, in the Capulet reception hall, we enter the Friar's cell, see the Nurse being accosted on her way to church, before we end up in the cemetery and the ancestral tomb of the Capulets, away from the city itself.

It seems reasonable to interpret Shakespeare's "ruralisation" of Verona as part of a deliberate technique of "familiarisation" used to bring the place of action closer to the experience of his spectators, while also suggesting his ambivalence to the metropolis. Returning briefly to *The Merry Wives of Windsor*, we encounter a whole spectrum of characters belonging to a provincial town, and Falstaff, who represents the urban Other. He is in the end transformed by his meeting with the good-natured people of Windsor, a town nostalgically representing the prelapsarian green world of the village.[18] This illustrates, I think, the mind-set Shakespeare brought to London, and which is also emplotted in his first play, *Two Gentlemen of Verona*, where Valentine initially sets up an antithesis between "the wonders of the world abroad" (1.1.6) and the "shapeless idleness of home" (1.1.8):

> Cease to persuade, my loving Proteus;
> Home-keeping youth have ever-homely wits.
> Were it not affection chains thy tender days
> To the sweet glances of thy honoured love,

> I rather would entreat thy company
> To see the wonders of the world abroad
> Than, living dully sluggardize at home (1.1.1–10)

The set of urbane and opportunistic values is inverted in the final act in favour of those of a simpler life in the country, when Valentine enters to contrast the soothing green world of country life and "flourishing peopled towns":

> How use doth breed a habit in a man!
> The shadowy desert, unfrequented woods
> I better brook than flourishing peopled towns.
> Here can I set alone, unseen of any,
> And to the nightingale's complaining notes
> Tune my distress and record my woes (5.4.1–6)

This ending must surely have made the audience of Stratford, where the play may have been written and first performed, nod approvingly (Wells 1997, 89). The apprentice play would appear to delineate the dramatist's mind-set when he embarked on his remarkable career on the London stage, but this simple dichotomy was soon to be revised and refined. It is obvious that *Romeo and Juliet* appears to be withdrawn from aspects of urban life treated by such Dekker, Lodge, Marston, and Stow, but on closer inspection it emerges that Shakespeare was indeed concerned with the city as a shared but contested human habitat. "Civilitie" is indeed on his mind as signalled already in the Prologue: "In fair Verona, ... [w]here civil blood makes civil hands unclean" (2, 4).

ABSTRACTING URBAN SPACE

At the same time that Shakespeare avoids the sordid physical aspects of city life he conducts an analysis of city contingencies in terms of a deft use of *inventio*, *dispositio*, and *elocutio*, in his capacity of "chief architect and plotter".[19] The symmetrical design of the play's two phases and its "bipolarity" (Maquerlot 1995, 59) is solidified by the placing of the three "pillars" (Rose 1972, 146), being the public scenes in which Prince Escalus appears: 1.1, 3.1, and 5.3. These allocations and the underlying "disegno interno" turn the play into one of Shakespeare's most carefully composed plays.[20] However, whenever he repeats a configuration of characters in scenes like the three "pillar" scenes, or in the scenes between Juliet and the Nurse (2.5 and 3.2), he significantly changes what he repeats, transposing them as it were, to a different mode or key.[21] To claim, therefore, that he uses "an identical structure for all three of these episodes" (Maquerlot 1995, 39) fails to capture what these scenes really do in the play, as Escalus's verbal performance in them changes in ways that bear directly on how he governs the city.

Arthur Brooke underlines that

> There were two auncient stockes, which Fortune high dyd place
> Above the rest, indewd with welth, and nobler of their race,
> Loved of the common sort, loved of the Prince alike,
> And like unhappy were they both, when Fortune list to strike. (ll. 25–8)

When Shakespeare later in the Chorus stresses that the houses are "alike in dignity" (Prologue 1) and equally matched within the city, he also underscores the fragility of such a power balance. The families match each other but seemingly occupy distinctly different spheres within the state and Shakespeare foregrounds their different social standing. Underlying this discourse is the difficult problem of nobility by birth versus nobility by merit in Elizabethan society.[22] In fact, the noble Capulets jealously guard their status, and particularly so do Lady Capulet and Tybalt. She expects Juliet to marry young like Veronese "ladies of esteem" do (1.3.70):

> Well, think of marriage now. Younger than you
> Here in Verona, ladies of esteem
> Are made already mothers. By my count
> I was your mother much upon these years
> That you are now a maid. Thus then in brief:
> The valiant Paris seeks you for his love. (1.3.69–74)

The Capulets clearly belong to ancient nobility, and Juliet's "dearest cousin" (3.2.66), Tybalt, undoubtedly feels superior to the Montagues. Whereas both families are noble in Brooke (25–6), in the play the Montagues no longer are, but appear to be an affluent merchant family.[23] In the eyes of Tybalt they belong to an inferior class, and he refers to Romeo as "slave" (54) and "that villain Romeo" (63). In the central scene he again calls Romeo "a villain" (3.1.60). Lady Capulet later refers twice to Romeo as "villain" (3.5.79–80). As for Capulet, he appears to be pragmatic and appreciates qualities in Romeo initially, but is eager to marry Juliet to Paris, "this noble earl" (3.4.21), who is a kinsman of Prince Escalus. Capulet is pleased for "having now provided" (3.5.178) for his daughter:

> A gentleman of noble parentage,
> Of fair demesnes, youthful and nobly lign'd,
> Stuff'd, as they say, with honourable parts,
> Proportion'd as one's thought would wish a man. (3.5.179–182)

The match will consolidate the family's standing in the upper echelons of Verona and strengthen its alliance with the Prince.

I, therefore, take Shakespeare's emphasis on "alike in dignity" to mean equally worthy of respect, regardless of birth, and to indicate the social balance of Verona. He may have done this bearing in mind the much publicized and well-functioning social balance of the Republic of Venice. Shakespeare may have wanted to allude to Gasparo Contarini's advice to rulers:

> If you will have your commonwealth perfect and enduring, let not one part be mightier than the other, but let them all (in much as may be) have equal share in public authority.
>
> (Lewknor 1599, 67)

In fact, the socio-economic machinery of Venice was well known to and admired by Elizabethan policy makers and intellectuals ever since Sir Thomas Smith published *De Republica Anglorum: the Maner of Gouernement or Policie of the Realme of England* (1583).[24] Sir Dudley Smith compared the city-state to "a clock going with many wheels, and making small motions, sometimes out of order, but soon mended, and all without change and variety" (1907, 1.55). This was a system based on law and equity that allowed citizens considerable individual freedoms and also fostered a measure of tolerance. The civic policies of Escalus in the Venetian city of Verona could be seen to allude to the delicate socio-economic balance achieved by the Venetian system of government. However, the strengthening of the alliance between the Capulets and the Prince would seem precisely to render "one part ... mightier than the other".

The policies of Escalus have proved successful for some time and have brought quiet to the streets and piazzas of Verona and, hence, the weapons of the Capulets and the Montagues are "canker'd with peace" (l. 95) for lack of use. The citizens also support the Prince's policies, issuing armed and in force into the street to confront the antagonists and restore civic order:

> *Citizens.* Clubs, bills and partisans! Strike! Beat them down! Down with the Capulets! Down with the Montagues! (1.1.70–3)

The citizens who wish business as usual lend added authority to the Prince, but rather than punishing the fighting factions, he will conduct separate talks, albeit he also threatens with capital punishment. The Prince concludes his furious speech by summoning Montague to "our common judgement-place", which Shakespeare significantly gives the name "old Freetown", possibly in reference to the freedoms enjoyed by citizens under English Common Law (van Caenegem 1988, 98ff.). More importantly on this occasion, we note that Escalus does not summon both heads of family to "our common-judgement place".[25] Escalus prefers to talk to his fellow nobleman in private first, before he summons the citizen Montague to appear later at "Freetown", thus signalling a difference in rank.

The initial skirmish between the rivalling families, the citizens, and the Prince's men bears on the question that was the concern of John Barston's *The Safeguard of Societie* (1576), namely "how was the government of a commonwealth to be organized?" (Peltonen 1995, 67). Unfortunately, the Prince who governs Verona is unable to disregard what benefits his own class and therefore falls short as head of a city of free and law-abiding burghers. Discussing the Elizabethan brand of Ciceronian republicanism, Peltonen argues that to a political theorist like Barston

> liberty could be realised only if everyone led the civic way of life, was willing to disregard his own private good and to promote wholeheartedly the good of the whole community, without which it was impossible to avoid servitude.
>
> (Ibid., 163)

The Prince acts too late and lamely and ironically promises his citizens "to be general of your woes / And lead you, even to death" (5.3.218–19). His failure to stand firm and to disregard private interests comes across in the way Shakespeare fashions Escalus's speeches – from the initial attempt to impose order in 1.1.79–101 to his uninspired rhetoric in 3.3 and 5.2.

When the Prince enters to break up the riot in 1.1.79, he misreads the situation and chooses an inflated form of address that would seem to be more appropriate at a public ceremony. He simply relies too much on an inflated perception of himself as ruler:

> *Prince.* Rebellious subjects, enemies to peace,
>   Profaners of this neighbour-stained steel (1.1.79–80)

The three parallel phrases in elevated and antithetical style, simply do not succeed in capturing the attention of his unruly subjects, who are not only busy fighting each other, but are also attacked by citizens on all sides. Escalus is shocked at the lack of obedience and bursts out in bewilderment and frustration "Will they not hear?" (l. 81). He then furiously starts to shout at the top of his voice, changing his former rhetorical formality to a threatening, impassioned speech "What ho! You men, you beasts!" (l. 81). He attempts to control his subjects in what can be likened to an incantation marked by periodicity.[26] He virtually casts a spell of words that marks the trajectory of his angry outburst:

> ... What ho! You *men*, you beasts!
> That quench the fire of your pernicious rage
> With purple fountains issuing from your veins,
> *On pain of* torture from those bloody *hands*
> Throw your mistemper'd weapons to the ground
> And hear the sentence of your moved prince.
> Three civil brawls bred of an airy word
> By thee, *old Capulet*, and *Montague*,
> Have thrice *disturb'd* the quiet of *our streets*

Shakespeare as 'Chief Architect and Plotter' 91

> And made Verona's ancient citizens
> Cast by their grave-beseeming ornaments
> To wield *old* partisans, in *hands* as *old*,
> Canker'd with peace, to part your canker'd hate.
> If ever you *disturb our streets* again
> Your lives shall pay the forfeit of the peace.
> For this time all the rest depart away;
> You, *Capulet*, shall go along with me,
> And *Montague*, come you this afternoon,
> To know our farther pleasure in this case,
> To *old* Freetown, our common judgement-place.
> Once more, *on pain of* death, all *men* depart. (1.1.81–101; emphasis mine)

It is symptomatic that this speech, the Prince's longest, is the only one to exhibit a carefully orchestrated system of verbal repetitions linking its beginning, middle, and end.[27] That is, it represents order and reason. The words are arranged around the central lines that stress how "ancient citizens", who ought to behave with dignity, break decorum and "Cast away grave-beseeming ornaments / To wield old partisans"(ll. 91–2). The Prince's agitation also appears in his excessive use of alliteration and two examples of chiastic patterning in single lines ("*canker'd ... pe*ace, to *p*art ... *canker'd*" and "*old* partis*a*ns, in h*a*nds as *old*").

When the Prince enters after the sword fights between Tybalt and Mercutio and Tybalt and Romeo, we immediately notice that his speeches no longer possess the firm structure of his first speech:

> ... And for that offence
> Immediately we do exile him from hence.
> I have an interest in your hearts' proceeding;
> My blood for your rude brawls doth lie a-bleeding, (3.1.188–191)

Then, too, the weakly ended couplet (proceeding/a-bleeding) seems old-fashioned and counteracts the seriousness of the situation, corroding our impression of the Prince as an impartial figure of authority. He repeatedly thinks of his own family (3.1.191, 193 and 5.3.294) and possibly justly so, but also partly gives in to the demands of Capulet by banishing Romeo. This falling off from a forceful and controlled rhetoric seen in the final act, where we note a return to a stilted formalism, seen for example in the line "Search, seek, and know how this foul murder comes" (5.3.197) and in the following speech:

> Seal up the mouth of outrage for a while
> Till we can clear these ambiguities
> *And* know *their spring, their head, their true descent*,
> *And* then will I be general of your woes

> *And* lead you, even to death. Meantime forbear,
> *And* let mischance be slave to patience.
> Bring forth the parties of suspicion. (5.3. 215–21; emphasis mine)

The iterated anaphoras, the alliterations in 219–21, and the parallelisms (216) express his frustration, but also appear oddly irrelevant, revealing his propensity for vacuous words rather than action. His promise to be "general of … woes" and lead the citizens "even to death" ironically comes far too late to be wholly convincing as a genuine willingness to control the haughty members of his own class, men like Tybalt, Mercutio, and even Paris who ill-advisedly confronts Romeo.

Tybalt is, after all, predictable in his unpredictability. Being an impulsive defender of the medieval code of family honour, he is conditioned to attack whoever he believes to have designs on the Capulets' sphere of interest. He ignites at the mere sight of a man from the rival family. His counterpart in the play is Mercutio, the friend of Benvolio and the Prince's kinsman, whose very name expresses his joco-serious nature. In contrast to Tybalt, who strikes like a bolt whenever he is provoked, Mercutio is predictable in his *sprezzatura* and "martial scorn" (3.1.163). In short, Tybalt and Mercutio constitute a recipe for disaster, the former being unable to change, the latter slipping Proteus-like into ever new guises. When they feel their honour infringed, they cannot check themselves nor foresee the consequences of their actions.

Prince Escalus attempts to the best of his ability to maintain a state of equilibrium in Verona, and fails to exploit the space for peaceful interaction and reconciliation existing in the city: "old Freetown, our common judgement-place". That space is both a mental and a material space, as we see in the attitudes of individual members of two families in orderly coexistence. The foremost to favour civility is Benvolio, who in the initial skirmish tries to break up the quarrel among the servants, but is attacked by Tybalt who "hates" the word peace, as he "hate[s] hell, all Montagues" (1.1.68). In 3.1 Benvolio also urges Mercutio to withdraw before they meet Tybalt and his men:

> I pray thee, good Mercutio, lets retire;
> The day is hot, the Capels are abroad,
> And if we meet we shall not 'scape a brawl,
> For now these hot days is the mad blood stirring. (3.1.1–4)

Benvolio also has the ear of the Prince, who after the deaths of Mercutio and Tybalt turns to him for an explanation: "Benvolio, who began this bloody fray?" (3.1.153). The young Montague, then, is at the outset presented as a peaceful man who belongs in an arena in which interaction across social divides is possible.

The same goes for Romeo before he causes the death of Mercutio. When he is insulted and challenged by Tybalt, he protests that Tybalt does not know him and that he has "never injuried" (3.1.67) him. His refusal to fight is inevitably taken to be cowardice, but his civil behaviour is in keeping with how he is described by Juliet's father in the opening scene and in his appeal at 3.1.85–9. Old Capulet speaks surprisingly well of the masked intruder and tries to calm Tybalt:

> Content thee, gentle coz, let him alone,
> A bears himself like a portly gentleman;
> And, to say truth, Verona brags of him
> To be a virtuous and well-govern'd youth.
> I would not for the wealth of all this town
> Here in my house do him disparagement.
> Therefore be patient, take no note of him.
> It is my will, the which if thou respect,
> Show a fair presence and put off these frowns,
> An ill-beseeming semblance for a feast. (1.5.64–73)

Capulet's speech confirms that there is a neutral ground and a shared mental space in the city, although it is fragile and constantly challenged.

The fourth character that is preoccupied with the hostilities between the Capulets and the Montagues is Friar Lawrence, but Shakespeare considerably weakens the character found in Brooke's poem, turning him into an unlikely peace broker:

> The bounty of the fryer and wisdom hath so wonne
> The townes folks herts, that welnigh all to fryer Lawrence ronne
> To shrive them selfe the olde, the young, the great and small.
> Of all he is beloved well, and honord much of all.
> And for he did the rest in wisdome farre exceede,
> The prince by him (his counsel cravde) was holpe at time of neede.
> Betwixt the Capilets and him great friendship grew:
> A secret and assured frend unto the Montegue. (ll. 575–82)

In *Romeo and Juliet* the Prince is not central in religious and civic life. The Prince does not turn to Lawrence for counsel and only acknowledges him as "a religious man" (5.3.269), who has failed despite his good intentions. This radical change in the character indicates that Shakespeare wished to undermine the two patriarchal figures of political and spiritual authority, Prince Escalus and Friar Lawrence. The Prince is too inclined to favour his own social class and family, limiting himself to vacuous threats, whereas Friar Lawrence quite clearly lacks the intellectual rigor and circumspection needed in a civic leader. Shakespeare turns the Friar into a pedantic and credulous figure, who is too confident in his own mindset of proverbs and commonplaces. No longer the Prince's trusted counsellor, but he nonetheless seeks to combine "la ragion di stato" (Botero 1589) with the matters of the heart. He emerges as a naive counterpart to Giovanni Botero, who some years earlier than *Romeo and Juliet* had tried to reconcile politics and morality in an influential treatise.

The central patriarchal characters – the Prince, Capulet, and Friar Lawrence – are ultimately responsible for the deaths of five young people due to their inaction and actions. The entire commonwealth suffers due to their incapacity for change. From their point of view a liaison between Juliet and Romeo – had they known about it – would have constituted "a threat to the patriarchal system of family and state" (Shakespeare 2000, 40). The lovers, therefore, indirectly and directly become sacrificed to maintain the status quo. The young impetuous lovers die, but perhaps not in vain, because Shakespeare shows us a Veronese society in which an incipient civic space, though fiercely challenged, gradually emerges. He sketches a possible contractual commonwealth where "virtuous and well-govern'd" men are recognized for their worth and not their birth, a society where disputes are resolved at "old Freetown, [the] common judgement-place". In such well-governed states citizens are unselfish ornaments of the commonwealth, of the kind seen in Leon Battista Alberti's dialogue *Profugiorum ab aerumna* (Alberti 1966b, 2.107).

The Prince in the end has to admit that he, too, is partly to blame for the tragedies that have struck the two families and even his own family:

> Where be these enemies? Capulet, Montague,
> See what a scourge is laid upon our hate,
> That heaven finds means to kill your joys with love;
> And I, for winking at your discords, too,
> Have lost a brace of kinsmen. All are punished. (5.3.290–4)

Perhaps too much remains in Escalus of the mentality of the patrician Menenius in *Coriolanus*, who cannot treat the Plebeians equally or accept their freedom. For as Markku Peltonen observes of the rising merchant class in Elizabethan England:

> Although people had at the beginning been 'content every where to subject themselves to kings & princes,' they had slowly discovered 'the mane defaltes in princes and Magistrates,' once they slowly had come 'to know civilitie' and to embrace 'freedom'. (2004, 67)[28]

By the carefully designed processes of ruralization and abstraction Shakespeare's experiment with "civilitie" and individual freedom in *Romeo and Juliet* points forward to his treatment of ideology and the polis in his great Roman tragedies. Like *Coriolanus* later, *Romeo and Juliet* emerges as a historically precocious text that anticipates humanist republicanism before the advent of a civic humanist polity in England (Pocock 1975, 349). At the same time he brings to the fore contemporary Elizabethan thinking on how to govern the commonwealth and fulfill the obligations of monarch and citizens, creating the ground-plot and backdrop for the gripping drama of young love made impossible by the interests of family and State.

NOTES

1. Gibbons cites Painter (1567, 94). The play is quoted from the Gibbons edition (Shakespeare 2002), were the sources discussed at pp. 32–7. The sources are reprinted in Bullough 1957, vol. 1.
2. Brooke 1562, l. 1975 (Shakespeare 2002, 266).
3. The French "ville" (both town and villa), therefore does not denote quite the same as the Italian "villa" (villa or fortified estate in the countryside). Boaistuau refers to the Capulets' magnificent estate "la magnificence & grandeur de leur maison, Villefranche, duquel nous auons faict mention, estoit vn lieu de plaisence ou le seigneur … qui estoit a vn mille ou deux de Veronne" (1567, 34).
4. A famous Italian "free town" or "free port" (It. *porto franco*) was the city of Livorno, established in the late 1580s, but opened up for multicultural and multi-national commerce between Europeans, Turks, and Jews already in the 1570s. Cf. d'Angelo 2004, 13.
5. He focuses on broad schemes of balance and contrast (parallelism and antithesis), repetition in a different key (mirroring scenes and diptychs), and balance elements around a centre-point (triptychs), but does not pursue the patternings down to the verbal texture (Rose 1972, 148).
6. In *De re poetica* Wills uses Alberti's term for design, *lineamentum*: "This was the first power of language, and soon its use was enlarged by the additions of certain dimensions and lineaments (as it were) to its unformed and shapeless body" (Fowler 1958, 51).
7. In *Certain notes concerning the making of uerse in English* (Gascoigne 1904, 1.46–57) Gascoigne connects the placing of ornaments, in his case rhymes, with the work's inner design, or "platforme of inuention" (469) in keeping with Alberti's coupling of architectural ornaments and the underlying design (Alberti 1966, 1.6.5).
8. In *An Apology for Poetry*, Sidney uses the image of "the house well in model" when discussing how poets "figured forth" "infallible grounds of wisom" "by the speaking picture of poesy" (1973, 107).
9. He uses e.g. the English term "plot" – corresponding to "site", which is to receive the "ground-work" of a building (Eriksen 2001, 1–10)
10. In *The Tempest* (4.1.148–54) he appears to disclose a critical attitude to ideal cities like La Sforzinda (Pavia 1994, 25–8).
11. See e.g. how Valentine describes the importance of his love in his life with architectural terms:
    O thou that does inhabit in my breast,
    Leave not the mansion so long tenantless
    Lest, growing ruinous, the building fall. (*The Two Gentlemen of Verona*, 5.4.7–9)
12. For a different view, see Höttemann 2011, 373.

13. The ideological clash in *Julius Caesar* is between the republican elite and the idea of kingship or dictatorship, whereas in *Coriolanus* Shakespeare challenges "the idea of innate nobility" (Dollimore 1984, 220).
14. Whether the plots are set in Venice, Rome or Verona the settings and dialogue show few traces of the achievements of early modern civic society in reference to the buildings or urban designs of Italian ideal cities, whether painted by Piero della Francesca and Francesco Laurana, or realized in the urban designs of Pienza and Sabbioneta.
15. Rose points out how in addition to the three "pillars", that structure the plot, the play's comic and tragic movements texutally balance, in terms of text mass, around the central scene (3.1.1–195): 1346 lines / 195 lines / 1423 lines. Besides, he notes how "the two lovers' scenes" form "a large, pathetic diptych" (147) that frame the central scene (Rose 1972, 144–7; 145–50).
16. The lack of order in Verona possibly contrasts with the clock-work socio-economic mechanics of Venice, made known to the Elizabethans due to the translation of Lewknor (London, 1599) of Contarini (Venice, 1551).
17. Park Honan observes that the contemporary views of London differed greatly, being either gloatingly positive or glaringly negative: "Perhaps both views are true – by the end of the sixteenth century London was one of the largest, liveliest and most sophisticated cities in Europe, but it was also overcrowded, squalid, corrupt, crime-ridden and plague-infested" (2007, 36).
18. In contrast, in *2 Henry IV* Falstaff is evicted from the *polis*, being a representative of the predatory forces that threaten the order of the State from within.
19. In *Titus Andronicus* (5.3.121) Aaron, who works from a hidden design on his opponents' lives, is by his victims dubbed the "architect and plotter of these woes" (Shakespeare 2006).
20. He subordinates in all eleven scenes a symmetrical design on the pattern of abcde/a/edcba, where 3.1 is the pivot. The scenes forming this architectonic or structural grid are: 1.1, 1.3, 2.3, 2.4, 2.5, 3.1, 3.2, 3.3, 3.5, 4.2, and 5.3.
21. Good examples are 2.2 and 4.1 where the Nurse is the messenger of love and death, respectively, providing good examples of a pattern that is repeated in a different key.
22. Against the discourse on nobility Shakespeare pits the radical equality of Juliet and Romeo as lovers and human beings.
23. Höttemann assumes that both families are "aristocratic" (2011, 101).
24. On Venice as an economic template for Elizabethan England see Hutson 1989, *passim*.
25. Benedikt Höttemann wrongly claims: "the Prince sends Capulet and Montague to old Freetown, our common judgement-place" (2011, 226).
26. Michael Baxandall underlines that "the periodic sentence is the basic art form of the early humanists", and that its inherent principle of a "necessary balance of opposites" "ranges from antithesis within a single line of poetry to the alignment of phrases and clauses in a Ciceronian period and from the employment of contrastive plots and ideas in individual plays and poems to the pairing of separate works espousing different concepts" (1971, 21). Aristotle reminds us in *The Art of Rhetoric* that repetitions are not merely formal manipulations and that "style expresses emotion" (3.7.3), singling out three types of rhetorical repetitions that perform this role: *antitheton* [antithesis], *parisosis* [equality of clauses], and *paromoisis* [similarity of final syllables … at the

beginning and end of the clauses] (3.3.9). Francesco Robortello commented on Aristotle's definition of plot unity in drama with reference to the similarly structured period in which the beginning, the middle, and the end are linked (1548, 72).
27. We notice *epanalepsis* with *epanados* ("you *men*", l. 81; "*on pain of* torture", l. 84) *versus* ("*on pain of* death, all *men*", l. 101) and the use of large-scale *antimetabole* in arrangement of repetitions on either side of the speech's centrally placed "peripety" in line 91P, which is marked by a verb expressing change ("cast by"). The balance is furter underscored by the following repetitions around the central line: "old Capulet and Montague (l. 88) and "disturbed ... our streets" (l. 89) versus "disturb our streets" (l. 94) and Capulet (l. 97) and Montague (l. 98). The references to age at the centre of the speech ("ancient", l. 90; "old ... old" l. 92) are picked of in the penultimate line (l. 100), being yet another example of linkage between the middle and end of the speech so typical of the periodos. As a result the speech displays a variant of what Alastair Fowler terms "recessed symmetry" (1970, 95).
28. See also Philip Withington on the topic of the commonwealth and civic freedom (2005).

WORKS CITED

Alberti, Leon Battista. 1966a. *L'Architettura (De re aedificatoria)*, 2 vols. Edited by Giovanni Orlandi and Paolo Portoghesi. Milano: Edizioni il Polifilo.
Alberti, Leon Battista. 1966b. *Opere Volgari. Rime e trattati morali*, 3 vols. Edited by Cecil Grayson. Bari: Laterza.
Aristotle. 1926. *The Art of Rhetoric.* Translated by John Henry Freese. Cambridge, MA: Harvard University Press / London: Heinemann.
Averlino, Antonio (Il Filarete). (1462–66) 1972. *Trattato di architettura*, 2 vols. Edited by Anna Maria Finoli and Liliana Grassi. Milano: Il Polifilo.
Barston, John. 1576. *The Safeguard of Societie.* London: John Bynneman.
Baxandall, Michael. 1971. *Giotto and the Orators: Humanist Observer of Painting in Italy and the Discovery of Pictorial Composition, 1350–1450.* Oxford: Clarendon Press.
Boaistuau, Pierre. 1567. *Histoires tragiques, extraicté del Bandel, & mises en langue Francoise*, Tome Premier. Anvers: Chez Iean Waesberghe.
Botero, Giovanni. 1589. *Della ragion di stato. Libri dieci.* Venezia: Gioliti.
Brooke, Arthur. 1562. *The Tragicall Historye of Romeus and Juliet.* London: Richard Tottell.
Bullough, Geoffrey. 1957. *Shakespeare's Dramatic and Narrative Sources*, vol. 1. London: Routledge and Kegan Paul / New York: Columbia University Press.
Callaghan, Dympna C. 1994. "The Ideology of Romantic Love: The Case of *Romeo and Juliet*". In *The Weyward Sisters: Shakespeare and Feminist Politics*, edited by Dympna C. Callaghan, Lorraine Helms, and Jyotsna Singh, 59–101. Oxford and Cambridge, MA: Wiley-Blackwell.
Contarini, Gasparo. 1551. *De Magistratibus et Republica Venetorum.* Venezia: Sabinus.
Cunin, Muriel. 2008. *Shakespeare e l'architecture. Nouvelle inventions pour bien bâtir e bien jouer.* Paris: Honoré Champion.

D'Angelo, Michela. 2004. *Mercanti inglesi a Livorno 1573–1737. Alle origini di una 'British Factory'*. Messina: Istituto di Studi Storici Gaetano Salvemini.
Dollimore, Jonathan. 1984. *Radical Tragedy. Religion Ideology and Power in the Drama of Shakespeare and his Contemporaries*. Brighton: Harvester.
Eriksen, Roy. 1985. "What Place Is This: Time and Place in *Dr. Faustus (B)*". *Renaissance Drama* XVI: 49–74.
Eriksen, Roy. 2001. *The Building in the Text: Alberti to Shakespeare and Milton*. University Park, PA: Pennsylvania State Press.
Fowler, Alastair. 1970. *Triumphal Forms: Structural Patterns in Elizabethan Poetry*. Cambridge: Cambridge University Press.
Gascoigne, George. 1904. *Certain notes concerning the making of uerse in English*. In *Elizabethan critical essays*, edited by G. Gregory Smith, 46–57. Oxford: Clarendon Press.
Hieatt, Kent A. 1960. *Short Time's Endless Monument: The Symbolism of the Numbers in Edmund Spenser's "Epithalamion"*. New York: Columbia University Press.
Honan, Park. 2007. *The Lodger: Shakespeare on Silver Street*. London: Allen Lane.
Höttemann, Benedikt. 2011. *Shakespeare and Italy*. Berlin-Münster-Wien: LIT Verlag.
Hutson, Lorna.1989. *Thomas Nashe in Context*. Oxford: Clarendon Press.
Jonson, Ben. 1976. *Ben Jonson's Timber: or, Discoveries*. Edited by Ralph S. Walker. Westport, CT: Greenwood Press.
Lewknor, Lewes. 1599. *The Commonwealth and Government of Venice*. Edmund Mattes: London.
Maquerlot, Jean-Pierre. 1995. *Shakespeare and the Mannerist Tradition: A Reading of Five Problem Plays*. Cambridge: Cambridge University Press.
Painter, William. 1567. *The Palace of Pleasure*. London: Henry Bynnemann.
Paster, Gail. 1985. *The Idea of the City in the Age of Shakespeare*. Athens: The University of Georgia Press.
Pavia, Rosario. 1994. *L'Idea di città. Teorie urbanistiche della città tradizionale*. Milano: Franco Angeli.
Peltonen, Markku. 1995. *Classical Humanism and Republicanism in English Political Thought, 1570–1640*. Cambridge: Cambridge University Press.
Pocock, J.G.A. 1975. *The Machiavellian Moment: Florentine Political Thought and the Atlantic Republican Tradition*. Princeton: Princeton University Press.
Puttenham, George. (1589) 1936. *The Arte of English Poesie*. Edited by Gladys Doidge Willcock and Alice Walker. Cambridge: Cambridge University Press.
Robortello, Francesco. 1548. *In librum Aristotelis De arte poetica explicationes*. Firenze: Laurentii Torrentini.
Rose, Mark. 1972. *Shakespearean Design*. Cambridge, MA: The Belknap Press.
Røstvig, Maren-Sofie. 1979. "A Frame of Words. On the Craftsmanship of Samuel Daniel". *English Studies* 60: 122–37.
Scott, William. 2013. *The Model of Poesy*. Edited by Gavin Alexander. Cambridge: Cambridge University Press.
Smith, Logan Pearsall. 1907. *The Life and Letters of Sir Henry Wotton*. 2 vols. Oxford: Clarendon Press.
Shakespeare, William. 1999. *The Tempest*. Edited by Virginia Mason, Alden T. Vaughan. London: Cengage Learning (The Arden Shakespeare).

Shakespeare, William. 2000. *Romeo and Juliet*. Edited by Jill L. Levenson. Oxford and New York: Oxford University Press.

Shakespeare, William. 2002. *Romeo and Juliet*. Edited by Brian Gibbons. London: Methuen (The Arden Shakespeare).

Shakespeare, William. 2006. *Titus Andronicus*. Edited by Jonathan Bate. London: Thomson Learning (The Arden Shakespeare).

Shakespeare, William 2008. *Two Gentlemen of Verona*. Edited by Roger Warren. Oxford: Clarendon Press.

Sidney, Sir Philip. 1973. *An Apology for Poetry*. Edited by Geoffrey Shepherd. Manchester: Manchester University Press.

Smith, Gregory R., ed. 1904. *Elizabethan Critical Essays*, 2 vols. Oxford: Clarendon Press.

Snyder, Jon R. 1989. *Writing the Scene of Speaking: Theories of Dialogue in the Late Italian Renaissance*. Stanford: Stanford University Press.

Snyder, Susan. 1979. *The Comic Matrix of Shakespeare's Tragedies*. Princeton: Princeton University Press.

Van Caenegem, Raoul Charles. 1988. *The Birth of the English Common Law*. Cambridge: Cambridge University Press.

Wells, Stanley. 1994. *Shakespeare: A Dramatic Life*. London: Methuen.

Withington, Philip. 2005. *The Politics of Commonwealth; Citizens and Freemen in Early Modern England*. Cambridge: Cambridge University Press.

4 Inside-Outside
Love, Household, and City in *Romeo and Juliet*

Mera J. Flaumenhaft

Romeo and Juliet, known to most readers as a 'tragic' love story, suggests that the romantic love of individual human beings is viable only in the context of the families and cities that surround them. The play is not 'tragic' in the vulgar sense of 'extremely sad'. Nor is it a tale of bad luck. The true causes of the deaths of the "star-crossed lovers" (Prologue 6) lie in human nature itself, in hatred and in love, and in the distorted versions of human communities these passions produce. The long-lasting feud and the short-lived love affair frame the story and characterize Verona. The city itself, and the households and young lovers within it, are incomplete in their development; they do not mature to the full human forms of such associations. Both hatred and love distort the meanings of 'inside' and 'outside', in time and place. We can learn much about the play itself by reading from the 'inside out', by considering what is present in Verona, and what is absent from it.

Romeo and Juliet are often taken as paradigm human lovers by the millions of people, especially the young, who watch them fall in love and who, themselves, fall in love with them, and with love itself. In one way, Romeo and Juliet are paradigms; they exhibit some of the highest desires that define us as human beings: our freedom to attach ourselves to one other person by choice rather than by nature, to pursue lives of beauty and nobility, as well as mere life, and to make a 'world', a time and place, for ourselves, rather than accommodating the authority and needs of others. At the same time, they reveal the consequences of such freedom. Their love is 'tragic' in the deepest sense: the very thing that makes them beautiful young human lovers precludes other features of their humanity, and prevents them from maturing into full adult love. The feud and their young passion combine to make death, not life, the end of their love.

CITY

Inside Verona

We might expect a small and ancient city like Verona to consist of numerous households integrated in their political, economic, and social relations. Each would consist of a house – its family, servants, material 'holdings' – and a father who holds it together, ruling his own household by himself, and the city in association with the heads of other households. The patriarchs of such independent households also hold them together as parts of a whole of shared activities, places, times, and memories.

In Verona, however, "two households" have from time immemorial regarded the city as a public stage on which to enact their private feud, which regularly erupts when "civil blood" makes "civil hands unclean" (Prologue 4).[1] There is no history of the "ancient grudge", and, therefore, no account of its origins. If there were, there could be rational conclusion.

Verona's gates, closed at night, provide protection from outside dangers; sickness is the only once mentioned. Although there are watchmen, there is no mention of civic officials with specific responsibilities. The city is nominally governed by an ineffectual Prince who appears only when there is trouble among his "rebellious subjects" (1.2.79). Aside from his unplanned appearances, he is not seen. He has kin in Verona, but we hear of no wife or plan for succession. Two stage directions call him "Escalus", but the Veronese do not use his name. Rulers who wish to govern effectively must be visible and talked about. Although the Prologue does not name the "two households", the first scene makes clear which names matter in Verona. "Escalus" is not among them.

Young men from both clans prowl the streets seeking their counterparts in the other household and provoking street fights. They travel in packs; one is referred to as "the Capels" (3.1.2). The unindividuated enemy is even given a singular verb: "here comes the Capulets" (3.1.34). Retainers have only first names; they too are considered Montagues and Capulets.

These young men have no more interest in the future than in the past. Their masters also lack the signs of approaching maturity. Their masculine spiritedness expresses itself in insults and dirty jokes. They do not anticipate deliberating or fighting on behalf of their city. Nor do they expect to protect women (and children) rather than use them. Romeo has heard a lot of their talk. He leaves their world behind, but, for different reasons, his pure new life will not mature much further than the dirty adolescent life of his friends.

Mercutio, mostly Shakespeare's invention, is the most interesting of Romeo's companions. The summer heat intensifies his hot temper. He and his friends focus on sex, but Mercutio is more interested in words than in women. Before his fatal wounding, he expresses no interest in the feud. He does not mention his own family, although he is kin to the Prince and to Paris, and has a brother, Valentine, who is invited to Capulet's ball. Mercutio's 'freedom' is negative; there is nothing for which he wants it. His most remarkable trait is the quick imagination exhibited in his Queen Mab speech; it reveals how unbounded and ungrounded he is. Even his folklore comes from 'outside', not from his native Verona or Italy. Mercutio leaps and turns, but does not go anywhere. He runs through the dreams of lovers, courtiers, lawyers, ladies, parson, and soldiers, responsible insiders in functioning cities, mocking them all. When Romeo interrupts him,

Mercutio admits that his dreams are "the children of an idle brain, / Begot of nothing but vain fantasy" (1.4.98–9). This is the only time he refers to children. Still spouting doubletalk, Mercutio dies on a pun, a "grave" (3.1.100) one. His last word is "houses" (3.1.110). Four times, he curses "both" the "houses" whose feud has caused his death, and asks only to be carried into "some" house (3.1.107). In death, as in life, he will not be grounded; unlike Tybalt, he is not bound for a family grave. His vigor and intellect never mature to take part in household or city life. After Act 3 Mercutio is never mentioned. His death removes him from Verona, but he has never lived in real time and place.

The rest of the population steers clear of the ancient enemies, gathering in public places when they get caught in the frequent street fights, or come to watch them. In the BBC film (1978), a glimpse of a stabbed, bleeding baby emphasizes that these "civil brawls" are matters of life and death for all of Verona's families. Neither clan is of noble lineage; their prominence is economic: "My master is the great rich Capulet" (1.2.80). He lives in a palazzo inside the city, not far from the Montagues.

After the first brawl, the Prince commands Montague and Capulet to come, separately, and at different times, to "old Freetown, our common judgment-place" (1.1.100). No witnesses are mentioned, and his judgments are spread by hearsay, not by official 'decree'. Verona has no public place or council where citizens participate in judicial or other 'common' deliberations. Shakespeare has eliminated Brooke's allusions, in the source story, to a council and decrees (ll. 2985–6).[2] After Romeo kills Tybalt, Lady Capulet cries out to the Prince alone for "justice" (3.1.182). This is the only time this word is used.

Inside and Outside the City: Friar

One person in the play has a life that is intended to transcend the city. Friar Laurence is attached to Verona in something like a local, even 'civic', position. Unlike wandering Franciscan friars, he seems to be stationed here, familiar to other inhabitants, and he presides at church weddings and, probably, other events.

Although Capulet says, "All our whole city is much bound to him" (4.2.32), Shakespeare, unlike Brooke, does not say he counsels the Prince (l. 580). But the Christian Friar is not merely an insider serving the city, for his primary community is the universal Catholic Church, extending far outside it. Since Church teachings are in tension with the ordinary lives of human beings and their cities, its representatives may be disinclined or inadequate to participate in civic and family affairs. Shakespeare suggests some of the difficulties whenever the Friar appears.

Our first view of him reveals his thinking. He says that all plants are good by nature, but can be turned to evil ends. This suggests that, in the beginning – in the harmonious garden of Eden – no plant was poisonous. Presumably, human and vegetable incompatibility came with the Fall, and the Friar's mission is to prevent sinners from misusing wholesome herbs. But he does not make a theological argument. Shakespeare indicates the inadequacy of his opinions by putting them in the rhyming couplets he often uses to undercut such simplicity.

There is no indication that the resident friars previously have made any effort to end the Montague-Capulet feud. The Church has been as negligent or impotent as the secular Prince, but, here, perhaps, there is a political-theological explanation. Christianity may tend to weaken the authority of the worldly city and attachment to it. It deals with the salvation of individual souls and their final destination in another 'time' and 'place'. After Juliet's fake death, the Friar consoles her parents: they should rejoice that she has died young and been elevated from this inferior world to heaven. Presumably, he would also champion "reason" over "nature's tears" (4.5.83) were she happily married to Romeo and had died early.

When the Friar ventures into politics, he substitutes himself for the secular ruler, and, perhaps, risks playing God as well. He hopes that love and the virtuous use of herbal power will overcome hate without resort to violent power. This Christian hope is not fulfilled.

Outside: Mantua

There is no mention of previous or present relations with other cities. Verona needs somewhere to banish those not punished at home, but we hear nothing of external politics or commerce. Shakespeare's city lacks neighbours. Three brief remarks suggest some private outside contact. Juliet's parents (1.3.29), Lady Capulet (3.5.88), and, perhaps, Romeo (5.1.37–8) seem to have visited Mantua, but how much time they have spent there is unclear. Shakespeare mentions no other city. Mercutio refers once to Italy (3.1.12), a geographical, not political, place. Romeo hires post-horses to return from Mantua (5.1.26), but, for most of the play, Verona seems to be a place unto itself.

HOUSEHOLDS

Verona's two leading families live near each other in town, but like the city, they do not participate in outside relations; they are 'neighbours' only spatially. The Prince uses the word after the first brawl ("neighbour-stained steel", 1.1.80), as does Romeo, to signify location ("neighbour air", 2.6.27). It does not refer to social interaction among the adults of these households. Their older offspring 'socialize' in the streets, but their game is murder.

Despite their insistence on their difference, Verona's enemies are very much alike. Of common ethnic stock and religion, they speak the same language. The feud that divides them has made them even more alike: they withdraw from city affairs. Viable cities are strengthened by insiders with differing pasts, and even by outsiders, resident aliens. A multiplicity of others makes possible shifting alliances on different issues. Here, however, two foes have only one interest, and two is too few. Shakespeare depicts the two families in different ways, but shows that the ruling principle in both is the inside life – the household – rather than the outside life – the city.

Montagues

The Montagues remain indoors for most of the play; we see little of their private life. They emerge from their house into the 'public place' only after the street brawls. Lady Montague speaks only three times; her husband, eight. She and Lady Capulet suggest the limited development of women in clan societies. They seem less like mature individuals than means to increase the families into which they marry when they themselves are young and immature. After the first fracas, Romeo's parents withdraw into their house, leaving others to investigate what his father "and many other friends" (1.1.144) have failed to discover. We never see these other friends. The Montagues are tighter, less extended, than the sociable Capulets. Romeo is their only child, but they say nothing about his marriage or a Montague heir.

The Romeo we meet at the beginning of the play is a peculiar member of the Montague household. We never see him with his parents, and he spends much of his time roaming away from home. Benvolio says he saw him "abroad" (1.1.118) near a grove of sycamore trees that "rooteth" (1.1.120) on the west side of the city. Sprouted on its own, it suggests independence from its origins and cultivation. Romeo's tears and sighs are drawn to nature's distant dew and clouds. He seems to be freeing himself from city, family, and feud, and only distractedly asks about his father. When he is "private in his chamber" (1.1.136), he locks out the daylight, preferring "artificial night" (1.1.138). Later, he cries out, "I am not here. / This is not Romeo, he's some otherwhere" (1.1.95–6). Always on the move, he seems always out of place, out of time.

His first love might be an attempt to escape oppressive family bonds. Perhaps he pursues Rosaline instead of Capulets. But, although he flees the feud, he is not enjoying romance. Rosaline dwells in his imagination. Thinking he wants her, his attention is on himself, and on love, about which he speaks at length. But unlike many lovers, he does not speak Rosaline's name. Even when he reads it in Capulet's invitation, he does not react. He laments her chastity, which precludes 'posterity', but he does not speak of extending his own family. Shakespeare's decision not to show Romeo's first 'love' prepares us for what happens when he meets the embodied, responsive Juliet. Rosaline temporarily distracts him from family and feud. It is Juliet who will radically detach him from household and city.

Capulets

Like Old Montague, Old Capulet emerges from his house at the first street fight. A stage direction says he is in his "*gown*". It is morning, and he is in no hurry to leave his house. The Montagues withdraw into their home for most of the play. But we see the Capulets' hall, orchard, kitchen, bedroom, and, finally, family tomb. The feud has turned both families inward. Montague and Capulet are not city fathers, but only household patriarchs. We see this clearly in the more fully depicted Capulet.

In his first appearance, he calls for a sword that he is too feeble to use. His wife suggests that a "crutch" would be more appropriate (1.1.73–6). Montague's wife also tries to discourage her husband. The patriarchs instinctively assume their fighting posture. But the very feud that has made them enemies has attenuated their fighting spirit and they withdraw. It is not the feeble, idle old, but the vigorous, idle young, who fuel the feud.

In his next appearances, Capulet is absorbed in family matters. The first is his conversation with the County Paris about Juliet, his only child. His authority in his mostly female household seems gentle at first. He is a loving father, and will not force his daughter to marry against her will. Capulet is cordial to his outside visitor, and invites him to the ball "At my poor house" (1.2.23). The comic routine of the invitation list reveals the serious fact that the invited are mostly Capulet kin. Soon he will welcome into his home a mix of inside-outside guests.

We next enter female quarters deep inside the Capulet house. Lady Capulet, rather cold and hard, is much younger than her husband; she probably married him, not for love, but to produce an heir. Nothing is said about children other than Juliet, who calls her "Madam" (1.3.7), not 'Mother'. We hear of no social contact with other women in the city. The house holds her, providing safety and bodily needs, at the cost of isolation and limited freedom. Restricted in time and place, she does not initiate and is not consulted. She seems stunted.

The second adult woman, Juliet's Nurse, is the embodiment of body, the birth and nurture of which are the special responsibilities of the household. Affectionate and motherly, she is, perhaps, responsible for the capacity for love that Juliet could not have learned from her cold mother. It is the Nurse who has touched and held, dressed, and tucked in the Capulet child.

Such servants are typically absorbed, as permanent sub-units, into the main families and their activities. The Nurse's own child made her mother's milk flow for Juliet. When that child died, Juliet soon replaced her in her parents' affections. Nurse has only this name, although her master once calls her by her incongruous given name, Angelica (4.4.5). Like all servants, she has no family name of her own. She married a man whose name is not mentioned, into whose household she never moved. But the Nurse repeats his conversations and jokes with such gusto that we almost remember him as a real character. They seem to have had the only cheerful marriage in the play.

Despite her vulgarity, this homebody's down-to-earth perspective gives her a moral solidity and loyalty that some of her superiors seem to lack. In the midst of the grotesque feud, we are quickly drawn to this funny, affectionate, comfortable person. But it is precisely her taste for comfort that betrays Juliet. The earthbound Nurse is unmoved by principle, law, or spiritual love. Her soft heart does not understand the passion of the child she is so fond of, and why she cannot adjust to necessity and marry Paris. We, like Juliet, are shocked, especially when we understand that our appreciation and our anger are reactions to the same thing.

The Nurse's prominence sets the domestic tone of the Capulet household. The patriarch who called for his sword soon metamorphoses into a genial host, concerned with the bodily pleasures of his guests. Welcoming his relatives, Capulet speaks of his lost youth. Perhaps this sense of encroaching age has moved him to entertain Paris's proposal; for one not engaged in the affairs of an enduring city, marriage and family are a way to counter mortality. Capulet reminisces with an elderly cousin, also named Capulet, about a family wedding in the distant past; a clan coheres by remembering shared times, places, people, and events. The Nurse's many memories are understandably confined to the events of the household. From babies to earthquake, her time and place are given by the natural world. But it is unusual for a "great rich" man never to refer to political and military events, foreign affairs, leaders, public places, and other features of ordinary city life.

At Capulet's ball, Tybalt recognizes Romeo, and reaches for his rapier. Old Capulet will not mar the "feast" (1.5.73) "in my house" (1.5.69) by insulting Romeo. But he worries about a "mutiny among my guests" (1.5.79). This word appears elsewhere only in the Prologue, when the Chorus says the "ancient grudge" gives rise to "new mutiny". 'Mutiny' usually refers to an upheaval against a legal authority. Capulet's authority derives from nature, from age and sex, not from law. He asserts it entirely at home. When his will is thwarted, he becomes an irascible indoors tyrant. After Romeo meets Juliet, he and his friends prepare to depart, disappointing their host, who has prepared yet another "banquet" for his guests. While the feud has focused spirited young men on outdoors street fights, it has turned the attention of older men from typically masculine, often antagonistic, outdoors civic activity to typically female, cooperative indoors, domestic activity. The latter is preferable to deadly fighting. But the withdrawal from public to domestic life is a regression from the full life of a mature man. Later, when Capulet is fussing in the kitchen, applying all the managerial skill he has never exercised in the city to the preparation of the wedding feast, he recognizes that he is playing "the housewife" (4.2.43). The Nurse calls him a "cotquean" (4.4.7), a man who does a woman's work. Whatever kind of 'robe' he wears when he first appears in public, here he should wear an apron.

After the deaths of Tybalt and Mercutio, Juliet's formerly considerate father decides to marry her to Paris. He now treats her as an instrument for household ends. His repeated changing of the wedding day feels like a tyrannical attempt to control even time. He asks if his wife has delivered "our decree" (3.5.138), as if he were a public magistrate. Old Capulet, previously unable to lift his sword against his male foe, is now ready to attack a girl. He will banish her from his household: "Graze where you will, you shall not house with me" (3.5.189), but "hang, beg, starve, die in the streets ..." (3.5.193). Given his previous solicitude, and that the household is what defines them, the threat of unnatural eviction is shocking.

The Nurse articulates a more natural distancing of a human being from the household of birth. One would expect a talkative nurse to refer to her main qualification for her occupation. But in this Nurse's chatter about her breasts – she has a large vocabulary of synonyms for them – we also discern the meaning of nursing and weaning in a human life. In the beginning, one is literally attached, through one's mother (or her surrogate), to the family; our first 'household' is the womb. The nursing infant, held and nourished, has little desire for independence. It must be forced to give up safe attachment for risky freedom; the child is weaned by making the breast bitter. In this second 'birth', the child is further uncoupled, and begins to live in its own place and time, although still within those of the family household. The Nurse recalls an odd detail about Juliet's weaning. On that day, "My lord and you [Lady Capulet] were then at Mantua" (1.3.29). Juliet's distant mother was doubly distant almost from the beginning.

A third birth occurs for most young adults when they fall in love. It too is like entering a new time and place. The new tie can be strengthened by the intense temporary focus on an unrelated person, and the desire for freedom from previous, even all other, bonds. But in healthy communities, the natural self-isolation, in place and time, of passionate new lovers is restricted and shaped by the participation of families and city in their marriages.

Our first views of Juliet emphasize her extreme youth. The Nurse vividly describes her as a lively toddler. As an adolescent, she seems more passive. Like Romeo, she is an only child; but she is an indoors – household – child who has never roamed "abroad" from her parents, and has no friends. Lady Capulet's arguments for the marriage to Paris emphasize family obligation: He is handsome and of good birth, and Juliet is old enough to bear his child. Innocent and obedient, the fourteen-year-old girl respectfully replies that marriage is "an honour that I dream not of" (1.3.67). But perhaps her response is merely careful, and she does have a mind of her own, a desire for independence, and the will to defy, even deceive, her dominating parents.

Inside and Outside the Household: Friar

Romeo calls the Friar "father", and he calls Romeo "son" (2.3.27–30). Romeo is a sort of orphan in his biological family, and the Friar is almost a substitute father, as well as a "ghostly [spiritual] sire" (2.2.192), but he will never generate his own children. He loves Romeo, but has no experience of the passionate attachment families have to their own flesh-and-blood.

Hope, not prudence, propels the Friar's plan to end the feud by marrying the young lovers. He does not consider that generations of hatred might lead to the violent disowning of children who refuse to marry according to their parents' choice. That is exactly what Capulet threatens to do. The Friar's plan to reunite the lovers after Juliet's false death also fails because of his limited personal experience. As Romeo tells him, "Thou canst not speak of that thou dost not feel" (3.3.64). He does not anticipate that the beautiful boy will die for love as soon as he thinks Juliet is dead. It seems that years of hearing the confessions of haters and lovers have failed to deepen his understanding of the human heart.

Christian teachings, as well as his personal inexperience, may also limit his appreciation of the passionate attachment of blood relatives. Biological ties may be in tension with Christianity's claims that all human beings are children of God and 'brothers' in Christ: "Whoever does the will of my Father is brother, sister, and mother to me" (Matthew 2:50). Friar Laurence and Friar John come from different families, but their last names are never mentioned. The friars live in an incomplete community where they have not been generated; nor do they themselves generate future members. The universal brotherhood of the Christian 'family' teaches that attachment and hostility based on natural origins be eliminated or, at least, moderated. In his tidy 'household' of one, in the quiet Franciscan abbey, the Friar may underestimate human resistance to attempts to weaken biological and erotic ties.

LOVERS

Capulet Ball

Romeo's arrival at the Capulet house is surely the first time a Montague has crossed the threshold of the ancestral foe. Tybalt calls it an "intrusion" (1.5.90). Uninvited, the guest comes nameless; his mask obscures his own face and any family features it might reveal. This is the first of four times in the play – ball, balcony, bedroom, and tomb – that Romeo penetrates the Capulet household and violates the fundamental human custom that outsiders must be invited to enter the homes of insiders.

Romeo's friends persuade him to compare Rosaline with other women at the ball. His first glimpse of an unnamed dancer convinces him that this new "lady" (1.5.41) is "beyond" comparison. She is a "saint", her hand a "holy shrine"(1.5.93). Exceeding both the dull earth and anything accessible to him, she is celestial, out of his world. His frequent use of the word "yonder" indicates how far above him she seems. She, too, picks up this word (Shakespeare 2012, 169, n. 42). But, unlike Rosaline, Juliet is a touchable angel. Romeo's first speech, in closed couplets, is his alone. Their interwoven words then couple them, as their dance does, in a world that excludes all others. When they speak to each other, they generate a sonnet, first exchanging separate quatrains both ending with "kiss", then a quatrain of intertwining lines closed by a shared couplet and a real kiss (1.5.92–105).

Their love is spontaneous and, thus, can have no history. To say they love at first 'sight' is strange because Romeo's face is masked. The torches burn bright, but his face is in the dark. Neither lover has a name, the undeniable evidence that we come with strings attached. They offer themselves, alone.

Reasons for this original attraction are no more available than for the origins of the feud. People often remark on how undeveloped and unindividualized these young people are. They have not had time and experience to become people about whom one can articulate reasons for loving. Just as Verona does not complete the activities of the households within the city, and just as the Capulets are incomplete because they do not participate in civic activities beyond the household, the lovers are incomplete. Turning inward, they exclude family, household, and city from their newfound world. Since they have eyes only for each other, and must be seen by no one else, immediate vicinity is their world. Time too, is restricted to the present. Oddly, they are, like Mercutio, in no place ('utopia') and in no extended period of time.

Romeo's unusual courtship and marriage are depicted against the background of conventional customs. Paris displays all the elements of ordinary courtship. He is not 'blinded' by love; and does not 'fall' in love 'at first sight', thinking only of the present. With eyes open to the community around him, he is attentive to time and place. He visits and negotiates with Juliet's father, who recognizes his offer of an aristocratic connection and the possibility of grandchildren and a future for his family. Paris sets a date, and arranges the customary church wedding, procession, and music. His future in-laws look forward to a place of honour when they give their daughter to her husband.

Capulet Balcony

The erotic explosion that undermines Paris's conventional courtship simply rejects both household and civic life. It is unanticipated and unplanned. Except for his desperate wedding night, Romeo makes no 'dates'. After the ball, he finds his way to the orchard, another private Capulet place that separates the household from the town. Its walls are guarded by Capulet kinsmen, a family militia protecting one household from another. The young men of other cities might scale enemy walls with fellow citizen-soldiers. But Romeo invades an orchard. "Love" allowed him to "o'erperch these walls" (2.2.66). This leap of love will be repeated several times – Juliet picks up the word (3.2.7) – but without the sanction of city, parents, or other kin. Their 'courtship' moves directly from 'leap' to a marriage that more resembles an 'elopement', a word appropriately derived from that word.

Although the so-called 'balcony scene' is the most famous in the play, there is no actual balcony in *Romeo and Juliet*. Shakespeare probably thought of Juliet leaning out upon a wide windowsill. Nevertheless, nearly every production of the play is done this way, because a balcony is the perfect place for a forbidden courtship. Like porch and parlour, it is a conventional courting location, a place between inside and outside for potential spouses between single life and marriage. It is the threshold to the courted woman's household and family, who must also be courted. Although not physically present, they are acknowledged participants in such visits. But Romeo and Juliet reverse all the conventional customs of balcony courtship.

For the ball, Romeo enters the house through the brightly lit public front door. But, now, invisible in the dark, he ascends to a place never meant to be an outside entry to the house of Capulet. Her family has no idea he is there, but here he will "stay ... / forgetting any other home but this" (2.2.175).

Juliet's famous lines about Romeo's names refer to his enemy origins. But they also express her own rejection of any independent origin. "Deny thy father and refuse thy name ... and I'll no longer be a Capulet" (2.2.34–6). His name, unlike his hand, foot, or leg, is no "part" (2.2.41) of him. In exchange for his name, she says Romeo can "take all myself" (2.2.48). Their love suggests self-generation and self-possession. It feels infinite, as "boundless" and "deep" as the sea (2.2.133–5). He agrees: "Call me but love and I'll be new baptized. / Henceforth I never will be Romeo" (2.2.50). Born again, as if in a new time and place, the lover renames himself "love", and feels liberated from his old identity. Exogamous love ordinarily binds individuals to two families, retaining the first, and adding a second. But the feud and their own early passion have combined to make these lovers belong only to each other, only in their own place and time. As soon as they are married, Juliet says, she will give Romeo all her fortunes, leave Verona, and follow him "throughout the world" (2.2.148). But it does not matter where as long as they are together. They do not relate private present passion to the communal future of households and cities. They have not yet seen that balcony passion does not endure forever, and that marriage means more than making sonnets and making love. They never refer to children. Unlike her Nurse, Juliet does not associate love and sex with hungry babies who must be fed on time.

Friar's Cell: Wedding

In the morning, Juliet joins Romeo in the Friar's cell. He quickly marries them there, not in the church, and speaks more about keeping them apart – sexually – than uniting them. The 'balcony' scene goes on and on; they do not want it to end. But, in this extremely short scene, Shakespeare does not even stage the wedding. There are no wedding clothes, rings, vows, procession, witnesses, or recognition of the union by civil authorities – all are included by Brooke (ll. 767–70). No one knows that Juliet now legally bears the name of Montague. The omissions all point to the absence of the wider community. In ordinary times such omissions are typical of lovers who regard marriage as a private matter.

Juliet's Bedroom: Wedding Night

In Act 1, even before we first see Romeo, we hear how, "private in his chamber" (1.1.136), he avoids daylight and seeks night. Like most of the meetings of Romeo and Juliet, their first time together as a married couple takes place at night. On the balcony, Juliet worries that the "mask of night" (2.2.85) obscures the modest blush on her cheek. But now she yearns to "bring in cloudy night immediately", and speed the coming of "love-performing night" (3.2.4–5). Rapturously, she uses the word 'night' eleven times (Shakespeare 2012, 247, n. 4). Perhaps young love begins by preferring the dark, where it is easier to eliminate distance and merge with a lover. The illuminated faces of more mature lovers reveal the particulars, the experiences, sufferings, joys, that make particular people love particular others. These marks define them as distinct and interesting individuals for whom merging might be a less compelling and immediate end of love. Perhaps Romeo and Juliet, despite their sweet intensity, have not had time to become interesting in this way.

On their wedding night, Romeo again enters Juliet's home without the knowledge of her parents. Again he climbs a twisted ladder through a port not meant for entry, and leaves unseen. Juliet crosses no threshold into adulthood, new identity, and new household. Rather, she and her husband go backward in time to her parents' home and her childhood chamber, still prepared by her childhood nanny. According to custom, the bride and groom are in exactly the wrong place. Echoing the 'balcony' farewell, they pretend to extend dark night, finally acknowledging that, "more light and light it grows. / More light and light, more dark and dark our woes" (3.5.35–6). Her last view of him alive, descending his ladder, reappears in her later vision of him "dead in the bottom of a tomb" (3.5.56).

When Juliet seeks a "remedy" to avoid marrying Paris, Friar Laurence turns with "hope" (4.1.68) to his beneficent herbs, never thinking that plague, an undelivered message, and a lover's suicide might destroy his plan. Before Juliet swallows the potion, she has another vision of the family tomb, imagining herself dashing out her own brains with "some great kinsman's bone" (4.3.53). Not only the Montagues, but the Capulets themselves, have destroyed their Capulet descendants. Juliet knows that she will be their next victim.

CITY

Outside: Mantua

Act 5 is set outside central Verona: in Mantua, at the Friar's cell, and in the Capulet tomb in the churchyard. Romeo and Juliet are about to leave Verona forever. There is no place or time for them in this world, and no suggestion of reunion, redemption, or afterlife (cf. Brooke, ll. 2674 ff.) in another. Their final exodus does, however, initiate the revival of the city and those who remain inside it.

Dazed by the false news of Juliet's death, Romeo wanders through Mantua. Brooke speaks of his acquaintances and lodging there (ll. 1738–42), but, in the play, he is utterly alone. He seeks an Apothecary's shop, which is closed because of a holiday. If the stage street is also empty, the audience will feel beforehand the grim approach of Romeo's separation from the world of the living. The Apothecary, half dead from poverty, sells Romeo poison in order to keep himself alive. Separated from city, household, and the lover

112 Mera J. Flaumenhaft

who displaced them all, Romeo now arranges his transit beyond the time and place of all human beings. On the way, he turns the Apothecary into an agent of death, murders Paris, and is responsible for his own and Juliet's suicides. Whatever Mantua is to Verona, for Romeo, it is on the road to death.

Inside: Capulet Tomb

The city cemetery in the churchyard of St Peter's is a dead microcosm of Verona, with a separate vault or mausoleum for each family. Family 'remains' remain together, apart from others, in a 'household' of the dead. In the living city, the Montagues and Capulets are prematurely dead to each other: they do not interact, and they send each other to the dead world early. Here, too, we see the inside of only the Capulet 'household'. Juliet's two visions (3.5; 4.3) have given us a preview.

The world of the tomb is not horizontal like the living world where only a few generations are alive at the same time. The vault is vertical; successive generations now 'dwell' together out of all time, except for their different times of arrival. Ordinarily, it is a silent, motionless "place of peace" (5.3.143), but now, in the Verona cemetery, the living are still killing each other or themselves.

Paris comes to Juliet's tomb in the crypt of the family that would have been his. Again, the contrast with Romeo is striking. Conventional and decent, Paris brings flowers, speaks in rhymes, and vows to maintain his "nightly ... obsequies" (5.3.20), the proper times for mourning. He is, in his fashion, bereaved, but would probably recover and find another wife among the daughters of Verona.

Romeo's arrival brings the street brawls of the living city into the Capulet monument. As in his previous "intrusion[s]" into Capulet territory, he arrives unrecognized, a "torchbearer" on a dark night. In another irregular entry, instead of ascending, he descends into a tomb "low" (5.1.20) in the ground. Literally breaking in, he is now a burglar. The ring he pretends to recover reminds us of the lack of a wedding ring. Moving into the "maw, thou womb of death" (5.3.45), Romeo leaves behind household and city forever. Juliet imagined him among the eternal stars; he now anticipates eternity on earth, among the worms. His end in the Capulet vault echoes the consummation of his marriage in the Capulet bedroom. Both reverse the custom that a wife moves from her household to that of her husband. From beginning to end, Romeo is still at the wrong time in the wrong place.

The Friar's unfitness for worldly action is painfully underlined as he rushes about the tomb. When he discovers his plan has failed and that both Romeo and Paris are dead, he says he will 'dispose of' Juliet in another incomplete 'household', a "sisterhood of holy nuns" (5.3.157). This would, in effect, kill the loving girl, turning her into a living corpse a second time. All that remains of the Friar is his fear: "I dare no longer stay" (5.3.159), as the braver Juliet refuses to leave her dead husband: "for I will not away" (5.3.160).

Hearing of another eruption of the feud, "the people in the street", crowd into "our monument", as Lady Capulet says (5.3.191–3). Ordinarily, it would always be closed to outsiders (Brooke, ll. 2520). Surely no Montague has ever been there. A Watchman brings back the Friar, caught slinking away from the church with his tools. Many townspeople crowd in, some, perhaps, recognizable from the earlier street scenes. Alarmed and noisy, they cry out what they have heard. The two most interesting characters of the earlier acts, the Nurse and Mercutio, are notably absent, probable obstacles to the reconstitution of the city that is beginning to take place before our eyes.

Most important is the reappearance of the Prince who responds to the early calling of "our person from our morning rest" (5.3.189). Finally impressed by the consequences of his lax leadership, he awakens to the need to use force, even "death" (5.3.220), rather than Christian love, weak reprimands, and banishment, to impose order in the earthly city. "Fair Verona" will henceforth be 'fair' in another way: it will be 'just' and will make justice vigorous and visible.

The Friar confesses his responsibility for the deaths, although he says nothing about his plan to use the marriage to end the feud, and the Prince pardons him. He offers himself as a "sacrifice ... / Unto the rigour of severest law" (5.3.268–9), continuing to think in Christian terms – confession, pardon, sacrifice – as he tries to support the Prince – and save his own skin. But Friar Laurence has nothing to offer the city, households, and young people of Verona. He no longer merits even partial 'insider' status. Brooke reports that he went to a "Hermitage" (ll. 3001), a last 'household' two miles outside Verona, from which, we can assume, he will not return again. Shakespeare apparently regards him as irrelevant and does not even report his last move.

The Prince's justice is not enough to heal the fractured city. Old Montague informs those gathered in the Capulet tomb that his wife is dead. Patriarch of a clan with no future, he himself now heads a household of one. At this point, Capulet addresses him as "brother" (5.3.296), and offers him his hand; the last time they met, their old hands reached for swords. Montague says he will erect a golden statue of Juliet, which Capulet says he will match with another of Romeo. These statues will constitute the first public monument mentioned in Verona, not a dark, subterranean family "monument", a tomb for dead bodies, but a visible, outdoors memorial of a shared event in the past. Verona will now have a "story" (5.3.309) to become the subject of "talk" (5.3.307) among adults with a past and young people with a future, of history books, and, perhaps, of stage plays. In erecting this civic monument, the family patriarchs, now "brothers", act, for the first time, as city fathers. The Friar's scheme to resurrect Juliet ends in a bloody sacrifice, but the sacrifice has begun to resurrect Verona as a viable city.

What must be buried in the tomb, or at least restricted, by the restored city are the isolating detachment of hatred based on love of one's own, and the isolating attachment of erotic love for another. The debasements of the former are easy to see, but audiences often misunderstand the implications of the latter. The play exhibits it in all its beauty: young, free, undiluted by other responsibilities, and expressed in the lyrical language of first love. We would be less extraordinary beings, indeed, less human, if we never felt this way. But Shakespeare also shows that the exclusive love of Romeo and Juliet, withdrawn into their own time and place, is not a lasting love on which to base stable marriages, families, cities, and other aspects of our full humanity.

There are other changes at the end of the play. The language flattens when the feud and the lovers die. The fast, funny, dirty talk of Mercutio and his pals has been silenced. And the stars and sonnets, puns and similes, leaps and "yonders" of the lyrical love speeches have been brought down to earth. They are replaced by the Prince's sober political speech, the Friar's dull report, and the sad exchange of the two old enemies. The play ends with the famous sing-song couplets rhyming on the lovers' names: "set / ... Juliet" (5.3.301–2) and "woe / ... Romeo" (5.3.309–10). They are as flat as the Friar's speeches about herbs and the afterlife. Perhaps, as the city develops into a complex whole of integrated parts, it may give rise to personal, political, and even philosophical speech, of the sort we hear in the complex communities Shakespeare depicts in other plays. But here and now, inside Verona, Romeo and Juliet are silenced forever and the saddened households and city have not much to say. The new statues will be beautiful and visible to all, but they will be as immobile as the corpses in the tomb. And gold is cold.

NOTES

1. All line references to the play are to *The Arden Shakespeare* (Q2), edited by René Weis (2012).
2. Line references to Arthur Brooke, *The Tragicall Historye of Romeus and Juliet* (1562) are to Bullough 1957, vol. 1.

WORKS CITED

Bullough, Geoffrey. 1957. *Narrative and Dramatic Sources of Shakespeare*, vol. 1. London: Routledge and Kegan Paul / New York: Columbia University Press.

Shakespeare, William. 2012. *Romeo and Juliet*. Edited by René Weis. London: Bloomsbury (The Arden Shakespeare Third Series).

5 Defiance and Denial
Paradigms of Civic Transgression and Transcendence in *Romeo and Juliet*

Silvia Bigliazzi

THE CIVIC AND THE INDIVIDUAL

Framing a much more complex action, the Chorus's prologic narrative together with the Prince's famous final couplet on Romeo's and Juliet's deaths as the most woeful story of two star-crossed lovers provide a simplistic narrative of tragic scapegoating that has been popularized over the centuries. Sentimental feelings of easy compassion have been aroused by this story of doom at the expense of the complex tragic design they find themselves in and to which they respond with wilful opposition. The final reconciliation of the feuding families only helps to occult this tension in the name of an eventually restored peace. And yet a perceptible ambiguity creeps into the concluding exchange between the two heads of the families competing for the Prince's favour.[1] Conflict, either externalized within the highly agonistic society of Verona, or internalized within the characters' own psychological lacerations, remains at the core of the play down to its conclusion. It has often been remarked that issues of violence and sacrifice, rebellion and coercion, social individualization and erotic self-loss, individual choice and social responsibility, reshape the conventional narrative of ill-fated love, of classical and Italian origin, encrusting it with a number of unprecedented tensions. However, the extent to which this re-articulation delivers the play from the mechanical iteration of received topoi has not been sufficiently investigated in the dialectic between the individual and civic society. For instance, it has not been sufficiently pointed out that the degree of conflict between different potential tragic outcomes is largely dependent on a reconceptualization of the position of the individual within the civic space, and that this space is deeply and troublingly traversed by social disrupting forces bearing political consequences on different levels: the household, the public space and the maintenance of peace, the role of the governor. As Reynolds and Segal have suggested, Verona "is constituted by feuding ideologies that generate dueling subjective territories", and their "common parlance is the language of commerce" (2005, 49). This fact has political implications that rescue the tragedy from a romanticized idea of a love-and-death all-transcending story.[2] Nonetheless, the dialectic between this composite civic dimension and its social stances is based upon relational paradigms of behaviour which have been underexplored in their basic structure. Attentive to the relation between the civic dimension and the individual, Hunter and Lichtenfels have noticed the relevance of "the difference between a feudal family-based civil world and a civic order based in the law, and the separation between socially approved behavior and individual desire" (2009, 191). The relational paradigms I have in mind point precisely to this kind of separation.

It has been contended that to an Elizabethan audience Romeo and Juliet's self-destruction would have appeared as the natural outcome of their transgression of family and social norms (Stone 1977, 87). Although this moralistic view is clearly put forward in Brooke's preface to the poem, confirming that it is no peregrine assumption, it does not strike quite the right note in the play. In it morality is subjected to diffracting perspectives, such as the Friar's critical attitude towards both the all too rash love of the two youths and Capulet's enforced will on Juliet's marriage with Paris (5.3.237–9).[3] It has also been remarked, contrariwise, that it is rather the abusive and constraining social system that brings about tragedy, and that the "suicides of Romeo and Juliet represent one version of ideology's destructive power" (Snyder 2007, 95). Albeit antithetical, these two stances need to be looked at in conjunction because Shakespeare here seems to intersect different models and worldviews in order to draw from within the frame of a traditional story of doomed love and death the potential for reassessing issues of individual awareness and responsibility in the face of a violent society. What he comes up with is a new sense of the radical alternative between transgression and transcendence, defiance and denial in respect to the civic order and its bearing upon a revitalized tragic pattern of violence and sacrifice.

Romeo and Juliet is a political play, and the love it portrays *is* intrinsically political, because implicated in the political conflicts of the town, *while*, or *by*, being politically transcendent. What may sound as an oxymoronic concept joining politics and its negation in fact helps explain the seemingly irreconcilable views the play elicits. I will try to show how a rethinking of the tragic here involves both the ideas of transgression and transcendence and a redefinition of the subject within the civic dimension. This will entail a reconsideration of the individual's awareness of citizenry and citizenship and his/her position in respect to both. I will argue that the action, situated within a highly conventional format smacking of lyrical experimentalism, with its widespread lyricism and patterned exchanges, scattered with choruses, sonnets, aubades, epithalamions, and lamentation pieces, shows the story's resistance to formal and thematic fetters,[4] which it struggles with and eventually remodels, providing a new tragic garment for an evidently ritualistic scheme of scapegoating that no longer affords a viable pattern. This involves a re-assessment of the individual through an interrogation of the meaning of one's freedom in respect to the communal demands. This interrogation is triggered by the elemental yet complex relation between violence and sacrifice, bringing the scapegoating issue a step ahead towards a questioning of the Renaissance preordered world-view as a system of hierarchy threatened by gradually collapsing stances of power and authority.[5] It is precisely in the interstices that open within this once solid system of social scales and universal analogies that a fresh sense of the tragic emerges from the inside, laying bare new unanswered questions regarding the subject and society. In particular, the pervasive acts of defiance and denial featuring in the course of the play reveal a deep affiliation with Shakespeare's early reformulation of age-old schemes of violence and sacrifice and their tragic potential.

As will be seen, the interaction between the scapegoating model, providing a privileged focus upon the community, with new dynamics of civic disorders and their repercussions upon the individual, is precisely what allows for the emergence of an original configuration of the tragic out of the collapse of old community rituals and the inauguration of a new dialectical relation between the individual and the civic context. My view is that the emerging of a complex conception of subjectivity here occurs precisely through the tragic experience of staking one's life in response to the demands of the society. This is the result of a necessary dialectics leading to self-affirmation through self-denial as the ultimate response to the overbearing demands of a community seeking to find stability in an transitional age of class tensions. Without those demands, no tragic experience would simply subsist. It is by interrogating that civic dimension in its dialectical relation with the scapegoating frame that a rethinking of the tragic subject is here carried out. I will examine the actions of denial and defiance as two opposed possibilities the individual may resort to for achieving freedom. I will also look at how this achievement is made at the tragic cost of one's life within the civic frame. My starting point are some preliminary considerations on those two paradigms in relation to an idea of individuality linked to separateness. Discussion of the civic relevance to these issues will follow and will be connected with different relational paradigms of behaviour in respect to the community; this will unveil the existence of a fundamental ambiguity at the of core of the system, casting light on the manifold conflicting stances that shape the tragic course of the play.

PARADIGMS OF SEPARATENESS: PREMISES

It has often been suggested that the articulation of the subject's tragic experience in *Romeo and Juliet* may be referred to two elemental dynamics: fighting and erotic desire. In either case, it has been argued, the main issue is how the subject may achieve freedom and self-affirmation by accessing an awareness of the self as separated from the other (Kottman 2012). The idea of separation evidently entails one of individuality, which at the time was gradually taking shape according to new parameters. The semantics of the term 'individual' fluctuated between the antithetical, but complementary, ideas of wholeness and inseparability, on the one hand, and, on the other, separableness from the general. In the mid-seventeenth century the verb 'to individualize' began to signify 'marking something out' by means of individual characters, thus suggesting the idea of 'separating from others' what is not further divisible but retains intrinsic compactness (1637; *OED*, 1; 1655; 2). However, at the beginning of the century, the word 'individual' primarily identified an 'indivisible entity' as well as the quality of being 'inseparable' (1600; *OED*, A1 and 2), thus focusing on the fact that something may exist as a 'separable identity' by being 'numerically one' (1593; *OED*, A4). In other words, it mainly expressed the ideas of 'integrity' alongside that of 'distinctness' from others, as well as 'opposition to the general'. It indicated an individual entity (A1c, 1425) that cannot be separated (A2, 1555), a single organism (A3a, 1570), different and distinguished from others (A5, 1646); as a noun it identified a single human being as distinct from a particular group or from society (N1, *a*1500, but the earliest examples date from 1618), although the predominant meaning was that of internal cohesion and distinctness from the others. In 1605 Francis Bacon claimed that "As touching the Manners of learned men, it is a thing personal and individual" (*The Advancement of Learning*, I), thus referring to what pertains to a 'singular person' (A3a), and the social acceptation of 'individual' as opposed to Society and the Family gradually became relevant in the course of the seventeenth century. In 1646 Sir Thomas Browne in his *Pseudodoxia Epidemica* (1.4.19) would write that "A man should be something that men are not, and individual in somewhat beside his proper nature", that is, "[d]istinguished from others by attributes of its own; marked by a peculiar and striking character" (*OED*, A5), thus stressing peculiarity as a trait of individuality. Evidently, the late sixteenth and the early seventeenth centuries focused alternatively on the two opposed ideas of 'indivisibility', or internal integrity, and 'separability' from the general, thus suggesting, when combined, that the individual was something at once intrinsically indivisible and separated from the general. The language to define this concept in its social and philosophical acceptation was gradually being established.

And yet, by the end of the sixteenth century this language and the alternative notions it conveyed had not yet stabilized themselves along clear social coordinates. As Martin puts it, "most Renaissance men and women were not detached from social groups and networks, from the family and the parish or the guild and confraternity", since identities "could be defined by social location but also by a self-conscious awareness of the complexity of community" (2004, 17–18). An individual could be recognized as such precisely because belonging to a group, not because separated from it. However, separation was (and is) precisely what establishes the individual as such. Broadly speaking, it is by positing oneself as separated from the other that one affirms individuality. The notion of separation, as the prerequisite of self-asserted individuality, assumes relation with, and, at the same time, division from, the other, be it singular or plural. By extension, the extreme instance of otherness is what is ultimately opposed to one-self and one's life: death. It follows that in order to assert oneself as a separate individual, one must paradoxically affirm one's life by staking it individually. It is by willingly confronting the horizon of mortality represented by the fight (and the duel as its best example) that one achieves an awareness that one is more than one's instinctual desire to live. This experience is reciprocated in the fight, in that also the enemy is risking his life and only one of the fighters will survive the duel, thus implying that it will be impossible for them to see each other dead. Only by staking one's life does one measure its value. It is already evident at this point that this issue is deeply ingrained in the dynamics of *Romeo and Juliet*.

This argument, that briefly sums up Kottman's position as put forward in 2012 and 2014, provides the starting point of my own argument too. Yet contrary to Kottman's claim, I will hold that this idea of staking one's life is central to, and not separated from, a dialectic with the civic dimension in which the drama is set. While it is true that in "Shakespeare's drama the tethering between individual actions and the demands of culture or the claims of nature slackens", it is less arguable that the "dialectic can no longer tighten it" (Kottman 2012, 4). A conflictual relation between the individual and the community is inevitable because self-affirmation occurs only through self-emancipation, and this is the testing ground for the actualization of the individual's freedom. This involves a primary focus on how the subjects participating in the conflict achieve freedom, including the ultimate option of freely choosing death. A secondary, but no marginal focus, is on how the tragic outcome affects the community and how the community reacts to the tragic event. As will be seen, this is part of the revision of the tragic experience elaborated in the play, and it would be impossible without this dialectic.

Staking one's life does not mean resorting to fight only. Sexual desire too may involve a similar degree of separateness when it brings about a conscious wish to be recognized as a freely desiring subject separate from its object and itself a freely desired object in a context of mutual recognition. What matters here is that fighting and sexual desire form the two basic paradigms of a play in which both are at odds with acceptance of civic peace and norms. In Verona, conforming to civic rule requires the debunking of the individual aspiration to separateness. Separation, in line of principle, is the opposite of togetherness and involves rejecting or defying the rules and constraints which lead to that togetherness. Therefore, civic bond hinders individualization, which in order to assert itself needs to face the ideas of otherness, separateness, and mortality as its ultimate stance, not of community. In other words, civic bondage unmakes self-realization, if realizing oneself consists in freely claiming one's separateness, including the ultimate option of death. It follows that realizing oneself signifies being un-civic: this is the implied corollary of a line of reasoning that sees the duel as the quintessential example of the self's attempt to prove one's life's value, and likewise considers love as providing a way to assert oneself freely in a context of enmity. I will add that suicide provides an alternative to the mechanism of defiance underlying the duel pattern, and that in this play it occurs as the result of a sequence of actions transgressing the logic of defiance in order to achieve an ultimate form of separation through utter denial. Although the critical focus has mostly been on the topic of love (and upon sexual desire), it is the fight that provides the wider horizon of self-affirmation in the play; and it can hardly be claimed that there is a debunking of the role of civic disorder due to the initial 'aborted' duel (Kottman 2012, 8). Indeed, the play does not open on a duel but on a general brawl, and its interruption is no proof of the irrelevance of the fight to the death, but rather of the dialectic underlying civic violence and the Prince's ineffectual authority; it also provides the pretext, on a dramatic level, for leaving the fight open to sequels, since what the two families receive here is only a strong rebuke. In other words, there is no demoting of the civic challenge implied by the stopping of the first bout of street disorder, and, therefore, no freeing the play from its dialectic with the civil dimension. Both fighting and sexual desire are situated in it, although their relation to the civic sphere will take different forms. For the moment, suffice it to mention that both offer significant paradigms of separateness, and it is precisely upon those paradigms that the play builds its tragic value by relying on an ambiguous conception of civic and civility.

CIVIC, CIVILITY, AND CITIZENRY

Much has recently been written on the notion of civility in the Renaissance (see for instance Appelbaum 1997; Bryson 1998; Richards ed. 2003, esp. Shrank 2003 and Peltonen 2003), unveiling its deep-rooted ambiguity (Clark 2011). While civility conveys the meaning of refined manners and civilized behaviour, it also implies its contrary, or uncivilized violence and source of civic disorder. The root of an idea of 'uncivil civility' contrary to peaceful cohabitation has been tracked within an ebullient, but socially declining, aristocracy that considered mannered violence, especially in the form of duels, as a distinguishing feature of its power and status. This implication surfaces in the play's first Prologue whose account of Verona's outbreak of violence mentions a new "mutiny" where "civil blood makes civil hands unclean" (ll. 3, 4). If "civil" here simply signifies 'civic', the bloodshed and shame alluded to concern both households qua citizens as well as the general citizenry involved in the riots. More intriguingly, though, "civil" may imply 'civilized', indeed 'aristocratic', thus referring to the blood of noblemen whose shameful responsibility would turn out be the cause of the sullying of "civic hands", as a synecdoche for peaceful citizens. This interpretation entails a neat divide between aristocrats ("civil blood") and citizens ("civil hands") with ensuing class-struggle implications. Along these lines Clark (2011) has claimed that *Romeo and Juliet* portrays a more subtle enmity than the one manifest between the two families, involving an outright, yet creeping, social antagonism between the masters and their subordinates. The often quoted ambiguity of Sampson's and Gregory's exchange on the quarrel between the two families hints at the possibility that the servants fight not only among themselves on behalf of their masters, but also with their own masters ("The quarrel is between our masters and us their men", 1.1.17). Sampson's remark that "'Tis all one" and his further boasting that he will show himself a tyrant, before voicing fantasies of male violence and rape (ll. 18–20), confirms this ambiguity. What is all one? The quarrel, equally involving the masters and servants of the two opposing houses, or/and the quarrel between the masters and servants of the same house, thus making the two quarrels ideally conflate within one? Emulation is evidently at work in the servant's fantasies of male omnipotence, making him a tyrant and an 'aristocratically mannered' and 'erotically refined' lover with the maids he claims he will be civil with. Boasting about civility with women, meaning violence, is clearly an ironic twist for the sake of understatement, before brutal outspokenness ("I will cut off their heads", ll. 19–20); and this implies an awareness of the contiguity between civility and violence, which he imitates here, rather than blaming.

Undeniably, though, the notion of civility is also antithetical to violence,[6] and this contributes to foregrounding the ambiguity of an idea of civilization here dramatized in the pangs of its self-questioning. Does being civil with Romeo make Capulet civilized? Does his violence with Juliet unmake his civility? In the civic microcosm of his house, Capulet is both enemy to the Montagues and ruler of the family. His display of civility towards Romeo confirms his wish to "keep the peace", as avowed to Paris in 1.2 (l. 3); it is a show of wisdom and gentleness as the apt and diplomatic response to the city of Verona's high regard for the young Montague, who is deemed to be a "portly gentleman" (l. 65) and "the wealth of all this town" (l. 68).[7] Confronted by his hothead nephew and "princox" (l. 85) who challenges his own power ("You must contrary me!", l. 84) by challenging Romeo, he is inflexible in rebuking Tybalt's "cock-a-hoop" fieriness (1.5.80), whose impatience risks "making a mutiny" (l. 79) among the guests. As Clark again suggests, Capulet seems to signify that "Tybalt will create an embarrassingly violent fracas in a properly joyful setting", implying that "he fears Tybalt is determined to 'make' or promote a domestic coup or rebellion among the guests" (2011, 282). I am not sure what "domestic coup or rebellion" means here, unless it refers to general domestic disorder. Surely, though, the word 'mutiny' echoes its former use by the Prologue, projecting within one single household the feeling that rebellion may penetrate domesticity, thus causing in the head of the family anxiety about lack of control. This word entered the English language through Fenton's 1567 translation of Matteo Bandello's *Certaine tragicall Discourses*, where it refers precisely to domestic discord or even minor dispute – "He … (besides a thousand pettie mutynies that fall out in housekeping,) escapeth seldom without a sprit of grudge or cyuill discension, disturbynge hys quiet" (vol. 1, f. 34 sig. Eii^v). In his own house Capulet does not fear a minor quarrel, but danger of downright violence, which he evidently perceives as a serious menace for what Aristotle called *oikonomia*, or rule of the house, with an implied parallel with the government of the city.[8] The challenge of his own authority from within his own family obfuscates the 'scorn at their solemnity' supposedly perpetrated by the enemy. Yet another challenge he will receive at a later stage by a Juliet determined not to comply with his own choice, and at that point he will prove even more fierce than with Tybalt. Civility towards the outside world of the city, including the enemy, does not correspond to indoors civility, precisely as civic diplomacy does not correspond to the exercise of absolute power in the household.

According to a pattern of duplication implied in the same *oikonomia* notion recalled above, the episode in Capulet's house iterates the potential crisis of authority already perceived in town at the end of the first scene with the arrival of the Prince. Escalus too is the guarantor of civic peace; he is the Lord of the town and presides over the citizens whom he treats as "subjects" (l. 72), that is, citizens bound by the "laws and the state" and "agreeing to fight for the nation" (Hunter and Lichtenfels 2009, 189). Like Capulet in his own house, he makes show of wielding power with the threat of an inflexible law. Mutiny, in either case, implies a subversion of social household/civic order as well as a challenge of the master's/Lord's authority. While in the course of the play Capulet will demonstrate increasing rigour in respect to the Prince's leniency, in Act 1 both symbolize threatened and largely ignored rule: Tybalt's appeasement is only momentary, and he will soon send Romeo a letter of formal challenge which will not be read, because on the Sunday night Romeo does not return home. Civic peace is restored for the short time lapse of one day and will be broken again on the Monday afternoon by yet another brawl consequent to Romeo's failing to respond to Tybalt's challenge. This time the fight will involve two distinct duels as the thwarted versions of fights to the death dislocating the one-to-one opposition for self-affirmation to a logic of triangulation: Tybalt will kill Mercutio while aiming at Romeo, and Mercutio will fight Tybalt in the place of Romeo, but not in defence of the Montagues, since he is a kinsman to the Prince and no member of the feuding families; Romeo will kill Tybalt because of Mercutio's death, thus finding a more tangible reason for hatred than the groundless enmity of the opposing households: revenge for a friend.

All this descends from an ambiguous notion of civility as a double-edged category that exhibits the blurring of the dividing line between gentleness and violence, leniency and inflexibility, complacency and blind authority. Shakespeare was so keen on foregrounding this ambiguity that he construed a pattern of repetitions and variations already in Act 1 and then developed out of it a sequence of actions leading to the turning point in 3.1 through a series of challenges. This is a crucial episode not only in the course of the action, which suddenly swerves towards tragedy, but also in the same mechanics underlying civic feuding. If so far quarrels had been but an extension of the logic of staking one's life individually, thus transposing to the level of the household's social visibility and ontological raison d'être the struggle for self-individualization, Mercutio's death is rooted elsewhere: in a wish to substitute himself for his friend in an attempt at self-affirmation and defence of a code of male honour, which he interprets as having been violated by Romeo's leniency. All this goes beyond household opposition. Romeo's subsequent reaction is likewise a defence of that same code when he realizes that its violation due to amorous 'effeminacy' has been the cause of his friend's death, not of an offence to his family. These two mortal duels resulting from the logic of the households' vindication of social visibility through seemingly groundless fights to the death turn that logic against itself: the fight is grounded in revenge, friendship, and male honour; Mercutio curses the two families as incongruously responsible for his own death; Romeo kills the murderer of his friend. The magnates' feud has been emptied of its self-affirming value as a challenge to both the Prince and the community of the citizens, and has been replaced by a variation upon the Achilles-Patroclos paradigm involving male, rather than family, bondage.

This is an entirely new and highly relevant addition to the story by Shakespeare since the fight in Brooke is a general brawl in the streets started off by Tybalt and involving first two groups of Capulets and Montagues, and then other citizens who have joined in,[9] before Romeo arrives and urges them to stop from "confound[ing] all this our commonweal" (l. 1001). Strictly speaking in the poem there is no duel but, within a general fray, a one-to-one fight between Tybalt and Romeo, who eventually "thrust him through the throat, and so is Tyablt slain" (l. 1034). In Shakespeare things are evidently more complicated, and the addition of Mercutio makes it palpable. Civil mutiny is going beyond clan feuds, and is getting closer to civic disruption referable to individual involvement and wilful commitment.

In this context, where 'civil' violence in the streets is presented as a way for the magnates (and their young generations especially) to achieve social assertion in respect to the community, citizenry plays a crucial role (see Weinberger 2003, 363 and ff.). Anonymous citizens, in small numbers (three or four) representing the collectivity, enter in 1.1 (ll.64–5) with clubs or partisans to stop the fray by combating the Montagues and the Capulets alike. They enter again in 3.1, with a similar function of civil militia, and one of them orders Benvolio to follow him in the name of the Prince. Finally, in 5.3 we hear Lady Capulet say that there are "people in the streets" who "cry 'Romeo' / Some 'Juliet', and some 'Paris'", all running, as in Brooke, "With open outcry toward our monument" (ll. 191–3). This is an evidently different type of civic outburst from their previous interventions, as they now show grief and despair at the loss of individual youths, significantly called by their first names, rather than intolerance of family feuds and fury against both households ("Down with the Capulets, down with the Montagues!", they had inveighed in 1.1.71). Besides, they are not shown on stage but only talked about by Lady Capulet who mentions their disordered manifestations of grief in the streets. They are simply called "people" as opposed to the citizens who in 1.1 and 3.1 were dubbed "Offi.[cers]" (Q2 1.1) and "Watch." (Q1 10, corresponding to Q2 3.1). In those previous scenes the civic role of the townsmen was that of supporters of the Prince, and their presence was more prominent and dramatically effective. Their role in stopping the fray in 1.1 (Fitter 2000, 169) is yet another original addition by Shakespeare, since in the only brawl recounted by Brooke, in which Tybalt is slain, the Prince sends his own troops to face the feuding families (l. 1039) with no military intermediacy on the part of the town. Thus citizenry has a weightier role in the play in respect to its source, where "townsmen" is used to identify the riotous Capulets and Montagues as well as other citizens who have joined them in the street fight. Against them all the Prince sends his own army ("The townsmen waxen strong, the Prince doth send his force", l. 1039). In this passage Brooke makes clear that the fight to the death *is* a form of self-affirmation in which only one of the two fighters will survive. The metaphors he chooses are of a feral thirst for the blood of the enemy that conveys physical, primitive connotations to the staking of one's own life ("Who thirsteth after other's death, himself hath lost his life", l. 1036). Romeus's survival at this point provides a way for his family to experience through him what it means not to succumb in staking one's life, while the Capultes experience the contrary feeling of self-loss through the loss of Tybalt ("The Capulets are quailed by Tybalt's overthrow, / The courage of the Montagues by Romeus' sight doth grow", ll. 1037–8). Here, the townsmen are no civic militia supporting the Prince, but the fighting enemies themselves. In a general civic derangement, they too appear rebellious to the Lord, having grown audacious and strong by intermingling in the fight with the original quarrellers and eventually become indistinguishable from them; thus all need to be stopped. The family feuding has infected Verona, and citizenry has fallen prey to swaying violence much more radically than in Shakespeare's version, despite the unique combat actually engaged in the poem.

Indeed, in Escalus's words citizens are not just everybody, nor are they quite as potentially dangerous as those we find in Brooke. Escalus calls them "ancient", meaning both citizens of long-standing families, and old citizens, in accordance with a use of the word signifying old age.[10] Reference to their old stock, however, is particularly relevant, because it contributes to defining the community as a closed system whose solidity is proved by the antiquity of its citizens' lineage. To a traveller like Fynes Moryson, for instance, who journeyed throughout Europe between 1591 and 1595, Verona appeared as a "strong Town" (1617, Part 1, book 2, ch. 4, 175), "ennobled by the ancient nobility of the citizens, who are endowed with a cheerful countenance, magnificent minds, and much inclined to all good literature" (ibid., 176). Located within a space surrounded by walls, as it actually appeared to Moryson, and yet projected back in time, to a period when still under the Scaliger control, the city looks self-sufficient and careful to keep itself safe from foreigners and the plague, so that access and exit at night are regulated by a watch.[11] To be an ancient citizen means being part of, and responsible for, the city; it implies being known in town and respected, and, as other uses of the word suggest, venerable and wise too (see OED, II 7, *Taming of the Shrew*, 5.1.66, "You seem sober, ancient gentleman by your habit").

As recalled earlier in this chapter, citizens provide support for those who govern them, in accordance with an idea of the city as a communal system aiming at order and peace within itself, but lacking professional city guards employed by the Prince. In "A Discourse of the Names and First Causes of the Institution of Cities and Peopled Towns" appended to his *Survey of London* (1598), John Stow wrote that the "common weals, cities, and towns, were at first invented, to the end that men might lead a civil life amongst themselves, and be saved harmless against their enemies" (1842, 200). Developing closed societies, however, open to foreigners (as contended by Stefano Guazzo in the second book of his *The Civil Conversation*, 1587), meant favouring civility, by this signifying improvement of social relations and peace-keeping by the respect of the common weal. Stow further observed that "men by this nearness of conversation are withdrawn from barbarous feritie and force to a certain mildness of manners, and to a humanity and justice; whereby they are contented to give and take right, to and from their equals and inferiors and to hear and obey their heads and superiors" (ibid., 200). The law itself of God may be more easily enforced "by reason of the facility of common and often assembling; and consequently such inhabitants be better managed in order, and better instructed in wisdom" (ibid.). In cities, "men by mutual society and companying together, do grow alliances, commonalities, and corporations" (ibid., 201), which favours the excercise of "love and goodwill of one man towards another". Finally, and foremost, "the inhabitants be a ready hand and strength to men, with munition to oppress intestine sedition", while also being "continual bridle against tyranny" (ibid., 201). Citizens, in short, are the necessary civil force for a political and military containment of all excess in town, whether on the part of seditious intestine forces or on that of the ruler.

Verona is all but the fit example of the perfect concord, civility, and good commonweal here described, but its citizens seem to play precisely this function of a double-edged control, manifest in their attempt to redress the violation of the common weal by aristocratic struggle for self-affirmation, but also in the political consideration the Prince diplomatically reserves to them. There is fairly general agreement on considering the Capulets and the Montagues as representatives of a class apart, a gradually declining nobility (Weinberger 2003; Clark 2011), although it is nowhere openly stated that they are aristocrats. The fact that Capulet hurries to sign the matrimonial bond for his daughter, showing great pride for the very good match with a nobleman he has negotiated, might in fact be a hint to the contrary.[12] It has also been suggested that they might be of a middle-class status,[13] and that their domestic life in fact resembles that of "English merchants rather than renaissance Italian nobility" (Shakespeare 1980, 38). In noticing that the "name of Capulet's castle, in Painter, is Villafranca, and in Brooke, Freetown", Gibbons underlines that "Shakespeare visualizes Capulet as living in a merchant's house rather than in a castle", and that this "dignity he transfers to Escalus" (ibid., 87). What is sure is that they are both rich; Capulet deploys his abundant wealth in the preparation of feasts and banquets in times of crisis and plague (Fitter 2000, 156ff.); Montague might even enjoy "a more stable financial security" by never showing in the course of the play mercantile eagerness (Reynolds and Segal 2005, 48). On the other hand, there is no precise indication of the social status of the "ancient citizens", and from Escalus's mention of their "old partisans" wielded by "hands as old" (1.1.85) in the opening fray it may be inferred that they too might be of some noble lineage. Before becoming weapons "borne ceremonially by civic and other guards" (1611; *OED*, 1b), partisans were part of the gentleman's equipment for duelling, normally alongside a round shield. They were famously mentioned in well-known treatises of fencing and fighting such as Antonio Manciolino's 1531 *Opera Nova per Imparare a Combattere, & Schermire d'ogni forte Armi* (book 6), and Achille Marozzo's 1536 *Opera Nova Chiamata Duello, O Vero Fiore dell' Armi de Singulari Abattimenti Offensivi, & Diffensivi* (book 4). Whatever their social position, though, it is clear that they serve as a kind of civic militia as opposed to the historically documented military support of the aristocracy that used to side with the King; this support was gradually coming to an end in the Tudor era, due to the reduction of retinues and the increasing royal independence from them (Stone 2008, 96–107),[14] and this adds to the political connotation of civic support replacing them.[15] At the same time, the good citizens' temporary deafness to the Prince's command on his arrival in 1.1 contributes to rendering the sense of his isolation and precariousness, at least at a symbolic level.

On the whole, the play dramatizes on different planes the complexity and extreme consequences of social imbalance and unstable order; it hints at class tension between master and subordinates in different civic and domestic spaces, plays on the inherent ambiguities of the notion of civility, and dramatizes the creaking of the hierarchical relation between magnates, citizenry and the city Lordship.[16] This articulated network of social forces and its radical instability come to radicalize a struggle for self-assertion investing the two households whose fighting for the sake of fighting provides the clan phenomenology of the elemental dynamics of individual self-affirmation through fighting as mentioned earlier in this chapter. They supply an extension of it in terms of family groups who strive to assert themselves through quarrels in which the notion of individuality is reduced to that of family representativeness, at least until Mercutio and Romeo take the duelling logic in their own hands and reshape it in the name of revenge and friendship. Civilly invoked by Tybalt (the refined fencer in the Spanish fashion),[17] who resorts to a formal challenge of Romeo, but fails to receive response and satisfaction, the household's feud is eventually turned against itself. Tybalt is slain for reasons other than those he has invoked for the duel; the family logic of fighting to the death for once looks defeated not by the Prince or the citizens, but the fighters themselves.

VIOLENCE, SACRIFICE, AND THE LAW

Besides alluding to civil mutiny, the Prologue recounts also a story of scapegoating as the manifest backbone of a drama of violence and final reconciliation focused upon the inveterate hatred of the fathers, as opposed to the youths' love. How partial, if not entirely wrong, the Prologue is one does not need to wait long to verify: it is only at the opening of 1.2 that Capulet avows to Paris that "'tis not hard, I think, / For men so old as we to keep the peace", being both "in penalty" (ll. 2–3), and in 1.5. Tybalt proves that hatred is fomented by the younger generation instead. However, this is the linear rationale of the story as offered prior to the beginning of the play. It should be recalled that the Prologue's peculiar position in an in-between space connecting audience and actors (Weimann and Bruster 2004; Bigliazzi 2015a) gives it special authority. Despite being only a version of a well-known tale circulating at the time in prose and verse, as well as in several different languages, it supplies a clearly ideological perspective that is entirely missing from Brooke's opening Argument – a piece roughly corresponding to the Prologue with a short summary of the tragedy. Thus it is worth pointing out that what the Prologue selects to say agrees with what could arouse interest. Mention of the sacrifice of two star-crossed youths must have sounded quite appealing, while providing a good ground upon which to build a more complex tragic design in the course of the play.

But let us look at this basic structure first. It has become common knowledge, at least since the popularization of the idea of an existing bond between the sacred and violence in ancient tragedy, that the tragic has much to do with a maddened agonistic system that needs the sacrifice of a scapegoat to be purified and appeased. In René Girard's seminal formulations (2005), violence is the breeder of violence, which is triggered by mimesis, or emulation, when the moral and social differences within the cultural order collapse. Once erased, everybody acts violently in response to, or as a prefiguration of, the perceived aggressiveness of the neighbour. In order to prevent or check the violent chain reactions, the religious institutions are assumed to come first, and then the legal ones follow at a later stage. The sacrifice of a scapegoat, and his/her expulsion from the city, provides the way for the community to converge its own violence onto a single victim and purify itself by restoring the difference between good and bad aggressiveness, punishment and crime.

However oversimplified, these are the latent contours of the basic anthropological ground upon which *Romeo and Juliet*'s own system of violence and sacrifice is claimed to rest by the Prologue. And yet, from very early in the play we perceive that something is not quite right, from the mediation of the religious institution, whose function, according to that scheme, can in no way be taken up by the Friar, to continue with the idea of the convergence of the community's violence upon one sacrificial victim: while being victims sacrificed to the altar of civic peace ideally, in practice the two youths are not selected by the community as scapegoats. Indeed, they happen to play the role of sacrificial victims by chance, or better, following choices of their own making that end up being unlucky: what eventually looks like a sacrifice is the effect of a chain of events making up a plot that everybody ignores, families and community alike. Reconciliation thus ensues without the restoration of a moral code by the active agency of the religious institution and the Law, and, as hinted at at the outset, the actual family appeasement remains dubious to the end. This is why to concentrate on the death of the two youths in search for a sacrificial pattern provides a false route. If a sacrifice is truly being carried out, it needs to be searched for elsewhere and at a later stage in the course of the play.

Before coming to that, though, it may be worth noticing that contagious violence is clearly at work and this makes true at least that part of the scheme. It has been noted that in the Renaissance, as much as today, both power and authority relied on relational violence in order to claim a role within society; nevertheless, this violence was often based on a fairly opaque distinction between what was acceptable and what was not. "Society", it has been argued, "was composed of a series of reciprocal hierarchical relationships in which protection and care were exchanged for deference and obedience" (Amussen 1995, 4). More generally, "violence was legitimate when used by superiors against inferiors; those who used violence outside of its accepted forms often sought to claim much superiority – or at least equality – through their actions" (ibid.). Within a system of analogical correspondences between the state and the domestic government, the head of the household behaved as the governor of the state, and handled the punishing and disciplinary power over his subordinates (wife, children and servants) in ways that could easily turn into downright abuse. Although the words 'violence' and 'violent' were utilized with a whole range of different meanings, and not always within formulaic expressions indicating legal infringement, they mostly suggested an inappropriate or illegitimate behaviour (see ibid., 3).

Criticism has often pointed out that the rivalry dramatized in spectacular episodes of violence in the play reflects the historical riotous circumstances of London in 1590s (Power 1985; Levenson 1995; Fitter 2000; Herman 2008), as well as the intemperance of metropolitan aristocracy testified to by street brawls and a gradually increasing fashion for duels (Stone 2008, 118-24). Yet, apart from the historicity of civic feuding, which, as suggested earlier, contributes to articulating socially the agonistic scheme at the root of a tragic conception of scapegoating, the play enucleates the master-and-servant-alike type of quarrelling as an elemental paradigm of self-assertion that calls into question the role of the law itself. The ambiguity of the antagonism between masters and servants elaborates on the basic idea of quarrelling in a civic state of crisis, modifying the anthropological scheme of emulation of violence preceding scapegoating by adding shades of social tension. Whatever Gregory's 'all one' means in his 1.1 cue, the city *is* traversed by an undifferentiated form of antagonism, foregrounding that everybody fights everybody else, and all are entangled in a chain of crimes resounding with accents of tribal male and sexual aggressiveness that pushes back in time, to a primitive state of brutal ferality, the notion itself of a paradoxical 'civic civility'. According to this 'uncivil civility', the fight is precisely what allows to identify the fighters; the Capulets may be the Capulets by not being the Montagues, and both strive to achieve recognition through opposition to, and separation from, the 'other'. Citizens, instead, appear on stage unnamed, as undistinguished figures who watch over civic peace. This is not coincidental, because it demarcates different social positions and conceptions of civility, according to which citizenry is opposed to feuding households and vindication of clan individuality. As Snyder has argued following Eagleton, "'This' can only be distinguished when set against 'that', however arbitrary such distinctions are in language and other social constructions (2007, 91). "The feud", therefore, "is not a matter of contrary ideas, not a matter of ideas at all, but of repeated, habitual actions that keep reasserting the defining distinctions between 'us' and 'them'" (ibid.). In this scheme of obsessive actions of self-affirmation reflecting a 'crisis of differentiation' that subverts the ethical order, confounding right and wrong, crime and punishment, there is no place for civic peace, because the civic bond bans antagonism and arbitrates disputes through the law.

Yet here we encounter a problem, because ambiguity characterizes also the law and this confounds the scapegoating scheme. Suspicion of a double-edged illegal legalism is spurned at the levels of both governance and citizenry, and an idea of violence as quintessential to this system, as well as equivocal in its manifestations, appears to be assumed at the system's own core. Its inconsistency is what makes it irredeemably flawed and therefore useless. In a context of emulation of violence, not only does it claim to respond with equal violence, but it wavers in effecting it, thus showing to rest on unstable judicial paradigms of behaviour, tacitly, and contradictorily, mingling leniency and hardness. The examples in the play which underline both fear of the law and its arrogant violation, as well as accusation of arbitrariness in its exercise, but also freedom of self-arbitration, point to a confused system and to an equally confused perception of the function of law in presiding over the common bond. Only few instances may suffice. It has often been remarked that the Prince is a weak governor, and that his weakness principally resides in his failing to keep his word. Typically, he proves lenient towards Romeo, whom he bans instead of sentencing to death. However, the Friar interprets this choice as a show of mercy, calling it as a "rush[ing] aside [of] the law" (3.3.26), and advocating a rule of pardon and humanity. Within a context of anti-communal patterns of behaviour, as the one in force in Verona, this pardoning would provide a way out of the spiral of violence. However, the Prince does not back up his choice with reasons of understanding and equity, and rather raises the suspicion that he might simply wish to be cautious about using 'legal violence' with a gentleman Verona brags of. Be it as it may, he covers up the leniency of his decision with sententious words that resound with Machiavelli's contrary inflexible teaching on the necessary severity of the Prince, thus clearly underlining the divide between speaking and acting: "Mercy but murders, pardoning those that kill" (3.1.197).[18] From a dramatic point of view, this ironically anticipates the criminal side-effect of his 'merciful' act, paving the way for the murder of yet another youth. Thus the question of how the law should castigate civil riot and murder is left unanswered, and discrimination between right and wrong falls prey to incertitude. The only outcome is that in a context dominated by a crisis of differences, crime does not seem containable by a violent law, nor does leniency succeed in preventing the prosecution of crimes.

Although demoted in the Prince's hands, however, even braggart subordinates are afraid of the law, which is perceived in its coercive potential.[19] Also peace-maker Benvolio is aware of the consequences of talking with the enemy "in the public haunt of men" (3.1.49), following the Prince's proclamation.[20] Besides, legal language traverses the play as a "strong undercurrent" counterpointing the widespread unlawfulness of the fighting (Hunter and Lichtenfels 2009, 193–4). This same law decreeing death penalty is conceived of in town as an instrument of criminal redress that anyone may handle, thus demonstrating the weakness of a civic bond based upon a rule that lends itself to individual exercise. After all, whether it is the Prince, or one of the citizens, who punishes a murderer by murdering him, the logic of violence as breeder of violence for the sake of self-affirmation is untouched. Crime, in other words, appears to be the reverse of a coin showing law on the front. Montague's claim that Romeo has only righteously enforced Escalus's law, which would have put Tybalt to death for the murder of Mercutio (3.1. 175–6), unveils precisely the extent to which the civic bond has been thwarted. The law may be taken in private hands, and, by extension, this justifies the feuding logic itself and its chain of crimes in a sequence of incessant responses. Thus while showing a deep misunderstanding of the function of the law in respect to communal peace, Montague acknowledges private revenge as its proper enactment, yet again pointing to the crisis of the Prince's authority the moment the Prince attempts to centralize it in his own person. On the one hand, he unveils the potential arbitrariness of the law when exercised by one person only; on the other, he reveals the extent to which the mentality underlying feuding is incompatible with a healthy civic rule.

To go back to the Prologue's simplistic narrative, it is now apparent that there is a perceptible rift between what it says and what actually happens on stage. In its basic narrative, the Prologue had clearly deprived the characters of responsibility, as well as temperamental determinism: the two lovers are doomed to die by a heavenly design which intervenes to quench the rampant time-old violence between two Veronese families (Q2, l. 3). The apparent arbitrariness of violence[21] is why their strife has no prospect of ceasing. There is no religious institution that carries the sacrifice out, as posited in ancient rituals. Yet the account assumes that there is a transcendental will, or design, presiding over the whole story. This is made quite clear from the initial reference to the stars: if in sonnet 15 they are said "in secret influence [to] comment" (l. 4) upon the shows of men, here they do more than that. They predetermine the tragic events, and a transcendental will replaces the hero's free choice in causing the catastrophe: if the community, and the law embodied by the Prince, fail to check the self-destructive violence of Verona, Heaven provides the metaphysical explanation for scapegoating. As the Prince will conclude in 5.3, inviting the Capulets and the Montagues to reconcile, God has laid a scourge upon their hatred and everybody has been punished (ll. 292–5).

In the course of the play, though, it becomes increasingly less clear whether it is God, or some black fate, or blind fortune or chance, or all of them together, to guide the events, thus revealing the actual weakness of the idea of a transcendental design. Black fate is evoked by Romeo in 3.1, after Mercutio's death; fortune, and misfortune, are mentioned ten times, (most significantly when Romeo calls himself "fortune's fool", 3.1.127, for thinking he has been tricked into killing Tybalt in his present predicament); chance, instead, recurs six times, twice with the meaning of lamentable event, accident or hazard, with reference to the slaughtered youths in the tomb. Linked with the feeling of a design inherent in life are also the premonitions and dreams scattered through the play, starting with Romeo's sensing "Some consequence yet hanging in the stars" (1.4.107) right before fatally going to Capulet's house. All this is connected with the rationale offered in the Prologue's narrative, which frames and contains the problematized moral and epistemological views dramatized in the course of the play, which fuel the centrifugal drive of a new sense of tragic. In the light of what we have seen so far, this tragic is much more mundane than metaphysical, and implies a dual focus upon the community and the individual through its manifold conflictual phenomenology. The multiplication of plots through Romeo's and Juliet's secret agency and the complicity of the Friar and the Nurse complicates the levels of the tragic discourse, which in fact comes to be diffracted into two basic paradigms of action irreducible to each other, as well as to a unified conception of conflict and self-affirmation. Moving from the collapse of differences and civic defiance to the tragic affirmation of the individual outside the system through denial, and self-denial, the narrative of Romeo and Juliet becomes, with Shakespeare, the tragedy of an impossible wish for transcendence and the need to affirm a new perspective outside the agonistic models of transgression and repression problematized at the level of civic feud and governance. And this passes through a peculiar patterning of rebellious attitudes.

DEFIANCE AND DENIAL

Although both 'defiance' and 'denial' may signify 'to disavow' (*OED*, defy, 1b, obs.; deny 4), their general meaning is not the same. Defiance mostly implies a declaration of hostility (1a), a challenge or a revolt at (21, 4, 5) something or somebody, so that it may also be synonymous with 'reprobating, cursing' (archaically: 6). While both implicate a rebellion, defiance does not stand for a refusal to acknowledge the existence of something or its claims, like 'denial' (I, 3; II, 4); it rather affirms that something is existent and as such is challenged or contested. Therefore, while denying may lead to nihilism, defying sets off agonism; they rely on different conceptions of being, and non-being, and on different forms of violence: one transcends drama, the other triggers it, one is a-civic, the other one un-civic, and most of all, one posits one's individuality and freedom, the other one risks it.

The relation between the two families is clearly agonistic: they neither deny each other nor the authority of the law, which they acknowledge either by attempting to curb it to their own interests and take it on their side, or by trying to escape it, as when Benvolio invites Mercutio and Tybalt to withdraw to some secluded place to avoid being seen together and prevent their cut and trust from being noticed (3.1.43-6). Antagonism here is based on open and formal challenge, as the one Tybalt sends to Romeo, but also on implied forms of defiance, as in Tybalt's revolt in Capulet's house. The violence seen so far is always the result of various forms and degrees of challenges; they destabilize the system, functioning like "resistive conductors" of a transgressive ideology "whose disruptive effects point toward the decentralization of Verona's state [and household] power" (Reynolds and Segal 2005, 46). Yet to this end they must acknowledge established order, as the 'other' from which they claim separation. This is the logic of the duel or fight to the death as the matrix of a chain of possible variations upon the idea itself of challenge as a form of self-affirmation.

The case of Romeo and Juliet is different, and it is precisely by looking at how they relate themselves to the 'other' as the site of civic and civil order that their agency comes to provide a radical alternative to the un-civic dimension of the challenge – or its 'uncivil civility'. It has been argued that the two youths transcend the feud-ideology and make it visible in a way that "it would never be if everyone continued to operate inside its unspoken premises" (Snyder 2007, 92). Yet, they belong to that ideology and fall victim to it. This belonging and transcending at the same time is precisely what allows Shakespeare to experiment on new forms of violence and sacrifice as the basic scheme upon which to build a new sense of the tragic. And here is where the defiance/denial alternative and its implication with the civic dimension play a role.

Juliet shows a potential for defiance vis-à-vis the clan's rule of domestic discipline and family bonds only at an early stage, and then again shortly (yet firmly) when she refuses her father's marital offer. Before then, in 1.3, her impatience with orders surfaces in her subtle reply to her mother's recommendation to love Paris ("Speak briefly, can you like of Paris' love", l. 98) with a witty punning on "look" and "like". Balancing individual choice and family bonds, she avows her wish to like him as long as his looks will please her, making sure that her passion will not escape parental control; defiance takes the shape of ambiguity and impatient compromise (1.3.98–100). Her lines provide an unconscious response to Capulet's exchange with Paris in 1.2, where he too had called into question the relation between his own consent in matters of marriage and Juliet's freedom to dissent, an issue which resonated troublingly and ironically in his final rhyme "her choice" / "my voice" ("within her scope of choice / Lies my consent, and fair according voice", 1.2.18–19). No surprise, his strong affirmation of her daughter's liberty will soon be taken back in 3.5 when the time comes for Juliet to say no. At that stage, differently from Brooke's poem, where the girl is reminded of the old Roman law as a solid proof of paternal power,[22] Shakespeare first only hints at domestic law by having Capulet use a legal language ("How now, wife? / Have you delivered to her our decree?", he asks his wife in 3.5.138, by "decree" meaning my "sentence", *OED*, 1 and 4). Then he shows the abuses inscribed within that law by giving voice to Capulet's violence against the recalcitrant girl, who in his eyes contradictorily becomes a greensick carrion and a harlot for not agreeing on becoming a wife (not for proof of sexual licence!). That the idea of scope of choice expressed in 1.2 is double-edged becomes apparent at this point, when the contradiction between freedom and authority translates into conflict. Now it is clear that the scope Capulet talked about regarded the girl's capacity for desire (*OED*, 6a) only in so far as it was in accordance with his own decision, which in fact confined it within a precisely allotted space (*OED*, 8a), which measured its reach by setting boundaries.[23] Within that range and measure the tragic conflict between the individual and society, daughter and paternal authority, unfolds.

This conflict bursts out when Juliet meets Romeo. It is the authoritarian notion of scope of choice that makes clear that no compromise, mediation, or reconciliation will ever derive from their union, as the Friar will naively expect. Since no dialectic is allowed within that scope which is regulated by the authority of the father, the only radical choice they are left with is one of denial. Denying the 'other' means doing as if the 'other' did not exist. It does not mean staking oneself, but asserting selfhood and freedom in solitude. The paradox lies in the fact that in order to assert one's own freedom one has to free oneself *from* something (the 'other'), and, therefore, solitude may provide no actual dialectic, and, therefore, no freedom. In deciding from the start to escape confrontation, Romeo and Juliet evade this issue and paradoxically delude themselves into believing that secrecy may instead ensure it. This is an intermittent delusion, as the second balcony scene beautifully suggests, but it is enough to draw the contours of their basic choice. They know that if they conform to the family code and the feudal system of violence, they have to renounce the liberty to choose; if they opt for choosing, instead, they must defy that code. If they negate that code, they pre-empt the dialectic necessary for achieving freedom and posit it through its own negation. In the first case they renounce individuality, and accept to be acknowledged as belonging to the family and the city; in the second case they renounce the family and the city, but vindicate their own individuality; in the last case they only act *as if* they were free. The first two alternatives lead to no possible synthesis, the last one offers a compromise between the two as a way out of immanence through transcendence. Once defiance, which is immanent rebellion, is replaced with denial, which is revolt leading to transcendence, one goes beyond violence, but also beyond self-affirmation, as well as reconciliation. In so doing, they take upon themselves the responsibility of ignoring the other, overlooking the side-effects of this ignorance, as well as their own potential for being turned into the scapegoats they are not. Agonism failing, nihilism takes on in the name of radical denial: of names, family bonds, social system, ultimately, if necessary, metaphysical constraints, as well as the right to assert oneself freely and openly in the face of the 'other'.

This shift from a potentially defying attitude to one of denial, starting from the family bonds and names as markers of their civic attachment to a household, occurs very early in the play, in fact soon after the youths' encounter. In the first balcony scene, the word 'deny' punctuates Juliet's famous "what's in a name" speech, where it means refusing the names of Montague and Capulet alike (2.2. 33–6). A few lines later, Romeo wishes literally to "tear the word" if he had "it written" (l. 57). Writing as the locus of logos and power is targeted here to signify getting out of the social system of names, and yet transcending society and the town is no easy task. It has been remarked that "if the language of Romeo and Juliet, apart from ... lapses [such as Juliet's "bookspeak" as a Capulet when she thinks on Romeo the murderer of Tybalt in 3.2.73–85], hints at a journey beyond the prevailing ideology, the constraints implicit in the play's action leave them with nowhere to go, nothing to do except die" (Snyder 2007, 95). This has been seen as the accomplishment of a process of excommunication started with Romeo's banishment from Verona. Yet, it should be underlined that this banishment is not directed at the expulsion of the two lovers, while remaining its indirect cause. Rather, it is the reaction of the law to violence and its agonistic chain of defiances. As seen earlier, the Prince punishes Romeo the revenger of Mercutio involved in a street brawl originating in family feuding, not the lover and husband of Juliet and denier of names. This makes a difference in terms of the defiance/denial alternative and its dramatic and ontological outcomes, because the two stories Romeo and Juliet find themselves in are simply not manifest: no-one, except the Friar and the Nurse, knows that they are married; their secret agency implies doing *as if* the family and the social constraints were non-existent. They marry with no outspoken intention of reconciling the families (this being only a wish on the Friar's part), then meet cautiously after Romeo is banned, avoid confronting the fathers to the end, and finally plan to meet again outside Verona through the help of the Friar. Their transcendence concerns the family and the town alike.

Thus, while by banishing Romeo the law waves its blow against crime, it is unequal to the name-transcending language and logic of the two lovers. What may appear as the exemplary sacrifice of the criminal punished for the sake of the town's purification is in fact the result of the involuntary intersection between the law's repression of a side-effect of feuding as degenerate agonism and the two youths' secret agency, which impedes confrontation and consequent decision-making attuned to actual circumstances. In all this, chance (or heavenly design) scarcely plays a role, and Romeo's ban escapes the logic of scapegoating while being dependent upon the Prince's unexpressed reasons of leniency and ignorance of their secret actions.

BEYOND SCAPEGOATING: DEFIANCE AND/OR DENIAL

Scapegoats need to be recognized as guilty of some crime. Though no one makes them scapegoats intentionally, Romeo and Juliet are responsible for a crime which happens to be assimilated to the language of the feud-code in the name of violence. In the Friar's words, their too intense and rapidly sparked love is the sign of an unnatural behaviour that can only end violently. Loving too quickly and strongly means consuming their passion too fast, as he says in 2.6 before celebrating the secret marriage (ll. 9–15). This spokesman of Christian morality offers his censorious word on immoderate desire after foreboding punishment from above for the act that he is about to sanctify ("So smile the heavens upon this holy act / That after-hours with sorrow chide us not", ll. 1–2).[24] Divine judgement has thus been voiced through him, and this ominously opens to the possibility of retribution coming from above. All too easily ready to go beyond established ideologies and family codes, Romeo and Juliet may prove eager to make further radical choices; but this is not exactly what the Friar has in mind, because what he dreads is divine punishment for what they have already done with his own help. Laurence' fear of inflexible divine retribution for defiance of civic law, as opposed to the lovers' serenity in the face of God's law, already at this point marks a divide underlining the potential catastrophic effect of compromising between different behavioural paradigms. The youths' backing out of family codes does not entail their backing out of the religious codes presiding over their matrimony, which in fact they want 'holy', and to this end they secretly access the civic space of the church.[25] In their conforming to one code (the religious one) while ignoring its civil dimension, they open to the possibility that their denial may be taken as a defiance, either by God, as hinted at by the Friar, or by their own families once the marriage is made public according to the Friar's plan. It is in this rift that lies the potential for a scapegoating interpretation of the tragedy: the Friar expects retribution precisely because the marriage is secret to the city but open to God, and this divinely presided-over action, in his view, forcibly enters a transcendent retributive design. The divine design failing as a viable interpretation, there remains the concrete possibility of discovery, and breach of family prescriptions may have unpredictable consequences, including that of sacrifice in various ways.

By manipulating this old, but easily reconfigurable, scheme, Shakespeare in fact is posing a question of free will as an expression of conscious responsibility in respect to consequences of agency: to what extent is agency dependent on individual freedom, and what are the options available? What does it entail to conflate alternative and mutually irreducible paradigms of behaviour? To what extent will things go wrong as a consequence of the impossibility for agency to backing out of otherness, be it someone else, or Chance or Heaven? So far we have seen that the first event triggering a chain of reactions leading to the final catastrophe is the Prince's ban of Romeo, and his decree comes unawares of Romeo's bond with Juliet, causing marital separation besides civic exclusion. Up to this point no element of Chance or Fortune appears to be involved in the action. The sequence of events is clearly based on a logic of cause and effect, and this sequence starts with a first act of denial on Romeo's part. His initial covering up of his own identity to intrude into Capulet's house is no overt challenge according to the feuding code, but a way to wipe out his own face and name by doing *as if* he were a nobody. All the same, Tybalt takes it as a challenge instead, and there follows a sequence of further challenges (the formal letter, the challenge in 3.1 and the ensuing duels). In 2.1, Romeo and Juliet wish to deny their own names and afterward they go on negating the feuding-code by resorting to secrecy in getting married (2.6); then, in her famous soliloquy of 3.5, Juliet reverses all received *topoi* of female education and civility and attributes to "civil Night" the subversive function of teaching her sexual love rather than modesty (see Bigliazzi 2015b); finally, by repudiating domestic rule, she turns her own room, which belongs to the household, into the paradoxically transcending site of totalizing love. Denial of the other, whether it be a social code, family rule, household space, or even God, is a radical form of self-assertion which, compared to the logic of the challenge underlying the fight-to-the-death pattern, does not posit free individualization as an achievement, but as its premise. By assuming that I am freely myself in solitude, I may safely do as if the other were non-existent; I may safely make the other non-existent without killing the other. Going by this logic, ultimate denial will turn out to be self-denial as the extreme enactment of the denial of all ban, self-slaughter included. It is precisely when the sacrificial design requested by agonistic violence, as recounted by the Prologue, intersects this process of negative transcendence involving the two lovers that a rethinking of the tragic potential of the story becomes perceptible, entailing their solitary assumption of responsible choice.

There are two crucial scenes when this happens, and precede the moment when each of them commits suicide in the presence of the dead body of the beloved other, which will then make their decision not only irrevocable but also urgent. Before then, they experience the prospect of self-annihilation as a possibility to be faced, although they confront it with different frames of mind: Juliet consciously stakes her life by taking the potion without being sure of its effects in the hope of seeing Romeo in this life again; Romeo renounces his own life when he becomes aware that he will see Juliet no more. Albeit moved by different motivations, they likewise step outside the scope of all kind of predetermination and accept the (potentially tragic) burden of individual choice. Here is where Shakespeare reshapes its narrative source and makes out of it a wholly new drama of tragic self-denial.

The first to deal with a choice is Juliet. In 4.3 she confronts her fear of death before taking the potion in a soliloquy when, closely following Brooke, she passionately wavers between a desperate need to be freed from her freedom of choice, and the awareness that she must act alone "that dismal scene" (4.3.19), finally showing a resolute, masculine willpower that pushes her to drink the potion (l. 58). Then it is Romeo's turn. This occurs when he is misinformed about Juliet's death in a scene where, in the short space of a few lines, two opposed attitudes towards predetermination and freedom are put face to face. 5.1 opens on Romeo's self-deceiving dream of Juliet's arrival to find him dead and restore him to life with a kiss. A dream of final happiness. Only the first part will prove truthful, though, which marks for the first time a disaccord between Romeo and supernatural premonitions, which eventually confirms Mercutio's sceptical words on the insubstantial nature of dreams that had since very early undermined the validity of mysterious correspondences and designs (1.4.96ff.). Yet, even more deceiving, and fatally so, is Balthasar's denial of Romeo's expectations when he relates a false report of Juliet's death. It is the first time that, misled by both presentiments and agents of Chance or Fortune, Romeo faces the prospect of definitive solitude and loss, for which no compensation or mending is now possible. It is at this stage that he changes radically. The posing melancholy youth, later turned into a passionate lover caught between transcendence and immanence, denial and defiance, is finally at a dead end. The time has come to choose responsibly and discard all conditioning, including that of the stars:

> Is it e'en so? Then I deny you, stars! –
> Thou know'st my lodging. Get me ink and paper,
> And hire post-horses. I will hence tonight. (5.1.124–6)

Interestingly the two quartos here offer different solutions. The word 'deny' appears in Q2, while Q1 has 'defy'. Since Pope most editors have opted for Q1's reading, arguing that Romeo either curses the stars or challenges them with a more mature rebellious fury than in 3.3. Which is possible, of course. As John Dover Wilson contended in his 1955 Cambridge edition, "In 'defy' a tragic hero challenges the universe to do its worst; in 'deny' a philosopher 'repudiates' judicial astrology'" (Shakespeare 1955, 212). Later Gibbons, among others, expounded on this and embraced the defy variant:

> Evidently, Romeo admits the influence of the stars ("Is it even so?"). His hysterical reactions to news of his banishment in 3.3 ... might be a precedent for supposing him here equally hysterical, rather than the resolved, furious and defiant hero of 3.1.125–126: "Away to heaven respective lenity, / And fire-eye'd fury be my conduct now". Yet by this late stage of the play Romeo has clear awareness of the powerful influence of the stars; the parallel with 3.1.125–126 is striking: on receiving the news Romeo is death-defying. In Brooke Romeo's reaction to news of the banishment is "he cryed out (with open mouth) against the stares above" and "he blamed all the world, and all he did defye". Cf. Ham., 5.2.211: "we defy auguries". (Ibid., 218)

In turn, Atkinson has rightly pointed out that in Brooke's precedent "'defye' and 'the starres' ... remain some twenty lines apart" (at ll. 1347 and 1328, respectively), so that his inveighing against the stars has nothing to do with his "blam[ing] all the world" and his defying all ("and all he did defy", l. 1348) (1988, 50). It can also be added that if Romeo really anticipates Hamlet's defiance of auguries, as suggested by Gibbons, Romeo's challenge would turn out drastically to differ from what one would expect, because it would mean that Romeo trusts Providence beyond bad omens.

Strangely enough this is precisely what Ribner argues in order to support the deny reading in an attempt to reconcile the Christian framework with a stoical perspective: Romeo's denial of the stars, in his view, would be a casting off of fortune's "control as the child may cast off that of a father" in order to accept "death as the necessary end of man", thus supporting the stoical idea of "suicide as noble and heroic" for the sake of "rebirth of good" (Ribner 1960, 33). Although avowing that a "true Christian might not have committed suicide", he finally contends that

> the simple point which Shakespeare wishes to make is that Romeo has grown to maturity, has learned to accept the order of the universe with all it may entail, that he is ready for death, and that he can accept it bravely and calmly as the necessary means towards the greater good of reunion with Juliet. (Ibid., 34)

What sounds deeply wrong in this position is precisely this quietistic acceptance of death which locates Romeo within a tragic vision which, for Ribner, will be developed in later tragedies towards an achieved confidence in God's ultimate plan. This view is not only disputable in general, but here it is Romeo himself who says that he is a "desp'rate man" (5.3.59); and desperation has nothing to do with one's confidence in heavenly plans.

The deny variant, which I think plausible in Q2, is more sensibly supported by Atkinson, who argues in favour of "a new sense of personal responsibility for his actions at this moment of crisis", when in fact Romeo does not challenge the stars, but rather "rejects the idea that [the end] is supernaturally fated and takes it upon himself" (1988, 51). Consistently, Romeo goes straight to buy the poison and in 5.3 is ready to take upon himself the freedom to "shake the yoke of inauspicious stars / From this world-wearied flesh" (5.3.111–12). This decision is all his own, as he seems to hint at Paris when, threatened with death by him, shows indifference, because he has gone armed against himself to meet Juliet in the tomb (l. 65). At this stage, while Paris enters the violent circuit of murder and revenge, still enmeshed in a logic of defiance (but not for feuding reasons), Romeo is already beyond strife and ready to get free from the book of misfortune into which his name has been written alongside that of Paris (l. 82). It is only because Paris keeps challenging him ("I do defy thy conjuration, / And apprehend thee for a felon here", ll. 68–9), that Romeo responds to the provocation and is for the last time dragged into the circle of violence: Death at his own hands, at Juliet's side, is what he is after; no other death previous to his joining her in the solitude of his own death can be accepted. Anticipating Juliet's, this is meant to be his own self-affirmation through self-denial as the consequence of his radical denial of heavenly forbiddance of self-slaughter.

Romeo is clearly beyond the logic of conflict, as well as of 'uncivil civility', and it is with tragic irony that he eventually fulfills the stars' design, as recounted by the Prologue, by deciding to commit suicide; at this point he acknowledges his freedom to assert his own liberty through no challenge or social defiance, but through absolute negation (and self-negation). Atkinson again is right in reminding us of Cassius's realistic precept in *Julius Caesar* (1599–1600), a play which would follow soon after the publication of Q1 and Q2 (1597–1599): "Men at some time are masters of their fates. / The fault, dear Brutus, is not in our stars, / But in ourselves, that we are underlings" (1.2.140–2). Now Romeo wishes to be absolute master of his own fate, and this entails ultimate self-denial.

But what the defiance/denial alternative shows beyond doubt is that the deny reading here makes the action consistent to the end, fulfilling an idea of the tragic related to choice and a questioning of responsibility subtly encrusted on one of predetermined sacrificial ritual which forms only a blurred residue of old schemes providing the simplified frame of the action. For Romeo to deny the stars which he had sensed to be presiding over his fate from the very beginning, means eventually asserting himself master of his own choice and fate without staking it, but by claiming it; it means reaching the climax of a process of transcendence that follows from the denial alternative, and which fatally brings full circle the two lovers' impossible metaphysics of desire (Belsey 1993) as a form of self-individualization in the beloved one. This is the most radical change Shakespeare made to his source, where Fortune is never challenged by Brooke, as is instead the case here with a continuous alternation and tragic intersection between civic defiance and a-civic denial, immanence and transcendence.[26] Ironically, and tragically, Romeo's resolutely self-inflicted death accomplishes the ultimate sacrificial ritual that the narrative of the two star-crossed lovers requires of them from the start, situating a new sense of the tragic precisely in the crossing of boundaries between violence and transcendence, scapegoating and its denial. The illusion of absolute freedom and self-realization in death is its final tragic irony; the ultimate promise of the 'idolatrous' erection of golden statues mystifies their radical denial, celebrating within the boundaries of civic life all aspiration towards individual transcendence of civic space, in a competition to appropriate and commodify that transcendence into the sacrificial icons that Romeo and Juliet are not. The city has eventually expelled the scapegoats and translated them into the glorious symbols they need to erect for the community: two shining statues of pure gold. The scapegoating scheme has finally taken place in a 'post-sacrificial' space.

NOTES

1. For a insightful discussion of this issue see Reynolds and Segal 2005, 48; see also chapters 6, 7, and 12 in this volume.
2. Among some relevant readings, see Callaghan (2001, 92), who concentrates on the Protestant and Puritan construction of desire linked with economic instances, and on the political dimension of the play, showing that the "move from the family allegiances associated with feudalism to those identified with centralization of the state constitutes the overarching narrative of *Romeo and Juliet*"; Snyder (2007), instead, offers an Althusserian interpretation that demonstrates the ideological constraints of subjectivity, while Weinberger (2003) focuses upon the interrelation between religious and secular authorities.
3. References to *Romeo and Juliet* are to Shakespeare 2003, while those to Q1 are to Shakespeare 2011. All other quotations are from Shakespeare 1988.
4. The more conventional that design is, the more revolutionary the alterations in form and dramatic content appear. To this end a revision of formal and generic conventions is crucial, involving also what Colie calls the unmetaphoring of forms: "One of the most pleasurable, for me, of Shakespeare's many talents, is his 'unmetaphoring' of literary devices, his sinking of the conventions back into what, he somehow persuades us, is 'reality'". This makes conventional forms wholly naturalized, such as the *topos* of love at first sight: it "is here made to seem entirely natural ... its conventionality forgotten as it is unmetaphored by action" (1974, 145). On Shakespeare's revision of formal conventions and

Defiance and Denial 141

their relation with Brooke's source see for instance Laird 1964; Brisman 1975; Belsey 1993.
5. Cf. for instance Herman 2008.
6. The *OED* definition of "order; orderliness in a state or region; absence of anarchy and disorder" (n. 2), recasts older ones such as Thomas Wilson's own in the Preface to his *Art of Rhetoric* (1553), where he clarifies that it was precisely by the art of eloquence, as expression of man's reason, that people could start to live in cities: "Neither can I see that menne coulde have bene brought by anye other meanes to lyve together in felowshyppe of life, to mayntayne Cities, to deale trulye and willyngeye to obeye one another, if menne at the firste hadde not by Art and eloquence perswaded that, which they ful oft found out by reason (1553 A7r); see also Shrank 2003a and 2003b.
7. Household peace, as the counterpart of civic peace in town, wins over individual self-affirmation through enemy challenging, so that all attempt to go for a fight inside the domestic walls must be stifled.
8. "For some holde opinion, that the government of a master is a kinde of science, and that the authoritie of a master and Oeconomie, or ordering a familie, and the government of a Cittie or Common-wealth, and the kingly state and government are all one and of the selfe same kinde and nature: as wee haue alreadie touched at the beginning", Aristotle 1598, 21e. The first French edition, several times reprinted afterwards, dates from 1568. On the parallel between the master of the house and the Prince see Hunter and Lichtenfels 2009, 186–7.
9. "The noise here of anon throughout the town doth fly, / And parts are taken on every side;" (ll. 983–4).
10. "Ancient" qualifies the Nurse in Mercutio's sarcastic farewell to her as an "ancient Lady", 2.4.121, and in Juliet's curse: "Ancient damnation!". 3.5.235; besides, also the Friar's ears are "ancient" in 2.3.74: "Thy old groans yet ring in mine ancient ears".
11. Romeo is advised to leave the town either before the guard arrives or at dawn, 3.3.165–6; see also Brooke, ll. 1729–1732: "The weary watch discharged did hie them home to sleep / The warders and the scouts were charged their place and course to keep, / And Verone gates awide the porters had set open, / When Romeus had of his affairs with Friar Laurence spoken".
12. A kinsman to the Prince, Paris is called "a nobleman in town" by the Nurse, 2.4.145, a "noble earl" by Capulet, 3.4.21, who also defines him as a worthy gentleman whom Juliet does not deserve, 3.5.144, and "A gentleman of noble parentage, / Of faire demesnes, youthful and nobly lignéd", 3.5.179–80.
13. "The two families, at least to me, are not representative of aristocratic values but instead appear to be bourgeois intrusions into an older and rapidly disintegrating social order. They are not directly allied to the Prince and are therefore not of the ruling class. Escalus, for example, never addresses either family with a feudal title. The Capulets' servants describe their masters merely as 'rich' (1.2.81), and according to the invitations to the party, most of the Capulet guests are referred to as 'signor' (which Shakespeare used frequently as a nonspecific courtesy title in his Italian plays, giving it, for example, to Baptista in *The Taming of the Shrew*, Antonio in *The Merchant of Venice*, and Benedick in *Much Ado about Nothing*). There is nothing about the Capulets or the Montagues that is remarkable other than their wealth and shared hatred. That Escalus's family has sought an alliance with the Capulets could be attributed more to their wealth than to the desire of

Paris and his family to associate with one of the principal parties in Verona's civil unrest" (Gridley 2009, 92). See also Reynolds and Segal (2005, 58) where the Romeo and Juliet bond "bears the potential to bridge an alliance between two merchant households 'alike in dignity' (l.P.l)", and "[a]lternatively, Paris and Juliet's wedding was capable of producing a merger between merchant class and royalty". See also Eriksen's chapter in this volume.

14. For instance he recalls that "At the time of the Armada the National levies were assembled, but a corps of shock troops of 1,500 foot and 1,600 horse was supplied by the tenants and servants of the nobility and leading gentry. The letter written to the Queen by the Earl of Pembroke ... was as reassuring in its expressions of loyalty as it was alarming in its medieval implications ... It is a measure of Elizabeth's caution that, even in this great crisis of the reign, this offer of a sizeable private army was not accepted" (Stone 2008, 101).

15. Weinberger, in particular, blames the Prince's ineffectiveness and his reliance upon a popular militia "made up not of robust soldiers, but of *old men*, Verona's 'ancient citizens,' ... Brooke makes no mention of the militia ... By the end of the play, Verona, with a popular militia of old men and a soft Prince who depends on them and a decimated and effeminated aristocracy, stands defenseless before the world". This is why the "Veronese regime – made up of aristocrats, Prince, and people – is diseased, suffering as it does from an absence of vigor and defensive strength in all of its orders" (2003, 370, 371, 372).

16. In Clark's view "*Romeo and Juliet* anticipates the later tragedies in its recognition of the breadth and depth of subordinate disaffection for a social order in which the behavior of those who claim superiority has begun to appear unnatural or grotesque. To the extent that the play reveals the longing for something more comforting and more civil than hierarchy, it fails to stabilize any sort of dominance or coercion" (2011: 300). See also Fitter: "For the play's demystifying criticism of the city's ruling classes could claim to be a dutiful echo of higher authority, since its barbs echoed the ancient civil ideal of Commonweal paternalism shared by monarch, church, and Privy Council. *Romeo and Juliet* takes advantage of the contemporary conflict between levels and traditions of authority to establish its skeptical portrayal of the urban rich, since 1594–97 saw considerable friction between city leaders and the Crown" (2000: 182–3)

17. About Tybalt's Spanish technique and the fashion of duelling in the Spanish and Italian modes much has been written; see for instance Soens 1969; Holmer 1994; Levenson 1995; Limon 1995; Peltonen 2003; Hunter and Lichtenfels 2009.

18. "Therefore, a prince, so long as he keeps his subjects united and loyal, ought not to mind the reproach of cruelty; because with a few examples he will be more merciful than those who, through too much mercy, allow disorders to arise, from which follow murder or robbery; for these are wont to injure the whole people, whilst those executions which originate with a prince offend the individual only" (Machiavelli 1908, 133; chap. XVII, "Concerning cruelty and clemency, and whether it is better to be loved than feared").

19. See Sampson's preoccupation to "take the law of our side" in the first brawl, 1.1.33; see also l. 40 ("Is the law of our side if I say ay?"), as well as Peter's claimed readiness to "draw as soon as another man" if there is "occasion of a good quarrel, and the law on [his] side", 2.4.131-2.

20. By the 1590s several proclamations had been issued to ban duelling and unlawful assembly. Some of these documents may be found in Callaghan 2003; on the relation between sword-fighting and the Prince's role in banning them in *Romeo and Juliet* see also Hunter and Lichtenfels 2009, 188ff.
21. Which Snyder relates to Althusser's a-historical conception of ideology (2007, 88). "The feud", Snyder continues, "like ideology, flattens out personal differences, slotting individuals into predetermined roles" (ibid.).
22. "How much the Roman youth of parents stood in awe / And eke what power upon their seed the father's had by law?" (ll. 1951–2).
23. On the experiential values of metaphors see Lakoff and Johnson 2003. Of primary importance here is the metaphorical rendition of freedom in terms of spatial measure and boundary-setting which at the same time quantifies and limits free-will.
24. It should be recalled, though, that scene 9 in Q1 is radically different in showing a more joyful encounter between Romeo, Juliet and the Friar, who does not voice reprimands and calamities but hastens to make their happy: "Without more words I will do all I may / To make you happy, if in me it lie" (ll. 3–4).
25. In this respect, Reynolds and Segal (2005, 51) notice that "Romeo recognizes that in Verona's official culture Church blessings are required to legitimate his purchase through marriage, and therefore convinces the Friar to assist him in securing his possession with the 'holy words' (2.6.6) necessary for Romeo to 'call her mine' (2.6.8)". Besides, "That their union must be legitimized through 'the rite' of the official auspices of the Church, and thus recognized under God's law, is further evidence that their relationship, although in defiance of their families, remains delimited by the state-supporting ideological structures within which they have been reared" (ibid., 55–6). I only point out that this is not carried out "in defiance of their families", but in their denial, and that it is precisely this denying that causes misunderstanding and the consequent chain of tragic events, including the sacrificial-type of appropriation of their deaths upon which the play closes. Contradiction is further elucidated here in respect to Juliet, whose "decision to choose a mate rather than allow her father to assign her '[a] gentleman of noble parentage' (3.5.179) may be an act of rebellion against an earthly patriarchal order; yet, since she insists that her individual choice be legitimized by an official other and through conventional means, it reconfirms the conception of a hierarchy based on a heavenly father whose image is conducted through the offices of a Church whose higher purpose is to support the state" (56).
26. Cfr. Atkinson 1988, 52. He also notices that "Romeo and Juliet are among the very few Shakespearian characters to commit suicide outside of the classical world, and their conscious involvement in their own destruction is surely a part of the tragedy" (ibid.).

WORKS CITED

Amussen, Susan Dywer. 1995. "Punishment, Discipline, and Power: The Social Meanings of Violence in Early Modern England". *Journal of British Studies* 4 (31): 1–34.

Appelbaum, Robert. 1997. "'Standing to the Wall': The Pressures of Masculinity in *Romeo and Juliet*". *Shakespeare Quarterly* 48 (3): 251-72.

Aristotle. 1598. *Politiques or Discourses of Government. Translated out of Greeke into French ... by Loys Le Roy, called Regius, Translated out of French into Englishe by I.D.* London: Adam Islip.

Atkinson, David. 1988. "Romeo and Juliet V.1.24". *Notes and Queries* 35 (1): 49-52.

Belsey, Catherine. 1993. "The Name of the Rose in 'Romeo and Juliet'". *The Yearbook of English Studies* 23 (*Early Shakespeare Special Number*): 126-42.

Bigliazzi, Silvia. 2015a. "Chorus and Chorality in Early Modern English Drama". *Skenè. Journal of Theatre and Drama Studies* 1 (1): 101-33.

Bigliazzi, Silvia. 2015b. "Female Desire and Self-Knowledge: Juliet's Soliloquies in *Romeo and Juliet*". *Rivista di Letterature Moderne e Comparate* 3: 243-65.

Brisman, Leslie. 1975. "'At thy word': A Rereading of 'Romeo and Juliet'". *The Bulletin of the Midwest Modern Language Association* 8 (1): 21-31.

Brooke, Arthur. (1562) 1908. *Romeus and Juliet*. Edited by John J. Munro. New York: Duffield and Co. / London: Chatto & Windus.

Bryson, Anna. 1998. *From Courtesy to Civility: Changing Codes of Conduct in Early Modern England.* Oxford: Oxford University Press.

Callaghan, Dympna C. 2001. "The Ideology of Romantic Love: The Case of *Romeo and Juliet*". In Romeo and Juliet. *Contemporary Critical Essays*, edited by R.S. White, 85-115. Houndmills, Basingstoke: Palgrave Macmillan.

Callaghan, Dympna C., ed. 2003. *William Shakespeare.* Romeo and Juliet. *Texts and Contexts.* Boston and New York: Bedford / St Martin's.

Clark, Glenn. 2011. "The Civil Mutinies of *Romeo and Juliet*". *English Literary Renaissance* 41 (2): 280-300.

Colie, Rosalie. 1974. *Shakespeare's Living Art.* Princeton, NJ: Princeton University Press.

Fenton, Geoffrey. 1567. *Certaine Tragicall Discourses written out of Frenche and Latin.* London.

Fitter, Chris. 2000. "'The quarrel is between our masters and us their men': *Romeo and Juliet*, Dearth, and the London Riots". *English Literary Renaissance* 30 (2): 154-83.

Girard, René. (1977; 1988) 2005. *Violence and the Sacred.* London and New York: Continuum.

Gridley, Carl James. 2009. "'We're Everyone you Depend On': Filming Shakespeare's Peasants". In *Shakespeare and the Middles Ages: Essays on the Performance and Adaptation of the Plays with Medieval Sources or Settings*, edited by Michael Almereyda and Dakin Matthews, 89-104. Jefferson: McFarland.

Guazzo, Stefano. 1581. *The Ciuil Conuersation.* Translated by George Pettie. London: Richard Watkins.

Herman, Peter C. 2008. "Tragedy and the Crisis of Authority in Shakespeare's *Romeo and Juliet*". *Intertexts* 12 (1/2): 89-11.

Holmer, Joan Ozark. 1994. "'Draw, if you be Men'": Saviolo's Significance for *Romeo and Juliet*". *Shakespeare Quarterly* 45 (2): 163-89.

Hunter, Lynette, and Peter Lichthenfels. 2009. *Negotiating Shakespeare's Language in* Romeo and Juliet. *Reading Strategies from Criticism, Editing and the Theatre.* Farnham: Ashgate.

Kottman, Paul A. 2012. "Defying the Stars: Tragic Love as the Struggle for Freedom in *Romeo and Juliet*". *Shakespeare's Quarterly* 63 (1): 1-38.

Kottman, Paul A. 2014. "Duel". In *Early Modern Theatricality: Oxford Twenty-First Century Approaches to Literature*, edited by Henry S. Turner, 400–22. Oxford: Oxford University Press.

Laird, David. 1964. "The Generation of Style in 'Romeo and Juliet'". *The Journal of English and Germanic Philology* 63 (2): 204–13.

Lakoff, George, and Mark Johnson. (1980) 2003. *Metaphors We Live By*. Chicago and London: The University of Chicago Press.

Levenson, Jill. 1995. "'Alla stoccado carries it away': Codes of Violence in *Romeo and Juliet*". In *Shakespeare's Romeo and Juliet: Texts, Contexts, and Interpretation*, edited by Jay L. Halio, 83–96. London: Associated University Presses.

Limon, Jerzy. 1995. "Rehabilitating Tybalt: A New Interpretation of the Duel Scene in *Romeo and Juliet*". In *Shakespeare's* Romeo and Juliet: *Texts, Contexts, and Interpretation*, edited by Jay L. Halio, 97–106. London: Associated University Presses.

Machiavelli, Niccolò. 1908. *The Prince*. Translated by W.K. Marriot. London: J.M. Dent / New York: E.P. Dutton.

Martin, John Jeffries. 2004. *Myths of Renaissance Individualism*. Houndmills, Basingstoke: Palgrave Macmillan.

Moryson, Fynes. 1617. *Itinerary. Contayning His Ten Yeeres Travell*. London: John Beale.

Peltonen, Markku. 2003. "Civilized with Death: Civility, Duelling and Honour in Elizabethan England". In *Early Modern Civil Discourses*, edited by Jennifer Richards, 51–67. Houndmills, Basingstoke: Palgrave Macmillan.

Power, M.J. 1985. "London and the Control of the 'Crisis' of the 1590s". *History* 70 (230): 371–85.

Reynolds, Bryan, and Janna Segal. 2005. "Fugitive Explorations in 'Romeo and Juliet': Transversal Travels Through R&JSpace". *Journal of the Early Modern Cultural Studies* 5 (2): 37–70.

Ribner, Irving. 1960. *Patterns in Shakespearian Tragedy*. London: Methuen, 1960.

Richards, Jennifer, ed. 2003. *Early Modern Civil Discourses*. Houndmills, Basingstoke: Palgrave Macmillan.

Shakespeare, William. 1955. *Romeo and Juliet*. Edited by John Dover Wilson and George Ian Duthie. Cambridge: Cambridge University Press.

Shakespeare, William. 1980. *Romeo and Juliet*. Edited by Brian Gibbons. London: Methuen (The Arden Shakespeare).

Shakespeare, William. (1984) 2003. *Romeo and Juliet*. Edited by G. Blakemore Evans. Cambridge: Cambridge University Press.

Shakespeare, William. (2007) 2011. *The First Quarto of Romeo and Juliet*. Edited by Lukas Erne. Cambridge: Cambridge University Press.

Shakespeare, William. 1988. *The Complete Works*. Edited by Stanley Wells, Gary Taylor, with John Jowett, and William Montgomery. Oxford. Oxford University Press.

Shrank, Cathy. 2003a. "Civil Tongues: Language, Law and Reformation". In *Early Modern Civil Discourses*, edited by Jennifer Richards, 19–34. Houndmills, Basingstoke: Palgrave Macmillan.

Shrank, Cathy. 2003b. "Civility and the City in 'Coriolanus'". *Shakespeare Quarterly* 54 (4): 406–23.

Snyder, Susan. (1996) 2007. "Ideology and the Feud in *Romeo and Juliet*". In *Shakespeare Survey, 49:* Romeo and Juliet *and its Afterlife*, edited by Stanley Wells, 87–96. Cambridge: Cambridge University Press.

Soens, Adolph L. 1969. "Tybalt's Spanish Fencing in Romeo and Juliet". *Shakespeare Quarterly* 20 (2): 121–7.

Stone, Lawrence. (1967) 2008. *The Crisis of the Aristocracy 1558–1641*. Abridged edition. Oxford: Oxford University Press.

Stone, Lawrence. 1977. *The Family, Sex, and Marriage 1500–1800*, New York: Harper & Row.

Stow, John. (1598) 1842. *A Survey of London*. Edited by William J. Thoms. London: Whittaker and Co.

Weimann, Robert, and Douglas Bruster. 2004. *Prologues to Shakespeare's Theatre. Performance and Liminality in Early Modern Drama*. London and New York: Routledge.

Weinberger, Jerry. 2003. "Pious Princes and Red-Hot Lovers: The Politics of Shakespeare's *Romeo and Juliet*". *The Journal of Politics* 65 (2): 350–75.

Wilson, Thomas. 1553. *The Arte of Rhetorique*. London: Richardus Graftonus.

6 Tying the Knot in "fair Verona"
The Private and Public Spaces of Marriage in *Romeo and Juliet*

Lisanna Calvi

> ... stony limits cannot hold love out.
> (2.1.110)

THE CIVIC FUNCTION OF MARRIAGE

In his *The Arte of Rhetorique*, published in 1553, Thomas Wilson offered an example of persuasive rhetoric introducing an Englished version of Erasmus's 1518 *Encomium Matrimonii*, which he rendered as "An Epistle to perswade a young ientleman to Mariage".[1] The text pays much reverence to married life as a privileged state in life, as it is "more honest, more profitable, and also more pleasaunt ... to marie, than to lyve otherwyse" (Wilson 1553, 22). Also, the ancient Roman custom of bestowing civil offices only on married men is highly praised thus yoking this status with the public good of the "commune Weale" (ibid., 24). This same idea is further asserted in the "Epistle" through a distant reference to Psalm 127, which gets rhetorically coupled with the idea that marriage can prevent social disruption:

> A Citie is lyke to fall in ruine, excepte there be watchmen to defend it with armour. But assured destruction muste here needes folowe, excepte men throughe the benefite of Mariage supplie issue, the whiche through mortalitie, doe from tyme to tyme decaie. (ibid.)

The Geneva Bible itself would accordingly gloss the term "citie" (Psalm 127:1)[2] as "the publicke estate of the commune wealth" (2007, 263), alluding to the existence and condition of a town as a community of citizen. In the "Epistle" the ruin of an unguarded "citie" is equated to the renunciation of marriage, which is accordingly praised because of its public import and socially conservative function as an instrument of civic defence (Shrank 2003). It does not come as a surprise then that this idea of marriage is completely devoid of any reference to personal fondness or affection, let alone to love. If the scope of individual liking includes private needs and tastes and therefore implies the recognition of the role of subjective will, the conception of marriage as civic duty apparently curbs any individual partiality and gives back the idea of marriage as a sort of 'public benefit' for the exclusive sake of the community. However, despite the views provided by Erasmus (and Wilson), when it comes to the different reasons and manners that assisted the choice of a partner, the situation in early modern England was definitely not so black and white and indeed stressed a problematic "separation between socially approved behaviour and individual desire" (Hunter and Lichtenfels 2009a, 191).

Andrew Gurr has first drawn the attention to marriage as a recurrent dramatic theme in late Elizabethan drama and, with regard to *Romeo and Juliet*, argued that the play's "invocation of love was a serious challenge in a repertory much of which was based on settled ideas about arranged marriages" (1987, 195).[3] However, as James N. Loehlin justly foregrounds, if "stories of young lovers confronting parental opposition were familiar enough", they were "mainly limited to comedy" (2002, 5). The topic is here transferred into a tragic context as the play both echoes and challenges the contemporaries' "settled ideas" by introducing different concepts as well as different types of nuptials: Capulet's arranged union of his daughter with Paris, and of course Romeo's and Juliet's contract in the garden and their secret wedding. The topic of marriage problematically attends the staging of issues of power and control against paradigms of individuality, through the dramatization of the difficult intersection between parental authority over children and children's liberty of choice, which the characters – old Capulet, the Friar, and the protagonists themselves – unpredictably or capriciously endorse, deny, vindicate, or even exploit in order to satisfy the need for civic reconciliation in violence-ridden Verona. In a context of both crisis in the Renaissance conception of the subject and bourgeois unrest, such friction sets off an intricate and at times violent conflict between private and public issues. The two wedding contracts themselves (the one scheduled by the father and the one entered by Romeo and Juliet) trigger a dialectics of spaces, through an ambiguous intertwining of private-domestic and public-civic implications which opens up an intriguing outlook on the function of marriage at the turn of the sixteenth century and on the role an individual might or might not play with respect to it.

JULIET'S GETTING MARRIED

In Erasmus's dialogue "Colloquium Proci et Puellae" (1523), translated by Nicholas Leigh in 1568 as *A Modest Meane to Mariage*, Maria, the beloved, responds to her suitor's proposal by calling into cause parental consent: "I will tell you", she says, "what were a better way for us both. You shall treate with your Parents and myne, and with their will and consent let the matter be concluded" (1568, Ciii^v). Although, the woman adds, this procedure seemingly belongs to "olde time", she deems herself to be "not at liberty" (ibid.) to make a decision, and moreover supposes the marriage will be "more luckie, if it be made by the authoritie of … [the]

parents" (ibid., Ciii^r). Had Romeo and Juliet followed this piece of advice, their story might have been different or at least differently told. Back to Erasmus, though, the allusion to an "olde time" custom seems to imply that new traditions have set in, and that parental permission is therefore no longer necessary, albeit maybe advisable, in order to choose a spouse. During the sixteenth century, marriage regulations actually rested on shaky ground and civil authorities and divines alike hotly debated their substance and enforcement, leading to legal perplexity, with special regard to the question of parental consent. At the same time, as B.J. and Mary Sokol correctly remarked, the "[c]onfusion about spousals was a lively topic which often inspired Elizabethan or Jacobean playwrights" (2003, 15) who expatiated on it by making it serve different dramatic functions.

The contemporaries largely pondered over the question and mostly agreed that a perfect balance between authority and affection was tellingly hard to reach, although ideally advocated, as stated in the anonymous *Tell-Trothes New Yeares Gift* in 1593:

> ... it is most requisite that the children should have their free liberty in likinge, as the fathers had theirs in choosing. For as those matches are best, wher there is a mutuall agreement betweene parentes and their children, so do those for the most part, love best, that have the priviledge of choosing for themselves, My cheefest reason may bee drawne from contentment in love, which is satisfied with any thinge according to the saying Love hath no lacke. (A4^v)

If "Love hath no lacke", when marriage was concerned, the law was similarly faulty or at least defective. After the break with Rome in the 1530s, matrimonial regulations had remained virtually unchanged and, as Eric Carlson points out, "the Roman canon law of marriage ... survived virtually unchanged until the seventeenth century" (1994, 8). The Canons of 1585, confirmed and royally sanctioned in 1597, tried to put some order into the matter with special regard to secret marriages, celebrated without family consent but legitimate and legally binding: "The ministers shall not solemnize this marriage, without the consent of their parents or governours, who are hereby licenced to marry" (*Capitula sive constitutiones ecclesiasticae*, 1597, 23). The obtainment of a licence was accordingly subdued to parental consent, although it appears that the procedure was not sufficiently implemented and the problem remained virtually unsolved, as proven by the many complaints against unduly granted licences (i.e. without the assent of the family) and the dispensations for marriage without banns raised in the Commons after the enforcement of the Canons.[4] The issue was, therefore, rather popular in those days, and was also debated in academic disputations, at times leading to rather surprising verdicts. A set of anonymous Latin verses, probably published between 1585 and 1590 at Cambridge, clearly states that *Consensus parentum in contrahendis nuptus non est necessarius* [*Parental consent is not necessary to contract a marriage*]; and since forced love – it continues – is doomed to death, "parents may command but not forbid" (1585–90?, 27).[5] This kind of 'lawfully established', if partial, independence naturally clashed with coeval ideas about children as 'goods' whose destination hung upon parental decisions and wishes. This is the idea expressed by Barthelemy Batt in his *The Christian Mans Closet*, translated from Latin in 1581. The text is constructed as a dialogue and the main speaker, Theodidactus, states that "[a] daughter is another possession unto the father", therefore, disobedience is considered as a "detestable sinne" and those who "intangle them selves unto marriage without the consent of their Parentes" commit "not only great disobedience, but rather verie great madnesse" (1581, 76, 99). In this scenario, arranged marriages were ordinary business, although Batt himself raised some objections against the reasons that often lie behind certain choices:

> *Theodidactus:* ... Marrie thy daughter and so shalt thou performe a weightie matter: but give her to a man of understanding.
>
> *Amusus:* Truly it is very godly councel, if so be parents woulde alwaies beare it in remembrance: & follow it. But for the most part in the bestowing of their daughters & sonnes nowadaies, they rather regard wealth then wisedom, beautie, then bashfulness: fineness, then fidelitie or any other good gifts or qualities either of bodie or minde. (ibid. 8)[6]

Unwise matching could lead to the situation described by Charles Gibbon, writer and member of Cambridge University. Gibbon offered an interesting perspective on this question in a treatise he published in 1591 under the peculiar title of *A Work worth the Reading*. Structured as a fictional dialogue between Philogus and Tychicus, "two lovers of learning" (1591, 1), Gibbon's text raises the question "Whether the Election of the Parents is to be preferred before the affection of their Children in Marriage" (ibid.). Philogus supports the idea that parents should try to second their children's likings in the choice of a partner, whereas Tychicus, backing his argumentation with Biblical examples and norms, purports and justifies the absolute and lawful prerogative of parents over children. In fact, *Romeo and Juliet* echo both Philogus's and Tychicus's opinions. An imposed *mésalliance*, Tychicus says, means death for the bride:

> Alas, you doo not consider the innumerable inconveniences to those parties which bee brought together more for lucre than love, more for goods than good will, more by constraint than consent ... [and] such a marriage is the beginning of al miserie, and no doubt he that bestows his daughter no better, shall abridge her grief, by following her to the grave.
> (Gibbon 1591, 7)

Such an untimely ending is what Juliet envisages for herself in the play when the prospect of her wedding to Paris is disclosed to her:

> *Juliet.* Delay this marriage for a month, a week;
> Or if you do not, make my bridal bed
> In that dim monument where Tybalt lies. (3.5.199–201)

On the other side of the dispute, recalling Job's children, whose example was often quoted to substantiate the issue of parental authority over children, deemed to be as their father's own substance,[7] Philogus equals children to goods, therefore "a man may give ... [them] to whome hee will" (Gibbon 1591, 7). In 3.5 this instance is voiced, almost *verbatim*, by Capulet's retort to his recalcitrant daughter whom he considers as a piece of property he can dispose of at pleasure: "And you *be mine*, I'll *give you* to my friend." (191, my emphasis).

Gibbon's *A Work* once again demonstrates that when the choice of a spouse was concerned, the dividing line between individual liking and the family pick was rather hazy. "At every level of society", writes David Cressy, "the freedom of the couple to conclude their own affairs was counterbalanced by the interests of parents, kinfolk, and friends ... [and t]he tension between patriarchal authority and individual choice produced many domestic dramas" (1997, 235). If we take Lawrence Stone's model of the restrictive patriarchal and nuclear family (1979, 93ff.) as the representative of early modern households, it does not come as a surprise that strict obedience to parents was expected from children in every phase of their life; nevertheless it would be rather simplistic to depict sixteenth-century homes as exclusively ridden by oppression, constraint, and duress, and even though economic and dynastic reasons certainly played a significant role in matrimonial matters, selecting a mate was not solely aimed at satisfying a "pragmatic calculation of family interest" (ibid., 128).[8] In his *A Godly Form of Householde Government* (1598), Robert Cleaver describes spousal commitment as a "voluntarie promise ... mutually made betweene one man and one woman, both beeing meete and free to marry one another, and therefore allowed so to do by their Parents" (116). Parents did have share in the game, but – as Capulet would have it early in the play – their consent was "but a part" (1.2.17) of it. Cleaver further discusses the issue of 'voluntariness' and claims that "wee call this promise of marriage voluntary, because it must not come from the lippes alone, but from the wel-liking and consent of the heart" (ibid., 119). Nevertheless, if love between the betrothed was not flouted or brushed aside ("there must and ought to be a knitting of hearts, before striking of hands, ibid. 321) and forced marriages were heavily censured ("I crye out upon forcement in Marriage, as the extreamest bondage that is", Whetstone 1582, F1), marriages performed without the parents' consent were condemned as rash, unwise, and especially foreboding future unhappiness and bitter regret. Parents were consequently called to cool down foolish ardours and warn their children against imprudently entering a marriage only on the basis of infatuation or sexual ardour:

> ... every saucy boy, of ten, fourteen, fifteen, or twenty yeares of age, catch up a woman and marry her, without any feare of God at all, or respect had, either to her religion, wisdom, integrity of life, or any other virtue, or which is more, without any respect how they may live together, with sufficient maintenance for their callings and estate. No, no, it maketh no matter for these things, so he have his pretty pussy to huggle withal, for that is the only thing he desireth. ... This filleth the land with such store of Beggers, as we call them, that in short time (except some remedy be provided to prevent the same) it is like to grow to great poverty et extream misery, which God forbid.
> (Stubbes 1583, 65)

In the play, the secret marriage itself, although – as we will see – endorsed by the Friar because of its potential peacemaking outcome, is depicted as dangerously rash rather than passionately romantic, echoing the Book of Common Prayer's advice against too hasty unions.[9] Laurence himself early censures its foundations when he sententiously anticipates:

> *Friar:* These violent delights have violent ends,
> And in their triumph die like fire and powder,
> Which as they kiss consume. ... (2.5.9–11)

He calls for prudence and wisdom ("Wisely and slow; they stumble that run fast", 2.2.95) in front of Romeo's eagerness and his critical attitude severely resounds of Biblical echoes from Ecclesiastes 1:2, in the admonishment against vanity (2.6.20), but also from Proverbs 25:16 when he refers to honey's cloying sweetness:

> *Friar:* ... The sweetest honey
> Is loathsome in his own deliciousness,
> And in the taste confounds the appetite.
> Therefore love moderately: ... (2.5.11–14)

The Geneva Bible ("If thou have founde honie, eat it that is sufficient for thee, lest thou be overful, and vomit it", Proverbs 25:16) applies this metaphor to the "pleasures of this world" that one should "use moderately" (2007, 25:16[n]). Despite this censuring attitude, the Friar will later condemn Capulet's intention to have Juliet "married perforce ... / To County Paris" (5.3.238–9), which again voices contemporary 'instructions' to the parents. While they should try to ward off from their children the unpleasant consequences of a too hasty union, they likewise should not abuse their authority. In 1564, Thomas Becon, theologian and Church of England clergyman, spoke against imposed marriages, especially when dictated by financial reasons. In spite of the fact that mutual consent of bride and groom was necessary and could not be extorted or ignored,[10] parents, especially among the nobility, too often bullied their children into marriage.[11]

In the play, as in history, the two positions that have children bound to obey and parents instructed not to force them are ambiguously yoked together and prove hard to disentangle. The question of the arranged marriage with Paris, which articulates the expression of Capulet's paternal power, is the first to be called into question and is introduced in the play even before Juliet herself appears on stage. In 1.2, Capulet examines the Count's suit for Juliet's hand but honestly shows some reluctance at the prospect of marrying off his "child" too soon:

> *Capulet:* My child is yet a stranger in the world,
> She hath not seen the change of fourteen years;
> Let two more summers wither in their pride
> Ere we may think her ripe to be a bride.
> *Paris:* Younger than she are happy mothers made.
> *Capulet:* And too soon marred are those so early made.
> The earth hath swallowed all my hopes but she;
> She is the hopeful lady of my earth. (1.2.8–15)

Although old enough to be a bride (the legal age for marriage was set at 12 for girls and 14 for boys),[12] Juliet may be not ready to be a mother yet. The same piece of wisdom is actually echoed by William Vaughan in his *The Golden Grove*, published in 1600, in which parents are warned not to "marre their children by marrying them, during their minorities, neither cause them against their willes to be assured [i.e. engaged]" (1600, N8). Capulet actually hesitates in front of Paris's insistence for fear that his only daughter, who is also the only heir to his substance (that is, earth, land) and with whom lie his expectations of posterity as a grandfather ("of my earth", also means 'of my body', OED, 'earth', *n*.14a), could be ruined by a premature and potentially dangerous pregnancy.[13] Capulet 'plays by the rules', as it were, and wishes to act by consent rather than by constraint. The choice also depends on Juliet's agreement, to which – he says – "My will ... is but a part" (1.2.17). And yet, the girl's liberty to act (her "scope of choice", 1.2.18) is limited by his permission, his "according voice" (1.2.19) that seems here already favourably attuned to Paris's request, as he encourages him to woo Juliet and win her heart. In fact, the establishment of a dynastic alliance with a kinsman to the Prince would definitely enhance Capulet's social position and possibly earn him civic prestige as well as economic and political benefits.

As we have pointed out earlier, in Renaissance England the children's field of action was actually circumscribed within the limits imposed by their parents. It is again Thomas Becon who distantly echoes Capulet's words, when writing that "the chyldren be not so at their owne libertie, that they may do what they will; but rather so in the power of their parentes" (1564, xxiii^v).

Although tinged with fatherly protectiveness, Capulet's voice exerts patriarchal and economic power that curbs Juliet's autonomy and directs her action. Later on, oblivious of former concerns about age or opinion, he will ultimately curtail any autonomy by violently imposing his choices. The logic of civic and political convenience forcefully enters the territory of personal affection and short-circuits individual choices by fulfilling private ambitions and desires through public commitments and obligations. From the very beginning, Juliet's father seems to care for "more for lucre than love" (Gibbon 1591, 7) when looking for a potential son-in-law, and his wife, Juliet's mother, is no different from her husband and seems to care for "wealth ... [and] beautie" (Batt 1581, 8) above all things. In 1.3 she introduces to her young daughter the prospect of marrying Paris. According to Lady Capulet, by marrying Paris, whose face has been 'written' "with beauty's pen" (1.3.84), her daughter would have a portion in her husband's assets and prestige: "So shall you share all that he doth possess, / By having him, making yourself no less" (95–6), a thought vulgarly glossed by the Nurse ("No less, nay, bigger – women grow by men", 97). Juliet does not seem much impressed by the suggestion and, at her mother's insistence, plays the docile and bashful daughter:

> Lady Cap: Speak briefly, can you like of Paris' love?
> Juliet: I'll look to like, if looking liking move.
>   But no more deep will I endart mine eye
>   Than your consent gives strength to make it fly. (1.3.98–101)

She hides her reluctance behind the limits imposed by her parents' counsels and assent, showing she is aware of the rules by which children should abide but, at the same time, she also vindicates her own preference by yoking the "looking" to the "liking". From this point onwards, Juliet will in fact act her mind fully conscious of her feelings; she will independently commit herself totally to her love and her words (as well as Romeo's) will also bear a 'legally' tragic force.[14] In the so-called balcony scene, the two young lovers' exchange of vows is interestingly similar to what was defined as "spousals", that is, "a mutual Promise of future Marriage, being duly made between those Persons, to whom it is lawful" (Swinburne 1686, 5). Although overwhelmed by the suddenness of passion, Juliet pronounces a formally correct and binding promise:

> Juliet: Three words, dear Romeo, and good night indeed.
>   If that thy bent of love be honourable,
>   Thy purpose marriage, send me word tomorrow,
>   By one that I'll procure to come to thee,
>   Where and at what time thou wilt perform the rite,

And all my fortunes at thy foot I'll lay,
And follow thee, my lord, throughout the world. (2.1.185–91)

Her words, spoken in the future tense ("all my fortunes at thy foot I'll lay, / And follow thee my lord ..."), sound as a promise *per verba de futuro*, which occurred "[w]hen the Parties contracting Spousals do use words of future time" (Swinburne 1686, 56). This kind of matrimonial promise signalled "the entrance and beginning of Marriage" which became effectual and binding after it had been sanctioned by a Church minister, who, through marriage, made "the Man and the Woman ... one flesh" (ibid. 16) or, as Friar Laurence has it, "holy church incorporate two in one" (2.6.37). The secret marriage is afterwards further and irrevocably sanctioned by the night-time sexual encounter between the newly-weds, which Juliet eagerly awaits. In her "Gallop apace" monologue (3.2.1ff.), she voices the wholly personal dimension of a love which no one is allowed to talk of or see: "Spread thy close curtain ... and Romeo / Leap into these arms, untalked and unseen" (ll. 5–7). This love, whose "rites" (l. 8) are performed behind closed doors and veiled by night, is sacred and sealed by its very privacy and this emphasis on the consummation of love and marriage into an emotionally private space clashes with the parents' idea of marriage as an instrument of preservation of an established social order. Indeed, another contract is soon to be agreed upon, and it will overtly speak the language of patriarchal and economic power. In 3.4, after avowing that he has not found the time nor the occasion to talk to Juliet because of Tybalt's untimely death, Capulet ventures into speaking for her: "Sir Paris, I will make a desperate tender / Of my child's love. I think she will be rul'd / In all respects by me; nay, more, I doubt it not" (3.4.12–14). His intention was in fact to "move" (l. 2) her, that is, to persuade her (*OED*, 'move', v26.a and 26†d), but his status as *pater familias* induces him to give Juliet's abidance to his will for a fact. His "child's love" accordingly becomes a "tender", which means a formal offer, especially of money (*OED*, $n^2$1a and b). Capulet's words reveal the economic value of love, which is here almost equated to currency in what looks more and more like a commercial transaction. Besides, we could even assume that Capulet's haste in having Juliet married into the Prince's family were dictated by the contingency of Mercutio's and Tybalt's deaths. We may expect that these killings will rekindle the feud, therefore, not only may an advantageous dynastic alliance with Escalus expand the Capulets' social prestige, but also possibly protect them from civic penalty and further retaliation.[15]

The voice of paternal power suitably becomes a "decree" (3.5.137), a term Shakespeare probably got from Brooke,[16] but which is significant here as it veils the abuse of authority with a lawful hue which makes him the domestic homologous of the Prince and its civic authority and function as law-giver. Capulet's decision is meant to have the force of law, and it is a law to which there is no amendment. Individuality is completely crushed, and Juliet's will is ultimately debased to that of an animal. She is compared to a horse that needs to be groomed or fettled ("But fettle your fine joints 'gainst Thursday next", 3.5.152) or to a pasturing sheep abandoned in the field ("Graze where you will, thou shall not house with me", 3.5.188).

In front of her father's hardheartedness, Juliet turns to Friar Laurence who will devise for her the notorious potion plan. Once she returns to her father, she plays the meek and obedient daughter and speaks the words Capulet wishes to hear:

> Capulet: How now, my headstrong, where have you been gadding?
> Juliet: Where I have learned me to *repent* the sin
> Of *disobedient* opposition
> To you and your *behests*; and am *enjoined*
> By holy Laurence to fall *prostrate* here
> And *beg your pardon. Pardon*, I beseech you.
> Henceforward I am ever *ruled* by you. (4.2.15–21, my emphasis)

Her speech is overcrowded with allusions to disobedience and command and she appears now as completely bereft of her willpower. Her disobedience is a sin of which she has repented; she falls on her knees before her father, not to beg him to free her from hateful nuptials, as she has done before, but to be pardoned and "ruled" (l. 21) by him. In fact, she engages here in an equivocal manipulation that makes use of the vocabulary of submission with the actual intent to fake it. Being legally married to Romeo she cannot be "ruled" by anyone but her husband; besides, she is only performing a part in a metatheatrical game she will carry on until her simulated poisoning in 4.3. Juliet's newly found conformity to the contemporary urging of filial obedience is of course make-believe, as she seemingly complies with her father's intentions and desires. To make it more credible, her discourse even resounds of Capulet's words ("I think *she will be ruled* / In all respects *by me*", 3.4.13–14; "Henceforward *I am* ever *ruled by you*", 4.2.21, my emphasis) and such mimicking voids the strength of paternal power, which is critically emptied of its authority both from a legal (Juliet is not a daughter anymore, but a lawfully wedded wife)[17] and performative point of view in that she is faking her repentance; indeed, the artificial nature of her plead emerges when she rhetorically encloses it into the formalized structure of a chiasmus:

> To *beg* your *pardon. Pardon*, I *beseech* you.

In the end, though, no power will have its final say and death and general woe will set everything at zero. No claim, no legal bond or parental rule eventually prevail and the dispute over paternal authority *versus* children's self-determination remains unsolved and laden with dreary ambiguity.

"TO HAVE HER MATCHED": THE PRIVATE AND PUBLIC SPACES OF MARRIAGE

As we have seen, in *Romeo and Juliet* the question of 'making a match' invests and gives rise to a set of problems that span from the role of patriarchal rule and its conflict with the emergence of individual will and likings in younger generations to the discussion of passion and responsibility; however, the issue of marriage seemingly mirrors some further and possibly more complex interweaving of diverse and ever conflicting intentionalities. This blurs the distinction between the categories of private and public causing a tension/interaction between domestic and civic spaces. Indeed, the two nuptial contracts – the one scheduled by old Capulet and the one entered by Romeo and Juliet – trigger what we may term as a dialectics of spaces, with special regard to where marriage is talked of or 'performed', that is, Capulet's house and the adjacent orchard and Friar Laurence's cell. These spaces in particular betray some ambiguity in their private and civic implications: the Capulets mansion, where Juliet is 'given' to Paris, is a private and domestic space, but at the same time it opens itself towards a civic perspective of political and economic rules and visibility. The 'verbal' contract Romeo and Juliet pronounce takes place in the liminality of the garden, a hard-to-reach, open-air yet walled space, private and yet crucially close both to the house and to the streets. The Friar's cell, where the secret nuptials are celebrated, is again a closed area, but it hosts the representative of a civically recognised authority, that is, the Friar and the Church, from which – as we have argued above – derives the celebration of a publicly valid undertaking.

As Riitta Laitinen and Thomas Cohen have justly emphasized, "amidst so many early modern changes in conceptions of personal and shared, secret and open, and domestic and communal, 'public' and 'private' have proven useful terms, demanding caution but difficult to avoid" (2009, 4). But how did the contemporaries view the spaces they lived in, especially the domestic or 'para-domestic' ones (such as the garden) in which the marriage dynamics take place? In his seminal study on the social and cultural evolution of family and household systems in England from the Renaissance to the eighteenth century, Lawrence Stone argues how the "most striking change in the life-style of the upper classes in the seventeenth and eighteenth centuries was the increasing stress laid upon personal privacy" (1979, 169). Indeed, a changing conception of housing, starting as early as in the fifteenth century, played a fundamental role in this process. Some ten years after Stone, Philippe Ariès pointed out how:

> [a]fter remaining fairly stable from 1100 to 1400, housing began to undergo a complex series of changes that have continued up to the present day. The size of rooms was reduced. Small rooms first appeared as annexes to main rooms, as offices or alcoves but soon most activity was concentrated in them and they took on a life of their own. (1989, 6–7)

This phenomenon[18] apparently goes hand in glove with William G. Hoskins's debated notion of Great Rebuilding which he referred to the architectural improvement and modernization of houses that took place in England between 1570 and 1640.[19] According to Hoskins, this transformation was mostly due to economic reasons (i.e. a greater monetary abundance among the gentried classes), but also to an increasing need for privacy, and "privacy demands more rooms devoted to specialist uses" (1953, 54). This tendency has been discussed and freshly foregrounded by recent studies, too. Among the others, Nicholas Cooper has suggested that this architectural shift towards domestic spatial exclusivity is due to "a mental climate that was increasingly concerned with the cultivation of the individual and with the enjoyment of privacy as a good" (1999, 300). In fact, Hoskins himself offered a vivid description of a typical refashioning of a fifteenth-century hall-house, which does not appear to be too distant from how Elizabethan audiences may have pictured Capulet's house interior:

> This reconstruction usually took the form of inserting a ceiling in the medieval hall, formerly open to the rafters, so producing a living room and parlour on the ground floor and bedrooms above. This necessitated in turn the making of a staircase leading to the bedrooms, itself a major structural alteration. (1953, 45)

This new space, the parlour, would testify to the shift towards a growing specialization in the uses of rooms and "a concomitant increase in the attainment of privacy" (Cooper 1999, 273). Indeed, physical seclusion was not the only concern and, by focusing on interior spaces, these structural changes entailed not only an increasing privatization of domestic areas but also contributed to the growth of the concept of selfhood or, we should say, inwardness as the fertile ground for the birth of the individual subject.

If Tudor homes obeyed to Hoskins's configuration, Capulet's parlour could very well be the imagined setting for 1.2 and 3.4,[20] when he and Paris discuss Juliet's marriage before the feast, and later on 'seal the deal' and fix the wedding for the following Thursday. But should (individual) privacy be considered the 'specialized' use of the parlour-space in the play? The answer unsurprisingly presents some ambiguous turns. In 1.2, Capulet's apparent resistance to Paris's request of Juliet's hand shows his concern with his young daughter's feelings and betrays a perhaps unsuspected leaning towards fatherly affection ("Earth hath swallowed all my hopes but she", 1.2.14). He appears reluctant to disrupt his domestic and familial circle, even the privacy of it, by giving away his only daughter. Unwilling to let his child go, as it were, he (with tragic irony) equates her wedding to his other sons' funerals. At the same time, by alluding to her "scope of choice" (l. 18), if limited by his authority, he seemingly wishes to foster her individuality which may further mature only if nurtured, for a couple of years more, in the privacy of his own home. Nevertheless, a prospective marriage, its social and, therefore, public dimension and its implications of civic visibility – Paris is not only a noble and probably wealthy suitor but also related to the Prince – are soon to invade the private sphere of family life and its spaces. Later in the play Capulet will change his mind and abruptly decide to have his daughter hastily "married to this noble earl" (3.4.22). Juliet's "scope of choice" (1.2.18) is drastically pronounced null and void, and a date is set without even hearing her preference. This harsh imposition of a father's will takes place most likely in that same parlour that hosted his tender worries about age, courtship, and consent. Juliet is absent in both scenes (1.2. and 3.4), but while in 1.2 the attention is concentrated on her as a potentially active, if naive, protagonist in matters of courtship ("*My child* is yet a stranger to the world", "*She* hath not seen", "*her* ripe to be a bride", "all my hopes but *she*, / *She's* the hopeful lady", "woo *her* ... get *her* heart, / My will to *her* consent ... / And *she agreed*, within *her* scope of choice ...", ll. 8–18), in 3.4 she is completely 'objectified' as the totally passive receiver of someone else's actions: "*I will make* a desperate tender of my child's love", "*she will be ruled / In all respects by me*", "*bid her* ... – on Wednesday next –", "*She shall be married* to *this* noble earl" (12–23). Juliet has lost all rights and may only abide by her father's decision. As already pointed out, in 3.4 Capulet seems to be managing a commercial transaction whose economic, social, political, and therefore exclusively public effects penetrate the domestic space of the parlour and open it up to the logic of civic convenience. The business dynamics of the *piazza* is applied here to the stipulation of a marriage contract,[21] blurring the boundaries of this private space. Its former 'inward-oriented' purpose (the endearing of Juliet's heart) is definitively erased and transformed into an 'outward-oriented' one (the earning of a high-status son-in-law). Indeed, the staging of this twofold perspective problematically records the very historical nature of Renaissance domestic spaces. In her study on the early modern conception of privacy, Lena Cowen Orlin explores the multi-functional nature of an interior space such as the parlour. Much as it was naturally inclined towards the attainment and preservation of domestic intimacy, the parlour was also a "showpiece" space (2008, 109). If, as Hoskins hypothesized, the Great Rebuilding was a consequence of a demographic and economic improvement, "people who accumulated more possessions needed space in which to employ, store, display, and enjoy them" (Cowen Orlin 2008, 105). Eager to add a socially prestigious and politically advantageous alliance to his wealth, Capulet showcases his most precious commodity (i.e. his daughter) letting his civic ambitions and public meanings penetrate and act inside his own house. Therefore, as Louis Montrose has argued, the domestic "is not a place apart from the public sphere so much as it is the nucleus of the social order" (1996, 96) and the patriarchal decrees that govern it not only mirror the pyramidal order that controls the city, but also the new value on economic power that attended the birth of modern 'proto-bourgeois' society.

While the marriage negotiations carried out in the parlour dramatize the public capacity of a private sphere, another contiguous and yet separate area of the house will be the privileged space that the lovers elect as the original abode of their own concurrent marital pledges: the garden. The early modern garden, located "immediately beyond betraying internal walls", was conceived as the best place "for the pursuit of private conversation" (Cowen Orlin 2008, 232-3). In fact, if compared to indoor spaces, often inhabited by inconveniently loquacious servants – as would be the case with Juliet's garrulous Nurse – gardens offered greater opportunity for both privacy and secrecy. And this is exactly what Romeo and Juliet look for when they reach for the Capulets' orchard in 2.2.[22]

Open-air and penetrable but also guarded by hedges and walls,[23] the garden hosts in its liminality the "erotic explosion" – as Mera J. Flaumenhaft has it in this volume – of young love. The logic of the feud would have Romeo killed by Juliet's kinsmen and the one of convenient marriage alliances, pursued by Juliet's father in the parlour, would bar their union but in the moonlit garden names are forgotten and love becomes absolute. Nevertheless the place is no idyllic retreat. Hard to reach and potentially deadly, it is threatened by the code of violence that rules the streets of Verona:

> Juliet: The orchard walls are high and hard to climb,
> And the place death, considering who thou art,
> If any of my kinsmen find thee here. (2.1.106-8)

Moreover, it is also encircled by the logic of submission to parental requests, here possibly voiced by the Nurse's calling her young mistress from within. However, both codes are discarded. Romeo penetrates the walls of the garden, potentially disrupting the truce imposed by the Prince, and Juliet ignores the 'logic of acquisition' that earlier on her mother and the Nurse herself applied to love and marriage. Juliet rejects this perspective and in the space of one night, her love grows deep and unreserved, and eventually voices a promise of unconditional devotion: "And all my fortunes at thy foot I'll lay / And follow thee, my lord, throughout the world" (2.1.190-1), she says, echoing the ancient Roman wedding formula *ubi tu Caius ego Caia*.[24]

In the space of the garden, Romeo and Juliet carve out a niche for themselves and find a voice of their own.[25] As Mary Thomas Crane pointed out in an illuminating article on early modern gardens, despite the "deep-seated cultural reasons for our tendency to connect enclosure ... with the shaping of the subject ... outdoor spaces might provide a more open and liberating environment for the formation of the self" (2009, 7). This is what happens to the young Veronese lovers who, in an area so dangerously close to the patriarchally ruled parlour and the riotous streets of Verona, build up a space of independence going well beyond the scope they would be allowed.

Yet the promise they exchanged in the garden needs to be formalized by means of a proper, albeit clandestine, celebration.[26] The ceremony is not performed on stage, but the way in which the different characters view and interpret it is enough to make it into a site of contention between private and public issues and expectations.

Marriage inherently and culturally implies the mutual commitment of the couple in front of society, entailing lawfully established reciprocal duties and, as James L. Calderwood justly observes, "although love itself may be a fine and private thing marriage is by nature public" (1971, 95); therefore, despite its secrecy, Romeo and Juliet's union places them, as husband and wife, into a public dimension. Significantly enough, the space in which this action is undertaken is once again one of private-public hybridity. The Friar's cell, where the secret nuptials are celebrated, is a sheltered and exclusive area, not freely accessible (as a church would be) and devoted to personal prayer and individual confession. These functions primarily shape it as a private and almost secretive space in which inner thoughts and feelings may be safely revealed either through devout and intimate worship or sacramental penance. Nevertheless, this same space hosts the representative of a public and civically active authority. The Friar is revered by both households (Laurence is made privy of both Romeo's and Juliet's secrets throughout the play), and by the Prince himself, who acknowledges his much respected role in Verona: "We still have known thee for a holy man" (5.3.270), he will declare.[27] Indeed, when he agrees on Romeo's request ("That thou consent to marry us today", 2.2.64), Laurence's aim, although performed in the private and literally cloistered space of his cell, inhabits a wholly public and namely civic sphere. He does not act out of sympathy with young love, nor to save Romeo from wantonness – although he had earlier worried about him spending the night with Rosaline (2.2.44). In fact, he seconds the marriage plan because, in spite of its rashness, Romeo's union with Capulet's daughter could eventually quench the feud and the names that Romeo and Juliet had scoffed off in the orchard are irresistibly reasserted:

> *Friar:* In one respect I'll thy assistant be:
> For this alliance may so happy prove,
> To turn your households' rancour to pure love. (2.2.90–2)

As Jerry Weinberger remarks, "the friar is willing to offer the children as hostages to fortune, for the sake of possibly uniting the city by means of their love" (2003, 356). His plan proves to be a recipe for disaster. Of course fortune and fate have a hand in what happens next, but the tragic outcome of the story may also be ascribed to a conflict between two different conceptions of love and marriage: public/civic on the one hand and private on the other. The Friar's plan to transform a private bond of love into an instrument of civic appeasement may in fact have sounded reasonable enough to the contemporaries in that it echoes a common attitude towards marriage. The same was made into a tale in "The woorthy Historie of Phrigius and Pieria", a short prose account of Plutarchian derivation included in

George Whetstone's *Heptameron* (1582). The "woorthy Historie" tells how the love of princes Phrigius and Pieria, begun in the civic space of Diana's temple, is exploited by Lord Miletus, counsellor to the Ionian Duke Nebeus, to stop the protracted hostility between the cities of Miletus and Myus: "… in this love he foresaw an end, of the ancient envie and enmitie, betweene the Cittizens of Miletum and Myos: whose civill Fraies, had buried more young men in the Fieldes, then aged in the Churches and Churchyardes" (1582, Y.iv^v). The solemnization of the marriage is here civically endorsed and corresponds to the issuing of "an Edict of Amyty" (ibid., Zii^v), unanimously applauded and celebrated by "Nobles", "Gentlemen", "Citizens", "Cleargy", and "common people" alike (ibid., Ziii^r).

In the same way, the Friar does not approve of Capulet's rushing his daughter into a forced marriage with Paris, which not only would put him into trouble because he has just celebrated the girl's marriage with another man, and a Montague, but also imply the disruption of that civic harmony he seems so eager to achieve. Indeed, the parents' duress in disposing their children's choices could equally produce discord within the family but also in the community. As George Whetstone once again warns, a forced union engenders hatred between bride and groom and:

> … hatred between the Married, breedeth contention betwixt the parents, contention betwixt the parents, raiseth quarrels among the kindred, and quarrels among the kindred, occupieth all the neighbours with slander. (1582, Fii^r)

This is exactly what Friar Laurence wishes to avoid; still his view stands at odds with the conception of love and marriage the two young lovers voice in the play. When the wedding is about to be celebrated, impatient Romeo urges the Friar to carry on with the rite since "… love-devouring death do what he dare, / It is enough I may but call her mine" (2.5.7–8). The emphasis is on the exclusive and all-important possession of the loved one; no other concern is taken into account, not even life itself, as death would be nothing compared to the loss of Juliet. The same sentiment can be found in 3.3, when Romeo equates banishment to death since it bereaves him of Juliet's presence. Significantly enough, the Friar announces the Prince's decision to banish Romeo as a "gentler judgment" (l. 10), possibly because it does not mar his civic intent. Contrariwise, Romeo's perspective is devoid of any public implications. The compass of Verona's walls, outside which "there is no world" (l. 17), becomes in his eyes a private space whose boundaries are defined by his love for Juliet and the space of her embrace overlaps and engulfs any other space, and ultimately the whole city.

Nevertheless Friar Laurence's plan will somehow eventually work and Verona's warring families will achieve reconciliation in the gloomy space of the tomb, but this will come at the cost of erasing the private dimension of love as Romeo and Juliet had lived it. Eternized in gold (the statues) and narrative ("For never was a story of more woe", 5.3.309), their love will ultimately, if dolefully, play a civic role of appeasement. Yet this closure is veiled with ambiguity. After the Friar has finished his sad recapitulation of misfortune and death and old Montague and Capulet have shaken their hands in front of their children's dead bodies, the final cues are given to the Prince:

> *Prince:* A glooming peace this morning with it brings;
> The sun for sorrow will not show his head.
> Go hence to have more talk of these sad things;
> Some shall be pardoned, and some punishèd.
> For never was a story of more woe
> Than this of Juliet and her Romeo. (5.3.305–10)

He talks of peace, forgiveness, punishment, and woe but this closure sounds disturbingly artificial and "highly formalized" (Bigliazzi 2012, 337) in its being contained into a six-line stanza, rigidly disciplined by a rhyme scheme (ababcc). This stylization seems to agree with the promise to realize two statues – carved resemblances of the two lovers – earlier pronounced by Capulet and Montague in order to honour their children's sacrifice.

For sure their initiative may be interpreted as a symbolic seal of reconciliation between the feuding families or even as a monumental celebration of love. As James L. Calderwood has it, "if their [Romeo and Juliet's] love has aspired to a lyric stasis, here too in the fixity of plastic form is that stillness" (1971, 117). In fact, while an aspiration of "lyric stasis" could possibly fit Romeo's unrequited infatuation with Rosaline, which he had early voiced in stiff Petrarchan "numbers" (2.3.37–8), what he shared with Juliet was indeed no stasis but a sudden and prodigious passion, which overwhelmed their hearts, overwrote their very identities, tinged their desire with erotic anticipation and endowed their actions with impatient expectancy (2.5.3–8 and 3.2.1–31).

In the unhappy site of the tomb, whose liminal capacity of dividing the living and the dead is here almost subverted in a world in which the young are survived by the old, we are presented with the last act of what is still a business mediation. The funeral mausoleum, private in that it piously hosts the bodies of the deceased members of a family and stands as a cenotaph of the survivors' grief, is also public in its monumental display of genealogic antiquity and social position, and Juliet herself describes it as "… a vault, an ancient receptacle, / Where for this many hundred years the bones / Of all my buried ancestors are packed" (4.3.38–40). With regard to post-Reformation burial practises, David Cressy points out:

> The Elizabethan and Stuart élite continued to use their churches as mausoleums, … to assert the lineage and status of the living. … Premium placement, with appropriate memorial masonry, would demonstrate to posterity the position one held in this world. (1997, 460–1)

Family tombs then functioned as "a striking reminder of power, continuity, and cohesion" (ibid., 462). In his *Ancient funerall monuments within the united monarchie of Great Britaine* (1631), an historical overview of burials and funeral monuments since early medieval times, John Weever wrote: "Sepulchres should bee made according to the qualitie and degree of the person deceased, that by the Tombe every one might be discerned of what ranke hee was living" (1631, 10). By giving their children a static memorial or possibly a properly adorned burial place[28] the parents wish to exalt, perhaps even parade, their children's (and their own) rank. As Peter Sherlock points out in his study of funeral memorials in early modern England, "monuments made claims about a person's heraldry, genealogy and hereditary rights to improve the status of the families they represented" (2008, 4). In fact, this is exactly what Romeo and Juliet tried to overrule by erasing their own names as the verbal symbols of enmity and unmotivated hatred. Moreover, perpetuating the remembrance of the dead as a permanent memorial for future generations sounds like a rather sterile, hollow, and self-referential display since there will be no posterity for either Montague or Capulet.[29] Yet the two fathers seem strangely oblivious of this bleak predicament and they carry on their scheme pursuing their usual exchange logic and transform the enclosure of the tomb into a civic space of (commercial) negotiation that reminds of what had earlier gone by in the parlour:

> *Capulet:* O brother Montague, give me thy hand.
> This is my daughter's *jointure*, for no more
> Can I demand. (5.3.296–8, my emphasis)

Capulet's reference to Juliet's "jointure", either her dowry or her dower,[30] while implicitly acknowledging her marriage with Montague's son, monetizes his loss and casts a veil of ambiguity on peace itself whose price is equated to a sum of money. He had previously equated her love to an offer (a "tender", 3.4.12) and now measures her death in terms of an economic settlement. The private dimension of the tomb is utterly muted and is now ruled/violated by profit-making dynamics becoming the site for a civic display not of memory but of wealth:

> *Montague:* But *I can give thee more*;
> For I will ray her statue in *pure gold*,
> That whiles Verona by that name is known,
> There shall no figure *at such rate be set*
> As that of true and faithful Juliet.
> *Capulet:* *As rich* shall Romeo's by his lady lie,
> Poor sacrifices to our enmity.
> (5.3.298–304, my emphasis)

The rich materiality of "pure gold" – earlier despised as poisonous by Romeo himself (5.2.80) – refers both to the wealth of Montague and "great rich Capulet" (1.2.82) and the durability of the patriarchal power that Juliet especially tried to resist. Metal, precious and durable, will assure its worth ("rate") against devaluation and yoke its permanence to that of Verona itself.[31] Truth and faithfulness are given a solid value[32] and the two fathers actually seem to compete over it ("I can give thee *more*", "*As* rich ...") as if, possibly still mindful of their rivalry, neither of them wanted to be inferior to the other. The statues carry out the incorporation of the represented subject into a category of typification: in Juliet's case, of epitomized female 'loyalty and faithfulness' to be set as a model in front of the whole city. Crystallized into their sculpted likenesses, Romeo and Juliet eventually become civic 'idols' of reconciliation. The question of idolatry surprisingly (even though obliquely), resurfaces here after the lovers themselves had explored it on their first encounter (in 1.4.218 and, more explicitly, in 2.1.156-7). While the 'created object' of Juliet's idolatry was Romeo's "gracious self" (2.1.157), that is, his being an independent subject severed from his familial and civic identity as a Montague ("Verona brags of him", Capulet said of him in 1.4.180), individuality is now dissolved into a solid item meant for the public display of the families' civic and now seemingly peaceful virtue. In fact, this shift is no assurance of devotion and may even trigger new acts of violence dictated by iconoclastic and "barbarous rage against the dead", that is, the "images ... erected, set up, or pourtraited, for the only memory of them" (Weever 1631, 50-1),[33] which sets an even gloomier light on an already lightless (5.3.306) day and marks the failed reconciliation of the private and the public while the Prince himself, the representative of civic power, cannot but acknowledge the opacity of a scenario in which "All are punished" (5.3.295).

NOTES

1. The Epistle has been seen by many as influential in Shakespeare's creation of his first twenty-one sonnets (see, for instance, McKernan 1989, De Grazia 1993, and Callaghan 2008).
2. "[E]xcept the Lord kepe the citie, the keeper watcheth in vaine", Psalm 127:1.
3. See also Knutson 1988 and Gurr 1988.
4. See Carlson 1994, 86 and Peele 1915.
5. "Mitis amor cogita non vult, sed flectitur ultro. / Flectitur? hic durat, cogitur? ille perit. ... His [the parents] licet ut iubeant, non inhibere licet" (ibid., 17–18, 27).
6. Theodidactus's words are a quotation from Ecclesiasticus 7:25.
7. See Job 1:2–3 and Smith: "Therfore *Iob's* children are counted part of *Iob's* substance, shewing, that a man hath the disposition of his owne substance, so he hath the disposition of his own children" (1591, 35).
8. Stone's notions of the early modern family as "a structure held together not by affective bonds but by mutual economic interests" (1979, 88) and of parents' "fierce determination to break the will of the child" (ibid. 116) have been partially challenged by subsequent scholarship (see, for instance, Houlbrooke 1984; Macfarlane 1986; Cressy 1991, 1997).

9. "[Matrimony] is not to bee enterprised, nor taken in hande unadvisedlye, lightelye, or wantonly, to satisfie mens carnal lustes and appetites, like brute beastes that have no understanding: but reverentely, discretely, advisedly, soberly, and in the feare of God" (*BCP Book of Common Prayer*, "Of matrimony", 1549).
10. "... the consent of both parties ought to be free, not enforced, not compelled, not constrained. It is then counted to be free, when neither the authority of the parents, nor the power of the rulars, nor the enforcement of the tutors drive them to consente in contractinge Matrimony, but theyr owne redye bente good wyl one toward another without all force and constraynte." (Becon 1564, D.C.xviii).
11. "Those Parents, therefore which take unto them such and so great authority and power over theyr Children, that they many times mary them to suche for lucres sake, as the children can by no meanes favour, nor abyde to dwel with them … are greatly to be discommended. … many Parents at these day, namely such as be of the nobility, do so handel their children, as the Grazier both his oxen and sheepe. … and that also many tymes in so tender and yonge years, as neither of them bothe knoweth, what Matrimony meaneth, nor what between them is concluded and confirmed" (Becon 1564, D.C.xix).
12. "Understand therefore, That a Man so soon as he hath accomplished the Age of *Fourteen* years, and a Woman so soon as she hath accomplished the Age of *Twelve* years, may Contract true and lawful and individual Matrimony … The Reason is, that because at these years the Man and the Woman are not only presumed to be of discretion, … but also to have Natural and Corporal Ability to perform the duty of Marriage" (Swinburne 1686, 47). Swinburne's *A treatise of spousals, or matrimonial contracts*, from which this quotation is taken, was presumably composed around 1600, and posthumously published in 1686. Juliet's young age (she is sixteen in Brooke and not even fourteen in Shakespeare) has been frequently pointed out by scholars, and historians have debated over the average age of first marriage for women, which varied from 17 to 26 (see Houlbrooke 1984, 61–8; Macfarlane 1986, 125–6; Cressy 1997, 285; see also Cook 1991, 19–20 and Carlson 1994, 106). Although not setting a recommended age for marriage, an anonymous tract, published in 1616, advised parents to "be wary, constant and unweary" in educating their children and to "neglect nothing, no time nor labour, which may further and make perfect the formal bringing up of their children, till a fit time of marriage, or 28 yeares of age" (*The Office of Christian Parents* 1616, 135). This does not mean that people always married in their late twenties but at the same time it does not exclude this possibility. Oddly enough, even the behaviour of young adults – as we would call them today – was considered as typically adolescent, "[f]or betweene 14 and 28 the child is most sensible, full of strength, courage, and activeness, easily drawne to libertie, pleasure, and licentiousness" (ibid.).
13. See Kahn 1981, 93–4.
14. As Ann J. Cook has it, "[w]ith two minors whose parents would violently oppose any alliance, it is essential to show how and why the young couple are truly married" (1991, 208). To this reason I would add another (and perhaps obvious) observation as to the necessity to have them "truly married" which is an exquisitely dramaturgical one. Should Juliet be still unmarried when her father agrees on her marriage with Paris, her desperate resistance to it would sound less justified.

15. A further hypothesis is made by Hunter and Lichtenfels who underline how "[d]espair at Tybalt's death turns Capulet father from a tolerant head of household into an abusive father; having lost his only male heir he becomes desperate to place his remaining daughter" (2009a, 88). See also Dash 1981, 74.
16. Capulet himself refers to his decision of having Juliet marry Paris as to a decree ("... How now, wife? / have you deliver'd to her our decree?", 3.5.137–138), following Brooke where he reproached her saying: "How much the Roman youth of parents stood in awe / And eke what power upon their seed the father's had by law?" (ll. 1951–2).
17. Early modern marriage "redefined social and sexual roles, and conferred new duties of statuses, authority and dependency". No more subdued to patriarchal power, a married couple could actually exercise it since "marriage signified a passage into adulthood, a mark of social maturity" (Cressy 1997, 287–8). Of course, given the clandestine nature of her wedding, Juliet cannot 'go social', as it were, but this does not change the substance of her being a married woman, and therefore no more subjected to the authority of her father.
18. In his discussion of the notion of 'private' in the transition between the Middle Ages and the Renaissance, Ariès famously defined England as "the birthplace of privacy" (1989, 5).
19. Hoskins's own influential definition of Great Rebuilding (Hoskins 1953, 44) was reassessed and partially challenged by Robert Machin (1977) and Chris Currie (1988). See also Johnson 1993.
20. According to Brian Gibbons, "Shakespeare visualizes Capulet as living in a merchant's house rather than a castle" (Gibbons 1980, 87).
21. Capulet's promise may be equated to a contract, whose validity is unequivocally sealed by his calling Paris "my son" (3.4.16).
22. For a discussion of the public-private space of the garden in the play's narrative sources see Henke in this volume.
23. Early modern gardening manuals advised about the best kind of plants and hedges to be placed in a garden to secure its perimeter: "[t]he comlie inclosure or hedge of a Garden be the same, which is made of the white thorne artely laid: that in few yeares with diligence cut, waxeth so thick and strong that hardly any person can enter into the ground, saving by the garden doore" (Hill 1657, 15).
24. Where you are Caius, there I am Caia.
25. As Stanley Wells points out, this attitude is anticipated during the ball at the Capulets mansion, when the stylization of their first conversation into a sonnet form sets it "off from the surrounding bustle of the dance, creating an enclosed, private world" (2010, 156).
26. When visiting Friar Laurence at dawn asking him to celebrate his marriage with Juliet, Romeo briefly summarizes what has happened the night before: "And all combined, save what thou must combine / by holy marriage. ... We met, we wooed, and made exchange of vow" (2.2.60-2). Although with extreme quickness, Romeo and Juliet have gone through all the phases of match-making and are now ready to tie the knot.
27. It is perhaps worth noticing here that the Prince uses 'we' and not 'I' as he is presumably speaking on behalf of the whole Veronese community which endows the Friar with a civic role and function.

28. Although the statues may be intended as freestanding sculpted memorials, I agree with the interpretation, mainly based on l. 303 ("As rich shall Romeo's by his lady's *lie*", my emphasis), that signifies them as funeral relief figures lying on a sarcophagus (see Hosley 1954; Roberts 1998, 98; Shakespeare 2000, 356n; Hunter and Lichtenfels 2009b, 508n). "Commemorative purposes were fulfilled in the century following the Reformation by some of the most massive and grandiose tombs ever set up in England. ... On the finer monuments the dead were portrayed with greater realism and in postures which brought them into closer rapport with the onlooker" (Houlbrooke 1984, 205). On the popularity and function of funeral recumbent effigies, see also Llewellyn 1996, 197.
29. Tybalt, Mercutio, Romeo, Juliet and, in Q1, Benvolio too are dead.
30. See *OED*, 'jointure', *n*a, b and †c. A jointure is specifically defined as "lands or income to be held jointly by the husband and wife, and then by the widow alone" (Houlbrooke 1984, 83).
31. Susan Snyder suggests that this reference to gold "also resonates disturbingly with Romeo's recent diatribe against gold as a poison, a murderer (5.1.81–5). Memorializing the feud's victims in a medium that is synonymous with corruption and death makes at best an inauspicious beginning for a new era of peace" (1996, 96).
32. Indeed, early modern funeral monuments were "typically ... elaborate structures of carved stone, often painted and decorated in bright colours and trimmed with gilding" which made them "extremely costly to their patrons" (Llewellyn 1996, 179).
33. In spite of Protestant tolerance of figurative sculpture in memorials, "in the post-Reformation England ... there was a great deal of uncertainty about the status of visual experience and particular worries about the legitimacy of religious imagery" (Llwellyn 1996, 179). Queen Elizabeth herself promulgated a decree (early in her reign and again in the 1570s) against the "breaking or defacing of Monuments of Antiquitie, being set up in Churches or other publike places for memory and not for superstition" (Weever 1631, 52–4).

WORKS CITED

An. 1585–90?. *Consensus parentum in contrahendis nuptus non est necessarius*, Cambridge: s.n.
An. 1616. *The Office of Christian Parents*. Cambridge: Cantrell Legge.
Ariès Philippe (with Roger Chartier). 1989. *A History of Private Life. Passions of the Renaissance*. Cambridge, MA: Harvard University Press.
Batt, Barthelemy. 1581. *The Christian Mans Closet*. Translated by William Lowth. London: Thomas Dawson and Gregorie Seton.
Becon, Thomas. 1564. *The Booke of Matrimony*. In Thomas Becon, *The worckes*. London: John Day.
Bigliazzi, Silvia, ed. 2012. *William Shakespeare: Romeo e Giulietta*. Torino: Einaudi.
Book of Common Prayer, "The Forme of Solemnizacion of Matrimonie". 1549. Accessed February 28, 2015. http://justus.anglican.org/resources/bcp/1549/Marriage_1549.htm.
Calderwood, James L. 1971. *Shakespearean Metadrama*. Minneapolis: University of Minnesota Press.

Callaghan, Dympna. 2008. *Shakespeare's Sonnets*. Oxford: Blackwell.
Carlson, Eric Joseph. 1994. *Marriage and the English Reformation*. Oxford: Blackwell.
Church of England. 1597. *Capitula sive constitutiones ecclesiasticae*. London: Christopheri Barker.
Cook, Anne Jennalie. 1991. *Making a Match. Courtship in Shakespeare and Society*. Princeton, NJ: Princeton University Press.
Cooper, Nicholas. 1999. *Houses of the Gentry, 1480–1680*. New Haven: Yale University Press.
Cowen Orlin, Lena. 2008. *Locating Privacy in Tudor London*. Oxford: Oxford University Press.
Crane, Mary Thomas. 2009. "Illicit Privacy and Outdoor Spaces in Early Modern England". *Journal for Early Modern Cultural Studies*, 9 (1): 4–22.
Cressy, David. 1997. *Birth, Marriage & Death. Ritual, Religion, and the Life-Cycle in Tudor and Stuart England*. Oxford: Oxford University Press.
Currie, Chris. 1988. "Time and chance: modelling the attrition of old houses". *Vernacular Architecture*, 19: 1–9.
Dash, Irene G. 1981. *Wooing, Wedding and Power: Women in Shakespeare's Plays*. New York: Columbia University Press.
De Grazia, Margreta. 1993. "The Scandal of Shakespeare's Sonnets." In *Shakespeare Survey, 46: Shakespeare and Sexuality*, edited by Stanley Wells, 35–50. Cambridge: Cambridge University Press.
Gibbon, Charles. 1591. *A Work worth the Reading*. London: Thomas Orwin.
Gibbons, Brian, ed. 1983. *William Shakespeare: Romeo and Juliet*. London and New York: Routledge (The Arden Shakespeare).
Gurr, Andrew. 1987. "Intertextuality at Windsor". *Shakespeare Quarterly*, 38 (2): 189–200.
Gurr, Andrew. 1988. "Intertextuality at Windsor: A Reply". *Shakespeare Quarterly*, 39 (3): 394–8.
Hill, Thomas. 1657. *The Gardeners Labyrinth*. London: Jane Bell.
Hoskins, William G. 1953. "The Rebuilding of Rural England, 1570–1640". *Past & Present*, 4: 44–59.
Hosley, Richard, ed. 1954. *William Shakespeare: Romeo and Juliet*. New Haven: Yale University Press.
Houlbrooke, Ralph H. 1984. *The English Family 1450–1700*. London and New York: Longman.
Hunter, Lynette, and Peter Lichtenfels. 2009a. *Negotiating Shakespeare's Language in Romeo and Juliet: Reading Strategies from Criticism, Editing and the Theatre*. Aldershot: Ashgate.
Hunter, Lynette, and Peter Lichtenfels, ed. 2009b. "The Text of the Play". Accessed March 12, 2015. http://www.romeoandjulietedition.com.
Johnson, Matthew H. 1993. "Rethinking the Great Rebuilding". *Oxford Journal of Archaeology*, 12 (1): 117–25.
Kahn, Coppélia. 1981. *Man's Estate: Masculine Identity in Shakespeare*. Berkeley and Los Angeles: University of California Press.
Knutson, Roslyn L. 1988. "Intertextuality at Windsor: A Rejoinder". *Shakespeare Quarterly*, 39 (3): 391–3.
Laitinen Riita, and Thomas V. Cohen, ed. 2009. *Cultural History of Early Modern European Streets*. Leiden: Brill.

Llwellyn, Nigel. 1996. "Honour in Life, Death and in the Memory: Funeral Monuments in Early Modern England". *Transactions of the Royal Historical Society*, 6: 179–200.

Loehlin James N. ed. 2002. *Romeo and Juliet. (Shakespeare in Production)*. Cambridge: Cambridge University Press.

Macfarlane, Alan. 1986. *Marriage and Love in England. Modes of Reproduction, 1300–1840*. Oxford: Basil Blackwell.

Machin, R. 1977. "The Great Rebuilding: A Reassessment". *Past & Present*, 77: 33–56.

McKernan, John. 1989. "The Influence of Erasmus on Shakespeare's Marriage Sonnets". In *The Portrayal of Life Stages in English Literature, 1500–1800: Infancy, Youth, Marriage, Aging, Death, Martyrdom: Essays in Honor of Warren Wooden*, edited by Jeanie Watson and Philip McM. Pittman, 57–91. Lewinston, NY: Edwin Mellen Press.

Montrose, Louis A. 1996. "Spencer's domestic domain: poetry, property, and the Early Modern subject". In *Subject and Object in Renaissance Culture*, edited by Margreta de Grazia, Maureen Quilligan and Peter Stallybrass, 83–130. Cambridge: Cambridge University Press.

Peele, Albert, ed. 1915. *The Seconde Part of a Register*. Cambridge: Cambridge University Press.

Roberts, Sasha. 1998. *William Shakespeare. Romeo and Juliet*. Plymouth: Northcote House.

Shakespeare, William. 2000. *Romeo and Juliet*. Edited by Jill L. Levenson. Oxford: Oxford University Press.

Sherlock, Peter. 2008. *Monuments and Memory in Early Modern England*. Aldershot: Ashgate.

Shrank, Cathy. 2003. "Civil Tongues: Language, Law and Reformation". In *Early Modern Civil Discourse*, edited by Jennifer Richards, 19–34. Houndmills, Basingstoke: Palgrave Macmillan.

Smith, Henry. 1591. *A Preparative for Mariage*. London: R. Field for Thomas Man.

Snyder, Susan. 1996. "Ideology and the feud in *Romeo and Juliet*". In *Shakespeare Survey, 49:* Romeo and Juliet *and its Afterlife*, edited by Stanley Wells, 87–96. Cambridge: Cambridge University Press.

Sokol, B.J., and Mary Sokol, 2003. *Shakespeare, Law and Marriage*. Cambridge: Cambridge University Press.

Stone, Lawrence. 1979. *The Family, Sex and Marriage in England 1500–1800*. Abridged edition. London: Penguin.

Swinburne, Henry. 1686. *A treatise of spousals, or matrimonial contracts*. London: S. Roycroft for Robert Clavell.

The Geneva Bible. A Facsimile of the 1560 Edition. 2007. Peabody, MA: Hendrickson.

Vaughan, William. 1600. *The Golden Grove, moralized in three bookes: a worke very necessary for all such, as would know how to governe themselues, their houses, or their country*. London: Simon Stafford.

Weever, John. 1613. *Ancient funerall monuments within the united monarchie of Great Britaine*. London: Thomas Harper.

Weinberger, Jerry. 2003. "Pious Princes and Red-Hot Lovers: The Politics of Shakespeare's *Romeo and Juliet*". *The Journal of Politics* 65 (2): 350–75.

Wells, Stanley. 2010. *Shakespeare, Sex, & Love*. Oxford: Oxford University Press.

7 Silencing the Natural Body
Notes on the Monumental Body in *Romeo and Juliet*

Silvia Bigliazzi and Lucia Nigri

BODIES AND MONUMENTS

"Deaths open up spaces in social and personal relations": this is how Nigel Llewellyn incisively introduces the idea of fragmentation produced by death at the level of familial and societal fabric alike. Crevices in the household order destabilize the family, but may also have repercussions at the level of the community, raising anxiety about loss of cohesion, as well as "loss of social differentiation" (1991, 104). Leveller Death treats everybody in the same way, making no distinction between the rich and the poor. In early modern England this sense of undifferentiated loss was to be "resisted by the ritual" (ibid.) and preserved through social visibility. The monumentalization of the natural body had the aim of occulting decay and, in its place, determining the permanence of the social body through a process "charged with the task of re-establishing social difference" (ibid.). To this end, "monumental bodies effected replacement of the deceased by registering what we might loosely term their personal identity and locating them as precisely as possible in social terms, even at the cost of fabricating and manipulating history" (ibid.). Peter Sherlock has more recently revised this argument, claiming that monumentalization did not invest everybody in the same way. His assumption is that this "legal fiction" was especially employed "to explain the transfer of sovereign power from a monarch to his or her successor",[1] and did not necessarily apply to all people, not even those "in positions of authority in that society" (2008, 44). On this account, he has contended that "most tombs" should rather be considered as "representations of the dead, not replacements for their social role" (ibid.). Whatever the case may be, *Romeo and Juliet* clearly relies on a different conception closer to Llewellyn's view. What emerges from the play, in fact, is that the funeral statues on whose promised erection the last scene ends are monumental symbols of finally achieved civic harmony entirely alien to the two natural bodies they portray. Indeed, this commemorative choice is itself shaped by unsolved conflicting stances emerged long before that scene. In that last scene, in fact, the agreement signed by the two families, and presided over by the Prince, provides a civic ritual that does not include a funeral procession, as customary at the end of tragedies (Neill 1984), but, as often contended, something more akin to a commercial transaction.

This negotiation incongruously set in the cemetery transfigures this place of memory into a wholly public place of reconciliation in which the city looks within itself and devises a way to come to terms with its intestine unruliness.

The relevance of the relation between the three bodies mentioned above (natural, social, and monumental) becomes apparent precisely because, as Carroll suggests, in that final civic ritual "[o]f the actual bodies, which still lie before us on the stage (along with those of Paris and Tybalt), there is no mention. They have already ceased to exist ... [t]heir story has been transmuted into an incomplete and passionless narrative" (1981, 68). This narrative in turn has been promised to be further translated into two celebrative and glamorous civic artefacts: the golden statues. In this regard, classical parallels with Ovidian metamorphoses pointing out that they too exemplify "a specific lesson to future generations" (Colie 1974, 146) have failed to acknowledge that the common moral teaching "elides the real difference" that "statues cannot breathe" (Carroll 1981, 68). No genuinely positive value of the silent simulacra can here be envisaged.[2] Indeed, the play appears to reflect the signifying power of "[m]onumental commemoration" in order to "secure a better future by rewriting the past, not merely preserving it" (Sherlock 2008, 3). Yet, rewriting the past means opening further gaps too.

The play dramatizes precisely this issue, overloading it with connotations of idolatry at a time when memory of massive "damage to funerary sculpture" caused by attacks "on superstitious imagery" was still fresh (Archer 2001, 95). In this context, though, it is the 'commercial bond' that calls for closer attention because it carries out the definitive transformation of the cemetery as a place of memory into one of civic politics. By looking back at the dramatic events leading up to it, this scene no longer appears as an accretion to the text, but intimately linked with the rest of the play. This becomes apparent not only by considering the rightly underscored monetary references scattered through the play (Reynolds and Segal 2005), but also, and especially, by looking at the discursive strategies that construct contrary conceptions of death and its commemoration. Introduced within the fabric of the drama, these conflicting perspectives contribute to producing different spaces suggested and reinforced also by an attentive dramaturgy of stage movements and properties' use. Precisely this tension between different relational and affective categories regarding the experience of death forms a latent discursive and dramatic undercurrent of the text. Its natural, albeit ironically tragic, outcome is the sublimation of the two lovers into symbols of an ideal of marital union legitimized by the community itself, but extrinsic to the couple's own (marital) conception of desire. Communal peace at this point needs the silence of the bodies.

SOLITARY TOMBS

Contrary to models of love sacrifice and funeral rituals uniting the lovers in a self-same urn or tomb,[3] no explicit mention of common burial is here made, although this might be suggested by the closeness of the two golden statues, supposedly lying side by side ("As rich shall Romeo's by his lady's lie", 5.3.303). Like the two bronze effigies of Elizabeth of York and Henry VII in Westminster Abbey,[4] Romeo's and Juliet's own statues might in fact be meant to adorn one and the same sarcophagus enclosing both corpses. If so, memory of this funeral sculpture would have triggered political overtones concerning household conflicts on a larger scale,[5] and it is undeniable that this might have greatly added to the dramatic effect. However, Capulet's line might also signify that the statues are simply positioned next to each other in a visible, if imprecise, site of the town. Be it as it may, the fathers' discourse pinpoints interest not so much in Romeo and Juliet visibly united in a 'marital crypt', as in their individual presence as well as in their 'dissolution' into single statues. Their names are evoked in sequence, by singular mention, and no reference is made to one articulated icon of their union in death. Furthering the feeling of separateness, Romeo and Juliet are not presented as equal symbols of faithfulness and sincerity, qualities which are attributed only to Juliet. She is the one who will come to represent the value itself of the city, like the statue of Lady Verona that Cansignorio ordered to be visibly placed right at the centre of Piazza Erbe in 1368.[6] No further indication, as to the size or the symbolic details of the statues, is supplied,[7] but attention is reserved to their precious material, exceeding both the marble of the novella tradition and the bronze of the Tudor effigies. That gold is a corrupting material risking sainthood and morality alike is a statement that lingers on in the memory (Romeo calls it "saint-seducing", 1.2.212, and "worse poison to men's souls", 5.1.79). That it is implicated in the social discourse of power is also clear from Lady Capulet's early metaphors of matrimonial union as an economic and social transaction (in the elaborate book metaphor she uses to describe Paris, Juliet is ominously metamorphosed "into the gold clasps lock[ing] in the golden story", 1.3.94). At this point Lady Capulet is only probing her daughter's readiness to marry the young nobleman, but considering that language transcends signification by displaying a constitutive power to construe reality,[8] she already suggests that there is more to it than innocent figurativeness. Similarly, the discourse of the fathers in the post-mortem contractual space of the cemetery is one of separateness that incongruously appropriates the language of marital bonds to seal, through Juliet's "jointure" or dowry (5.3.97), the reconciliation between the families.

For sure, though, no common tomb is openly mentioned, and this is one of the several deviations from the play's direct source. Brooke is explicit in relating of a "stately tomb, on pillars great of marble", with epitaphs set all above and beneath "in honour of their death"; a tomb that "even at this day ... is to be seen" and "worthy of the sight" (ll. 3014–19). Also Painter's "Rhomeos and Iulietta" is unequivocal about their common entombment:

> And to immortalizate the memorie of so intier and perfect amitie, the lord of *Veronna* ordained, that the two bodies of those miraculous louers shold be fast intombed in the graue where they ended their

liues, where was erected a high marbled pillar, honoured with an infinite number of excellent Ephitaphes, which to this day be apparent, with such noble memorie, as amongs all the rare excellencies wherewith the Citie is furnished, there is none more famous than the monument of Rhomeo and Iulietta. (1567, 247)

Before them, Luigi Da Porto had similarly mentioned only one monument for both,[9] and Matteo Bandello had referred to one and same "sepoltura dei dui amanti" ["tomb of the two lovers"], engraved with an epitaph in sonnet form (Romano 1993, 1.245).[10] None of these texts mentions statues, and by monument all signify a marble sepulchre ordered by the Prince himself, not by the fathers. Evidently, the mention of the statues in gold was Shakespeare's innovation, and it activated a whole set of implications.[11] In addition to the monetary and commercial practice that sets up here a public space of communal negotiation, the play clearly deploys a civic process of camouflage of the community's fear of fragmentation into subversive individual wills and private discourses. At the same time, it also strives towards a contrary direction aimed at asserting distinction and therefore at concealing the loss of social differentiation in death. This dual strategy that affirms class difference while doing away with individual wills suggests that class is the true marker of identity. To this aim, it elaborates on a public discourse and engages in a social practice of effacement of the natural body that construes a social body out of it through the public establishment of the monument.

In the play this process is triggered at a fairly early stage. It starts with Juliet's metonymical thinking on the wedding-bed as death-bed and grave, a concept she lexicalizes in ways that show how alien she is to the family and civic discourses that will later absorb and transfigure her. With tragic irony, the two lovers' relocation to a communal dimension that they do not belong to in the experience of their mutual love is in fact a process that they try to escape but will eventually undergo. The public exhibition of their own metamorphosed bodies into symbols, and reminders, of their 'sacrifice' will be the token for their families' (and the community's) definitive appropriation. They will be the glorious memento of legitimate love approved of by the city and a 'talisman' against family enmity. By legitimizing their transgressive desire, the city channels that transgression into its own social discourse, and translates it into a social practice of communal self-assertion. This is the truly, if thwarted, sacrificial act carried out by the community, one which takes place publicly in the play's coda, and makes use of the monument for the sake of self-purification and lasting memory of renegotiated peace and rule.[12]

The way to this final civic assumption of sacrifice as an experience that needs first to be acknowledged and voiced in words, and then carried out via civic symbolism, is in fact paved for by the gradual shaping of language and space as hybrid loci where the lovers clash with the familial and communal views, tacitly producing civic tension. Implying a neat divide between the private and the public spheres of the household, Romeo and Juliet appropriate the house in-cased space of the bedroom and the town in-cased space of the tomb as spheres of liberty. Yet power relations enforced by the households transform them into spaces of public interest and commercial transaction. This contrast, which is carried out both discursively and socially through agency, shows that, as Kilian has it, "[t]he power of exclusion and autonomy", which is "necessary to maintain one's right or one's identity", is doomed to fail if those actions are not based on "power relationships ... maintained through public intervention" (1998, 126). In other words, if exclusion, which leads to privacy, is not publicly acknowledged through social relations of power, it is simply ineffectual. From this perspective, if confrontation is missing spaces cannot be considered as purely 'public' or 'private', but they are sites where these categories coexist and change function according to their users (and producers), and this is true for both mechanisms of exclusion and of access. In *Romeo and Juliet* a drama (and dramaturgy) of space-construction and space-tension runs precisely through the shaping of the bed-grave metonymical discourse of Juliet; it permeates also Romeo's attempt to transform the civic vault into a private space of marital union in death, subversively establishing it inside the mausoleum of the enemy. To these discourses and actions the community responds by removing their bodies and rewriting their story: the answer is their transfiguration into 'solitary' monumental bodies.

THE BED-GRAVE DISCOURSE

Exploring the dramaturgy of the play, Andrew Gurr has underlined the "deliberately vague language" referring to the death-bed by terms like "'tomb', 'grave' and 'monument' ... intentionally non-specific, explicitly fictional configurations designed to allow the players to use whatever resources that day's venue could afford" (1996, 25). Yet it should be added that they are not always used casually. The first character to resort to the word monument is Juliet in her contrast with her parents (3.5.201); later Balthasar mentions it in his report of Juliet's death (5.1.18), and then it is the Friar's turn (5.2.23, 127); there follow Lady Capulet (5.3.190) and again Balthasar (5.3.274). "Vault" is also a word used by the Friar (4.1.111, 5.3.131, 254, 276, 290), by Balthasar (5.1.20) and finally by Romeo (5.3.85), when he eventually descends into it. Juliet uses it twice in the potion scene.

References to graves, not monuments and vaults, occur fairly soon in the play. They start off in Juliet's words to the Nurse soon after her encounter with Romeo, when she fears that he be already married and figures out for herself the sterile prospect of her wedding bed turned into a grave (1.5.134). Later, at the news of Romeo's banishment, while still intent on desiring sexual consummation, she wishes to be taken by Death in her still unused wedding-bed. Her voice troublingly betrays nuances of a masochistic wish of self-annihilation as a paradoxical self-inflicted punishment for bereavement, and strangely resounds male fantasies of female rape[13] similar to those we have heard in Sampson's opening sexist and bawdy lines ("I, a maid, die maiden-widowed. / Come, cords, come, Nurse, I'll to my wedding bed, / And death, not Romeo, take my maidenhead!", 3.2.135–7). Evidently Juliet too is part of the culture of male violence and sexist aggressiveness rooted in Verona, and her being 'spoken' by that discourse shows how deeply and subtly discursive models shape also her own imaginings. The same metaphor will obliquely crop up again in Romeo's words in the tomb, when, with grim images unveiling feelings of possession and jealousy under the hallucinatory effects of despair, he will believe to see in her rosy cheeks and still blooming beauty the visible sign of her reciprocated affection for the unsubstantial rival Death (5.3.103). Then, still in 3.2, Juliet unsuccessfully implores her father to delay the wedding, and her mother disparagingly wishes to see "the fool [Juliet] married to her grave" (3.5.140), using a word which does not belong to her language and therefore adds shades of scorn to her imprecation. In response Juliet too evokes images of bridal bed as bier; yet, for the first time, and contrary to her mother, she mentions "the dim monument where Tybalt lies" (3.5.201). It is not by chance that this happens when she talks to her family, because she needs to attune her language to her interlocutors for making herself understood: her death will be a loss for them, it will open up a gap in the household, and will increase by one the number of past losses memorialized in the stately vault. Discursive confrontation around the perception and conception of death are evidently taking place, producing contradictory spaces at the level of discursive exchanges in which Lady Capulet insults Juliet with implicit menace of a common burial in the ground; in turn, Juliet responds with threat of entombment in the crypt. By abandoning the grave image and resorting to the death-language of the family she tries to provoke a reaction by addressing their own discursive field. Death leaves the domain of private feelings and of social un-differentiation, and enters the space of social discourse with the re-establishment of class differences. This is no marginal issue because it underlines the contrasting discursive stances behind the divide between the private language of Juliet and the public language of the family she occasionally retorts against them: a partition that will later show in the translation of the two lovers' suicides into the language of sacrifice, on the one hand, and, on the other, in the transformation of their natural bodies into socially erected monumental bodies.

In these instances the wedding-bed and the death-bed appear as mutually permeable categories. This is true whether we consider Juliet's intimate implications of the sexual correlation between love and death as expression of her own most private dimensions,[14] or instead whether we turn to the social discourse, and practice, of the family, that seems to reflect a contemporary view on them both as sites of public intercourse. As Michael Neill suggests:

> In early modern culture the marriage bed had a peculiar topographic and symbolic significance. It was a space at once more private and more public than for us. More private because (with the exception of the study or cabinet) it was virtually the *only* place of privacy available to the denizens of sixteenth- and early seventeenth-century households; more public because as the locus of the most crucial of domestic offices – perpetuation of the lineage – it was the site of important public rituals of birth, wedding, and death. (2000, 266)

The connection between the room and the tomb containing the two beds is evidently very close. This is reinforced by their radical opposition along an idea of love as breeder of life (matrimony as procreation) and of death as breeder of corpses (as Romeo will voice in the 'tomb-womb-of-death' metaphor). This ideal connection between room and tomb solicits various options in terms of stage-practice. Shakespeare did not miss the opportunity to dramatize it, and, as Thomson has observed, "capitalized on the physical conditions [of the stage] to create thematic visual images", while also granting dialogue the peculiar function of "introduc[ing], describ[ing], confirm[ing], or embellish[ing] what the audience saw" (1995, 232). Critics have long discussed the stagecraft of this scene, suggesting the alternative choices of using either the discovery space or the trap door leading into the understage.[15] Taking the bed-bier metonymy literally, though, the closest pick would have been to exploit its potential visually. A bed is provided and it may serve two purposes, thus translating into the language of stagecraft the reinvention of space already at work through discourse. As Thomson aptly observed, this flexible use of one and the same property invites

> the spectators to perceive thematic connections in the transition from room to tomb. Thus when first Romeo and then Juliet die in the Capulet tomb the paradox-resolving transcendence suggested by the language and imagery (the two lovers united in death) would have been conveyed visually by the staging as well. (ibid., 234)

In terms of theatrical logistics, and its thematic and symbolic effects, the bed in 4.3 "would have been 'thrust out' from the tiring house" (ibid.), and as

> [t]he Q1 direction for the curtains to be shut at the end of the bed chamber scene ["*They all but the Nurse goe foorth, casting Rosemary on her and shutting the Curtains*"] makes it possible to speculate ... the bed was not pushed back into a tiring house recess but remained

> on stage with its curtains closed until the tomb scene, only 160 lines later, when Romeo finds Juliet dead. Not only the conventions of the unlocalized stage, but staging practicality would seem to dictate a verbal-and visual-metamorphosis of bed into bier. (Ibid., 241)

Whichever the case and performative options, it is undeniable that the proximity of the chamber and the vault scenes in the sequence of actions solicits a perception of spatial connections between the bed and the bier also at a symbolic level. This is reinforced by the transition provided by 4.3 with Juliet's own soliloquy in her room, which she transfigures into a hallucinatory vault. As Thomson again rightly remarks, "the vivid descriptions serve the practical purpose of creating the tomb in the mind's eye of the spectator even before the scene which takes place there". Indeed, "the action-describing words suggest that the oxymoronic ceremony of marriage-in-death has begun here, to be completed in the tomb by first Romeo, then Juliet" (ibid., 240).

This is the only case, among Juliet's solo-pieces, in which Brooke's source is dramatized almost literally. The poem provides an even longer passage than Shakespeare's Q2 (52 lines compared to 44), while not being as rich in psychological details. For instance, it fails to show Juliet's hesitation at remaining alone in carrying out her faked death in her bedroom, a subtle touch added in the play. Decision-making at that point is the testing ground to prove her manly courage, and this needs separation from the family and an imaginative rehearsal of what may mean experiencing her own death, as well as the alternative possibility of waking up in the vault before the time comes. No longer perceived as the private family locus of veneration of the dead, but as the horrendous charnel house of a burdensome line of progenitors, grimly fragmented into disjointed bones to be handled for dashing out her own brain, the vault is for Juliet a place of separation and solitude where she feels and pre-suffers the horror of the inert, putrefied vestiges of her own household. All sense of family belonging and memory is lost, and, filled with fear and dismay, she figures out that place of death as the monumental edifice of a rotting, death-generating family. In her grim phantasmagoria, the vault unveils the decayed natural bodies of the dead it contains; those bodies are not silenced by the monument, but terrifyingly talk to her. This monstrous 'dialogue of bodies' provides the potential, if imaginary, link between the room as a site of physical desire, as famously voiced in the "Gallop apace" piece, and the room-as-tomb inhabited by Juliet's fears and enclosing her lost feeling of belonging to a family she wishes to desert. What remains is an awareness of family feuding only, which invades the space of her mind with the final delusion of the imaginary fight between Romeo and Tybalt. Juliet's own bedroom as monument of her own death to the family has eventually, and imaginatively, turned itself into the civic space of hatred as well as of her own desire to escape from it.

HYBRIDITY AND LIMINALITY

Brooke's narrator recalls that "throughout Italy this common use they have" (l. 2515),

> That all the best of every stock are earthéd in one grave:
> For every household, if it be of any fame,
> Doth build a tomb, or dig a vault, that bears the household's
> Wherein, if any of that kindred hap to die,
> They are bestowed; else in the same no other corpse may lie. (ll. 2516–20)

No such comment may be found in the Italian novellas, which generically mention an "avello" (possibly a tomb or stone sarcophagus) outside the Church of San Francesco.[16] Differently from them, Brooke is keen on clarifying that by national custom the household tomb *is* a social symbol asserting the civic role of the family and its own revered past. This "avello" may designate either an overground edifice (as the novellas seem to suggest) or a semi-underground crypt, making for intimacy and privacy while aiming at showing off antiquity and elitism in grouping the "best" citizens in the same death-space. Being a family lodge for corpses belonging to the same stock, undifferentiated burial is not allowed, nor is intrusion admitted. And yet Brooke has Romeo clearly say that it is in the house of his enemies that he wants to lie in death,[17] precisely as it is the house of his enemies that he first intruded into, and met Juliet. Taking up this clue from Brooke, but only having Romeo voice his intention of lying with Juliet that night, as a prefiguration of a second marital consummation in the house of the enemy, Shakespeare innovates on the source and adds Paris – another intruder into the private space of family memory. A figure of public-private duplicity, he is both the responsible citizen, apprehending the outlaw Romeo in the name of the Prince, and the private mourner of a loss suffered even before erotic and marital fulfilment. Standing at the threshold between the outside and the inside of the vault – itself ambiguously located in an imprecise site –,[18] the last civic conflict takes place between two intruders: the bereaved bridegroom trespassing the gateway of a family mausoleum that he will never be allowed to access as a family member, and the bereaved secret husband and enemy to that house, who, despite being an outlaw, paradoxically belongs to that very house. The divide between the public and the private dimensions of the vault, as two opposed yet contiguous areas, is marked by a door (or cover), which significantly needs forcing to be opened and give access into the underground "womb of death" (5.3.45) through a symbolic descent. Imaginatively duplicating the public feast in Capulet house, the vault provides yet another feast scene, with light symbolically invading this second house, transfigured by Juliet's presence. Her natural body apparently devoid of life has already been the object of contemplation and lament several times, starting in 4.5, where a choral threnody has taken place transforming her bedroom into a room where the family's death ritual is celebrated;[19] a funeral rite has exhibited that body to the community, and the vault has been visited by the citizens, as Shakespeare seems to suggest by having Balthasar claim that he has seen her "laid low in her kindred's vault" (5.1.20). This detail further suggests the public dimension of the Capulet monument on the day of the funeral, which in Brooke is instead left unclear by the sole mention of the local use of having "whosoever dies, / Borne to their church with open face upon the bier he lies" (ll. 2523-4). Yet the body is later enclosed within the tomb and left visible only to the family – and to unlawful intruders. Brooke scans the timing of the town watchmen's arrival and of the suicides carefully: they pass by the vault and "spy" a candle-light "through the gates" (l. 2795) after the two suicides have already taken place, and no trace of interference is mentioned. Afraid of the presence of some "enchanter" abusing the place, they break into the monument only to find out the "husband and wife" "[i]n clasped arms y-wrapt" (l. 2801). Shakespeare quickens the dramatic pace and has Juliet hear and fear the arrival of the watchmen. They are bearers of civic norm and rule, but in order to enforce it, they too trespass the boundary dividing the outside public dimension of the vault and the inside private space of memory. Watchers over the monument of public distinction of the Capulet family, they invade Juliet's private space, in a vertiginous overlapping of civic and private categories. Juliet's private death chamber is the correlate space of her private household bedroom, where she first made love to Romeo, and where she experienced in solitude her own meeting with the dead by rehearsing her own death. The bed was then transformed into the death-bed she now lies upon in the vault, and as her own bed had been violated by the marital transactions carried out by her family, also this death-bed is now violated by the watchmen who hasten her suicide. The gathering of the citizens at the monument immediately after the two lovers' death (which in Brooke occurs the next day, when "[t]he news was by and by throughout the town dispread", l. 2808), prepares the ritual of symbolic sacrifice carried out by the community at a publicly acknowledged place of death. As mentioned earlier, it is at this point that social discourse, in a social practice of power negotiations, transforms this death-place into a communal site of self-interrogation and commercial dealings. Lamentation is heard, inquisition is carried out, the probing of witnesses and examination of evidence (including the perusal of Romeo's letter to his father), are accomplished and the final recapitulation may eventually take place. The vault has served the function of a civic court but also of a confessional, where the Friar, suspected of murder, has accused and absolved himself. The bodies, as already suggested, remain ignored. They are discursively transformed into social bodies, acquiring the identity of sacrificial victims for the sake of the community. They are soon to be metamorphosed into what they never wished to be, or become: the monumental bodies of family (and civic) peace, visually replacing the names they bore as signifiers of hatred. They are turned into the 'visual names' of their own bodily subtraction, of the concealment of their own erotic desire as the natural and essential prerogative of being natural and sentient bodies; they are the simulacra of the negation of their individual self-affirmation, and, contrariwise, of the communal acknowledgement of their boundary-crossing as the cause of their victimising. The town, by the offer of the fathers, and not on orders of the Prince, who is here drawn into a tacit transactional practice with the two feuding families (and the township asking for peace), celebrates a wedding already secretly officiated for the sake of the city. Through forgetfulness of their past desiring bodies, and ignorance of their corpses now, the city looks at the golden statues as the precious material of a festive occasion that transcends death through the sublimation of loss in a renegotiation of civic relations.

The "grave" as opposed to the "vault" as the indirect discursive clue of individual thinking on death outside of social practices aimed at occulting un-differentiation through maintenance of class distinction, is an early instance in the play of an attempt to go beyond monuments and reconfigure space privately. The conflation of bed and bier is another one, demonstrating a wish to cross boundaries and reshuffle social categories. Yet, the natural body is eventually silenced and there remains but the voice of the monumental body bespeaking excision and forgetfulness: the gap between society and the individual has not been filled in, but the community has found its own (ambiguous) and glamorous symbols of self-purification.

NOTES

1. Reference here is to Kantorowicz 1957.
2. Suggestion that they embody an artistic sublimation of the lovers' own ineffable desire, bridging the "communicative gap between the private secret love and the social order oblivious of the existence of that love" (Calderwood 1971, 117) has also missed the mark; as pointed out by Carroll, "the gap is in fact established by the statues" (1981, 69).
3. Reference is, for instance, to a myth Pyramus and Thisbe's, on which see Avezzù's chapter in this volume.
4. See https://henrytudorsociety.wordpress.com/tag/elizabeth-of-york/. Accessed March 25, 2015.
5. Evidently allusion is to the conflict between the houses of York and Lancaster, eventually reconciled after Henry's defeat of Richard III at Bosworth and marriage with Elizabeth.
6. The statue is part of a Gothic fountain designed by urban architect Giovanni Rigino, "who used one of the last remaining Roman statues still standing in the Capitolium of Verona" (Fabbri 2002, 26). It is worth pointing out that she holds a scroll in her hands showing the following municipal motto: "Est justi latrix urbs haec et laudi amatrix", which can roughly be translated as "This city is the bearer of justice and the lover of praise" (ibid.)
7. On the habit of requiring that the sculpture should show precise physical features as well as a precise posture of the dead, besides the size and the material of the effigy, see Llewellyn 1991, 106ff.

8. For a critical discussion of this concept, clearly derived from Foucault, see Fairclough 2013.
9. "E ordinato un bel monimento, sopra al qual la cagione della loro morte scolpita fosse, gli due amanti, con pompa grandissima e solenne, dal signor e da' lor parenti e da tutta la città pianti e accompagnati, seppelliti furono" (Romano 1993, 1.105) ["and a beautiful monument having been demanded, upon which the reason of their death should be inscribed, the two lovers were mourned and accompanied by the Prince and their parents and the whole city, and then buried with great solemnity"]. All translations from Italian and French are ours.
10. Boaistuau, of course, had provided the French translation of the Bandello version, although the idea of a magnificent marble sepulchre uniting the two corpses appears closely modelled on Da Porto: "Et pour immortaliser la memoire d'vne si parfaicte & accomplie amitié: Le Seigneur de Veronne ordonna que les deux corps de ces pauures passionnez demouroient enclos au tombeau auquel ils auoient finy leur vie, qui fit eirgé sur vne haulte colonne demarbre, & honoré d'vne infinité d'excellens epitaphes. Etest encore pour le iourdhuy en essence: de forte qu'entretoutes les plus rares excellences qui se retrouuent en la cite de Veronne, il ne sevoit rien de plus celebre que le monument de Rhomeo & de Iuliette" (Boaistuau 1567, 51) ["and to immortalize such a perfect and excellent friendship, the Prince of Verona demanded that the two bodies of these poor lovers would be buried together where they had ended their life. This tomb should be erected upon a high marble column inscribed with so many excellent epitaphs. The monument of Romeo and Juliet is still there nowadays, and among the many attractions in Verona there is nothing more famous than this"].
11. See Reynolds and Segal 2005; see also chapter 12 in this volume.
12. See chapter 5 in this volume.
13. See Watson and Dickey 2005.
14. This suggestion may be linked with other hints at the relation between the height of sexual pleasure and dying, which seems to emerge in Juliet famous "Gallop apace" soliloquy (see Kristeva 2001; Bigliazzi 2015b). It may also be recalled that, as Marshall suggests (2002), masochistic forms of self-effacement were common in the writings of the age and provided recurrent material onstage with cathartic functions for the audience.
15. For a detailed discussion see Gurr 1996, 22ff.
16. "Non avevano ancora questi frati conventuali il luogo di San Fermo in Verona, né gli altri osservanti, da essi dividendosi, aveva quello di San Bernardino fondato, ma in una chiesetta del nome di San Francesco intitolata, nella quale egli già stette e nella cittadella ancor si vede (la sua vera regola, a' nostri tempi dal loro licenzioso vivere guasta, perfettamente osservando), insieme dimoravano; presso le mura della quale, dal canto di fuori, erano allora appoggiati certi avelli di pietra, come in molti luoghi fuori delle chiese veggiamo: uno de' quali antica sepoltura di tutti e' Cappelletti era, e nel quale la bella giovane si stava ..." (Da Porto in Romano 1993, 1.99) ["These friars did not have San Fermo in Verona yet, nor the other Observants, having separated from them, had founded San Bernardino, but dwelt in a little church dedicated to San Francesco, where he had resided and which can still be seen in the Cittadella (in perfect observance of his true rule, nowadays corrupted by their licentious way of life) and placed against the outer walls of this church, there was a number of tombs such as we see outside the churches. One of

these was the ancient sepulchre of all the Cappelletti, in which the beautiful Juliet was laid"]; "con quegli strumenti e ferramenti che giudicarono esser al bisogno se ne andarono verso la Cittadella e senza trovare impedimento veruno giunsero al cimitero de la chiesa di San Francesco. Quivi trovato l'avello ov'era Giulietta, quello con loro ordigni destramente apersero ed il coperchio con fermi puntelli puntellarono." (Bandello in ibid., 1.151) ["taking with them all the tools that they deemed necessary, they headed towards the Cittadella and finding no impediment reached the cemetery of San Francesco. There they found Juliet's tomb, whose lid they skillfully opened with their instruments and propped up with appropriate supports"].
17. "Or else so glorious tomb how could my youth have craved, / As in one-selfsame vault with thee haply to be ingraved? / What epitaph more worth, or half so excellent, / To consecrate my memory, could any man invent" (ll. 2647–50).
18. Mention is made of a cemetery and of a yew tree, but, differently from the sources, which clarify its intramural position, no indication is provided on whether it is inside or outside the city walls. Going by historical evidence, vaults were in fashion also in England from the Middle Ages, although their great period started during the reign of Elizabeth. London extramural cemeteries were first established in 1569 but they were not the norm. See Houlbrooke 2000, esp. 338, 334.
19. On the choral original reinterpretation of this threnody, see Bigliazzi 2015a.

WORKS CITED

Archer, Ian W. 2001. "The Arts and Acts of Memorialization in Early Modern London". In *Imagining Early Modern London: Perceptions and Portrayals of the City from Stow to Strype, 1598–1720*, edited by Julia Merritt, 89–113. Cambridge: Cambridge University Press.
Bigliazzi, Silvia. 2015a. "Chorus and Chorality in Early Modern English Drama". *Skenè. Journal of Theatre and Drama Studies* 1 (1): 101–33.
Bigliazzi, Silvia. 2015b. "Female desire and self-knowledge: Juliet's soliloquies in *Romeo and Juliet*". *Rivista di Letterature Moderne e Comparate* 3: forthcoming.
Boaistuau, Pierre. 1567. *Histoires tragiques*. Anvers: Iean Waesberghe.
Brooke, Arthur. (1562) 1908. *Romeus and Juliet*. Edited by John J. Munro. New York: Duffield and Co. / London: Chatto & Windus.
Calderwood, James L. 1971. *Shakespearean Metadrama*. Minneapolis: University of Minnesota Press.
Carroll, William C. 1981. "'We were born to die': *Romeo and Juliet*". *Comparative Drama* 15, 1: 54–71.
Colie, Rosalie. 1974. *Shakespeare's Living Art*. Princeton: Princeton University Press.
Fabbri, Patrizia. 2002. *Verona. The City of Romeo and Juliet. A Love Story*. Firenze: Bonechi.
Fairclough, Norman. (1992) 2013. *Discourse and Social Change*. Cambridge and Malden, MA: Polity.
Gurr, Andrew. 1996. "The Date and the Expected Venue of Romeo and Juliet". *Shakespeare Survey* 49: 15–26.
Houlbrooke, Ralph. 1998 (2000). *Death, Religion and the Family in England, 1480-1750*. Oxford: Clarendon Press.

Kantorowicz, Ernst H. 1957. *The King's Two Bodies: A Study in Mediaeval Political Theology*. Princeton: Princeton University Press.

Kilian, Ted. 1998. "Public and Private, Power and Space". In *The Production of Public Space*, edited by Andrew Light and Jonathan Smith, 115–134. Lanham: Rowman and Littlefied.

Kristeva, Julia. (1987) 2001. "*Romeo and Juliet*: Love-Hatred in the Couple". In *Romeo and Juliet*, edited by R.S. White, 68–84. Houndmills, Basingstoke: Palgrave.

Llewellyn, Nigel. 1991. *The Art of Death: Visual Culture in the English Death Ritual, c.1500–1800*. London: Reaktion Books.

Llewellyn, Nigel. 1996. "Honour in Life, Death and in the Memory: Funeral Monuments in Early Modern England". *Transactions of the Royal Historical Society* 6: 179–200.

Marshall, Cynthia. 2002. *The Shattering of the Self. Violence, Subjectivity & Early Modern Texts*. Baltimore and London: The Johns Hopkins University Press.

Neill, Michael. 1984. "'Exeunt with a Dead March': Funeral Pageantry on the Shakespearean Stage". In *Pageantry in the Shakespearean Theater*, edited by David Bergeron, 153–93. Athens: University of Georgia Press.

Neill, Michael. 2000. *Putting History to the Question: Power, Politics, and Society in English Renaissance Drama*. New York: Columbia University Press.

Painter, William. 1567. *The Second Tome of The Palace Of Pleasure*. London: Imprinted in Pater Noster Rowe, by Henry Bynneman, for Nicholas England.

Reynolds, Bryan, and Janna Segal. 2005. "Fugitive Explorations in 'Romeo and Juliet': Transversal Travels through R&Jspace". *Journal for Early Modern Cultural Studies* 5 (2): 37–70.

Romano, Angelo, ed. 1993. *Le storie di Giulietta e Romeo*, vol. 1. Roma: Salerno editrice.

Shakespeare, William. (1984) 2003. *Romeo and Juliet*. Edited by G. Blakemore Evans. Cambridge: Cambridge University Press.

Shakespeare, William. (2007) 2011. *The First Quarto of Romeo and Juliet*. Edited by Lukas Erne. Cambridge: Cambridge University Press.

Sherlock, Peter. 2008. *Monuments and Memory in Early Modern England*. Aldershot: Ashgate.

Thomson, Leslie. 1995. "'With Patient Ears Attend': 'Romeo and Juliet' on the Elizabethan Stage". *Studies in Philology* 92 (2): 230–47.

Watson Robert N., and Stephen Dickey. 2005. "Wherefore Art Thou Tereu? Juliet and the Legacy of Rape". *Renaissance Quarterly* 58 (1): 127–56.

Part II
Civic Performances and R&Jspaces

8 "For these dead birds sigh a prayer"

Paul Edmondson

David Garrick's Stratford Jubilee of 1769 bristles in our cultural imagination. It was an occasion for consensual pageantry, flamboyant excess, quasi-theological underpinning, and political opportunities. Temporary performance spaces were erected, a special Jubilee ribbon was produced in nearby Coventry, a procession through the streets of Stratford-upon-Avon very nearly happened (it was rained off), and mulberry-wood objects were revered and solemnly presented, as though the tree from which they were made had stretched its roots all the way into Shakespeare's own veins. Although not a word of Shakespeare was spoken in the Jubilee's formal proceedings, Shakespearian fantasies were aired and formed part of Garrick's famous Ode. Thomas Arne's oratorio *Judith* was presented close to Shakespeare's grave in the chancel of Holy Trinity Church, an oratorio based on the fervently nationalistic biblical account of how the namesake of Shakespeare's second daughter, Judith – meaning literally 'the Jewess' – saved the Jewish nation. Garrick's Jubilee in part created a civic space for Shakespeare, allowing his potential for meaning to extend far beyond the realms of his actual works. What happened in Stratford-upon-Avon in September 1769 made it possible for people – anyone – to appreciate and to express a public love for Shakespeare without ever having read or understood a word he wrote.

That same Jubilee spirit is alive and well among the hundreds of thousands of people who visit Shakespeare's birthplace every year – they cannot all have actually read or seen *Hamlet*, or know a sonnet off by heart, *can* they? And the same Jubilee spirit is present among the crowds who flock to see Juliet's balcony, and indeed tomb, in Verona, who send letters to Juliet (she does not reply; I know because I once sent her one), and who write graffiti on the walls of the Casa di Giulietta – they cannot all have actually read or seen *Romeo and Juliet, can* they? I wonder how many visitors each year, for instance, pause to realize that Juliet's much-touched statue should be on the balcony, not below it? Jubilees make pageantry freely available to the people, permitting celebration for its own sake. The jubilee Garrick brought to Stratford-upon-Avon in 1769 marked the first time that Shakespeare was, literally, brought onto the streets and out of the theatres. Whether or not you agree with the politics of the anniversary (a long-reigning monarch, for example), you can still enjoy the firework display. Thinking about *Romeo and Juliet* in the context of the Garrick Jubilee, and in the mood of a civic Shakespeare that makes itself so easily felt in Stratford-upon-Avon and in, as it were, Romeo and Juliet's hometown of Verona, has made me begin to question the play's own civic rites and enactments.

I have long been troubled by the suicides of Romeo and Juliet and by the statues of both of them that are to be raised in pure gold by their surviving civic fathers at the end, cold and banal, like Čhekov's seagull that appears on stage stuffed, shortly after Konstantin has shot himself. The desire to see each other's dead child commemorated is already leading to an unattractive one-upmanship between Montague and Capulet:

> *Montague:* I will raise her statue in pure gold,
> That whiles Verona by that name is known
> There shall now figure as such rate be set
> As that of true and faithful Juliet.
> *Capulet:* As rich shall Romeo's by his lady's lie,
> Poor sacrifices of our emnity. (5.3.298–303)[1]

Since, as Biron in *Love's Labour's Lost* says, "honest plain words best pierce the ear of grief" (5.2.745), it might be hoped that the gold statues themselves be deferred and, in the end, avoided, though one suspects not. But no memorial can undo the suicides of the two young lovers, which remain an inextricable and inescapable part of the tragedy, and in the religious understanding of Shakespeare's early audiences – and many an audience since – uncomfortably and challengingly evoke a common belief that suicides shall burn in everlasting torment.

An overall condemnation of suicide was first articulated in the fifth century by St Augustine in *City of God*. Suicide is regarded as a sin because it is understood as self-murder, betraying a love of oneself as well as one's neighbour. In 1562 the Roman Catholic Church pronounced that all who committed suicide should be denied a Christian burial. John Florio's translation of Montaigne's essay, "A Custom of the Isle of Cea", which more than countenances suicide, was published in 1603. John Donne's famous treatise on 'self-homicide' was written in 1608 (and first published in 1647). Donne at once accepts a justification for suicide whilst at the same time contextualizing it within an incomplete and problematic theology. Suicide was a crime in England from the thirteenth century until 1961, and it was not until 1997 that the Roman Catholic Church decided that suicide might be a result of diminished responsibility as a result of extreme hardship, anguish, torture, or psychological disturbance.

Young suicide, and an audience's response to it, remains an indelible part of the true tragedy of Juliet and her Romeo. Perhaps Friar Laurence's testimony specially pleads for their deaths being a result of misadventure because otherwise – unlike Ophelia's drowning in *Hamlet* – there can be no ambiguity about Romeo and Juliet's intention to kill themselves. Or, perhaps that exchange between Montague and Capulet seeks to excuse Romeo and Juliet from the ignominy of not having a full Christian burial in consecrated ground because of their class and position in society? This is reflected in the reasoning of the two clownish gravediggers in *Hamlet*:

> *Second Clown:* Will you ha' the truth on't? If this had not been a gentlewoman, she should have been buried out o' Christian burial.
> *First Clown:* Why, there thou sayst, and the more pity that great folk should have count'nance in this world to drown or hang themselves more than their even Christian. (5.1.23–9)

Or perhaps Romeo and Juliet's suicides serve rather to challenge any easy assumption about divine justice that might enter into the audience's mind. Like the poor, unfortunate Ophelia, the loyal Horatio (who would have killed himself if only he could with the last drop of poisoned wine), and those transcendently loving pagans Antony and Cleopatra, the suicides of Romeo and Juliet challenge our expectations. Surely a pair as loving as they cannot really suffer any more beyond the grave. The play itself makes no answer. It is left to the audience to decide and reflect upon. Modern minds as well as early modern ones are troubled by the suicides of Romeo and Juliet.

In his writing about Dante, whose descriptions of Hell have burned in the Western imagination for 750 years, T.S. Eliot remarks that "it is a test (a positive test, I do not assert that it is always valid negatively), that genuine poetry can communicate before it is understood". The poet Craig Raine offers the following commentary: "[T]his means that genuine poetry *sometimes* communicates before it is understood and sometimes not" (2007, 139). Romeo and Juliet's suicides and the after-effect of them in the minds of Shakespeare's original audiences, as well as in the imaginations of readers and audiences in subsequent centuries, are a good example of a poetry in motion that communicates before it is understood. Quoting Christian doctrine and theological discourses around this brace of dead lovers will only emphasize the inadequacy of the rational, critical approach when confronted with the bodied-forth, imagined reality of life, love, and death. This is where a creative response may be more appropriate, and one rooted in civic enactment perhaps best. The truth about Romeo and Juliet's suicides can begin to be understood when read alongside and in relationship to Shakespeare's wider dramatic and poetic output.

So that is why I turn to Shakespeare's "Let the bird of loudest lay", also known as *The Phoenix and Turtle*, which I should like to read as a civic expression of grief, a civic space through which it is possible to conceive new fantasies about how Shakespeare's works relate to his thinking and imagination. I want to consider how *The Phoenix and Turtle* might be read as Shakespeare's own creative and civic response to *Romeo and Juliet*, a sort of

190 Paul Edmondson

publicly enacted meditation and lamentation not present in the drama itself. How might *The Phoenix and Turtle* be considered Shakespeare's own creative and perhaps redemptive reply to the questions raised by the two suicides he stages in Verona? "For these dead birds sigh a prayer". Here's the poem in full:

> Let the bird of loudest lay
> On the sole Arabian tree,
> Herald sad and trumpet be,
> To whose sound chaste wings obey.
>
> But thou, shrieking harbinger,   5
> Foul precurrer of the fiend,
> Augur of the fever's end —
> To this troop come thou not near.
>
> From this session interdict
> Every fowl of tyrant wing,   10
> Save the eagle, feathered king.
> Keep the obsequy so strict.
>
> Let the priest in surplice white
> That defunctive music can,
> Be the death-divining swan,   15
> Lest the requiem lack his right.
>
> And thou, treble-dated crow,
> That thy sable gender mak'st
> With the breath thou giv'st and tak'st,
> 'Mongst our mourners shalt thou go.   20
>
> Here the anthem doth commence:
> Love and constancy is dead;
> Phoenix and the turtle fled
> In a mutual flame from hence.
>
> So they loved, as love in twain   25
> Had the essence but in one,
> Two distincts, division none.
> Number there in love was slain.
>
> Hearts remote, yet not asunder,
> Distance, and no space was seen   30
> 'Twixt the turtle and his queen.
> But in them it were a wonder.
>
> So between them love did shine
> That the turtle saw his right
> Flaming in the Phoenix' sight.   35
> Either was the other's mine.

Property was thus appalled,
That the self was not the same.
Single nature's double name
Neither two nor one was called.   40

Reason, in itself confounded,
Saw division grow together
To themselves, yet either neither,
Simple were so well compounded

That it cried 'How true a twain   45
Seemeth this concordant one!
Love hath reason, reason none,
If what parts can so remain.'

Whereupon it made this threne
To the phoenix and the dove,   50
Co-supreme and stars of love,
As chorus to their tragic scene.

Threnos
Beauty, truth, and rarity.
Grace in all simplicity,
Here enclosed in cinders lie.   55

Death is now the phoenix' nest,
And the turtle's loyal breast
To eternity doth rest.

Leaving no posterity: —
'Twas not their infirmity,   60
It was married chastity.

Truth may seem but cannot be,
Beauty brag, but 'tis not she.
Truth and beauty buried be.

To this urn let those repair   65
That are either true or fair.
For these dead birds sigh a prayer.

That the *The Phoenix and Turtle* might be regarded as a civic poem can be easily associated with its first appearance in print, the occasion being to celebrate Sir John Salusbury being granted a knighthood by Elizabeth I in June 1601. It appears among a gathering together of fourteen poems under the title *Diverse Poetical Essays,* which are printed after Robert Chester's part appropriation of Arthurian myth, *Love's Martyr*. Chester's work evokes the Phoenix and the Turtle as "allegorically shadowing the truth of love". The poems that follow by George Chapman, Ben Jonson,

John Marston, William Shakespeare, the anonymous writer 'Ignoto', and 'Chorus Vatum', are all written on the same theme. The publication marks the civic patronage of Sir John Salusbury of "several modern writers", the four named authors – Chapman, Jonson, Marston, and Shakespeare – being the leading poets and dramatists of the day. *The Phoenix and Turtle* is the only time when Shakespeare allowed his work to appear as part of a book by another writer. Published by Edward Blount, the printer of *Love's Martyr* was none other than Richard Field, Shakespeare's old school friend who had also printed *Venus and Adonis* and *Lucrece* a few years earlier.

The Phoenix and Turtle has been called, by I.A. Richards, "the most mysterious poem in English" (Shakespeare 2002, 87). It has also managed to produce some of the most mysterious criticism in English. As Barbara Everett noted in a piece for *The Times Literary Supplement* on 16 February 2001, the poem qualifies Shakespeare as no less than "the first Symbolist in Europe", "we seem, even while finding it exquisite, to lack some expertise, some password". I cannot claim to have found a 'password', but I have, I hope, found a new way in, that is by thinking about the poem as a creative, civic response to *Romeo and Juliet*. Approaching *The Phoenix and Turtle* through and because of *Romeo and Juliet* is in part sanctioned by the poem's critical history. Here G. Wilson Knight's summary dismissal of all biographical approaches is useful: "[W]e need not commit ourselves to biographical details" (even though most readings of the poem still do). For Wilson Knight, the poem was in part a way "to gather up and transmute, the experience of the Sonnets, in its own particular fashion" (1955, 194). He also saw in stanzas two to six "a brief summing up of Shakespeare's total work" (ibid., 204). For C.S. Lewis, *The Phoenix and Turtle*, a poetical essay about the philosophy of love, represents Shakespeare's "last word, presumably, that he has given us in his own person on that subject" (1954, 508). Furthermore, it represents a Shakespearian high-watermark, the point at which "we have been admitted to the *natura naturans* from which the *natura naturata* of the plays proceeded: as though we had reached the garden of Adonis and seen where Imogens and Cordelias are made" (ibid., 509). For Lewis the poem holds within it a quintessential Shakespearian DNA and a creative life-force from which it is possible to understand, and to which it is possible to connect, all of Shakespeare's works. The metaphor about the poem being Shakespeare's point of creative origin, 'the garden of Adonis', no doubt arises from the poem's suggestion of the Garden of Eden. By conceiving a Shakespearian appropriation of Christianity through the poem, Lewis's metaphor also recognises the work's public and civic qualities. Inga-Stina Ewbank thought *The Phoenix and Turtle* Shakespeare's "furthest reaching out in words towards what cannot be articulated" (1971, 104). For her, the poem is the occasion when Shakespeare was able to convey meanings that were impossible to body forth on a stage.

The Phoenix and Turtle is rich with a language of civic expression and pageantry: "loudest lay", "herald", "sad trumpet", "troupe", "session", "obsequy", "surplice", "defunctive [or funereal] music", "requiem", and "mourners" all inhabit a public world of a grief which finds expression through liturgy and ritual. The metrical form is uncompromisingly regular, like a congregational psalm or hymn. And at the heart of the poem there is the singing of an "anthem", or hymn, about the Phoenix and her Turtle-dove. This anthem invokes the voice of "Reason" which goes on to make a "threne" or lamentation, printed in a separate section entitled "Threnos". There we find the Phoenix and Turtle consumed by fire and turned to ashes, or "cinders". There is mention of an urn in the final verse as part of a liturgical and civic directive for the public paying of respects:

> To this urn let those repair
> That are either true or fair.
> For these dead birds sigh a prayer. (ll. 65–7)

The Phoenix and her Turtle become no more nor less than "dead birds", entering into a collective, civic memory at the moment when the mourning for them is being enacted. As Colin Burrow remarks the poem "is not only about the dissolution of separate identities into a single whole: it enacts it" (Shakespeare 2002, 88).

Among Shakespeare's wider dramatic and lyrical output, the concerns and expression of *The Phoenix and Turtle* can be compared to Venus's mourning for Adonis ("The flowers are sweet, their colours fresh and trim; / But true sweet beauty lived and died with him", ll. 1079–80); to Claudio's funeral dirge for Hero in *Much Ado About Nothing* ("So the life that died with shame / Lives in death with glorious fame", 5.3.6–7), and Arviragus and Guiderius's funeral song for Innogen, who they suppose is dead, in *Cymbeline* ("Quiet consummation have, / And renownèd be thy grave", 4.2.281–2). Metrically, "The Phoenix and Turtle" is also similar to Shakespeare's own epitaph (whether or not we believe he had the foresight and taste to compose those lines himself). The poem's literary affinities also link it to the classical tradition of Ovid and Catullus and the later medieval tradition of Petrarch, Geoffrey Chaucer, and John Skelton. *The Phoenix and Turtle* is cast in a tone of voice and form that makes its civic expression similar to comparable moments in Shakespeare's other works and one that self-consciously harks back to earlier traditions. Shakespeare's mock-medievalism suits well the poem's chivalric occasion – a knighthood for John Salusbury – and the context of Robert Chester's evoking Arthurian myth in *Love's Martyr*.

"The Phoenix and Turtle" can be read as Shakespeare's own poetic testimony for all lovers whose social worlds (and whose own, secret imagined places) have not been able to sustain them, either because they have been forced to love across a divide (like Pyramus and Thisbe, Romeo and Juliet's comic counterparts, and the Wall that divides them) or because of conflict (for example, Troilus and Cressida). Shakespeare's canon of work provides many other examples: Silvia and the banished Valentine in *The Two Gentlemen of Verona*; Richard II and his Queen; Jessica and Lorenzo in *The Merchant of Venice*; Fenton and Anne Page in *The Merry Wives of Windsor*; the banished Rosalind and the fugitive Orlando in *As You Like It*; Hamlet and Ophelia; Viola and Orsino in *Twelfth Night, or What You Will*; Shakespeare's other Juliet and Claudio in *Measure for Measure*; Desdemona and Othello; Bertram and Helen in *All's Well That Ends Well*; and Posthumus Leonatus and Princess Innogen in *Cymbeline*. All of these couples can be presented as "allegorically shadowing the truth of love", as Shakespeare's poem was originally set forth to do; Lewis's "*natura naturata*" again, "where Imogens and Cordelias are made".

But it is the poem's illustration that two selves simultaneously equal two *and* one which makes it central to Shakespeare's wider poetic and dramatic vision:

> So they loved as love in twain
> Had the essence but in one,
> Two distincts, division none.
> Number there in love was slain. (ll. 25–8)

And later, "hearts remote yet not asunder" (l. 29, evoking the Book of Common Prayer's marriage liturgy "those whom God hath joined let no man put asunder"), "neither two nor one was called" (l. 40), "saw division grow together" (l. 42) and, radically, in terms of material possessions:

> Property was thus appalled
> That the self was not the same.
> Single nature's double name
> Neither two nor one was called. (ll. 37–40)

But being married in the poem seems to challenge, rather than build and encourage, social and cultural fabric. "Property" (and all that word may mean for the economic implications of marriage) becomes pale, is horrified that materiality can no longer be defined through an individual's possessions, since the marriage of the Phoenix and the Turtle makes individuality a nonsense. Furthermore, their marriage, like Shakespeare's Cressida when seen through the betrayed eyes of Troilus, "is and is not". The state of the relationship is compounded by the interdependency and intersubjectivity of the Phoenix and the Turtle's "married chastity" (l. 61). Here it is worth noticing the apparent absence of sex in the poem. Or perhaps the "married chastity", which should not be confused with 'celibacy', still allows for a sexual consummation, though one that has not produced children:

> Leaving no posterity
> 'Twas not their infirmity,
> It was married chastity. (ll. 59–61)

Hinted at here might be a fulfilling sexual union but one which remains chaste (sex untainted by lust). "Married chastity" does not mean a sexless marriage – marriages have to involve sex in order legally to be consummated – rather it points to a marriage that brings a spiritual awareness to the sexuality expressed within it: pre-Lapsarian, Eden-like, and entirely born of love and mutuality without a single mote of lust.

Shakespeare's fascination with selves which incorporate themselves one with another spans his whole career. In what is likely to be his earliest, single-authored work, Shakespeare's other play set in Verona, *The Two Gentlemen of Verona*, Valentine says of Silvia:

> She is my essence and I leave to be
> If I be not by her fair influence
> Fostered, illumined, cherished, kept alive (3.1.182–4)

In *The Comedy of Errors* Antipholus of Syracuse compares himself to "a drop of water" (1.2.35), lost in an ocean and longing to be incorporate, seeking

> ... another drop,
> Who, falling there to find his fellow forth,
> Unseen, inquisitive, confounds himself. (1.2.36–8)

The songs of the Owl and the Cuckoo at the end of *Love's Labour's Lost* come in place of a promise of marriage, but both are expressive of halves of a procreative union and interdependence between Spring and Winter. The waking Helena in *A Midsummer Night's Dream* still sees with a "double" (4.1.188) and a "parted eye" (189) and finds her "Demetrius like a jewel, / Mine own and not mine own" (191–2). Many of Shakespeare's Sonnets engage with the idea of selves incorporated: "... my soul which in thy breast doth lie / That is my home of love" in Sonnet 109 and "the marriage of true minds" in Sonnet 116 are just two immediate examples. The twins Viola and Sebastian see each other as intimate beings sharing a resurrection when they are reunited in *Twelfth Night, or What You Will* (5.1.224–5). And in lines which echo *The Phoenix and Turtle*, Antony says to Cleopatra:

> The nobleness of life
> Is to do thus; when such a mutual pair
> And such a twain can do't. (1.1.38–40)

With the "The Phoenix and Turtle", emphasizes James Bednarz in his excellent book-length study, "Shakespeare produced the first great published metaphysical poem" (2012, 80). Bednarz claims that Shakespeare's poem "helped shape" John Donne's "ensuing myths of incorporate selves" (ibid., 162), which we find, for example, in Donne's poems "The Extasie", "The Canonization", and "Epithalamion: or Marriage Song on the Lady

Elizabeth and Count Palatine being married on St. Valentine's Day". For all of the other birds in the poem, it is the gaze that the Phoenix and the Turtle hold between them that makes them like characters in a play, staring at each other intimately and finding, like Romeo and Juliet, the truth of love in how they perceive and see:

> So between them love did shine
> That the turtle saw his right
> Flaming in the Phoenix' sight.
> Either was the other's mine. (ll. 33–6)

This is not fancy, the poem re-iterates, it is reason, and the figure of Reason in the poem "is itself confounded" by what it sees, and cries out, that only "Love hath reason, reason none" because of the mystery and the truth of love that it sees incorporated in the Phoenix and her Turtle-dove. But the poem also draws clearly from Plato's *Symposium*, a favourite among Elizabethan writers of love poems. Shakespeare, who was compared to 'a Socrates in mind' by his family and friends for the inscription on his memorial bust in Holy Trinity Church, Stratford-upon-Avon, echoes and appropriates Socrates's own words from Plato's discourse:

> Do you not see that in that region alone where he sees beauty with the faculty capable of seeing it, will he be able to bring forth not mere reflected images of goodness but true goodness, because he will be in contact not with a reflection but with truth? And having brought forth and nurtured true goodness he will have the privilege of being beloved of God, and becoming, if ever a man can, immortal himself.
> (Plato 1987, 95)

It had long been a commonplace that 'Truth' and 'Beauty' were components of 'Love' by the time Shakespeare came to pen his poem. Crucially, in writing in response to his commission to show 'the true nature of love', Shakespeare adds three more qualities and dimensions to Plato's pre-requisites: "rarity", "grace", and "simplicity" (ll. 53–4). In fact, says the poem, if love were only dependent on 'truth' and 'beauty', then we would find them "buried" (l. 64). It is as if Shakespeare is taking up where Socrates left off and redefining a literary love for his own time (an interested determination that also made him the supreme exponent of the sonnet form, one suspects). "Rarity" and "grace" are the watchwords in Shakespeare's re-casting of the truth of love, and both are exemplified by the Phoenix herself. It limits Shakespeare's radical adaptation of Platonic thought to suggest that *The Phoenix and Turtle* should only be interpreted biographically and be 'about' Queen Elizabeth I (Duncan-Jones and Woudhuysen 2007); his project is altogether more philosophical and theological than this. Unlike Socrates, Shakespeare's poem does not present 'immortality' as an inevitability that true love makes available. The emphasis in his adaptation is on the "rarity" and "grace" of the Phoenix and the Turtle. Phoenixes are wont to arise from the ashes; Turtle-doves are not, and the end of the poem presents only ashes contained by an urn, and pair of dead birds.

In *The Phoenix and Turtle* it is as if Shakespeare's metaphysical thinking culminated, was distilled, and found most succinct expression. In order to achieve poetic truth, metaphysical realities require intense looking, soul searching, and reason. "His poem feels as though it is coming from another world", writes Colin Burrow in his exemplary Oxford edition, "as though it grows from thinking, and thinking gradually, about sacrifice in love, and about where Elizabethan poetry might go next" (Shakespeare 2002, 89). But surely, as enigmatic as the poem remains, it enacts its metaphysics almost as a brief poetic drama in miniature. The scene is visually set with the reference to the "sole Arabian tree" and the various birds taking their respective parts in a funeral. Shakespeare's Othello echoes the phrase just moments before he kills himself, imagining

> ... one whose subdued eyes
> Albeit unused to the melting mood,
> Drops tears as fast as the Arabian trees
> Their medicinal gum. (5.2.357–60)

Othello is climactic and self-dramatizing enough to mention a whole species of tree, possibly even a whole forest of "Arabian trees" weeping like him and with him. *Othello* is the poem's near-contemporary work, but, in contrast, the "bird of loudest lay" is heard "on the *sole* Arabian tree", as if there is only one such tree left – particular, isolated, splendid – and that all of its tears (its gum) are being shed for the Phoenix and the Turtle.

The Phoenix, too, is especially distinguished. Like the lonely tree, there is only ever one Phoenix seen at any given moment, but Shakespeare's Phoenix is awarded further distinction by being female. Shakespeare presents her in the mythical role traditionally understood to be male, and by so doing evokes something of the world of his own comedies. But the Phoenix is not pretending to be male and her sex, though unexpected, is a cause for celebrating her particular uniqueness. Perhaps this is Shakespeare's way of challenging any straightforward, purely emblematic reading of the poem, Christian, or otherwise. Any traditional view of the Phoenix will be and should be frustrated on the realization that his Phoenix is female. It is the distinctly Shakespearian Phoenix which re-appears in a 1935 book for children, *The Box of Delights*, by the then Poet Laureate, John Masefield, himself a Shakespearian. The protagonist, Kay Harker, is asked by the old magician-owner of the Box, Cole Hawlings, which bird he would most like to see. Their attention is turned to the fire-place:

> That seemed to open into a desert all glittering with jewels. Kay knew that it was an Arabian desert, for, somehow, Egypt with the Pyramids

were behind him, and mirages were forming far, far in the distance. Then, lo, in the midst of the desert was the sole Arabian tree, oozing gum, its leaves dropping crystals of spice, its flowers heavy with scent, and its fruit shedding sweetness. Leaves, flowers, and fruit all grew upon it at the same time.

As Kay looked, a wind poured through the boughs, and, within, on a next of cinnamon sticks, was a Phoenix, "It's a Phoenix!" Kay said. "And now I can say I have seen one. Oh, I wonder, will it begin to sing?" She lifted her head, and the plumes changed from white to gold, and from gold to orange. As the song increased, so as to shake the house, the plumes changed from orange to scarlet, and, lo, they were no longer plumes, but flames, which burned up the Phoenix, so that the song died away, and at last there was no Phoenix, nor any nest, only some ash blowing away in the wind and a few embers.

(Masefield 2007, 28)

Clearly, Masefield's is a distinctly Shakespearian Phoenix, female and singing on the "sole Arabian tree". In the context of the story, we learn that Shakespeare himself is said to have been among the previous owners of the Box of Delights. Just after the Phoenix has been consumed into ash, out of the embers, Kay notices some fragments of egg shell; another Phoenix has been born. Masefield's appropriation of Shakespeare's poem into his children's story is an important act of criticism in its own right. He identifies "the bird of loudest lay" as the Phoenix, the bird singing in the "sole Arabian tree", an identification not made within Shakespeare's poem; he also imagines the Arabian desert as a backdrop to the poem, not least, of course, because this would speak more readily of adventures to his young protagonist; and he envisions the Phoenix resurrected through its own off-spring at the end of the episode. In contrast, Shakespeare is keen not to present a new Phoenix and, instead, leaves any sense of a resurrection to our own imaginations.

The experience of the poem and its civic possibilities are life-giving when it is read in creative tension with *Romeo and Juliet*. *The Phoenix and Turtle* is pre-echoed in Shakespeare's imagination when Romeo first sees Juliet at the Capulet ball. Juliet here burns as brightly as a Phoenix and is compared to a dove:

> O, she doth teach the torches to burn bright!
> It seems she hangs upon the cheek of night
> As a rich jewel in an Ethiope's ear –
> Beauty too rich for use, for earth too dear.
> So shows a snowy dove trooping with crows
> As yonder lady o'er her fellow shows. (1.5.43–8)

Later she will become more Phoenix-like, looking out from her balcony like the sun arising in the east – like a bird on an Arabian tree, perhaps – and angel-like, with an extreme brightness, the fire of stars is in her eyes and cheeks (2.1.45, 57–9, 61–2, 68, 66), so much so "that birds would sing and think it were not night". Or, as the great biblical love poem *The Song of Songs* has it, describing a similar feeling, "the time of the singing birds is come, and the voice of the turtle is heard in our land'" (2:12). The lark, which Juliet mistakes for a nightingale "on yon pom'granate tree" (3.5.4), has its counterpart in the poem, "the bird of loudest lay / On the sole Arabian tree". Romeo and Juliet listen with increasing despondency to the lark:

> ... that sings so out of tune,
> Straining harsh discords and unpleasing sharps.
> Some say the lark makes sweet division;
> This doth not so, for she divideth us. (3.5.27–30)

The tragic trajectory will always divide and separate, unlike the metaphysical, which seeks instead to unite, as the poem has it "two distincts, division none" (l. 27). But the poem follows a tragic trajectory, too, at once celebrating and finding beautifully astonishing the union of the Phoenix and the Turtle-dove whilst at the same time mourning their great loss. Romeo and Juliet are bodied forth as "a pair of star-crossed lovers" and in "fair Verona, where we lay our scene" (Prologue 6 and 2). The Phoenix and the Turtle-dove are "co-supremes and stars of love" that have the voice of Reason "as chorus to their tragic scene" (l. 52).

Colin Burrow has suggested that Shakespeare wrote *The Phoenix and Turtle* to "keep the name of Shakespeare alive and to keep it associated with new forms, and to create a poem which could adapt itself to many circumstances by virtue of its refusal to individualize" (Shakespeare 2002, 89). Similar reasons might be given to explain the Garrick Jubilee of 1769: to keep the name of Shakespeare alive, to create new forms of aesthetic expression, to adapt Shakespeare – as Garrick was fond of doing – to different circumstances. Garrick, of course, in his own adaptation of *Romeo and Juliet* (which held the stage for ninety-seven years from 1748), could not let the lovers die without Romeo experiencing a momentary resurrection of Juliet, just minutes before he himself dies from the poison he has drunk, and she stabs herself.

And so, it seems very much in the spirit of Garrick – and possibly even in the spirit of Shakespeare himself – to read this most enigmatic of poems, especially in the context of Verona's civic identity, as the funeral rite for Romeo and Juliet. I can see the poem painted, in quasi-medieval, possibly even pre-Raphaelite style as a fresco on an unsuspecting wall of a prominent public building; I can hear it being set to music (as it often has been) with a Benjamin Britten-like spareness; and, if this were to be worked out into a physical, liturgical, performed expression, as a creative civic response to Shakespeare on the streets of Verona (or Stratford-upon-Avon), then all the elements for the consensual pageantry are clearly present. As *The Phoenix and The Turtle* is sung, or spoken, as was Garrick's Shakespeare ode against music, two golden statues of Romeo and Juliet come to life, like Hermione in *The Winter's Tale*: "dear life redeems you" (5.3.103). The other birds in the poem are represented by dancers holding effigies, or perhaps with appropriate banners or rod puppets. We see Romeo and Juliet representing the roles of the Phoenix and the Turtle-dove. The civic pageant performance I imagine would be presented as Shakespeare's own 'Masque of True Love, or a Funeral Rite for Romeo and Juliet'. It would show within it what Guiderius and Avriagus in *Cymbeline* sing as:

> All lovers young, all lovers must
> Consign to thee and come to dust. (4.2.275–6)

The Phoenix and her Turtle-dove are consumed by fire, but the Phoenix always rises again from the ashes. We need not see that (because Shakespeare does not allow us to in his poem), but we might be encouraged to hope for it. At the end of the first section, the effigy of the Phoenix bursts into flames, burning the Turtle-dove, too. As the Threnos begins, Romeo and Juliet continue to dance but return, slowly, to where they started from. As they do so, the figure of the Priest stands among the ashes and blesses them at the beginning of the final verse. They become statues again, and the music stops. My imagined masque presents a journey through dancing, a climax of flames and destruction, to arrive at a contrasting stillness, in which Romeo and Juliet themselves turn back into statues they started out from. The funeral rite is over and "the priest in surplice white" (l. 13) stands among the ash, reminding onlookers of the consolation and hope of Christianity. When the music stops, a successful presentation of the masque would inspire a collective sigh in the audience before the applause starts – the civic equivalent of a collective prayer that Shakespeare himself seems to want us to sigh each time we experience the poem afresh.

NOTE

1. All citations are from Shakespeare 2005.

WORKS CITED

Bednarz, James P. 2012. *Shakespeare and the Truth of Love: The Mystery of 'The Phoenix and Turtle'*. Houndmills, Basingstoke: Palgrave Macmillan.

Chester, Robert. 1601. *Love's martyr: or, Rosalins complaint. Allegorically Shadowing the Truth of Loue* … London: Imprinted [by R. Field] for E. B[lount].

Duncan-Jones, Katherine, and Henry R. Woudhuysen, eds. 2007. *Shakespeare's Poems*. London: Thomson Learning.

Everett, Barbara. 2001. "Set Upon a Golden Bough to Sing". *The Times Literary Supplement*, 16 February.
Ewbank, Inga-Stina. 1971. "Shakespeare's Poetry". In *A New Companion to Shakespeare Studies*, edited by Kenneth Muir and Samuel Schoenbaum, 99–115. Cambridge: Cambridge University Press.
Plato. (1951) 1987. *The Symposium*. Translated by Walter Hamilton. Harmondsworth: Penguin.
Knight, G. Wilson. 1955. *The Mutual Flame: On Shakespeare's Sonnets and The Phoenix and The Turtle*. London: Methuen.
Lewis, C.S. 1954. *English Literature in the Sixteenth Century, Excluding Drama*. Oxford: Clarendon Press.
Masefield, John. 2007. *The Box of Delights*. New York: New York Review of Books.
Raine, Craig. 2007. *T. S. Eliot*. Oxford: Oxford University Press.
Shakespeare, William. 2002. *The Complete Sonnets and Poems*. Edited by Colin Barrow. Oxford: Oxford University Press.
Shakespeare, William. (1988) 2005. *The Complete Works*. Edited by Stanley Wells, Gary Taylor with John Jowett and William Montgomery. Oxford: Oxford University Press.

9 "Wherefore art thou Marius?"
Otway's Adaptation of *Romeo and Juliet*

Loretta Innocenti

> As 'twixt two equal armies, Fate
> Suspends uncertain victory
>
> (J. Donne, *The Extasie*, 13–14)

What struck Shakespeare in Arthur Brooke's *Romeus and Juliet* was certainly the main theme of the star-crossed lovers: a story that in his times had already been rewritten by different authors, translated from one language to another, and transformed from a novella to a poem to a prose narrative, to end with drama. The starting point had all the potential for a play: the family feud preventing two young people to love each other and get married was a genre *topos*, though not one of tragedy. Comedies were usually based on the clash of generations, as well as on impediments to the fulfilment of young lovers' desires. The initial situation of Romeo and Juliet's story could lead to a happy ending: a similar plot – that of Pyramus and Thysbe – was turned into parody in *A Midsummer Night's Dream*, written in the same years. The finale, though, had all the features of a real modern tragedy, in which no fatal flaw stains the heroes and precipitates the events, but the mournful outcome depends on inevitable coincidences and on what Franco Moretti (1983, 159–62), though referring to children's narrative, called "Rhetoric of the Too Late".

In Shakespeare's *Romeo and Juliet* the tragic is rendered even more powerful by the presence of different registers, from the lyrical to the humorous, which seem hopeless efforts to steer the narrative thread towards comedy. Comic cues, characters, and situations appear as remnants of an impossible plot which slowly sink beneath the surface and become invisible. The pervasiveness of negativity also invests the social background of enmity and civil strife, which happen to be appeased only when reconciliation has become unnecessary. The family conflict is not given any motivation in the play, and it just appears as one of those gory wars of parties and factions dividing Italian Renaissance society – and maybe it also mirrors London riots at the end of the sixteenth century, as has been implied (Fitter 2000). Within the Capulet family Juliet's father imposes his rule and treats his daughter as someone – or something – that belongs to him:

An you be mine, I'll give you to my friend;
An you be not, hang, beg, starve, die in the streets,
For, by my soul, I'll ne'er acknowledge thee,
Nor what is mine shall never do thee good. (3.5.192–5)

The image of a patriarchal society, the violence of authority over needs and feelings, and the tragic scope of the civil conflict between two opposed factions are the characteristics of this play which later epochs 'appropriated' to convey political ideology and update a debate on power. As Michael Dobson writes: "Shakespeare, or a series of alternative Shakespeares, came to dramatize, sometimes imperfectly, specific contemporary conflicts, rather than coming to embody a single, monolithic consensus" (1992, 12). What the critic refers to is the practice of adapting Shakespeare's plays, a phenomenon that started with the reopening of the theatres at the Restoration in 1660.

Theatrical production is subject to change and adaptation almost by definition: at the very least, written dramatic texts are cut and reduced in performance. Yet, at the end of the seventeenth century, a different sort of textual rewriting took place, in order to make Shakespeare's plays fit for a new stage and a new sensibility. Alterations ranged from abridgment to amplifying inventions, to interpolating and mixing up different texts. If these were the main textual changes, motivations to transform the original plays obeyed different functions, from theatrical and spectacular needs to new social and political ideologies to illustrate.

Criticism has moved from an earlier phase in which the historical survey of adaptations was accompanied by a mainly negative aesthetic evaluation of the adaptors' work, as if they had insulted the sacred memory of the Bard (see Spencer 1927 among others). A more structuralist tendency in the 1970s started to consider the altered texts as the result of hypertextual operations (Genette 1982) and of changes dictated by the neoclassical rules newly imported from the continent during the Restoration and through the first half of the eighteenth century (Innocenti 1985; Walsh 2000). More recent consideration of political and ideological questions, in the wake of a New Historicist critical approach, has shifted attention from the 'neutral' notions of adaptation and alteration to that of 'appropriation', which Jean Marsden defined as a kind of usurpation for one's own uses, based on "a view of Shakespeare embedded not only in his own culture but in ours forcing us to consider both the impact we have on the plays and the impact they have on us" (1991, 8). If this can be taken as a general statement about the unavoidable application of our own standard and of present interest to the interpretation of any texts from the past, in my opinion it is only seeing adaptation – or appropriation – in a diachronic dimension and against different contextual backgrounds that can give us a clearer picture of specific ways of validating the present through existing past texts. In other words, adaptations can represent a kind of frozen exegetic practice which can tell us how Shakespeare and his ideas on communal welfare and political issues were interpreted and brought to date – i.e. made 'contemporary' – more than half a century after his death (Taylor 1989; Murray 2001).

In the 1680s many new political plays appeared on the London stage, mirroring the difficulties of the period and the conflict between Royalists and Protestants, which led authors to side with one or the other of the parties. Around 1678, during the reign of Charles II, news of a conspiracy was spread, accusing Catholics of planning the assassination of the king. Before the so-called Popish Plot was discovered to be fictitious and its inventor, Titus Oates, arrested under the accusation of perjury, fear had led to a widespread anti-Catholic sentiment in the whole nation. A false document was circulated, containing almost a hundred names of Jesuits allegedly involved in the plot. A sort of religious and political hysteria led to a number of executions and to a long parliamentary conflict. As the King's brother and heir to the throne, James Duke of York, was Catholic, Anthony Ashley Cooper, 1st Earl of Shaftesbury, publicly required that he should be excluded from succession and presented a Bill to the Parliament. The so-called Exclusion Crisis radicalized as a struggle between two newly founded parties – the Whig followers of Shaftesbury and the Tories supporting the King. The tension grew stronger and lasted for at least three years, up to 1681, when the Exclusion Bill was defeated in the House of Lords. The conflict mustered a large mass movement in the country, and it was commonly felt to be the prelude to a second Revolution, after the Civil Wars that had stained England in blood and whose memory was still vivid. Luckily the dreaded revolution would be "glorious" and peaceful, ending with James's abdication after less than three years of his reign, in 1688.

These events, which are well known, constituted the topical context portrayed or alluded to on stage. Dryden, in dedicating his comedy *The Kind Keeper, or Mr. Limberham* to Lord Vaughan, wrote: "The great plot of the nation, like one of Pharaoh's lean kine, has devoured its younger brethren of the stage" (Dryden 1992, 3), meaning that, as the seven lean cows had done with the fat cows in Pharaoh's dream (Genesis 41:1–7), the Popish Plot had swallowed up all the other plots, becoming the topic of all plays.

From explicit reference to political figures of the time to more or less covert allusions, similarities between historical facts and the present situation were always implied. Plays were under scrutiny by the censors, and some were held to be dangerous and disloyal. That is why Nahum Tate's *Richard II* was suppressed, and I am here referring to an interesting essay Silvia Bigliazzi (2010) has recently written on this subject, showing how playwrights were aware of the historical parallelisms that might be found in their plays, even while trying to deny any allusions and defending themselves and their work.

Around the 1680s not only were brand-new plays conceived, but also some adaptations made for political reasons, and Shakespeare's plays were appropriated, stressing some topics such as the miseries of the civil war (as John Crowne did with *Henry VI*), banishment, or usurpation (the topic of

Tate's *Richard II, or the Sicilian Usurper*), or even political ingratitude (as is the case of Tate's alteration of *Coriolanus*, re-entitled *The Ingratitude of a Commonwealth*).

Among these adaptations a special case is that of Thomas Otway's tragedy *The History and Fall of Caius Marius*, which was performed in 1679, just when the panic of an invasion by Catholic countries was starting to spread, after the 'discovery' of the Popish Plot. While preparing the play for the stage, Otway might well have read a book which became his source for *Venice Preserv'd*, and which had just been republished that year: *The History of the Spanish Conspiracy against the State of Venice* by the Abbé de Saint-Réal. As Philip Harth writes, the parallel between the Venetian conspiracy of 1618 and the Popish Plot would have been unmistakable (1988). The King was ill, and his illegitimate son, the Duke of Monmouth, had defeated the Scottish rebels and gained a wide popularity with the masses. He was not yet a danger, but Shaftesbury's faction, intending to cause alarm, flaunted the idea of his possible claim to the throne. The atmosphere then was one of political instability and social turmoil. This is also the topic of Otway's Roman tragedy of Caius Marius.

Lisanna Calvi in her book on kingship and tragedy (2005, 115–30) has made a detailed analysis of the political meanings and allusions in *Caius Marius*; I will here concentrate only on a few formal elements, related to the reuse of the Shakespearean text of *Romeo and Juliet*.

The plot of *Caius Marius* is taken from Plutarch's lives of Gaius Marius and of Sylla, besides echoing those of Caesar and Coriolanus, which had also been the sources for Shakespeare's plays of the same name. If what Hazel Batzer (1969) says is true, there were analogies between the situation of 1679 and that of 1607, with the political problems generated by the Midland County Revolt, when Shakespeare resorted to Plutarch and to Roman history to write his *Coriolanus*. Plutarch seems to have provided both playwrights with the example of political troubles and class conflicts. Another source for *Caius Marius* has been detected in Lucan's *Pharsalia*, translated into English by Sir Arthur Gorges as *The Civil War*. Though Lucan's text was concerned with the struggle between Caesar and Pompey, in the second book some veterans mention the strife between Marius and Sylla as a horrid precedent of the present "bloudy broiles and civill rage" (1.35), as the old Citizens complain, adding that

> Not *Famines* rage, nor wrackes of seas,
> Not *Earthquakes* dreads, nor *Plagues* t'apease
> The Heauens wrath; nor bloudy *Warres*,
> Euer gaue vs such deadly scarres. (Lucan 1614, 2.53)

And here a marginal note in the text comments: "Rome did never by any meanes suffer so great desolation as by *Marius* and *Sylla*" (ibid.).

The hatred between the two politicians and soldiers took place in an epoch of corruption leading to the end of the Republic and to the advent of the Empire. A Roman institution, namely the Senate, was the place of political manoeuvres and schemes, as well as of personal grudges. In the year 88 BC resentment for the Senate's decision to bestow on Marius the command of the army in the war against Mithridates, led to Sylla entering Rome with his legions: an act of overt hostility and the starting point of the civil war. Marius fled and took shelter in exile, but while Sylla was engaged in a military campaign in Pontus, he returned to Rome with his son, Marius junior. Repression against the rival faction was brutal: Sylla was proscribed and his estates were confiscated. Marius was elected consul for the seventh time but died soon after. Sylla defeated Marius junior in a battle near Preneste, where the young man committed suicide.

So far history, but the play tells only part of the story. Otway's play shows an ongoing conflict, without explaining its origin. I agree with Michael Dobson when he writes: "[I]ndeed, the original cause of the mortal hatred between Marius and Sylla is throughout the play left as obscure as possible, their rivalry serving only as a general warning against civil conflict itself" (1992, 78). Marius could easily be compared to Shaftesbury, as his siding with the popular party (*populares*) against the patricians (*optimates*) could resemble the position of the Protestant Whigs against the Royalist Tories. Like Antonio in *Venice Preserv'd*, he is a corrupt politician, ambitious and cruel, which could make us think that, as in that more famous play of his, Otway was delivering a Tory message in *Caius Marius* as well. Only a few critics, though – John M. Wallace (1988), for example – seem to be in favour of an Anti-Exclusionist Otway. Most critical interpretations of this play rightly recognize that there is no clear choice between the two factions. Neither party is right, and Otway's world, as Douglas Canfield writes, is "almost totally devoid of honor, trust, loyalty, constancy" (1985, 237) or, in Jessica Munns' words, "Otway's dramas are inescapably and intrinsically ambiguous, never univocal in their ideas, structures or characters" (1995, 207). But, as I believe that the author's position is not to be found in his own admissions or in his characters' statements, nor only thematically in plots, I would like to see more closely how this ambiguity is expressed in the fabric of the text.

And this is where Shakespeare comes to the fore. Because, besides echoes of *King Lear*, *Richard II*, and *Macbeth*, Otway inserted into the main political plot a love story between Marius junior and Lavinia, Metellus's daughter, who was promised to Sylla. The two young lovers belong to rival families, just like Romeo and Juliet, and it is from their Shakespearian tragedy that situations and even lines are borrowed and altered. Otway's play is always mentioned as an adaptation of Shakespeare, and not one of the best. To Ward, in his nineteenth-century *History of English Dramatic Literature*, it is "nothing short of a monstrous plagiarism" (1899, 3.415) and for Hazelton Spencer (1927, 296) it is an "abominable mixture of Roman and

Renaissance ... the execution of Otway's project is as grotesque as its conception". Even J.C. Ghosh, the editor of the Oxford Edition of Otway's works, unmercifully writes in his Introduction:

> Very little can be said in favour of this play. Otway has fallen between two stools and knocked his head against a third. The attempt to combine Shakespeare's romance with Plutarch's history has resulted in disaster to both, and matters have been made worse by the attempt to make the feud between the rival Roman factions suggestive of the Whig and Tory controversy of Otway's time. The different interests have not blended, and the play remains a clumsy patchwork with the seams staring.
> (Otway 1932, 46)

Yet, strictly speaking, *Caius Marius* is not an adaptation of *Romeo and Juliet*, but an autonomous Roman tragedy in which only the subplot is taken from Shakespeare.

Now, the question is: what is the function of a tragic love story – and particularly this one, which is embedded in a political tragedy?

From a theatrical and spectacular point of view, that is to say, in a practical perspective, Addison would later give a possible answer: love was a necessary device for the playwright to be successful with half of his audience, namely, female spectators:

> As our Heroes are generally Lovers, their Swelling and Blustring upon the Stage very much recommends them to the fair Part of their Audience. The Ladies are wonderfully pleased to see a Man insulting Kings, or affronting the Gods, in one Scene, and throwing himself at the Feet of his Mistress in another. Let him behave himself insolently towards the Men, and abjectly towards the Fair One, and it is ten to one but he proves a favourite of the Boxes. *Dryden* and *Lee*, in several of their Tragedies, have practised this Secret with good Success.
> (1711, 40: April 16)

Tate in his *King Lear* (1681) inserted a love story between Cordelia and Edgar, but this choice aimed at poetical justice so that in the end virtue would be rewarded and vice punished. The happy ending of Tate's *Lear* was evidence of a worldview made of absolutes, of black and white elements, far from the truth of life. Anne Righter (1965, 138) has written that Restoration tragedy was an artificial construct, while comedy was paradoxically serious and realistic. In this critic's opinion at the end of the century the two forms got closer and slowly came to refer to the same world: comedy became nihilistic and tragedy became increasingly based on the idea that life is deceitful. Otway represents this attitude and his play marks the passage from heroic to sentimental or affective tragedy. The plot taken from *Romeo and Juliet* becomes part of the civic story, not as a challenge to patriarchal society, but as the inevitable tragedy of obedience. In Otway's Rome there is no boundary between the public and the private. Lavinia was promised to Sylla by her father Metellus for reasons of political alliance, Marius junior will obey his father's request that Lavinia's name be no more called:

> I shall obey ...
> No, Sir, I'll speak that hatefull Name no more,
> But be as Curst as you can wish your Son. (1.356–9)

The love between the two is prohibited by their fathers, who are engaged in a bitter political strife; both Marius senior and Metellus threaten their children with banishment from their homes if they do not obey their wishes. Lavinia resists her father Metellus, and in plain Restoration style, calls marriage without love "a Lawful Rape" (2.107). In the third act, Marius junior confesses his father that he has married Lavinia, but is determined not to see her until he can show his military value and regain his father's affection. Love is here not opposed to public life, nor to family feud; it is a private condition which might be used for political purposes. Lavinia is a kind of war spoil, and the lovers' marriage is seen by Marius senior as a revenge against Metellus. The status of subplot is always stressed upon, since every private scene adapted from *Romeo and Juliet* ends with explicit references to the public plot.

Yet Shakespeare's play provides the metaphorical model on which Otway could base his work: there is a line in *Romeo and Juliet* that might be taken as the epitome of *The History and Fall of Caius Marius*, and it is a line that could not go unnoticed to an adaptor. The very opening spoken by the Chorus, "Two households both alike in dignity", already contains an idea several times repeated in Otway's play: that of two elements equal in value which can be opposed in hatred or united in love. Thus Marius junior remarks the coincidence and the difference of events within a binary system:

> When the unhappy Discords first took flame
> Betwixt my Father and the Senate; then
> A holy Priest of *Hymen*, whom with Gold
> I brib'd to yield us privately his Office,
> Joyn'd our kind Hands, and now She's ever mine. (3.130–4)

Two equal lovers, two equal fathers who are enemies, two equal factions which divide the State. Very acutely Jessica Munns states that Otway "found in both his sources that equality between rival sides to which he was always attracted. Shakespeare's Capulets are no better or worse than his Montagues. Likewise, Plutarch's Gaius Marius has magnificence as well as ambition, and his Sulla is a brilliant general as well as a dictator who destroys the republic" (1995, 99).

Equality can justify the idea that neither side is taken, not because both are good, but because "neither side is acceptable" (Wikander 1986, 349).

Nihilism is shown resorting to a figure that is different from the medieval wheel of fortune or from the ascending and descending movements of the two buckets Richard II talks about. Here, as in *Julius Caesar*, success and failure depend on the rabble, which is bribed or persuaded to oscillate between two opposite but similar, if not equal, poles. In the first act Antonius comments negatively on Marius's ambition and pride, highlighting just these elements: number two, equality, and the unpredictability of the mob:

> As 'tis not many years since two Great men
> In *Rome* stood equal Candidates together,
> For high Command: In every house was Riot.
> To day the Drunken Rabble reel'd to one;
> To morrow they were mad agen for t'other;
> Changing their Voices with their Entertainment:
> And none could guesse on whom the Choice would settle; (1.28–34)

As civil wars or urban turmoil are seen in terms of two equal rivals, winning should mean concentrating power in a single one, "Great, unequall'd and alone" (1.436), as Marius senior would like to be.

In the play other oppositions explicitly refer to a binary system: that between the private and the public, seen as a contrast between love and civic duties, is for Marius junior the object of a prayer: "Love and Renown sure court me thus together. / Smile, smile, ye Gods, and give Success to both" (2.391–2). His wish that the two could be kept together, and that he could be a Hero and a Lover at the same time, without being obliged to choose, is symbolized in the text by the recurrence of a term that belongs to both the military and the affective semantic fields: arms. "My arms" can thus either hint at a battle or at an embrace.

In the second act, Lavinia reveals to her father that she cannot love Sylla, implying the rivalry between two men: a duality in which the Nurse's words again refer to equality:

> *Marius* is a Man, and so's *Sylla*. Oh! but *Marius's* Lip! And then *Sylla's* Nose and Forehead! but then *Marius's* Eye agen! how 'twill sparkle, and twinckle, and rowl, and sleer? But to see Sylla a horseback! But to see Marius walk or dance! such a Leg, such a Foot, such a Shape, such a Motion. Ah h h … (2.182–7)

The Nurse, whose figure Otway maintained from the original text and emphasized, is a comic character, and her words are, of course, ironical. This role was successfully played by a famous transvestite actor, James Nokes, and his acting in drag intensified the comic part of the play. He was already known to the public as "Nurse" Nokes, having acted the nurse in Nevil Payne's *Fatal Jealousy*. Sexual innuendoes, puns, ironic cues or base expressions were added by Otway to the Shakespearian text, probably having this interpreter in mind. Their presence, besides stressing another duality – that of tragic and comic registers mixed together – has here the effect of cancelling the possibility for the general tone of the play to incline towards either. When Lavinia is found and thought to be dead, the cross-dressed actor announces to her father: "Your onely Daughter's dead: / As dead as Herring, Stock-fish, or Door-nail" (5.134–5), and promises:

> Nay, my poor Baby, I'll take care thou shalt not dy for nothing: for I will wash thee with my Tears, perfume thee with my Sighs, and stick a Flower in every part about thee … (5.152–5)

Events precipitate as in the original play, but the inevitable catastrophe of *Romeo and Juliet* was transformed by an additional device, which would have a long-lasting success: Lavinia wakes up to find that Marius has already drunk poison but is not dead yet. Thus the two lovers can talk before he dies transported by the joy of being with his beloved. What could be a tragic or pathetic ending becomes a little excessive to our sensibility as modern spectators. Marius senior enters as the winner with Metellus as his prisoner, and the latter dies in front of his daughter, slain by his rival. Marius recognizes Lavinia as the girl who once helped him and saved his life but, after accusing him of having butchered her father, Lavinia takes his sword and stabs herself.

This alteration of the original tragic death scene was later used by both Theophilus Cibber and David Garrick in their adaptations of *Romeo and Juliet*; the two playwrights appreciated the dramatic potential of Juliet's awakening and of a last pathetic dialogue with her lover. But David Garrick perceived that the "affective Circumstance" had not been fully exploited by Otway: "It is a matter of Wonder that so great a dramatic Genius did not work up a Scene from it of more Nature, Terror and Distress" (Garrick 1981, *Advertisement*, A3). He was right, because here, in Otway's adaptation, pathos, as well as the tragic, is barred. At Lavinia's death, Marius repents of his cruel nature, saying: "We might have all bin Friends, and in one House / Enjoy'd the blessings of eternal Peace" (5.466–7). "One House": an expression that refers to the private sphere of the family but may also topically allude to the public space of the Parliament. And, who knows, maybe to that of the theatre as well.

The finale bends toward the tragic. More sad news arrives: a messenger announces that Sylla is approaching Rome, "the Rabble are in new Rebellion" (5.472), and Sulpitius is mortally wounded. But just because Sulpitius is mentioned and enters, led by two guards, even the tragic events of the final scene are desecrated. His role, though drastically cut, is that of Mercutio, and he is alive till the end of the play, in order to have the very last word: he dies uttering Mercutio's tragicomic cue: "I am pepper'd, I warrant, etc." and dictating his own epitaph:

> Sulpitius *lies here, that troublesome Slave,*
> *That sent many honester men to the Grave,*
> *And dy'd like a Fool when h' had lived like a Knave.* (5.491–3)

Even more remarkable, he enters the stage while Caius Marius is lamenting his own ruin caused by ambition and advising rulers not to follow his example. Then Marius asks to be led away to a place where he will wait for death to come. Sulpitius comments, "A Curse on all Repentance! how I hate it!" (5.484). Underneath this cue, which is Otway's invention, I cannot help imagining that there lurks "A plague on both your houses!" which the wounded Mercutio exclaims four times before dying.

Whether this curse was in Otway's mind, to swear at both political factions of his own times, is not to be known. But *The History and Fall of Caius Marius* closes with "one House", as the emblem of peace, and with the implicit, background, reference to "both your houses", as the emblem of the civil war.

In my opinion 'Two' is the figure that links the Roman and the Shakespearian tragedies: a polarity where no choice is possible, and which is resolved only in death.

To end, I would like to quote John Donne, as no one expresses better this idea than he does, with his paradoxical and oxymoronic argumentation, in an epigram devoted to Pyramus and Thisbe, whose story recalls that of Romeo and Juliet:

> Two, by themselves, each other, love and fear
> Slaine, cruell friends, by parting have joyn'd here. (Donne 1912, 75)

WORKS CITED

Addison, Joseph. (1711) 1945. *The Spectator*. Edited by G. Gregory Smith, 4 vols. London: J.M. Dent & Sons.

Batzer, Hazel M. 1969. "Shakespeare's Influence on Thomas Otway's *Caius Marius*". *Revue de l'Université d'Ottawa* 39: 532–61.

Bigliazzi, Silvia. 2010. "Beyond politics: excision and revision in Nahum Tate's *Richard II*". In *Rehearsals of the Modern: Experience and Experiment in Restoration Drama*, edited by Susanna Zinato, 97–110. Napoli: Liguori.

Calvi, Lisanna. 2005. *Kingship and Tragedy (1660–1715)*. Verona: QuiEdit.

Canfield, Douglas J. 1985. "Royalism's Last Dramatic Stand: English Political Tragedy, 1679-89". *Studies in Philology* 82: 234–63.

Dobson, Michael. 1992. *The Making of the National Poet. Shakespeare, Adaptation and Authorship, 1660–1769*. Oxford: Clarendon Press.

Donne, John. 1912. *The Poems*. Edited by H.J.C. Grierson, 2 vols. Oxford: Clarendon Press.

Dryden, John. (1680) 1992. *The Kind Keeper, or Mr. Limberham*. In *The Works of John Dryden*, edited by Vinton A. Dearing, vol. 14. Berkeley, Los Angeles and London: University of California Press.

Fitter, Chris. 2000. "'The quarrel is between our masters and us their men': *Romeo and Juliet*, Dearth, and the London Riots". *English Literary Renaissance* 30: 154–83.

Garrick, David. (1748) 1981. *Romeo and Juliet*. In *The Plays of David Garrick*, edited by Gerald M. Berkovitz, vol. 2. New York: Garland.

Genette, Gérard. 1982. *Palimpsestes. La littérature au second degré*. Paris: Editions du Seuil.
Harth, Philip. 1988. "Political Interpretations of *Venice Preserv'd*". *Modern Philology* 85: 345–62.
Innocenti, Loretta. 1985. *La scena trasformata. Adattamenti neoclassici di Shakespeare*. Firenze: Sansoni. Republished 2010. Pisa: Pacini.
Lucan. (61–65 A.D.) 1614. *Lucans Pharsalia. Containing The Ciuill Warres betweene Caesar and Pompey*. Translated into English verse by Sir Arthur Gorges. London: Edward Blount. On line text: University of Virginia Library. Accessed March 12, 2015. http://xtf.lib.virginia.edu/xtf/view?docId=chadwyck_ep/uvaGenText/tei/chep_1.0389.xml.
Marsden, Jean, ed. 1991. *The Appropriation of Shakespeare. Post-Renaissance Reconstructions of the Works and the Myth*. London and New York: Harvester Wheatsheaf.
Moretti, Franco. 1983. *Signs Taken for Wonders. On the Sociology of Literary Forms*. London: Verso.
Munns Jessica. 1995. *Restoration Politics and Drama: The Plays of Thomas Otway, 1675–1683*. London: Associated University Presses.
Murray, Barbara A. 2001. *Restoration Shakespeare: Viewing the Voice*. Madison, NJ: Fairleigh Dickinson University Press.
Otway, Thomas. 1932. *The Works of Thomas Otway: Plays, Poems, and Love-Letters*. Edited by J.C. Ghosh, 2 vols. Oxford: Clarendon Press.
Righter, Anne. 1965. "Heroic Tragedy". In *Restoration Theatre*, edited by John Russell Brown and Bernard Harris, 71–91. New York: St Martin's Press.
Spencer, Hazelton. 1927. *Shakespeare Improved: The Restoration Versions in Quarto and on the Stage*. Cambridge, MA: Harvard University Press.
Taylor, Gary. 1989. *Reinventing Shakespeare. A Cultural History from the Restoration to the Present*. London: The Hogarth Press.
Wallace, John M. 1988. "Otway's *Caius Marius* and the Exclusion Crisis". *Modern Philology* 85: 363–72.
Walsh, Jaquelyn W. 2000. *The Impact of the Restoration Critical Theory on the Adaptation of Four Shakespeare Comedies*. Lewiston, NY: The Edwin Mellen Press.
Ward, Adolphus William. 1899. *A History of English Dramatic Literature*, 3 vols. London: Macmillan.
Wikander, Matthew H. 1986. "The Spitted Infant: Scenic Emblem and the Exclusionist Politics in Restoration Adaptations of Shakespeare". *Shakespeare Quarterly* 37: 340–58.

10 Brooke, Garrick, *Romeo and Juliet*, and the Public Sphere

Michael Dobson

> Juliet: Do not swear at all;
> Or, if thou wilt, swear by thy gracious self,
> Which is the god of my idolatry,
> And I'll believe thee. (2.1.155–8)

I want to look in this short chapter at some of the significances *Romeo and Juliet* held for the Enlightenment. Although I am going to start with a reconsideration of the play's main source, Arthur Brooke's poem *Romeus and Juliet* (1562), I am going to focus on a single figure, the actor-manager and writer David Garrick (1717–79), whose efforts as a publicist and self-publicist did much to guarantee Shakespeare's subsequent importance across Europe in the age of Romanticism. I am first going to consider one crucial aspect of Shakespeare's play proper in which it diverges from its source; then I examine its contrasting fortunes on the public and private stages of eighteenth-century Britain. I then want to look at the symbolic involvement of *Romeo and Juliet* in Garrick's pioneering Shakespearean festival, the Stratford Jubilee of 1769. In Shakespeare's hands, I shall argue, the story of Romeo and Juliet became almost accidentally a story about the Veronese public sphere. Thanks in part to Garrick, it has now modelled Shakespeare's presence in subsequent public spheres for two and a half centuries.

A TALE OF ONE CITY

The so-called 'balcony' scene (which famously never itself refers to a balcony), from which the opening quotation is drawn, has long dominated the popular image of *Romeo and Juliet*, and not inappropriately. Despite a rich and enduring tradition of dramatic representations of clandestine passion, elopements, trysts, and under-aged romance, this is one of comparatively few plays that dares to show us what its young lovers actually say to one another when in private, and hence the celebration of *Romeo and Juliet* in, for instance, Tom Stoppard and Marc Norman's screenplay for *Shakespeare in Love* (1997), as a work that "shows the very truth of love" (Norman and Stoppard 1999, 23). But the Romeo and Juliet story was always a narrative with an important civic dimension, too, and in adjusting it for dramatic purposes Shakespeare found himself obliged to make his play still more preoccupied with what it means to be and to belong in Verona even than his immediate source, Arthur Brooke's poem *Romeus and Juliet* (1562). Put simply, for the tragic last two acts of his play to look remotely plausible or necessary, Shakespeare had to make the idea of living away from the city more or less unthinkable for any of the characters concerned.

The subject of Shakespeare's modifications to the story he found in Brooke has long been a *locus classicus* of *Romeo and Juliet* criticism. Most commentators have been struck by the skill with which Shakespeare compresses events that in his source take place around nine months into an urgent, tight timescale of four days and four nights, a compression that requires Shakespeare's characters themselves (with the notable exception of the Nurse, her role wonderfully and digressively expanded from that of the poem's mere function-character) to display an impetuousness and impatience much less obvious among the cast of Brooke's poem. Many have also commented on the difference in tone between Shakespeare's sympathetic presentation of his ardent Romeo and Juliet and Brooke's more moralistic account, particularly in his preface "To the Reader", of his own Romeus and Juliet, who are, he tells us,

> a coople of unfortunate lovers, thralling themselves to unhonest desire, neglecting the authoritie and advise of parents and frendes ... attemptying all adventures of peryll, for thattaynyng of their wished lust ... abusyng the honorable name of lawefull marriage, the cloke the shame of stolne contractes ...
>
> (Brooke 1966, 1.284–5).[1]

This difference in moral attitude to the lovers, however, which has tempted some to dismiss Brooke as a drably orthodox Protestant, is connected, I would argue, to a simple but often unnoticed narrative question which potentially troubles all versions of this story, and to which Brooke and Shakespeare provide very different answers. That question – which nobody recounting the tragic tale of Romeo and Juliet can conveniently afford to allow their audience to ask – is this: why do the lovers just not elope to somewhere else? Why does Romeo descend the rope ladder alone after he and Juliet consummate their clandestine marriage, instead of taking Juliet with him to Mantua? Surely in practice any sensible Juliet would go off with her new husband to have a nice leisurely honeymoon at a safe distance from their feuding in-laws, instead of resigning herself to the rushed and furtive wedding night at home to which she consents in the play. It is a tribute to Shakespeare's dramatic sleight of hand that in performance audiences are deeply moved by the parting of the newlyweds in the aubade scene (3.5), instead of merely infuriated that Juliet should be doing anything as bizarre as waving Romeo off and herself staying behind in her parents' house.

In Brooke's poem, the answer to this question is scandalously different to that offered in Shakespeare's play, which is that the lovers are at first in no rush at all to start their shared life as acknowledged members of their own independent household. The hazardous business of getting to and from Juliet's bedchamber by rope-ladder, which for the play's Romeo is a desperate expedient for one stolen night only, will become for the poem's Romeus a matter of delightful routine which is to be repeated nightly for an indefinite period. The consummation of Romeus and Juliet's marriage is an altogether more leisurely business than that of Romeo and Juliet, concluded by a parting which is only to be for a few hours:

> And now in ease he doth possesse the hoped place.
> How glad was he, speake you that may your lovers parts embrace ...
> With frendly kisse in armes of her his leave he takes,
> And every other night to come, a solemn othe he makes. (Brooke 1966, ll. 923–4, 929–30)

This dubious state of affairs – by which the couple secretly enjoy the sexual pleasures of marriage without any of its social and economic responsibilities – continues for many weeks ("Yong Romeus clymes fayre Juliets bower by night / Three monthes he doth enjoy his cheefe delight", as "The Argument" puts it, ibid., 286), until Romeus's fatal encounter with Tybalt and sentence of banishment (brilliantly transposed by Shakespeare to take place between the marriage contract and the wedding night) forces him to leave Verona. (In fact it occurs only just in time, if then, to avert the other potentially troubling question which comes with this story, namely that of what the couple were proposing to do if Juliet became pregnant). As in the play, Brooke's Juliet permits her husband to go to Mantua alone only on the understanding that they will be reunited as soon as their families can be reconciled and their marriage disclosed. In the poem, however, it is Romeus who is to carry out the diplomacy involved rather than the Friar:

> Ere fowre monthes overpasse, such order will I take,
> And by my letters, and my frendes, such meanes I mynd to make,
> That of my wandring race, ended shalbe the toyle,
> And I cald home with honor great, unto my native soyle. (ibid., ll. 1673–6)

Furthermore, should this initiative fail within its finite set period, Romeus has a drastic plan B:

> But if I be condemd to wander still in thrall,
> I will returne to you (mine owne) befall what may befall.
> And then by strength of frendes, and with a mighty hand,
> From Verone will I carry thee, into a forein lande,
> Not in mans weede disguisd, or as one scarcely knowne,
> But as my wife and onely feere, in garment of thyne owne. (ibid., ll. 1677–82)

Once bounced out of the couple's illicit sexual idyll by banishment, in fact, Romeus belatedly gets on with assuming an active role in the public sphere, undertaking to work strenuously to turn the semi-adolescent, clandestine relationship into which he and Juliet had settled with such questionable ease into an acknowledged adult marriage – if not in Verona, then elsewhere. No sooner has he left Verona, accordingly, than he begins openly and diligently to plead their cause in Mantua:

> Warely he walked forth, unknown of frend or foe,
> Clad like a merchant venterer, from top even to the toe.
> He spurd apace, and came withouten stop or stay,
> To Mantua gates, where lighted downe, he sent his man away
> With woords of comfort, to his olde afflicted syre:
> And straight in mynd to sojorne there, a lodgeing he doth hyre,
> And with the nobler sort he doth himself acquaint,
> And of his open wrong received, the Duke doth heare his plainte.
> He practiseth by frendes, for pardon of exile,
> The whilst, he seeketh every way, his sorrowes to begyle. (ibid., ll. 1733–42)

In Brooke, the fact that Romeus and Juliet had already settled in to three months of secretly married life, and their confidence that by one or another of the means Romeus proposes they will soon be reunited (moreover, through his agency), makes their separation when he goes into exile in Mantua seem acceptable both to the lovers and to Brooke's readers. Furthermore, Mantua itself is shown as a bustling and hospitable arena in which a newly energized and adult Romeus promptly goes public as a husband. If all else fails he is evidently able as well as willing to settle with Juliet outside Verona in "a forein lande" (ibid., l. 1680).

Shakespeare's dramatic telescoping of the poem's events avoids the moral problem which troubles Brooke and animates his disapproving preface – namely that of having to invite our sympathy for a couple who behave at best sneakily in at first embracing a sex-only marriage at the Capulets' unwitting expense for a period of months – but for the play the narrative problem of making it look reasonable for Romeo to leave Juliet behind in Verona when he goes into exile becomes correspondingly more awkward. The poem's Juliet agrees to sleep with Romeo in secret indefinitely, long before his killing of Tybalt, but thereafter allows him to go into exile without her on condition that if all else fails they will live openly together elsewhere: the play's Juliet not only has to agree to consummate her marriage with Romeo after he has killed her cousin, but has to agree in advance that he will leave for Mantua without her immediately afterwards. With Shakespeare's new ordering of events, a shared departure from Verona to embark on marriage elsewhere is in danger of looking like a much more obvious option after Romeo's banishment than the one the lovers need to take if the remainder of the tragedy is to unfold.

This is one reason, I would argue, why Shakespeare takes such pains to persuade his audiences that in the universe of *Romeo and Juliet* banishment is the equivalent of execution: as Romeo says on learning of his sentence, in the course of his great set-piece on the subject, "There is no world without Verona walls, / But purgatory, torture, hell itself" (3.3.17–18).[2] The play implicitly agrees with him, whether banishment involves separation from Juliet or not, underlining the point by its structure and mode as well as by this sort of verbal statement. Only one scene in *Romeo and Juliet* takes place outside Verona, and, the least realistic in the play, 5.1, it seems designed to keep Mantua as shadowy and insubstantial as possible, even as we are allowed to see Romeo living there. All that happens in the Mantua scene is that Romeo (who unlike Romeus is living in aimless isolated privacy rather than lobbying among the city's rulers) recounts a dream, experiences a mood of what we know to be doomed optimism ("My bosom's lord sits lightly in his throne", 5.1.3), receives bad news we know to be false and instantly remembers an apothecary who seems every bit as dreamlike as anything in the scene's opening speech. (Brooke's Romeus is much more businesslike, even in his preparations for suicide: he purposefully goes out to seek an apothecary, carefully leaving his servant at home so that there will be no witness when he buys the poison, ll. 2561–88). The apothecary then promptly materializes, more like a wish or fantasy conveniently and magically made flesh than a concrete social being. In *Romeo and Juliet* the only important thing that happens in Mantua is that Romeo resolves to get back to Verona, where his life means something, in order to die. It is carefully never considered or represented as a place where there could be any sort of life other than a period of waiting dreamily in limbo before returning home to Verona.

This refusal to acknowledge Mantua as a possible alternative means that *Romeo and Juliet* focuses even more strongly than does *Romeus and Juliet* on the civic importance of the story's tragic outcome. Like Brooke, Shakespeare denies Romeo and Juliet a last private dialogue in the tomb; he then arranges for all the surviving Veronese characters to witness what has happened to the lovers and promise to erect public statues, which by commemorating their short-lived relationship will mark the end of the Capulet-Montague feud. The whole point and premise of the play, just in case we have not already got it, has been that Romeo and Juliet were first and foremost citizens of Verona and should as such have been perfectly at liberty to marry one another; their shared civic identity should have trumped their respective identities as a Montague and a Capulet. Whereas Brooke's poem sees the couple as Italians, who could have settled elsewhere, Shakespeare's play is obliged by its compressed time-scale to insist that Romeo and Juliet are strictly Veronese: as such, they should have been saved from the feud wished on them by their parents by their shared allegiance to the Prince.

A TALE OF ONE NATION

Romeo and Juliet is, in short, a play that (however accidentally) comes to encode the formation of a collective political identity at the expense of feudal loyalty to the family. As Benedict Anderson and others have pointed out,[3] such tales of young lovers tragically divided by the claims of rival clans, ethnicities, or factions tend to surface and proliferate in any society undergoing the making or unmaking of a national identity. Modern Western nation-states have indeed characteristically represented the liberty of marital choice as the definitive political right which the state exists to guarantee, and during the period of their emergence as such this regularly involved retellings of stories at very least analogous to *Romeo and Juliet*.

England, arguably, was already recognizing itself as a modern nation in Shakespeare's own time, but most historians agree that the most important period in the making of British national identity came between the 1707 Act of Union and the Napoleonic wars.[4] Exactly in the middle of that period came the career of David Garrick, and it is at least suggestive that throughout Garrick's career as an actor, a theatrical manager, and a writer, *Romeo and Juliet* – that play about the priority of collective identity over feudalism – was never far away. Although the play had fallen out of the repertory in the later seventeenth century – briefly supplied with a happy ending by James Howard in the 1660s, then laid aside except in the form of Thomas Otway's *Caius Marius* (1680), which is as much a new play as an adaption – the statistics compiled by C.B. Hogan in the 1950s place *Romeo and Juliet* as the most-revived Shakespeare play of the second half of the eighteenth century.[5]

Garrick himself is partly responsible for this. He took on the management of the Theatre Royal, Drury Lane, in 1747, and he took on the role of Romeo in the following year, adapting the play before he did so the better to make it fit eighteenth-century literary criteria (primarily by removing rhymes and puns), contemporary scenography (adding a funeral procession and dirge for Juliet), contemporary social mores (he raised Juliet's age to eighteen), and above all tailoring it to his own acting style.[6] Garrick's Juliet, like Otway's Lavinia in *Caius Marius*, awakens in the tomb before Romeo has finished dying of the poison, prompting Romeo at first to imagine he is in heaven, then to realize the full horror of his situation, then to become delirious before dying, an episode which allowed Garrick to give a characteristically energetic and twitchy histrionic display full of abrupt emotional transitions. (His performance in this scene is recorded by a 1753 painting by Benjamin Wilson, in which Garrick's Romeo is starting nervily back from the newly conscious Juliet, much as his Hamlet did on seeing his father's ghost).[7] The critic Francis Gentleman, for one, admired how fully Garrick's alterations worked the pathos in the Capulet tomb "to its tenderest pitch" in "melting incidents and expression", and his only reservation was that in its improved form the scene might be "rather too great a strain for tender sympathy" (1774, 2.152). The number of revivals enjoyed by this *Romeo and Juliet* was increased not only by the success with which Garrick had fitted the play to his audience's tastes, but by a feud-like instance of theatrical politics. The actor Spranger Barry, jealous that Garrick was taking all the best parts at Drury Lane, defected in 1750 to its only legal rival, the Theatre Royal, Covent Garden, and soon he and Garrick went head to head in what became known as The War of the Romeos. Both theatres staged their rival productions of *Romeo and Juliet* for twelve consecutive nights, each company waiting for the other to blink and be the first to advertise something else, and though many found Barry the more convincingly soulful and tender Romeo it was the energetic Garrick who won the day. (This was partly, it must be admitted, by default; Covent Garden's Juliet, Susannah Cibber, fell ill, possibly of exhaustion). In the new public sphere represented by the London playhouses, sometimes jokingly referred to at the time as a 'fourth estate of the realm' as if the theatres were a semi-official part of the national constitution, *Romeo and Juliet* had not only become a major canonical text about the relationship between marital choice and free citizenship, but it had actually been the only play anyone could see at all for the best part of a fortnight. Romeo would remain one of the Shakespearean roles with which Garrick was most closely associated as an actor, and it has remained a role in which aspiring Shakespearean performers have needed to prove themselves ever since.

The connections between the plot of forbidden marriage and the emergent discourse of nationhood would be more controversial, however, in two contexts: firstly, political situations in which nationalism was setting out to supplant older systems of social cohesion rapidly rather than gradually, and secondly in performances mounted not under the aegis of the State, as at the Theatres Royal, but under the aegis of the family. The political valence of the Romeo and Juliet story is nicely underlined little more than a decade after Garrick's death, for instance, by the poet, polemicist, and novelist Helen Maria Williams, whose pro-Revolutionary *Letters from France* (1790–96) begin with two topical, optimistic versions of the familiar tale. The Montague figure in the first is a tyrannical baron, passionately committed to the *ancien régime*, who has his son imprisoned in a bid to prevent him marrying his beloved Monique, to whom the Baron objects not because she belongs to a rival aristocratic dynasty but because she is a mere bourgeoise. This young couple, however, believe in getting out to the equivalent of Mantua, as a temporary measure at least; they succeed in eloping to that incorrigible neighbouring nation of shopkeepers, England, before at last feeling able to make a happy return from exile the day after the fall of the Bastille. The direct link between the politics of forbidden young love and those of the emergent nation-state is nicely articulated by the second modern Juliet in Williams' book. Madelaine is an impoverished gentlewoman whom her beloved Auguste's aristocratic father tries in vain to consign to a convent:

> Madelaine was a firm friend to the revolution, which she was told had made every Frenchman free. 'And if every Frenchman is free', thought

Madelaine, 'surely every Frenchman may marry the woman he loves'. It appeared to Madelaine, that, putting all political considerations, points upon which she had not much meditated, out of the question, obtaining liberty of choice in marriage was alone well worth the troubles of a revolution.

(Williams 1975, 174–5)

But back in Britain not everyone was as keen either on revolution or on the idea of marriages being contracted without parental consent, and even while *Romeo and Juliet* was enjoying its greatest popularity on the public stage it was all but banned from the private, non-professional, and semi-professional performances that proliferated in mid-eighteenth-century country houses. Garrick himself ridiculed a middle-aged couple who go in for private readings of *Romeo and Juliet* together in his play *A Peep Behind the Curtain* (1767); while James Powell's satirical play *Private Theatricals* (1787) depicts a scandalous country-house production of *Romeo and Juliet* in which the daughter of the house has ill-advisedly been cast as Juliet and is conducting a clandestine affair with the supposed professional actor hired in to play Romeo. Nor was it only playwrights who disapproved of such domestic productions of Shakespeare's play, fearing that it might corrupt the respectable daughters of ruling-class Britain. When the passionately stage-struck Earl of Barrymore went bankrupt in 1792, obliging the authorities to auction off the contents of his private theatre at Wargrave near Reading to pay some of the bills incurred during its construction, the judge in the case, Lord Kenyon, specifically invoked *Romeo and Juliet* while decrying the entire pastime:

> With respect to the tendency of private theatrical entertainments, his Lordship doubted very much whether they had ever inculcated one single virtuous sentiment. He had known instances where they had a contrary effect; and they usually vitiated and debauched the morals of both sexes; the performers seldom retired from the entertainment, but every Romeo knew the estimate of his Juliet's virtue.[8]

(This is the earliest instance I have found, incidentally, of the term 'Romeo' being used in a pejorative manner, as if it were the equivalent of 'Lothario'). This case was directly contemporary with Williams' composition of her two Romeo and Juliet-like vignettes of pro-revolutionary elopement, and it is hard to imagine Lord Kenyon reading her work with approbation. To those for whom the government of the realm still belonged by descent to a network of tightly defended families, *Romeo and Juliet* might just be acceptable as public entertainment, but the last place you wanted it was in the home. It is suggestive in this context that the only large-scale private theatrical enterprise of this period to have incorporated performances of *Romeo and Juliet* was the annual festival of charitable amateur theatre staged at Kilkenny in Ireland from 1802 to 1819. Significantly, this was a consciously civic event specifically designed to bring together rival political and religious factions in peace ("it often brought into the same social circle", remembered one local writer, "many who at other seasons of the year were separated by differences of politics or religion, that too frequently, and too fatally, divide us", *The Private Theatre of Kilkenny* 1825, 9), and even here the play's generational and sexual politics were partly defused by the hiring in of professional actresses to play Juliet.[9] The most notable of these was Eliza O'Neill, in the final, 1819 season, and she too did what she could to make the play more respectable by marrying her Friar Laurence and retiring from the stage altogether.[10]

A TALE OF ONE BOROUGH

So for the Enlightenment *Romeo and Juliet* was a highly popular play which, by aligning the right of young people to make their own marital choices in defiance of their parents with the kind of collective identity represented by the newly emergent nation-state, had come to occupy a special place on a key ideological faultline. How was Garrick to use this when setting out to declare Shakespeare the national poet of Britain at his great public festival, or perhaps fan-convention, the Stratford Jubilee of 1769? The answer, I think, is with considerable cunning.

The climax of the event which declared Shakespeare to be the voice of England's native soil was Garrick's own performance of his *Ode, upon dedicating a building, and erecting a statue, to Shakespeare, at Stratford-upon-Avon*, a text in which much of the event's enduring meaning would reside. Quite apart from maintaining a magnificent rhetorical postponement of the word 'Shakespeare', which the poem holds off until its 31st line, Garrick's baroque opening stanza makes alternating allusions to two different Shakespeare plays:

> To what blest genius of the isle
> Shall Gratitude her tribute pay,
>   Decree the festive day,
> Erect the statue, and devote the pile?
> Do not your sympathetic hearts accord
>   To own the 'bosom's lord?'
> 'Tis he! 'tis he! – that demi-god
> Who Avon's flow'ry margins trod
>   While sportive *Fancy* round him flew,
> Where *Nature* led him by the hand,
>   Instructed him in all she knew,
> And gave him absolute command!
>   'Tis he! 'tis he!
> 'The god of our idolatry!' (1769, 1)[11]

As the insular genius around whom an Ariel-like Fancy flies, Shakespeare is clearly identified here as royal Prospero to Britain's enchanted island – a trope which is still alive even now, as viewers of the opening ceremony of the 2012 London Olympics may recognize. But if Shakespeare is thus an authoritative and even authoritarian father in this stanza, he is also a disobedient, amorous son. If to admit to being emotionally moved by Shakespeare's plays is to own the "bosom's lord", then every sympathetic audience member is possessed by the spirit of Romeo; and this identification of Shakespeare with Romeo is reaffirmed when the playwright is declared, in words only slightly adapted from the balcony scene, the god of our idolatry. As Shakespeare's fans and fellow-islanders we are at once spritely Romeos and desiring Juliets, and as listeners to the Ode we are made whole in an act of public devotion conducted by a priest who is no less a person than David Garrick, the actor who won the War of the Romeos and is thus qualified to speak both for and as Shakespeare. According to the logic of the Ode, Romeo and Juliet both live on in the now avowedly public cult of Shakespeare, their golden statues subsumed into the statue of the playwright, which the poem gives to Stratford. Britain is Prospero's island, but it is also Shakespeare's imagined Italy; Garrick is the Prince, and Romeo, and Juliet, and above all Shakespeare; and Shakespeare's home town and that of his doomed young lovers are one and the same. The Enlightenment's canonization of Shakespeare promoted him to dominion over a public sphere partly imagined in terms borrowed from *Romeo and Juliet*, and according to the Jubilee Stratford is itself a version of Verona, the one true Shakespearean home from which exile would be not just inconvenient but unimaginable.

NOTES

1. See also Brooke 1966, 269–283; Shakespeare 1984 and Shakespeare 2012.
2. References to the text of *Romeo and Juliet* are to Shakespeare 2000.
3. See especially Anderson 1983.
4. See especially Colley 1992.
5. See Hogan 1952–7.
6. Garrick's acting version was published in the second volume of Bell's complete acting edition of Shakespeare in 1774. For an edited and annotated text, see Garrick 1981, vol. 3.
7. Wilson's painting is now in the Victoria and Albert Museum, as acquisition number S.1452–1986: it is catalogued under the rather unwieldy title "David Garrick as Romeo, George Anne Bellamy as Juliet and Charles Blakes as Tybalt in *Romeo and Juliet* adapted by David Garrick from William Shakespeare".
8. That is, without every Romeo knowing how much his Juliet's virtue was worth. These remarks were widely quoted: see, for example, the *Annual Register* 34 1799, 5.
9. The same point had been made by the *Dublin Evening Post*'s correspondent on 28 November 1809.

10. *The Private Theatre of Kilkenny* 1825, 121–2. See also *Gentleman's Magazine* 1819, 2.635. For an account of O'Neill's Juliet at Kilkenny, see *Ierne* 1861, 161–8. A hand-coloured print of Eliza O'Neill as Juliet in the 'balcony' scene (by Frederick Christian Lewis Sr, after George Dawe, 1816) now hangs in the Shakespeare Institute in Stratford: the same portrait is catalogued in the National Portrait Gallery as D35814. For a fuller discussion of the place of *Romeo and Juliet* in eighteenth- and nineteenth-century private theatricals see Dobson 2011, chapters 1 and 2.
11. On the Jubilee see especially Dobson 1992, chapter 5. See also Ewan Fernie's essay "Freetown! Shakespeare and Social Fourishing", forthcoming in *Shakespeare Survey*, and especially the live version at http://youtu.be/3id9cgynFSU. Accessed March 6, 2015.

WORKS CITED

Anderson, Benedict. 1983. *Imagined Communities: Reflections on the Origins and Spread of Nationalism.* London: Verso.

Brooke, Arthur. (1562) 1966. *The Tragicall Historye of Romeus and Juliet.* In *Narrative and Dramatic Sources of Shakespeare,* edited by Geoffrey Bullough, vol. 1. London: Routledge and Kegan Paul.

Colley, Linda. 1992. *Britons: Forging the Nation, 1707–1837.* New Haven: Yale University Press.

Dobson, Michael. 1992. *The Making of the National Poet: Shakespeare, Adaptation and Authorship, 1660–1769.* Oxford: Clarendon Press.

Dobson, Michael. 2011. *Shakespeare and amateur performance: a cultural history.* Cambridge: Cambridge University Press.

Garrick, David. 1769. *An ode upon dedicating a building, and erecting a statue, to Shakespeare, at Stratford-upon-Avon.* London: Becket and De Hondt.

Garrick, David. 1981. *The Plays of David Garrick,* edited Harry William Pedicord and Fredrick Lois Bergmann, 6 vols. Carbondale: Illinois.

Gentleman, Francis, ed. 1774. *Bell's Edition of Shakespeare's Plays, as they are now performed at the Theatres Royal in London,* 8 vols. London: John Bell.

Hogan, Charles Beecher. 1952–7. *Shakespeare in the Theatre, 1701–1800,* 2 vols. Oxford: Clarendon Press.

Ierne; or anecdotes and incidents of a life chiefly in Ireland ... by a retired civil engineer. 1861. London: Partrige and Co.

Norman, Marc, and Tom Stoppard. 1999. *Shakespeare in Love: A Screenplay.* London: Miramax Books.

Shakespeare, William. 1984. *Romeo and Juliet.* Edited by Gwynne Blakemore Evans. Cambridge: Cambridge University Press

Shakespeare, William. 2000. *Romeo and Juliet.* Edited by Jill Levenson. Oxford: Oxford University Press.

Shakespeare, William. 2012. *Romeo and Juliet.* Edited by René Weis. London: Bloomsbury (Arden Shakespeare Third Series).

The Gentleman's Magazine. 1819. 89 (2). London: John Nichols and Son.

The Private Theatre of Kilkenny, with Introductory Observations. 1825. s.l.: s.n.

Williams, Helen Maria. 1975. *Letters from France, 1791–96.* Edited by Janet Todd, 2 vols. Delmar, NY: Scholars Facsimiles & Reprints.

11 At Juliet's Tomb
Anglophone Travel-Writing and Shakespeare's Verona, 1814–1914

Nicola J. Watson

On November 6th, 1816, George Gordon, Lord Byron was making his way across post-Napoleonic Europe from Milan towards the pleasures of Venice, travelling in company of his friend John Cam Hobhouse. He reported in a letter to yet another old friend, the poet Thomas Moore, on his arrival at Verona and detailed his immediate sight-seeing plans:

> I shall remain here a day or two to gape at the usual marvels, – amphitheatre, paintings, and all that time-tax of travel, – though Catullus, Claudian, and Shakspeare have done more for Verona than it ever did for itself. They still pretend to show the 'tomb of all the Capulets' – we shall see. (1838, 326)

The next day, he added a postscript to the as yet unsent letter:

> I have been over Verona ... Of the truth of Juliet's story they seem tenacious to a degree, insisting on the fact – giving a date (1303), and showing a tomb. It is a plain, open, and partly decayed sarcophagus, with withered leaves in it, in a wild and desolate conventual garden, once a cemetery, now ruined to the very graves. The situation struck me as very appropriate to the legend, being blighted as their love. (ibid., 327–8)

As was Byron's custom during his travels, he had brought away such souvenirs of this visit as were available to send back to England. On this occasion, he filched "a few pieces of the granite [from the sarcophagus], to give to my daughter and my nieces" (ibid., 328). The very slight whiff of scepticism suggested by Byron's reference to Juliet's story as a "legend" and the sophistication with which he describes the garden as a suitable stage-set for that legend, recalls the accent of Byron's persona, the wanderer Childe Harold. *Childe Harold's Pilgrimage, Canto III*, upon which Byron was then at work, deftly assigned a series of similarly disappointing tourist experiences to a general sense of the decay and dilapidation of post-Napoleonic Europe, and strategically used such experiences, too, to underscore one of Byron's current self-dramatizations as the victim of blighted love in the wake of his social exile from England for having apparently had an adulterous affair with his half-sister. When Hobhouse recollected the episode many years later in 1859, however, he recalled it as a sentimentally authentic and less complicated experience; he wrote that Byron and he had both chipped into the fabric of the tomb very much in the spirit of "true believers" – believers, that is, in both the historical truth of Juliet Capulet and in the authenticity of the tomb itself (1859, 1.79).

The slight difference in tone between these two accounts might simply be attributable to the divergent personalities of the two friends, and it might also register the difference between an experience remembered immediately and an experience remembered many years later long after Byron's death, coloured by affectionate nostalgia for youth. However, Hobhouse's account taken in its entirety carefully performs an ideological change in the imaginative status of Juliet's tomb, from a powerfully sentimental to a semi-fraudulent place, and for that reason, draws a stronger contrast between romantic sentiment and Victorian hard-headed historicism. Hobhouse begins by noting that the principal "object of curiosity for Englishmen" visiting Verona at mid-century is "the stone coffin called the Tomb of Juliet" commenting that it "may be equally authentic with the Shakspearian relics at Stratford-on-Avon, for there is the same proof for it, namely, the positive assertion of the local authorities" (ibid., 1.78). Here Hobhouse sardonically alludes to the currently rather dubious cultural status of those Shakespearean relics as shown for a fee at the birthplace in Stratford where it was by then supporting a flourishing tourist economy (see Watson, 2007). He notes its position "above-ground in a garden without the city, where stood the Franciscan convent of Friar Lawrence", neatly and almost silently conflating play and topography, before deflating this satisfying congruence by observing in the following sentence that "a tradition tells us that it had originally been in a church, and sceptics assert that the old tomb has been lost" (Hobhouse 1859, 1.78). He notes, however, that by 1845 the divergence between play, tradition and actuality had been solved: "between my first and third visit, in 1845, to Verona, a picture of the church and tomb had been happily imagined, to satisfy the inquiries and silence the doubts of strangers" (ibid., 1.78–9). When he comes to remembering that first visit, however, he notes that "this was long before the days of handbooks"; as a result "we carried off a chip of the red marble from the tomb itself, like true believers" (ibid., 1.79).

Byron's letter, combined with Hobhouse's later memoir, raises a series of questions to do with the meaning and realization of *Romeo and Juliet* in Verona and beyond. When did tourists begin to seek out "Shakespeare's Verona" and why? When did a tourist industry spring up in Verona to cater to them, and what was its nature? What were the ideological meanings of such Shakespeare tourism and how stable were they? How and in what aesthetic forms, in short, did Shakespeare come to be naturalized and materialized within the civic culture of Verona, shadowing his contemporary career as a tourist attraction in Stratford? What follows endeavours to reconstruct the history of fluctuating tourist sentiment surrounding the rise of 'Shakespeare's Verona' from early eighteenth-century obscurity to its late-Victorian celebrity.

What one might term a glocal Shakespeare grew up in the aftermath of a succession of eighteenth- and early nineteenth-century world wars in which Anglophone culture eventually achieved a narrow victory at Waterloo in 1815. This glocal Shakespeare was everywhere courtesy of print culture. Yet at the same time it was increasingly thought of as locatable to somewhere in particular. This feeling was indebted for its shape and sensibility to a general aspect of nineteenth-century culture, a passion for sentimental objects and places, a strong desire to give the airy nothings of literariness a materiality, a local habitation and a home. The result was literary tourism, the visiting and representation of places of literary interest, a practice which typically brought about in its wake physical transformations in the places themselves, transformations which came about in an effort to make the place in question conform to tourist expectations (see Watson 2006). In Shakespeare's case, homing his works to material object and place was particularly desirable because of his status as a national and increasingly international figure. It was, however, particularly difficult because there was a good deal less of the material record left than people would have liked, and very little to connect him to the locales mentioned in his plays. Expressed in England, this impulse entailed the wholesale re-imagining and reconstruction of Stratford-upon-Avon over the course of the century coupled with a rather less successful push to retrieve Shakespeare's London from Goldsmith, Boswell, and Washington Irving onwards (see Thomas 2012; Watson 2006). It also translated into a strong desire on the part of the English, and even on the part of some foreigners, to 'home' Shakespeare in places beyond England, even in those places which Shakespeare was generally thought by scholarship to have known only by repute through the writings of John Florio and others – amongst them, the city of Verona.

'Shakespeare's Verona' in this sense has very little to do with the current scholarly interest in the depiction of the civic as disastrously dysfunctional in *Romeo and Juliet* (or for that matter in *The Two Gentlemen of Verona*). Popular culture from the nineteenth century onwards has generally read Shakespeare's tragedy as the story of star-crossed or parent-crossed lovers rather than as the story of how a state of civil feud and disorder brings about social disaster. As a consequence, it has been relatively unembarrassing for Verona to progressively accommodate to and capitalize upon *Romeo and Juliet* as a part of its heritage. This naturalization has been achieved over the last two centuries through place-specific iteration and reiteration by tourists through practices ranging from travel-writing and sentimental vandalism through graffiti, love-letters, and photography. But it has equally come about through local civic interventions which have progressively developed both Juliet's tomb and Juliet's supposed house as the 'Tomba di Giulietta' and the 'Casa di Giulietta' to more closely resemble places that successive generations of tourists can readily recognize as 'Shakespearean'.

Interest in Anglophone travel-writing in the possible actuality of the tomb of Giulietta Cappelletti seems to date from around the 1720s. The Scottish traveller, Andrew Balfour, writing in 1700, provides an extensive set of notes on the attractions of Verona, listing palaces and their associated gardens, grottoes, churches, and galleries, the ancient amphitheatre, three castles, the fortified walls, two stone bridges, and the opportunity to "herborize" on Monte Baldo, twenty miles distant, but makes no mention of Juliet's tomb (1700, 235–6). In this he is following the lead of writers before him, including Gilbert Burnet (1688), Charles Cotton (1689), William Acton (1691), John Dryden (1693), John Dunton (1694), and Maximilien Misson (1695). Even Acton, who made something of a point of visiting the tombs of Virgil and Ariosto, and certainly spent time in Verona, does not appear to have known of the tomb. The first mention of it appears in John Breval's influential and much-cited *Remarks on several parts of Europe* published in 1726. Breval's visit to the site of the tomb is prompted by an interest in what he supposes to be local history. His guide seems to have told him a story of how the tomb had been discovered by workmen: "three hundred years after" the entombment of the lovers, whereupon "all the city flock'd to see what was left of two such extraordinary Persons; since which time, what became either of the Stone Chest, or the Ashes that were in it, is what I never could learn" (1726, 2.103–4). This guide, however, showed Breval into the grounds of a monastery, then an orphanage, where the tomb of the lovers had reputedly formerly been located.

Although Breval's visit was not inspired by admiration of Shakespeare's play, it was nonetheless informed by it. He comments that the guide's story reminded him of Shakespeare's *Romeo and Juliet,* and notes that Shakespeare's account varies "very little either in Names, Characters, or other Circumstances from Truth and Matter of Fact" (ibid., 2.104), "Truth and matter of Fact" being here established by reference to Girolame della Corte's *History of Verona* (1560). This book retailed the story Matteo Bandello's novella "Giulietta e Romeo" (1554) (thought to be one of Shakespeare's sources) as historical fact, and had established Juliet as a historical figure not just for Breval but for editions of Shakespeare such as that by Lewis Theobald (1739).[1] Breval further expressed indignation that Thomas Otway's adaptation of the play *The History and Fall of Caius Marius* (1680) had transferred the action from Verona to Rome; his account, by contrast, set the whole story firmly back into Verona and effectively began the conflation of the stage-fiction of Shakespeare's Verona with the historical fact and geographical locality of Verona itself.

Sixty or so years later, although *Romeo and Juliet* was generally supposed to be based on historical record rather than upon an older fiction, it seems to have been accepted that there were no physical traces of the lovers still extant in Verona. This explains why it was that, when Hester Lynch Piozzi travelled through Verona in April 1785, she made no mention of Juliet's tomb, even though she expressed sorrow at having just missed a performance in Padua of a play entitled *Tragedia Veronese* (which she identified as a version of *Romeo and Juliet*), and even though she would comment on the way she experienced Venice through a Shakespearean lens: "I know not how it is, but to an English traveller each place presents ideas originally suggested by Shakespeare ... other authors remind one of things which one has seen in life – but the scenes of life itself remind one of Shakespeare" (Piozzi 1789, 157–8). Five years later, a traveller called Thomas Watkins showed up in Verona with a similarly Shakespearean sensibility but with nowhere to site it: "This city has been honoured by the attention of our Shakespeare, Romeo and Juliet, as well as his two gentlemen, were of Verona, but the times are much changed for the worse in the present age of apathy, as it would be impossible to find two such lovers on this side of the Alps ..." (1794, 2.370). On 17 October 1793, however, a young woman traveller, Mary Carter, noted in a letter to Lady Nelthorpe that she had "been a pilgrimage to Juliet's tomb" (Nelthorpe 1860, 9; see Sweet, 36).

The inference would seem to be then that, sometime between the early 1790s and 1816 when Byron saw it, 'Juliet's tomb' was simply invented. Given that English travel within continental Europe was restricted by war until 1815, and that it seems plausible that English enthusiasm for their newly nationalized bard would have been the driving force behind the production of this tomb from thin air, it seems likely that Byron saw it fairly early in its career as Juliet's tomb. Another early glimpse is afforded by the poet Samuel Rogers, who along with other aristocratic sight-seers had hurried over onto the continent during the short-lived peace of 1814 and had travelled down through Switzerland to northern Italy, only to be forced to flee back home by Napoleon's escape from Elba and his northward march back to Paris and power. Rogers recorded that he had visited a convent-garden and there viewed "with the eye of faith Juliet's stone coffin, the niche for her lamp, the spiracle for her respiration" (Pfister 1996, 92), and further, that the coffin was already showing signs of damage, which he attributed to the English passion for relics. This description of the coffin would become conventional, faithfully reproduced in account after account, suggesting the reproduction of a tourist-guide spiel that showed the coffin, and explained Juliet's survival by describing what may have been a drainage hole as a breathing-hole, and the stone ledge as variously a place to hold a lamp or as a stone "pillow".[2] Even so, it must have taken time for this (conjecturably Roman) sarcophagus in the convent garden to become secured as 'Juliet's tomb'. It does not seem to have been a must-see even for all English travellers, since neither James Wilson in 1816 nor Theodore Dwight in 1821 make mention of it. Equally, the local guides seem to have had only patchy awareness of it as a sight: for instance, in 1817, William Cadell reiterated, following Breval, that the tomb had been demolished, and does not seem to have viewed or been aware of the new pretender; on the other hand, in the same year, the perhaps more determined or simply more fortunate author of *Sketches in Italy*, Jane Waldie, seems to have been shown it as a regular sight (Cadell 1820, 1.116; Waldie 1820, 4.199).

Another woman visitor is recorded by the French traveller Jacques Augustin Galiffe at the tomb in the autumn of 1816:

> An English lady, who shall remain nameless, and who had paid her devotions at this shrine some weeks before us, had taken it into her head to lay herself at full length in this tomb, like a monumental figure, with her hands piously crossed on her bosom. But it is dangerous to tempt the devil, and especially in a monastery. The romantic visitor had no sooner clasped her hands on her breast, than a sudden gust of wind so disarranged her undefended garments, as to cause no slight confusion to herself, and some scandal to half a dozen male and female friends who accompanied her. (1820, 1.90)

This probably apocryphal figure of the discomfited English lady recurs throughout the tourist history of the tomb, and serves here to distance the French visitor from English enthusiasm. But as this punitive little story also suggests, viewing the tomb with "the eye of faith" seems to have been the order of the day, and English tourists were inventively romantic as to ways of consuming the experience. One feature seems to have been the type of self-staging that Galiffe satirizes. "With what feelings of fond, and pensive melancholy did I approach that shrine sacred to hapless, blighted love" mused the anonymous author of *A Classical and Historical Tour through France, Switzerland, Italy in 1821 and 1822* (1824, 1826), before indulging in extensive Shakespearean quotation on the spot, casting himself as an onlooker with Capulet mourning over Juliet's supposed corpse:

> All things [that] we ordained festival
> Turn from their office to black funeral;
> Our wedding cheer to a sad burial feast
> Our bridal flowers serve for a buried corse ...
> In thy best robes, uncovered on the bier,
> Thou shalt be borne to that same ancient vault
> Where all the kindred of the Capulets lie ... (*Classical and Historical Tour* 1826, 375–6)

He is the first to reveal that there was by now a visitors' book on-site of which he happily availed himself:

> I hastily inscribed, with a pencil, a slight effusion in the book kept for such purpose:
> Ah! hapless pair! at whose deep woes
> So oft I've sighed sincere;
> Here, at thy shrine, my heart bestows
> The homage of a tear ... (Ibid., 377)

Around the same time, again in 1822, the young actor William Charles Macready staged himself at the tomb as both Shakespeare enthusiast and as Romeo, visiting by moonlight in the teeth of his guide's lack of enthusiasm: "Our long walk had disinclined him for the visit, and he would have dissuaded me from going, insisting that it was nothing to see; to me it was all – it gave an interest to every step I took ...". The thought-experiment he conducts is a suspension of disbelief as to the authenticity of the tomb in favour of the authenticity of the sentimental experience: "It may be, I dare say, is fabulous, but yet the delusion was too pleasing to be admitted such. ... I stood like a fond and credulous pilgrim before her shrine, [and] ... as I stood in the broad moonlight, looking at the bright planet in full pure glory above me, I thought she must have looked just so when the love-sick boy invoked her beams in attestation of his truth" (Pollock 1879, 2.247).

Macready does not remark on whether he also takes souvenirs, but this practice seems also to have been established very early. In 1814, as I have already noted, Rogers claimed that the coffin was "lessened, they said, by the zeal of the English for fragments" (Pfister 1996, 92), and Byron was by his own admission an offender in this respect, too. Jane Waldie recalled the tourist-guide's patter with respect to this habit on her visit in 1817: "Every English visitor, she says, carries away a bit of the marble; a circumstance she greatly deplores – not considering that her telling them all so, is the very way to effect the continuance of the custom" (1820, 4.199). The appetite for such relics extended to other nationalities, too. François-René Chateaubriand, attending the Congress of Verona of 1822, remarked upon a pair of bracelets worn by Maria-Louise, Archduchess of Parma and widow of Napoleon, jewellery which had been made of the reddish stone of the sarcophagus (Chateaubriand 1838, 1.74). Antoine Claude Pasquin Valéry also mentions that "some illustrious foreigners and handsome ladies of Verona wear a small coffin of this same stone" (1839, 106); and in 1829, Maria Callcott, honeymooning in Italy, remarked on meeting a gentleman, who, being "dans le gens romantique", sported a fragment of the tomb set in a ring (Perry 1832, 20.265). Unsurprisingly, then, one of the earliest representations of the sarcophagus shows it in a very sorry state of dilapidation, with one side half chipped away (Duppa 1829, 158) although there is some evidence that the authorities started trying to protect the tomb "from the depredations of travellers" from at least 1831 onwards (Conder 1831, 2.85). The perceived neglect of the site began, curiously, to redound to the credit of English sensibilities. The essay on the tomb included in *Heath's Book of Beauty* for 1835 lamented rather smugly: "Beautiful daughter of Capulet! None care for thee, thy love, or thy memories, save the strangers from the Far Isle whom a Northern Minstrel hath taught to weep for thee!" (Heath 1835, 35).

Romantic effusion, however, did not survive Victorian historicism unscathed, and much of the reason for this can be found in John Murray's *Handbook for travellers in northern Italy* (1843), which in evaluating the comparative authenticity of the established sights in a decidedly cool tone threw a damper onto previous enthusiasms. Murray noted that although the families were real and celebrated (citing the authority of Dante), the Cappelletti and Montecchi seemed more likely to have been allies than deadly enemies, and that the story of the lovers originated with the sixteenth-century novelist, Luigi Da Porto. He allowed the possibility that the Casa de Cappelletti might have been the family dwelling, and further that there was once a possibly authentic tomb, long since destroyed, shown "before Shakespeare became generally known to the Italians". Of "the present one, in the garden of the *Orfanotrofio*" he simply remarks that it "does just as well" as the lost one although it was originally a "washing-trough". The entry concludes with a dig at the credulously sentimental, here exemplified by the ex-Empress and others: "Maria Louisa got a bit of it, which she caused to be divided into *hearts* and *gems,* elegant necklaces, bracelets etc., and many other sentimental young and elderly ladies have followed her Majesty's example" (Murray 1853, 298). The habit would also be satirized in *The Struggles and Adventures of Christopher Tadpole* (1848) in which the souvenir collection of a woman traveller, the silly and victimized Mrs Hamper, contained "all sorts of Juliet's tombs from Verona, to supply all of which that have been made from the monument itself, the original must have been an entire quarry" (Smith 1848, 218). In 1854, William Dean Howells dryly put such relic-acquisition down as eloquent proof of "a large amount of vulgar and rapacious innocence drifting about the world" (1883, 277). George Hillard is even more astringent the previous year, noting that "an old wash-trough serves well enough to call forth that unimaginative enthusiasm which is only aroused by some object addressed to the senses" whereas the true enthusiast sees that "the tomb which Shakespeare has built will outlast the amphitheatre" (1867, 58). What had once occasioned refined sentimental experimentation and secured the memory of it now laid bare vulgarity, rapacity, and materialism rampant – all embodied in silly middle-aged women. No wonder that by 1859 Hobhouse was sounding a little defensive about his youthful souvenir-hunting.

Although after Murray, the tomb would be officially regarded as a fraud, this did not deter tourists from coming to the site. In 1864 Henry Gaze's guidebook would sum up the situation: "Tomb of Juliet, doubtful; but it should be seen". A knowing Victorian sentimentalism explicitly rejected the tomb itself as an authentic auratic object but still used the site to invoke a localized experience of Juliet. Mary Wollstonecraft Shelley in September 1842, for example, conceding that the tomb itself was unlikely to be genuine, recuperates Juliet as an historical personage and the place as therefore an opportunity to co-locate with her sensibility: "Still such a scene – a garden, with its high antique walls, its Italian vegetation, and the blue sky, cloudless above – was a scene familiar to Juliet; and her spirit might hover here, even if her fair form were sepulchred elsewhere" (Shelley 1844, 2.76). In 1844, Dickens's characteristic sceptical waggishness gives away the tomb in

232   Nicola J. Watson

favour of preserving Juliet from tourism. He finds Verona a suitable "scene" for "one of the most beautiful and romantic of stories", and therefore reads *Romeo and Juliet* on the spot. He remarks on being shown what was, as far as he was concerned, clearly a water-trough, that "it was a pleasure, rather than a disappointment, that Juliet's resting-place was forgotten ... it is better for Juliet to lie out of the track of tourists, and to have no visitors but such as come to groves in spring-rain, and sweet air, and sunshine" (1957, 337–8). Both stances distance the elite traveller from Dean Howells' vulgar and rapacious innocents. They operate within a complex sentimental system which negotiates historical authenticity (there really were once Cappelletti and Montecchi), with investment in Shakespeare's character (Juliet as Victorian ideal), through a very Victorian investment in a sense of deep historical place. The tomb and the garden in which it lay provided even the most sceptical with a sense of physical continuity between past and present and between reading and reality through engaging with Juliet herself.

So far, I have been flirting with the possibility of constructing a history of the tomb as tourist attraction which starts off with outright belief in its authenticity and then, in the face of evidence to the contrary, tries to recuperate that belief in different modes so as to preserve the experiential possibilities. But looking at the ways in which later nineteenth-century tourists seem to have expended considerable empathetic effort at the site there are at first glance inconvenient continuities with earlier enthusiasts. There are, for instance, further accounts of tourists staging themselves as Juliet or Romeo. William Harrison Ainsworth retailed "an apocryphal story" told "of an English lady, who, being missed, was found half dead and in a state of ecstasy – in a white muslin morning dress and satin shoes – in the tomb itself" (1853–81, 113.258). The intention here is clearly satiric – but it is much less clearly so in an 1846 report of an English male enthusiast laid at full length within the sarcophagus (Costello 1846, 249). Perhaps the key here is that it is hard to find first person accounts after the 1840s of such rituals; rather they are effectively narrated as cases that have somehow violated sentimental decorum. There were other ways of putting oneself into the tomb that risked less ridicule; in 1887, a visitor reported the tomb's inside as "strewn with visiting-cards – travellers from all parts of the world paying this tribute of respect to the memory of the unfortunate girl-bride" and noted that there were even photographs amongst the litter, including one of a young lady superscribed with a message of sympathy for Juliet (Devereux 1884, 279–80). Occupying the tomb, stealing souvenir-chips to set into jewellery, dropping visiting-cards into the tomb, all expressed the desire to interpellate modern bodies with Juliet's in the tomb, an impulse still in evidence in the blogosphere, awash as it is with selfies of women posed by the tomb.

An alternative or additional strategy for the enthusiast was to seek out 'Juliet's house'. Samuel Rogers had first evoked this in his much-quoted poetic travelogue *Italy* (1822–28): "Are those the distant turrets of Verona? / And shall I sup where Juliet at the masque / Saw her loved Montague, and now sleeps by him?" (Rogers 1822). Rogers' note to these lines makes it clear that he had himself indeed sought out and viewed the house: "The old Palace of the Capelletti, with its uncouth balcony and irregular windows, is still standing in a lane near the Market-place" and further makes it plain that its aura is for him specifically Shakespearean, for "what Englishman can behold it with indifference?". In 1829, the party of Thomas Ireland had it pointed out to them (1836, 35). Appetite for the house increased, perhaps fuelled by the fact that Murray had both identified it and allowed the possibility that it was genuine. In the late 1840s, the Baroness Blaze de Bury and her party came in search of Shakespeare's Verona, and engaged in the sort of imaginative experiment typical of the literary tourism of the time. Blaze de Bury insists on the 'truth' of the story of Romeo and Juliet to Verona in a number of ways, adducing archival chronicles and comparing Shakespeare's plays to the original accounts, but her main system of authentication is the felt power of poetry to transform place. The house must be authentic, she argues, because she experiences it as authentic: "Why, if you will but take the trouble of listening, you may hear them within calling 'for dates and quinces in the pantry'; and as the evening shadows fall, masque after masque goes by to Capulet's feast. Never tell me that Juliet dwelt not there, and that it was not through that gateway that Romeo passed ..." (Blaze de Bury 1851, 416).

Despite the charm of the Baroness's imagineering strategy of inlaying the physical actuality of place with quotation from the play, other tourists did not find it an easy trick to pull off. Then, as now, the house was supposedly authenticated as having belonged to the Capulets by a stone plaque carved as a hat over the chimney-piece. Equally conveniently, for both visitors and proprietor, the house was an inn and therefore readily accessible to the public. There its suitability as a site for "poetic memories" ceased, as visitor after visitor, less adept than Blaze de Bury, complained. It was dirty, dilapidated and commercial and, very much worse, it was unaccountably short of the essential balcony: "[T]here is a balcony, certainly, but too high, I think, for even the ardent Romeo to have climbed" (Devereux 1884, 278–9). Shakespearean scholars will be aware that Shakespeare's play specifies no balcony. However, no contemporary stage-production would have been possible without a balcony; equally, as Frank Dicksee's famous picture of the lovers (1884) makes plain, no depiction in or out of the theatre of the lovers' mutual declarations could be imagined without a balcony, and a gothic balcony at that. No wonder Victorian tourists were disappointed.

On the one hand, then, visitors to Verona desired and expected to see sites associated with Juliet, whether they were sceptical or not; on the other hand, increasingly neither tomb nor house looked as visitors thought they should look. That is to say, neither resembled how they had come to look on stages right across Europe. (Something of the same problem was emerging at the same time in Stratford-upon-Avon where Shakespeare's house had ceased to convince as Shakespeare's house, something that prompted extensive intervention at mid-century). Civic intervention to redress this problem on the part of the Verona authorities had been minimal, although there is some suggestion by McLellan that in the 1830s the tomb was moved by the Austrian authorities from the garden into the courtyard of the orphanage. By the 1860s, however, the authorities seem to have become more interventionist and the tomb was developed to look more as it typically did on stage. The site seems to have been smartened up with a modern chapel and a sheltering portico in 1868 (compare "Chapel and Tomb of Juliet in Verona, *The Illustrated Sporting and Dramatic News* 1863 with Miller 1879). This process of making the place look as it had been imagined in other media took a dramatic leap in 1938, when, as Maria d'Anniballe has recently argued, the Fascist authorities repaired and restored the tomb to make it look more how it now should – that is to say, as it was represented in the new hyper-realism of film, specifically, by George Cukor's Hollywood blockbuster of *Romeo and Juliet* of 1936 (d'Anniballe 2012, 237). The tomb was now placed in a brand-new, purpose-built crypt, and a garden and approach ornamented with benches, columns, fountains and trees was provided. A similar transformation overtook Juliet's house, which between 1937 and 1942 was eventually provided with a rose-window, a gothic-style doorway, and a balcony, of which it is regularly said that it is either a sarcophagus or a water-trough, in unconscious reiteration of the old arguments as to the provenance of Juliet's tomb. Since then it has continued to evolve towards further realism, pressed on by Franco Zeffirelli's on-location filming in 1968. Innovations have included the inclusion of Zeffirelli's costumes, a replica of 'Juliet's bed', and the installation of a life-size bronze of Juliet herself in 1972.

To sum up – 'Shakespeare's Verona' as it came into being in Verona over the course of the nineteenth century has had little to do with the dysfunctional civic represented in the play. The power of this particular 'civic Shakespeare' is rooted in the celebration of English victory in the aftermath of Waterloo when the English sought to find that the continent was more English than it thought, to send back the proof of that to England in chips of red granite, and discovered that the continent's failure to recognize its own Shakespeareanism was a failing that only highlighted the superiority of English culture. It behoved those at the Congress of Verona to agree with them. By mid-century, Verona was providing a place to understand Shakespeare as global, where admirers of all nationalities, including and perhaps especially Americans, could encounter Shakespeare while insisting on the discrepancy between a true appreciation of the poetry of Shakespeare as experienced on the page and the credulous and effeminate literal-mindedness of tourism. However, the growing realism of stage-settings and the hallucinatory natural detail of pre-Raphaelite paintings of Shakespeare, precursors to the hyper-realism of photography and film, forced successive changes to the actuality of Verona from the late nineteenth century onwards, changes that have increasingly serviced tourists' desires to embody themselves in relation to Juliet – whether gazing at or from the famous balcony or wondering at and scrawling on her tomb – so celebrating the grand excesses of (mostly) heterosexual young love.

Although there are clear continuities between the Victorian view of Verona and modern day sensibilities and practices, what is striking is the extent to which Verona is not really Shakespeare's any longer, but altogether Juliet's; the story that has not naturalized well here is that of authorial celebrity, whether conceived as national or global. Verona has conscientiously erected at least three busts of Shakespeare, one at the gate through which Romeo flees the city and two at the site of the tomb; but it has to be admitted that seldom have busts of him looked more magnificently sheepish, creepily middle-aged, and altogether parentally and embarrassingly beside the point. The statue the tourists want to see and to touch and to be photographed with, is always Juliet's. Indeed, as of 2014 that statue was replaced by a replica because of damage caused by the new tourist custom of touching her breast to ensure good fortune in love, a very modern instance of that nineteenth-century investment in contiguity between the tourist body and that of Juliet.

NOTES

1. See Peck 1740, 256 which describes *Romeo and Juliet* as founded on a real tragedy, cites both Bandello and della Corte, notes the existence of Romeo and Juliet's tomb on Breval's authority, and cites Theobald's footnote in vol. 7, p. 124.
2. Compare Martin 1831, 426.

WORKS CITED

A Classical and Historical Tour through France, Switzerland, Italy in 1821 and 1822. 1826. London: for Baldwin, Cradock and Joy. Variant title *Mementoes, historical and classical, of a tour through part of France, Switzerland and Italy, in the years 1821 and 1822*, 1824.

Ainsworth, William Harrison. 1853–1881. *New Monthly Magazine.*

Balfour, Andrew. 1700. *Letters write* (sic) *to a friend by the learned and judicious Sir Andrew Balfour … containing excellent directions and advices for travelling through France and Italy, with many curious and judicious remarks and observations made by himself, in his voyages through these countreys, published from the author's original m.s.* Edinburgh: M. Balfour.

Blaze de Bury, Marie Pauline Rose Stewart. 1851. *Germania: Germany as it is …* 2nd edition, 2 vols. London: Henry Colburn.

Breval, John. 1726. *Remarks on Several parts of Europe, relating chiefly to their antiquities and history …*, 2 vols. London: Lintot.

Cadell, William Archibald. 1820. *A Journey in Carniola, Italy and France, in 1817, 1818,* 2 vols. Edinburgh: Constable.

Chateaubriand, François-René. 1838. *The Congress of Verona; comprising a portion of memoirs of his own times,* 2 vols. London: Richard Bentley.

Conder, Josiah. 1831. *Italy,* 3 vols. London: Duncan.

Costello, Louisa Stuart. 1846. *A Tour to and from Venice by the Vaudois and the Tyrol*. London: Ollivier.

D'Anniballe, Maria. 2012. "Form follows Fiction: Redefining Urban Identity in Fascist Verona through the lens of Hollywood's Romeo and Juliet". In *New Perspectives in Italian Cultural Studies*, vol. 2, edited by Graziella Parati, 223–44. Lanham, MD: Fairleigh Dickinson University Press with Rowman and Littlefield.

Duppa, Richard. 1829 (2nd ed.). *Travels on the Continent, Sicily, and the Lipari Islands*. London: Longman, Rees, Orme and Co.

Devereux, William Cope. 1884. *Fair Italy*. London: Kegan, Paul, Trench and Co.

Dickens, Charles. 1957. *American Notes; and, Pictures from Italy* (1842, 1846). London: Oxford University Press.

Dwight, Theodore. 1824. *A Journal of a Tour to Italy in the year 1821*. New York: printed for the author.

Galiffe, Jacques Augustin. 1820. *Italy and its Inhabitants; and account of a tour in that country in 1816 and 1817*. London: John Murray.

Gaze, Henry. 1864. *North Italy and Venetia; how to see them for fifteen guineas* London: Kent.

Handbook for travellers in northern Italy. 1843. London: John Murray.

Heath, Charles. 1835. *Heath's Book of Beauty*, London: Moyes.

Hillard, George Stillman. (1853) 1867. *Six Months in Italy*, 2 vols. Boston: Ticknor and Fields.

Hobhouse, John Cam. 1859. *Italy: Remarks made in Several Visits, from the year 1816 to 1854*, 2 vols. London: John Murray.

Howells, William Dean. 1883. *Italian Journeys from Venice to Naples and beyond*, 2 vols. Edinburgh: Douglas.

Illustrated Sporting and Dramatic News. 1863.

Ireland, Thomas James. 1836. *Extracts from a Journal during a Tour in Italy in 1829 and 1830*. Chiswick: Whittingham.

McLellan, Henry B. 1834. *Journal of a Residence in Scotland and Tour through England, France, Germany, Switzerland, and Italy*. Boston: Allen and Ticknor.

Moore, Thomas, ed. 1838. *Byron's Life, Letters and Journals*. London: John Murray.

Martin, Selina. 1831. *Narrative of three years' residence in Italy, 1819–22*. Dublin: Wakeman.

Miller, William. (1828) 1879. *Wintering in the Riviera, with notes of travel in Italy and France*. London: Longmans.

Nelthorpe, Frances, ed. 1860. *Mrs Mary Carter's Letters*. London: Clayton.

Peck, Francis. 1740. *New Memoirs of the life and poetical works of Mr John Milton*. London: n.p.

Perry, Reuben, and John Timbs, eds. 1832. *Mirror of literature, amusement, and instruction*, vol. 20. London: Hurst.

Pfister, Manfred. 1996. *The Fatal Gift of Beauty: The Italies of British Travellers*. Amsterdam: Rodopi.

Piozzi, Hester Lynch. 1789. *Observations and Reflections made in the course of a journey through France, Italy, and Germany*. Dublin: Chamberlain, White, Byrne, Wogan, Grubier and McAllister, Heery, Dornin, Moore, and Jones.

Pollock, Frederick, ed. 1879. *Macready's Reminiscences and Selections from his Diaries and Letters*, 2 vols. New York: Macmillan & Co.

Rogers, Samuel. 1822. *Italy: A Poem*. London: Longman, Hurst, Rees, Orme, and Browne.

Shelley, Mary Wollstonecraft. 1844. *Rambles in Germany and Italy in 1840, 1842, and 1843*, 2 vols. London: Moxon.
Smith, Albert Richard. 1894. *The Struggles and Adventures of Christopher Tadpole At Home and Abroad* (1848). London: Dicks English Library of Standard Works.
Sweet, Rosemary. 2012. *Cities and the Grand Tour: The British in Italy, c. 1690–1820*. Cambridge: Cambridge University Press.
Thomas, Julia. 2012. *Shakespeare's Shrine: The Bard's Birthplace and the Invention of Stratford*. Philadelphia: University of Pennsylvania Press.
Valéry, [Antoine Claude Pasquin]. 1839. *Historical, literary, and artistical travels in Italy*. Translated by C.E. Clifton. Paris: Baudry's European Library.
Watkins, Thomas. (2nd ed.) 1794. *Travels through Switzerland, Italy, Sicily, the Greek islands to Constantinople etc. in the years 1787, 1788, 1789* (1792), 2 vols. London: Owen.
Watson, Nicola J. 2007. "Shakespeare on the Tourist Trail". In *The Cambridge Companion to Shakespeare and Popular Culture*, edited by Robert Shaughnessy, 199–226. Cambridge: Cambridge University Press.
Watson, Nicola J. 2006. *The Literary Tourist: Readers and Places in Romantic and Victorian Britain*. Houndmills, Basingstoke: Palgrave Macmillan.
Wilson, James. 1820. *A Journal of two successive Tours upon the Continent in the years 1816, 1817, and 1818*, 3 vols. London: Cadell and Davies.
Waldie, Jane. 1820. *Sketches descriptive of Italy in … 1816 and 1817, with a brief account of travels in various parts of France and Switzerland in the same years*, 4 vols. London: John Murray.

12 Producing a (R&)Jspace
Discursive and Social Practices in Verona

Silvia Bigliazzi and Lisanna Calvi

CODA

Sometimes seemingly irrelevant details incidentally scattered in a story or left-out pieces suddenly recovered from memory take up unexpected meaning, as when the notoriously unreliable narrator of *The Good Soldier* closes his tale on the apparently forgotten marginal question of how "Edward met his death". All but fortuitous, the position of this final piece, mentioned only at the last moment as the unexpected surfacing of a lost, irrelevant memory due to occasional forgetfulness, provides the missing key to penetrate the narrator's own painful relation with the 'good soldier' and his secret emulative affection for him. Had he recounted it beforehand, with the appropriate emphasis and commentary, this bit would not have been equally revealing. Postponing is avoiding confrontation, even with oneself. Codas, however, are not the privileged space for procrastinated revelations or oblique avowals only; they may also be the site of recapitulations, thematic and narrative rounding off, recognitions, resolutions, indeed anything that is fit for a conclusion, even when this means supplying a cue for starting off again.

Romeo and Juliet offers precisely one such highly connoted and open-ended coda. Shakespearean endings are peculiar for making statements, but also for promising statements, thus closing the text while leaving it open to further elucidation, which the spectator will never hear, because destined to a time-space beyond the time-space of the performance. These promised narratives normally serve the purpose of cutting the story short while avoiding definitive recapitulations. *Romeo and Juliet* too promises one such narrative in the guise of "more talk on these sad events" (5.3.306), but it peculiarly provides also the last word on them, enriching the play with an assumedly authoritative comment. Following a full, if succinct, interrogation of the witnesses and the primary suspect alike, all shadows of doubt are eventually cleared,[1] and the sentence of the Prince is finally brief and unwavering, while significantly leaving the moral and civil responsibility of the Friar unjudged. Heaven has replaced the Prince in his judicial role and has laid a scourge upon the family's hatred; the two youths have been chosen by divine will as the sacrificial victims of enmity; their death has been carried out through love; the Prince has been punished for his "winking" (5.3.294) at the discord with the death of two kinsmen. Who else will be punished by his own sentence is left unsaid, because what matters is to clarify that the sacrificial scheme mentioned by the first Prologue has been accomplished and what has been promised has finally been offered; the action needs to be shown coherent with the framing narrative, and its claim of authority is thus finally exposed. So far the play has received its expected completion.

But this coda is not only a closing device mirroring the opening Chorus and offering the scapegoating rationale, while transposing it onto the transcendent level of the heavenly retribution of family hatred and civil weak governance. It also provides, retrospectively, the tacit subtext of the first Chorus's narrative, justifying why the spectacle has been worth attending to, and why it also will be worth attending to in the future. The final epigrammatic couplet tells us that the reason resides in its being the most woeful story ever heard. It eventually inscribes Romeo and Juliet within the verbal monument of an epitaph that ends up turning the play itself into their living tomb. The monumental dimension that the play thus acquires discloses a celebratory vocation that looks beyond the text, while being entombed in it. Epitaphs are mentioned also in Da Porto ("E ordinato un bel monimento, sopra 'l quale la cagione della lor morte in pochi giorni scolpita era"),[2] and in Bandello, who closes his novella on a sonnet that is said to be chiselled in their gravestone. It describes their death, and peculiarly dedicates ten of the overall fourteen lines exclusively to Juliet's pain and final passing away. Brooke too mentions the "Great store of cunning epitaphs, in honour of their death" (l. 3016) on every side of and beneath their stately tomb, but neither the novellas nor the poem advertise themselves as the monument of their tragic love.

The play's celebratory vocation in fact goes beyond these final lines and famously gives shape to one of its most ambiguous scenes in the name of what Reynolds and Segal have called the metallic metamorphosis of Romeo and Juliet, "symbolized by glorified golden figures, not the marble tomb monuments Brooke promises for his lovers at the conclusion of his poem" (2005, 60). Traced back to a discursive undercurrent of monetary and commercial references which, in their view, constraints the two youths' same conceptualization of desire, the promised erection of the two golden statues affords a tangible means for negotiating the pardon of the Prince:

> Mirroring the biocapitalitsic machinations of the Prince, in the final scene the fathers abstract their respective children into signifiers of Verona's prosperity, golden figures whose "rate" will "be set" for the length of time that "Verona by that name is known" (5.3.299). The planned commodification of Romeo and Juliet into displays of official culture is a response to the Prince's reprimand of society in general for allowing the families' feud to incur a wrath that has gone so far as to impeach upon his private property, taking the lives of his "kinsmen" (5.3.294). (Ibid., 48)

Official culture and commodification are precisely the message of this final piece, consigning clear instructions for the play's afterlife: as long as Verona will exist there will be no better ensign of truth and faithfulness than Juliet's simulacrum. Romeo's will be erected close to hers, but preference for Juliet is clear. Typically, the two statues, albeit possibly meant to be sepulchral, are somewhat independent of the tomb;[3] again in Reynolds and Segal's words, Romeo and Juliet

> have thus become objects in an auction of loyalty to the Prince, with each of their respective fathers using their children's images publicly to prove themselves more apologetic for the discord their feud has cost the state. Moreover, the transmutation of the lovers into golden financial "figures," serving as a compensation for the loss accrued by the state, simultaneously declares healthy, wealthy, and wise the socio-economic structures supportive to and supported by Verona's official culture. (Ibid., 48–9)

Public grief has been metamorphosed into a public show of opulence and has definitely entered the official discourse of power.

Turning to the afterlife of the play, to which the open-closed coda gestures by claiming authority over it and, at the same time, pointing to its never-ending iteration/circulation, this is also a major discourse that traverses the so-called "R&Jspace", that is, "a conglomeration of the official and/or unofficial historical, political, cultural, and social spaces through which Romeo and Juliet resound in various manifestations" (ibid., 38). Dominant and alternative discourses and practices are precisely a major issue when we come to think about what Verona as town and as a multidimensional cultural site is today, and what role the Romeo and Juliet myth plays in this respect. As suggested by the play's coda, Verona is the R&Jspace par excellence, if by space we mean something more concretely shaped than verbal discourses and mental territories, and consider it as a complex social space furnished with tangible objects, and shaped by civic practices, as well as social discourses, "including broader processe[s] of production and reproduction" (Kilian 1998, 117). The representation of its urban space, which depends on how "it is socially constructed" (ibid., 118), relies heavily on how 'a miniature city' has been embedded within the wider city, by being encrusted with simulacra of Juliet's life and death. Pretending to testify to the verity of a story still alive in town, in the assumed vestiges of a fictional memory aimed at the 'real thing', this built-in space in fact strives after purposes other than those of memory recovery. Taking Montague at his word, Verona has been turned into the city of Juliet, giving a pedigree name to the Lady Verona whose medieval anonymous statue dominates the central Piazza Erbe as symbol of "justice" and "lover of praise". This happened at a time, during the Fascist 1930s, when Shakespeare was being appropriated by Italian Caesarist culture (Isenberg 2012). The same culture in Verona, which in 1943–45 would become one of the governmental bases of the Fascist Salò Republic, pursued the intent of endowing the city with its own symbol and eventually found it in the trustworthy 'female' icon of the "true and faithful Juliet" (5.3.302). Little or no attention has been paid to Romeo, whose most remarkable memory in town is a plate set on the walls where the main access to the city centre opens, showing his "There is no world without Verona walls" (3.3.17ff.) speech, thus ideally enclosing the town upon itself with the authority of Shakespeare. Likewise, the Italian novella tradition, originally coming from the Veneto region and the Italian Northern area (Da Porto was from Vicenza Bandello from Castelnuovo Scrivia, and Gherardo Boldieri, better known as Clizia, author of *L'infelice amore de i due fedelissimi amanti Giulia e Romeo*, 1553, was a Veronese nobleman) receives no celebration in town. Whatever the reason, besides the revival that Shakespeare has been enjoying since the 1920s and the establishing of his myth in the Fascist period, the town has been redrawn according to a precise representation of space, or what Henri Lefebvre calls a conception of spaces planned according to a design (1991, 28–9), a "code to serve the alphabet and language of the town, its primary signs, the paradigms and their syntagmatic relations" (ibid., 47). This special code, concerning primarily a particular urban area, is imbued with a precise Shakespearean discourse, deriving from the potential of commercial refashioning provided in the play's own coda, and here appropriated and restyled according to the needs of the town. It applies only to a limited partition of the urban space and, as will be seen, is traversed by many power and market implications derived from the play itself. Drawing a path through the city linking Juliet's house to Juliet's tomb, a Shakespearean area within Verona's centre has been cut out, scattered with simulacra of a hyperreal city encased within the real dimension of everyday life and its social spaces. Akin to a hyperreal Disneyland (Baudrillard 1988, 171–2; Eco 1986, 43–8), but one which does not avow its fakedness, these Juliet spaces are replete with signs of remains deprived of an original referent; they signify her myth of sacrificed faithfulness, and conceal the power discourses that manage it, rousing expectation of encounter with reality. They are part of an entertainment machine that stimulates desire by fabricating "the absolute fake", as Eco called hyperreality, while passing it off as factual and historical. Thus they blur the "boundaries between game and illusion" and turn the town into "an art museum ... contaminated by the freak show" (Eco 1986, 38).

At the other opposite of the town, looking north, the Roman theatre is the site of another Shake-space, but of a different order. This is the locus of 'high' entertainment that has been hosting a summer theatre festival since 1948. It was inaugurated with a production of *Romeo and Juliet* in the translation of poet and Nobel Prize Salvatore Quasimodo, under the direction of Renato Simoni and a young Giorgio Strehler. The Festival marked the cultural and economic rebirth of Verona after Fascism and the Second World War. Over the years the Festival has been the site of international encounters including famous productions such as Peter Brook's *La Tempête* (itself an international enterprise based on Jean-Claude Carrière's French adaptation, 1991), the London Moving Theatre's *Antony and Cleopatra* (1995), the Royal Shakespeare Company's *Romeo and Juliet* (1998), the Propeller Theatre Company's *A Midsummer Night's Dream* (2003), the Dash Arts' *A Midsummer Night's Dream* (2006), and the Berliner Ensemble's *Richard II* (2007), to name but few.

However, Verona is more than this. As a multifaceted R&Jspace it displays yet another level of social production (and reproduction), corresponding to local practices of Shakespearean appropriation that overtly aim at civic cohesion and participation. These are forms of communal performance that vary in conception and implications: marathons, celebrations of Juliet's birthday, medieval festivals, literary prizes, street plays, all contribute to the production of a conglomeration of activities distributed over the year. These efface the dividing line between a genuine need of social identification and the civic appropriation of a hybrid Shakepearean discourse implicated with multifarious ideological interests. To a brief discussion of some of them, in their different sites and forms, we will turn now, by looking at the built-in Juliet space and its hybridized order of discourse, as well as at the official practices related to it in their dialectical relation with possible alternatives.

OBJECTS AND CIVIC BUILT-IN SPACES: THE HOUSE AND THE TOMB

Placed in the central via Cappello (at nr 23) and just outside the city walls, respectively, the house and tomb of Juliet, already the destination of uninterrupted pilgrimage for at least a century, were adroitly renovated as they look today in the 1930s. But how and when were they first identified and associated with the story of the two 'most unfortunate' lovers? It all started with the tomb.

In his *Dell'Historia della città di Verona*, published in 1596, the Veronese Girolamo Della Corte recounts "quel tanto infortunato caso di quei due infelicissimi amanti" (1596, 10.589).[4] Della Corte probably took and summarized the story from either Da Porto (1535) or Bandello (1554), but added a curious detail about the actual burial place of the two unfortunate lovers, blending – possibly for the first time – the real and the imagined:

> ... il signor Bartolomeo [Della Scala] ... ordinò, che fossero à quelli infelicissimi amanti fatto onorate esequie, le quali volontieri da Montecchi, e Cappelletti insieme furono molto pomposamente fatte, et i corpi poi de gli sfortunati amanti furono di commun volere di loro, riposte di nuovo nello stesso monumento, che di pietra viva era alquanto sopra terra, il quale io ho più volte veduto, per lavello al

pozzo di quelle povere pupille di S. Francesco, mentre si fabricava quel luogo a loro nome; e ragionando io di questo fatto co'l Cavagliere Gerardo Boldiero mio Zio, dal qual fui colà introdutto mostrommi oltra il predetto sepolcro un luogo nel muro quasi su' l cantone verso i Reverendi Padri Cappuccini donde, come egli affermava haver inteso, era stata, già molti anni adietro, questa sepoltura con alcune ceneri, et ossa cavata. (1596, 10.594)[5]

Fascinatingly enough, in Della Corte's prose account fiction and reality smoothly coalesce in a sort of narrative *continuum* and, in the same years that saw Shakespeare's dramatic creation, Romeo's and Juliet's tomb found an actual spatial collocation whose authenticity is guaranteed by an eye-witness ("io ho più volte *veduto*", "I have oftentimes seen"). Furthermore, in his version it is not the reconciled Montague and Capulet who decide to honour their children's death but the funeral directions come from Bartolomeo Della Scala, Prince of Verona until 1304. Civically established in fiction, the tomb is placed by tradition and civic memory[6] in a real (urban) space. This early identification, though seemingly silenced for at least two hundred years, resurfaced in the early nineteenth century when Lord Byron, among other famous visitors, notoriously pointed out how the Veronese people "of the truth of Juliet's story ... seem tenacious to a degree, insisting on the fact – giving a date (1303), and showing a tomb" (Murray 1838, 327).[7] Although revered by populace and visitors alike, the site received little or no attention from Verona's municipal authorities until the 1930s when – together with the supposed house of Juliet – it became one of the crucial points of a general reconfiguration of Verona's urban space.

In the last decades of the nineteenth century, after the Italian Unification (1861), Verona – for a long time under Venetian and later Austrian rule – was looking for its own cultural identity and, at the turn of the century, the city, although "historically resistant to myths", slowly started a process of "self-representation ... in the figure of Juliet" (Zumiani 2003, 203). During the summer of 1905 the municipality of Verona bought the medieval *hospitium a Capello*,[8] a five-story brick building conventionally associated with the Dal Cappello family. This traditional attribution of ownership derived from the presence of a blazon representing a hat ('cappello', in Italian) carved in the keystone of the house's entrance arch, and the assonance of the name Cappello with Cappelletti[9] or Capuleti did the rest. The acquisition of the house (the cost was 7,500 lire) somehow rounded off a rather heated debate that had animated the early-twentieth century Veronese cultural panorama. Poets Vittorio Betteloni and Berto Barbarani, who authored a poem "Zulieta e Romeo" (Betteloni 1905) and a brief verse account, *Giulieta e Romeo* (Barbarani 1905), both written in the local dialect, keenly supported the celebration of Juliet as Verona's own myth. In particular, in 1905, shortly before the public acquisition of the *hospitium a Cappello*, Betteloni wrote an impassioned defence of the 'cult' of the places that popular tradition assigned to Capulets and Montagues. He strongly advocated the intervention of the municipality to save the buildings from abandonment and degradation. Other prominent figures of Verona's cultural panorama, among whom Gioachino Brognoligo,[10] disfavoured the matter dismissing it as totally unimportant since Juliet was nothing more than a literary creation with no relationship whatsoever with history. Betteloni disagreed with what he reputed a prejudiced 'castling into erudition', and supported his reasons by means of a spatial metaphor:

> L'erudizione è fatta di studi, di ricerche, di ragionamento; il culto delle patrie memorie è fatto solo di sentimento. L'una abita la regione dell'intelletto, l'altro quella del cuore; l'una ci sta nel capo, l'altro nel seno. Abitando due quartieri separati, possono aver dimora nella stessa casa, cioè nello stesso uomo, senza litigare affatto. (2008, 55)[11]

The flaw in his line of reasoning lies in the assumption that sentimental memory may afford reality to a non-existent entity or event, precisely as in a hyperreal space the object is turned into a sign with no referent except for a fabricated concept or discourse behind it. An individual, Betteloni argues, is like a house with many rooms, therefore, erudition, which tells us that Juliet lived nowhere but in the poets' imagination and the cult of native memories, which instead gives her a home and an address within the city walls (and even a tomb, just outside), may coexist at peace in the same person (or house or city). This is in fact an avowal of the contradiction in terms lying at the root of his argument, according to which wishful thinking makes up for historical shortcomings. Juliet is, in Betteloni's words, "popolare nel vero senso della parola, cioè nota e cara ad ogni cittadino a qualunque ceto o condizione appartenga, senza eccezione" (ibid., 54).[12] True though Juliet may be considered, it is hard to say what made her dear to the citizens, unless it was her appropriated image of faithfulness entombed in her monumentalized icon of true love. Betteloni aptly speaks of "citizens", implying a properly civic bond between the myth fabricated out of the play, and the town: a myth which is materially made visible in the aptly chosen sites of reconstruction of the only two spaces Juliet inhabits: the house and the tomb, two private imaginary spaces which are metamorphosed into tangible public territories alluring visitors into a voyeuristic experience of (supposedly) private real life. These sites are central to the town, both physically and symbolically. They literally find a home within the urban space itself with the intent of reinforcing and emphasizing a secure relationship between the city and the people who inhabit it (Rykwert 2013). In Juliet's story, Betteloni writes, "tutto è bello ... puro, gentile, appassionato, eroico" (2008, 52).[13] Again, the story is here Juliet's, not Romeo's, or Romeo's and Juliet's, and eagerness to identify a heroine for civic purposes builds a romanticized discourse around it. Her qualities – the courage and steadfastness with which she faces adversity and eventually even death – and the date (1303) of her fictional existence place her into the city's medieval past, namely in the glorious age of the Della Scala's rule, often regarded by the populace and the municipal authorities alike as the period of Verona's most outstanding achievements (Zumiani 2003).

The urban setting accurately chosen for the reconstruction of her private spaces is intimately linked with the urban morphology, which had to incorporate them with minimum clues of anachronistic interventions. Those spaces had to be made public, available to the whole community to pay homage to their heroine but also to celebrate the city's own past, which in an idealized Juliet exhibited a morally ennobled origin. Back in the early 1900s, people in town, but also abroad,[14] had urged and later applauded the acquisition of 'Juliet's house'. Yet it was not until 1937 that both the house and the tomb (which the municipality had already purchased in 1894) were at the centre of a targeted architectural intervention, guided by Antonio Avena, local historian and director of the Civic Museums since 1915. Spurred by George Cukor's Hollywood film version of *Romeo and Juliet*, distributed in 1936 and premiered in Verona on 5 March 1937 (Guidorizzi 2003), Avena set up a plan to renovate the Dal Cappello house and refurbish its interiors.[15] In the same years, he also provided a whole new location for the 'Capulet's tomb' and, under his direction, Verona was turned into something of a theatrical or film setting, and was reanimated in the name of Shakespeare. Earlier on, in 1927, the "Bollettino Sindacato Provinciale Fascista Ingegneri" ["Fascist Provincial Bulletin of Engineers"] had published Avena's contribution to the debate around the renovation of one of the buildings overlooking the Piazza delle Erbe. Avena's closure may prove illuminating to clarify the conceptual underpinnings of his projects: "*Multa renovantur*", he had declared, "è il destino di una generazione forte ricondurre la vita là dove gli altri l'avevano spenta" (1927, 21).[16] Paraphrasing Horace's *Ars Poetica* ("Multa renascentur, quae iam ceciderre", l. 70; "Many [words] will be resuscitated that have fallen into disuse") and seasoning it with Fascist rhetoric by alluding to a "strong generation", Avena attributed his renovating zest to some kind of mission that should be pursued in order to bring back to life misused or formerly neglected areas (or possibly a whole city). This was the same principle that informed his interventions both at San Francesco al Corso (the site of what would become the reconstructed "ancient vault") and at the Dal Cappello house. However, what he was trying to reanimate was not simply a building but a legend through the creation, rather than renovation, of a new space which could provide a would-be historical substance and a visible texture to Juliet and her story of female steadfastness which the town was weaving for its own sake.

Looking at the flocks of tourists that still crowd the narrow space of the Dal Cappello courtyard every day, what Avena did is rather surprising and for some aspects anticipatory of what decades afterwards would develop as mass tourism, transforming the House of Juliet into one of the most visited spots in Verona.[17] His intervention radically changed the aspect of the house; its courtyard façade especially underwent a process of medievalization: the outer walls were revamped into exposed brickwork, a rose window was added, the upper-story openings were transformed into trefoil windows and the portal was similarly splayed to match the new gothic-like facelift which would intentionally (re)insert the building into an ideal Della Scala past. In fact, Avena took original elements from demolished buildings and literally 'patched' them onto the existing frontage. The most dramatic addition was, of course, Juliet's balcony. In his Metro Goldwin Mayer production, Cukor had used a custom made replica of Donatello's exterior pulpit of the Duomo of Prato, which possibly inspired Avena's approach when he decided to 'recycle' a marble slab decorated with carved lancet arches to replace the existing banister. This piece, part of which probably came from a medieval sarcophagus, was found during the renovation of the civic museum of Castelvecchio (itself the most renowned Scaliger military monument and yet another of Avena's urban projects which he had started in the 1920s).[18] In fact, the addition makes for a rather narrow box-like space which betrays its historical or at least functional implausibility as a proper balcony producing a strident effect that denounces its artificiality. However, not only did its strategic positioning – around eight feet above the ground – make its eye-catching decorative pattern perfectly visible from below, but also rendered it verisimilarly not too high for Romeo to have climbed his way to Juliet's bedroom with a rope ladder. Following the same line of reasoning, the house's interior was equally refurbished to suit an ideally conceived representation of a medieval or possibly early Renaissance home. Avena drew inspiration from both the early nineteenth-century miniature illustrations realized by Giovanni Battista Gigola for an edition of Da Porto's novella, published in 1819 in a limited number of copies, and the work of Venetian artist Francesco Hayez, who had authored a number of paintings on Romeo and Juliet, still very popular at the time. In particular, Hayez's 1823 *The last kiss of Romeo and Juliet*[19] provided a blueprint for Avena's internal arrangement of the house. In the painting, the scene is set in an imagined interior of a late-medieval house recognizable in the presence of a stained-glass window and an arched portion of an internal loggia. Similar details were almost identically reproduced on the first floor, easing the stagy identification of the place with the dwelling of the city's own beloved heroine. The legend, as it were, had found a home. This imitative layering of different artistic suggestions gave life to something of a permanent theatrical setting revealingly contiguous to the real theatrical space of the Teatro Nuovo, whose foyer is, not coincidentally, entitled to Juliet as a miniaturized performance and civic space called Piccolo Teatro di Giulietta. As the website instructs the reader,[20] this area opens on the courtyard surmounted by the famous balcony, and is equipped with a proper stage, duplicating on a small scale the larger one in the main hall. Acquired in 1931 by the Theatre itself and in 1949–51 turned into the site of the Cappello Theatre, thus dubbed because its access was through Juliet's house, the foyer is conceived of as a civic locus of intersection of different cultural and civic practices, providing a flexible space for exhibitions, conferences, gala dinners, and small-scale performances. Thus the physical contiguity between the balconied courtyard and this multifunctional theatre area blurs the dividing line between the pretended (hyper)real dimension of the house and the stage-setting of the real theatre, itself turned into an urban space where theatrical and social performances likewise take place. This extraordinary contiguity between, and blend of, the lifeworld turned into stage-life and stage-life turned into the lifeworld, in its various public declinations and actions, provides a living case study of how performances, in Richard Schechner's formulation,

> occur in many different instances and kinds', being 'construed' as a 'broad spectrum' or 'continuum' of human actions ranging from ritual, play, sports, popular entertainments, the performing arts (theatre, dance, music), and everyday life performances to the enactment of social, professional, gender, race, and class roles ... (2013, 2)

This meddling of physically and ideologically contiguous areas foregrounds the nature of social performance at the root of the production of, and participation in, the Juliet space as a fictional urban territory whose communicative and discursive potential asks to be activated through use. One way is to set off the fabricated objects' own talk, the balcony's, for instance. One such element is sufficient to convert the house into the larger-than-life location of passionate and yet tenderly naive young love, utterly erasing any dimension of violence, defiance, or struggle against oppressive patriarchal rule. In the 1930s, these issues certainly did not become the regime's male chauvinist concept of family life, but even nowadays they would probably ill-suit the commercial image of Verona as the 'city of love', which has found in the balcony one of its most popular post-modern icons and the ultimate destination of a lay pilgrimage. As Daniela Zumiani has justly foregrounded, "the spaces become a pretext to 'absorb' and 'consume' the myth, which materializes in the house and becomes tangible ... through the statue of the heroine and the balcony" (2003, 203). In fact, in 1969 Verona's Lions Club commissioned the realization of a statue of Juliet to local artist Nereo Costantini. Costantini possibly took inspiration from the feminine allegorical figures that adorn the fourteenth-century Arche scaligere[21] – the extraordinary open-air funeral monuments of the Della Scala that stand not far from the house – looking, as Avena had done before him, to the city's own celebrated past. It has also been suggested that Juliet's statue may be interpreted as a complementary modern-day figure to the Lady Verona mentioned earlier, a Roman feminine statue with medieval additions that stands at the centre of the Piazza delle Erbe (one of the two main squares of the town, the other being Piazza Bra where the Arena stands) as the "two fundamental components", Roman and medieval, "of the civic *genius loci*" (ibid., 217). Not funereal but celebratory of the city and the Shakespearean myth it cradles and upon which it feeds itself, Juliet's bronze figure, in imitation of its opulent golden predecessor, was placed in the courtyard of the house in 1972 and has been since then a very *tangible* icon, as her right breast has been worn shiny by the touch of hundreds of thousands of visitors: its "rate" (5.3.301), to which Montague alludes in the play, has become in fact one of good luck and modern-day "palmers" daily worshipping their "saint" (1.5.100, 102).[22]

The other pole of attraction for these 'pilgrims' is, of course, Juliet's tomb, whose present location was provided once again by Antonio Avena in the 1930s. His intention to have reality match dramatic fiction is once more at work. When he took charge of the project, the red-marble sarcophagus had been sitting for years under a late nineteenth-century Romanesque-like portico which, in Avena's eyes, must have appeared to have nothing in common with the "ancient vault / Where all the kindred of the Capulets lie" (4.1.111–12). He was, therefore, eager to find a remedy for such a deficiency and he actually commissioned a 'vault' to be built from scratch in an underground empty room (possibly a former cellar) of the seventeenth-century complex of San Francesco al Corso. The new 'burial chamber' was aptly given a medieval camouflage through the addition of double lancet windows and the insertion of false tombstones on the floor. The sarcophagus was eventually placed at the centre of the custom-built staging.[23] At the ground level, after walking through a gravel stone path, visitors are still welcomed by a bust of William Shakespeare realized in 1910 and moved here upon the inauguration of the 'new' tomb. They can thence experience their descent to the 'very place' in which the unfortunate lovers consummated the last act of their 'love sacrifice', as the story goes. A plaque quoting Romeo's words in 5.3 acts as a viaticum: "A grave? O, no; a lantern ... / for here lies Juliet, and her beauty makes / This vault a feasting presence, full of light" (ll. 84ff.). In order to be decodified and read, this space needs language, yet not any language, but Romeo's highly connoted words on Juliet's beauty and angel-like splendour turning the funeral vault into a bright and opulent palace. This is the language of the Juliet discourse fashioned out of the play by a civic ideology of moral rectitude and divine magnificence aimed at self-promotion and communal identity. Indeed, in July 1937, a local newspaper enthusiastically hailed the "felice rinvenimento della cripta" ["the happy recovery of the crypt"] which witnesses a more or less conscious hybridization between history and make-believe. Urban spaces were thus taken as fit loci in which extant elements from an anonymous past could be reused and converted into credible remnants of an imaginary past. A syncretic interpretation of historical and fictional memories, resulting in a deceptively 'authentic' construct in the eyes of visitors, was what was needed. In an enjoyable article published by the *New York Times* in 1996, Barbara Ascher reports her tourist experience in "fair Verona", a stopover at the House of Juliet included:

> Suspension of disbelief is your passport to pleasure. Bearing this in mind, I determine to venture to Juliet's house ... I strive for the frame

of mind that must have motivated the splash of graffiti on the red brick and peeling stucco walls of the 13th-century house with its Gothic door and charming balcony ... Near the rear of the crowded courtyard, Juliet stands demurely, forever nubile in bronze. Someone has left a note near the hem of her gown. It is written on a paper napkin stained with strawberry gelato. Shameless, I read it. 'Dear Juliet, I was here but you were not'. Indeed. (1996)

Juliet does not belong there, of course, but neither do the "Gothic door" nor the "charming balcony", and yet the representation of an imagined space appears and is regarded as authentic, because the legend has been incorporated into the urban fabric bending it to its own needs. What may seem to fall within the scope of what Henri Lefebvre dubbed as "representational spaces", in "which the imagination seeks to change and appropriate" and "overlays physical space, making symbolic use of its objects" (1991, 39), is in fact an accurately devised conceptual space. Conceived of as a material and mental territory, it is overloaded with a symbolic meaning ingeniously pre-set on the hyperreal artefact: verbal discourse, spatial location, and material objects here interlace in the articulation of a civic discourse inalienable from a clear, if multifarious, ideological meaning.

CIVIC PRACTICES

The appropriation of the R&J myth is possibly most evident in the singular experience of the so-called 'letters to Juliet' which, for almost eighty years now, has turned Shakespeare's heroine into the addressee of an untold number of letters written to her by people all over the world. Once again, it all started with the tomb.

In the Renaissance, funeral monuments "were concerned with establishing a permanent image of the social body", so that the "monumental effigy" set "for eternity the image of the deceased", preserving "his or her social body" and it was "happy to mislead the viewer about the whereabouts of the 'natural' side of the equation" (Llewellyn 1991, 68). In the twentieth century, preoccupation with Juliet's monument resulted in an expansion of the traditionally social significance of the tomb on a definitely larger scale than was common in the Renaissance; it did not concern the entombing of her natural body and the simultaneous visible preservation of her social body, but the visible entombing of her myth as a way to manipulate its monumental significance for the contemporary onlooker.

It was the tomb's custodian Ettore Solimani, whom the city council had appointed to the role in 1937, who inaugurated one of Verona's most enduring traditions: the letters to Juliet. As Lise and Ceil Friedman accurately describe it, Solimani "[a]n indefatigable showman ... understood the pull of the myth ... and devised a fanciful 'ritual of love'" (2006, 50).

The volcanic caretaker invited the couples who visited the site to exchange a kiss and make a wish in front of Juliet's tomb, and his idea was so successful that a few visitors even left written notes addressed to Shakespeare's heroine.[24] Soon afterwards, proper letters began to arrive, and Solimani spontaneously took upon himself the task of responding to every single one of them, becoming what people dubbed the 'Secretary of Juliet'. After his retirement, the letters piled up for nine years in the town hall tourist office until in 1967 the 'post' of Secretary was filled by Gino Beltramini, journalist and writer, founder of a monthly magazine, *Vita Veronese* [*Veronese Life*]. Surprisingly, Beltramini did not want his identity as Secretary to be disclosed and once it was revealed, in 1972, he resigned. Once again the city had to look for another secretary, and for a few years the letters were entrusted to a municipal employee, the city picking up the postage bill. When this person was moved to another office, around the mid-1980s, the letters went once again unanswered until, in the late 1980s, Giulio Tamassia, founder of the Juliet Club, a cultural local association, agreed to become the next Secretary. With a small group of volunteers, among whom his own daughter Giovanna, whose participation increased the sense of a family product, Tamassia and the Club – with a little help from the city[25] – have carried on the task until today making of the letters to Juliet a world-known phenomenon. Strange as it may seem, people come to Verona also to look for the famous Secretaries whose activity is carried out on behalf of the city council. Letters are left at the house of Juliet in two specially provided post boxes and also pasted on the walls of Dal Cappello house and courtyard – literally covered in notes and graffiti – where the 'Secretaries' collect them on a regular basis.

But who writes to Juliet? The vast majority are women, the largest group being made up of American teenagers and more than five thousands letters, sometimes simply addressed to "Juliet, Verona", are received every year.[26] It cannot be denied that this practice involving numbers of volunteers has a cohesive function in terms of civic participation. And yet the socio-cultural as well as political and ideological implications are very subtle. The letters tell about being in (or out of) love for the first time, but also about broken homes, interracial love and bereavement, and turn to Juliet for a word of wisdom or a piece of advice. Some even comment on Juliet's story wishing for a different finale or just refer to her as the embodiment of love and life: "Who knows who will read these messages, who will be curious to know the desires of strangers?", we read in one of these letters, where curiosity about who stands behind Juliet's pen name betrays awareness of the fictionality of the whole thing without disclaiming belief in it; and goes on: "Story or legend, it isn't rhetoric ... because Juliet exists. Yes, you exist and this is a prayer that everyday, more and more, you will be in me and in the heart of every man, and that you make him a dreamer, or lover, that you make him come alive!" (Friedman and Friedman 2006, 12). It is extraordinary how fiction and reality are here conflated when the story is admitted to being what it is, a legend, and yet deprived of the rhetoric of fiction. Juliet both exists and does not exist, she has no historicity but possesses mythical verity, and as Kenneth Burke would put it, seems to provide a peculiar 'equipment for living', precisely as works of art are *"equipments of living*, that size up situations in various ways and in keeping with correspondingly various attitudes" (1998, 598). This seems to suggest that in Juliet we encounter "the strategic naming of a situation", so that her myth "singles out a pattern of experience that is sufficiently representative of our social structure, that recurs sufficiently often *mutatis mutandis*, for people to 'need a word for it' and to adopt an attitude towards it. Each work of art is the addition of a word to an informal dictionary" (ibid., 596). Burke's reference is to *Madame Bovary* and Bovarysm, but the underlying logic is the same. The letter-writer grasps this logic and sentimentally recasts the concept in her own words. Her desperate wish to believe in Juliet's existence is a response to life's shortcomings and an attempt to make up for them by entering the self-deluding circuit of make-believe. Foucault (1981) many years ago warned about the dangers of confession as a mode of drawing "more of the person into the domain of power" (Fairclough 2013, 53), a strategy inherited today by therapeutic and counselling discursive practices. Letter-writing to Juliet affords precisely one such psychotherapeutic practice free of charge, where different orders of discourse intertwine. The fictional bond making for hyperreality provides an all-too-real love-icon, Juliet in therapeutic guise, who meddles conversational and familial discursive types, magazines' 'love section' or 'broken hearts' styles, and the confessional mode in globewise oriented exchanges advertising the city as the steadfast moral banner of love and peace. Hyperreality commingled with counselling therapy as a power-inducing form of the confessional mode serves the scope of commodifying Juliet's myth as a customer-oriented strategy – albeit with no other immediate profit than renown.

In and through the letters, Juliet herself comes alive and inhabits a space where people look for the averment of their own humanity. "Se ami credi in Giulietta" ["If you love, you believe in Juliet"] is a phrase Ettore Solimani early devised to be inscribed on a Romeo and Juliet souvenir pin he designed during his years at the tomb. Commodification becomes the portable gadget of a discourse of power absorbing and metamorphosing Juliet's story into the metal vehicle of civic self-advertising. If love, as Hedrick and Reynolds have it, is the "chief marker or signature of Shakespeare in the popular imaginary" (2000, 10), Verona has placed it at the centre of its very own 'Juliet-space'. The metal pin, representing a monogram with the letters R and J, was surmounted by the Dal Cappello carved emblem ideally blending Juliet's (fictional) love story and its would-be historical belonging to Verona's public space, reuniting the real and the imagined.

Articulated in the south-west-of-the-river built-in area of the house-tomb tourist path, as a commercial, popular, hyperreal accretion to a city traversed along this route by herds of global Juliet-pilgrims, and in the north-of-the-river high culture site of international theatrical performances at the Roman theatre, the R&J Verona space at times invades also the real lived-in space of the city. The occasion, not coincidentally, is Valentine's Day. The discourse of power impinging upon the perception of this town as the homeplace of love (a town notoriously a stronghold of the conservative and multiculturalism-resistant Lega Nord party) is appropriated through various forms of civic action. On 13 February 2015 an itinerant R&J performance, originating in the urban built-in R&J main area and then moving around the "splendide piazze circostanti, nel palcoscenico ideale della tragica storia dei due giovani amanti" ["the spendid squares, in the ideal setting of the tragic history of the two lovers"][27], crossed the spatial dimension of the city's daily life, thus confusing everyday spatial and tourist domains and bringing visitors and citizens alike within the meta-space, or super-space, of the civic R&J street performance. The same day, in the evening, yet another R&J performance, by the revealing name of *Opera in love*, took place at the Church of Saint Maria in Chiavica, "Un affascinante concerto spettacolo unico al mondo che unisce l'arte del melodramma all'ideale dell'amore eterno" ["A uniquely fascinating performance and concert that combined melodrama and the ideal of eternal love"].[28] Two days later, on 15 February, the eighth edition of the 'Giulietta and Romeo' half marathon cut across the city heading for its central Bra square, with its imposing Arena amphitheatre – again, a majestic opera theatre site chosen as the natural destination of a civic performance in the name of Shakespeare. A four-day tour-de-force 'love' celebration, from 12 to 15 February, rounded off the occasion in the downright commercial style of street markets scattered around the city centre, blending the perceived, routinely, everyday lived-in spaces and the consumerist-cast of the built-in R&J area. What is remarkable here is the mutual reinforcing of the physical space, conceptually devised in the hyperreal style seen above, and the multidimensional discourse accompanying it, in the dual form of Shakespearean quotes and appropriately devised commentary, interlacing information and publicity discourses – or the 'telling and selling' mixed discourse type (see Fairclough 2013, 113ff.). "Per la 11 edizione di Verona in Love", the website adverstises, "gli scorci più intimi di Verona si tingono di rosso: le vie del centro storico, il balcone di Giulietta, Piazza dei Signori, Cortile Mercato Vecchio e tanti altri luoghi magici si trasformano, per rivivere l'amore contrastato di Romeo e Giulietta" ["for the eleventh edition of Verona in Love, the most intimate corners of Verona are tinged in red: the city centre streets, Juliet's balcony, the Signori Square, the Old Market Courtyard and many other magical places are transformed to allow you to relive the contrasted love of Romeo and Juliet"].[29] This discourse shows familiar overtones in the direct address to an interlocutor who is allured into buying him/herself an exclusive experience of the "intimate" spaces of the town: its own most private and secluded area (and shops), as well as personal and, by implication, 'sexual' dimension of a feminized city, passionately, and violently, coloured in red.

Celebrations of Juliet's birthday on 16 September – a date that derives from some complicated calculations based on Luigi Da Porto's sixteenth-century novella[30] – is feted with the arrangement of a one-day medieval festival with costumed performers, an open-air painting marathon, arts and crafts stalls, toasts, and public readings that take place at the town's old commercial core between the Piazza delle Erbe and the Cortile Mercato Vecchio. The tourist built-in R&Jspace is thus exploded into a wider urban area more directly concerned with the cultural practices involving citizens, as part of an entertainment machine geared towards construing a sense of belonging while conveying a message of physical appropriation of a myth that transfigures the urban everyday space into a stage setting. Juliet and her 'myth' *are*, therefore, rooted in the city's multilayered cultural, commercial, and urban space, providing the discursive and ideological backdrop of civic and tourist performances. Millions of sightseers come to Verona every year,[31] rarely missing a visit to the House and Tomb of Juliet, thousands of letters addressed to the Shakespearean heroine arrive every year from all around the globe, and at least three international prizes have been inspired by her ("Cara Giulietta",[32] "Scrivere per amore",[33] and Premio Giulietta). The "Cara Giulietta" ["Dear Juliet"] award, whose winners are presented with on Valentine's day, is granted every year to the 'best' letter addressed to Juliet, while "Scrivere per amore" ["Writing for Love"] is dedicated to the best published romantic novel of the year, and the "Premio Giulietta" ["Juliet Award"] is annually given since 1991 to a female personality whose career achievements have been particularly outstanding.[34]

CODA TWO: ALTERNATIVE PRACTICES

The Juliet (and Romeo) discourse thus reinscribes itself in the urban space with practices of writing and rewriting love-letters and novels, strenuously casting a romantic, sentimentalized veneer upon commercial and civically cohesive practices. Mawkish sentimentality is the keyword of this official discourse in neat contrast with potentially subversive (or perceived as such) R&J counter-discourses. In a place where overall peaceful citizenry occasionally still suffers from local youth feuds and street brawls,[35] one feels the need of alternative practices evading stale commodification of romantic love and inaugurating a more multicultural way of conceiving and performing the play's afterlife and its complex message of peace. Eventually promoted and subsidized by a very supportive municipality, the project of an alternative civic *Romeo and Juliet* workshop run by Lindsay Kemp has been one of these examples. Whether or not initial wariness towards the project was due to Kemp's fame as transgressor of bourgeois chichés, potentially threatening the postmodern hyperreality of solidly set models of sublimated femininity and its urban extension, the one-month workshop was finally approved and held. Indeed, it received full backing and encouragement on the part of both the Head of the Shakespeare Summer Festival and the Town Hall, and culminated in a production/master-class event at the Teatro Nuovo in Verona on 12 April 2013.[36] In the same week, when a University international conference was taking place on *Romeo and Juliet* and the possibilities for its civic performance, a public reading too was set in the garden of Verona's medieval Castelvecchio museum, conducted by a well established local theatre company, the Teatro Scientifico. The reading followed and complemented a round table focused on the topic of *Romeo and Juliet* before Shakespeare, which was held a couple of hours earlier in one of Castelvecchio's main conference rooms. The reading blended different 'versions' of the story of the two "star-crossed lovers" ranging from Luigi Da Porto and Matteo Bandello, to Pierre Boaistuau and Arthur Brooke, but also including Alessandro Carli's edited collection of Veronese historical accounts, published in Verona in 1796, and local early twentieth-century poets Berto Barbarani's and Vittorio Betteloni's own Romeo-and-Juliet-inspired works ("Giulieta e Romeo", 1905, and "La storiela de Zulieta e Romeo", 1906, both mentioned earlier in this chapter). Extracts taken from all of these texts were read in the different original languages (Italian, English, and French) and the performance featured, in a sort of dumb counterpoint, also two Romeo and Juliet performers who made fugitive appearances on a balcony and on Castelvecchio bridge, both overlooking the green courtyard space. Live painting – carried out by artist Maurizio Zanolli – and music, especially composed by Valerio Mauro, accompanied the reading, which was orchestrated as a full score played by the actors almost 'chorus-like' walking around the garden. While subversion of the R&J official discourse was not the aim, these civic events, involving citizens and tourists alike, took place in the official urban site of that long-established official discourse, while offering alternative routes. International boundary-crossing experiences of different cultures, traditions, disciplines, and performative media and styles, from dance, to recitation and music, for once relocated Romeo and Juliet back to their overtly fictional dimension: by traversing urban, performative, textual, and multilingual territories, it offered an alternative way for doing it civilly without playing on the hyper-realism of the town-inscribed R&J space. Whether this was a new start in the production of a public perception and civic performance of *Romeo and Juliet* is hard to tell; yet it certainly was a fresh way to question that space from its inside.

NOTES

1. Which, contrary to Kottman's contention, are not "disjointed facts and accidents", failing to provide "a tragic *mythos* of consequential actions, reversal, and recognitions" (2012, 4), but the mere temporal and causal sequence of the secret marriage, the street fray with Tybalt's death, Capulet's plan to assuage Juliet's pain through marrying her, the faked death plot and the equivocation causing the death of the three youths in the vault. These facts are not fragmentary; they

rather reflect the intersection of different lines of action only partially known to their protagonists.
2. "And a beautiful monument was ordered, above which the cause of their death in few days was engraved". All translations of the Italian texts are ours.
3. See chapter 7 in this volume.
4. "that most unfortunate case of those two most unhappy lovers".
5. "... the lord Bartolomeo [Della Scala] gave orders for a dignified funeral homage to be paid to the two most unhappy lovers, which Montagues and Capulets willingly and very solemnly did, and the bodies of the two unfortunate lovers were, by their common will, placed in the same monument, which, made of vivid stone, stood noticeably above ground, and which I have oftentimes seen being used as a washing basin at the well by those poor wards at Saint Francis, while the site was being renovated for them; discussing this fact with Cavaliere Gerardo Boldiero, my uncle, who introduced me there, he showed me a place in the wall, beyond the abovementioned sepulchre, on the corner of the Capuchins' convent, from which, as he says, he had understood, this tomb was removed together with some ashes and bones many years before". An interesting addition to this is that, unlike what happens in both Da Porto's and Bandello's novellas, in Della Corte's narrative – as is in Shakespeare – Romeo dies before Juliet wakes up: "Giulietta, havendo già la polvere fornita la sua virtù, rinvenne e vedendosi Romeo morto a lato, ... si maravigliò molto" (1596, 10.593) ["Juliet, having the powder already released its effect, woke up and seeing Romeo dead by her side ... was very much surprised"].
6. Annamaria Conforti Calcagni hypothesizes that the stone coffin was removed and its content scattered or even destroyed by order of religious authorities, since it preserved the mortal remains of suicide lovers (2003, 197). Fascinating as it may sound, this hypothesis does not seem to be supported by Della Corte's description, which documents only the removal of the sarcophagus – possibly a menial drinking trough (Martelletto 2001, 138) – from its ancient collocation against the Convent's wall next to the well, where it served as a washing basin.
7. The quotation comes from a letter to Thomas Moore dated 7 November 1816 (on nineteenth-century foreign travellers to Verona see Watson's essay in this volume).
8. The *hospitium*, literally a lodging, was actually a modest travellers inn which possibly also included a shelter for horses. Its existence is documented as prior to 1364 and therefore it pre-existed (and survived) the realization of the so-called *broilum magnum*, a green area planned by Cansignorio della Scala within a larger project of urban reconfiguration in the second half of the fourteenth century (see Zumiani 2003, 204–12). The so-called House of Romeo, identified with the medieval Casa Nogarola (also known as Stallo alle Arche), is now a private residence. The relation with the house of Montague comes from an ancient chronicle that recounts of a terrible civil fight occurred in 1206 between the Count of San Bonifacio and the Monticuli (Montague) family which ended in the destruction of "le case de Monticuli appresso il Ponte Nuovo" (Zagata and Rizzoni 1797, 220) ["the house of Montague near the Ponte Nuovo bridge"]. For a historical overview of the site see Martelletto 2001, 129–34.
9. In Da Porto the name of Juliet's family is Cappelletti. He probably took it from Dante's *Purgatory* ("Vieni a veder Montecchi e Cappelletti", 6.106; "Come and see Montecchi and Cappelletti"), where the poet alludes to two northern Italian

rival families belonging to the Ghibelline and Guelph factions, respectively (see Romano 1993, 1.13 and 52, n. 17).
10. Literary critic and historian, Brognoligo, born in Verona in 1867, produced some of the earliest critical studies on both Matteo Bandello and Luigi da Porto.
11. "Erudition is made of study, research, reasoning. The cult of national memories is only made of sentiment. The former inhabits the regions of the intellect, the former the ones of the heart. The one harbours in our heads, the other in our bosoms. Albeit dwelling in two separate areas, they can live in the same house, that is, in the same individual, without quarrelling".
12. "popular in its truest meaning, that is, known and dear to every citizen of whatever class or condition, with no exceptions".
13. "everything is beautiful ... pure, gentle, passionate, and heroic".
14. It is again Vittorio Betteloni who writes: "Nello scorso mese di Aprile o di Maggio [1905], non ricordo bene, l'*Arena*, antico e serio giornale veronese, recava la notizia che la casa di Giulietta stava per essere messa all'asta al prezzo di lire 7.500, ed eccitava il Municipio a provvedere perché quel monumento non cadesse in mano di barbari [e] ... consigliava il Municipio stesso a comprare addirittura la casa per conto suo. Questa faccenda a Verona fece un certo effetto, e anche i giornali fuori se ne occuparono. Il *Figaro* di Parigi pubblicò una caricatura: anche in Francia Giulietta è nota, per la tragedia di Shakespeare e per l'opera di Gounod. E un gran giornale di Roma stampò che se il Municipio di Verona non comperava la casa lui, l'avrebbe comperata la Regina Margherita. Erano riscaldi e gonfiature: ma ciò prova che la cosa destava interesse" (2008, 54) ["Last April or May, I do not remember well, *L'Arena*, an old and serious Veronese newspaper, reported the news that Juliet's house was going to be put up for sale at auction for 7,500 lire, and urged the municipality to act lest the monument fell into the hands of barbarous people [and] ... advised that the municipality itself should buy it. This episode had some effect ... the Parisian *Le Figaro* published a cartoon: Juliet was known in France too, because of Shakespeare's tragedy and Gounod's opera. A big newspaper in Rome wrote that, if Verona's municipality did not buy the house, Queen Margherita would do that. This was all puffery but proved that the matter had awakened some interest"].
15. On the impact of Cukor's film on Avena's project of urban reconfiguration see D'Anniballe 2013.
16. "Many things will be renovated: it is the fate of a strong generation to bring back life where others have extinguished it".
17. Indeed, back in 1905, Vittorio Betteloni had pointed out the potential economic benefit that the restoration of Juliet's house an tomb could bring to the city: "Questa leggenda e le memorie che vi si collegano, apocrife certo, ma ad ogni modo visibili e palpabili come le case, la tomba e che so io, servono efficacemente a mantener viva ed alimentare l'industria del forestiere" (2008, 56) ["This legend and the memories linked to it, apocryphal of course, and yet visible and tangible just like the house, the tomb, and I do not know what else, can efficaciously maintain and nourish tourist industry"].
18. See on this Grimoldi 1994 and Bozzetto 2003.
19. This painting (Tremezzo, Villa Carlotta) was one of four works Hayez realized on a subject he admired for its Romantic implications of conflict between

subjectivity and social constraints, also cast in the light of the political struggles of Italian Risorgimento.
20. Accessed March 26, 2015. http://www.teatrostabileverona.it/incentive_foyer_del_teatro_nuovo.html.
21. The original four statues (ca 1382) were removed from the Arche in 1967 and have been recently (March 2014) substituted by replicas. They represent Justice (personified as Judith carrying the head of Olophernes), Temperance and the towns of Verona and Vicenza, at the time subjected to the Della Scala rule.
22. In June 2014 the original statue, which showed severe signs of wear, has been removed and transferred to a local museum, while a 'true and faithful' replica now stands at the original spot underneath the balcony.
23. On the administrative turns that led to the authorization of this renovation see Grimoldi 1994, 182.
24. As a nineteenth-century photograph of the tomb shows, Juliet had inspired people to write to her since much earlier times. This particular image represents a young woman kneeling in front of the sarcophagus, above which are appended hundreds of cards and notes (see Friedman and Friedman 2006, 11–12).
25. This contribution is actually barely adequate to cover the postage bill and at the beginning of 2015 the Juliet Club has indeed benefited from a donation of a Veronese private foundation which provided them with new premises in the city centre, not far from the House of Juliet. "In a while", Giovanna Tamassia says, "we may also become one of Juliet's sites" ("E-mail to the authors", 21 March 2015).
26. Upon their arrival – sent through regular mail, email or, as already mentioned, left in the two post boxes placed at the house of Juliet – all letters are catalogued and archived by the Juliet Club's volunteers. Recently e-mailed letters are also accepted and can be written on a specially provided computer placed inside Juliet's house.
27. Accessed March 15, 2015. http://www.teatrostabileverona.it/sulle_tracce_di_giulietta_e_romeo-p106e.html.
28. Accessed March 15, 2015. http://www.operainlove.it/.
29. Accessed March 15, 2015. http://www.cittadiverona.it/eventi/scheda531/sagre/verona-in-love-per-san-valentino.html.
30. In Shakespeare's play she was famously born on Lammas Eve ("Come Lammas Eve at night shall she be fourteen", 1.3.19), that is, on 31 July.
31. Over two million people visited Verona in 2014 (Accessed March 15, 2015. http://www.tourism.verona.it/it/servizi-e-info/statistica/flussi-turistici).
32. Accessed March 15, 2015. http://www.julietclub.com/it/notizie/eventi.html.
33. Accessed March 15, 2015. http://www.premioscrivereperamore.it.
34. Among the others, ballet étoile Carla Fracci (1991), sopranos Cecilia Gasdia (1996) and Katia Ricciarelli (2010), poet Alda Merini (2003), Beijing and Moscow Olympic gold medalists Federica Pellegrini (2009), and Sara Simeoni (2013).
35. The latest traumatic instance was the aggression in the night of 30 April 2008 of 27-year-old Nicola Tommasoli, battered to death by a group of youngsters for trivial reasons. A commemorative plaque denounces the slaughter which took place in the city centre, close to Juliet's house.
36. For a discussion of Kemp's workshop, see Bessell's essay in this volume. See also Nigri 2014.

WORKS CITED

Ascher, Barbara. 1996. "Trying to avoid Romeo and Juliet". *The New York Times* May 12.
Baudrillard, Jean. 1988. *Selected Writings*, edited by Mark Poster. Stanford: Stanford University Press.
Betteloni, Vittorio. (1905) 2008. "La leggenda di Giulietta". *Bollettino della Società Letteraria di Verona*:51–7.
Bozzetto, Lino Vittorio. 2003. "Indagini preliminari di studio sul restauro Forlati-Avena di Castelvecchio". In *Medioevo ideale e medioevo reale nella cultura urbana. Antonio Avena e la Verona del primo Novecento*, edited by Paola Marini, 133–53. Verona: Cierre.
Brooke, Arthur. (1562) 1908. *Romeus and Juliet*. Edited by John J. Munro. New York: Duffield and Co. / London: Chatto & Windus.
Burke, Kenneth. (1938) 1998. "Literature as Equipment for Living". In *The Critical Tradition: Classic Text and Contemporary Trends*, edited by David Richter, 593–8. Boston: Bedford St. Martin's.
Conforti Calcagni, Annamaria. 2003. "La tomba di Giulietta a San Francesco al Corso". In *Medioevo ideale e medioevo reale nella cultura urbana. Antonio Avena e la Verona del primo Novecento*, edited by Paola Marini, 195–201. Verona: Cierre.
D'Anniballe, Maria. 2013. "Form Follows Fiction. Redefining Urban Identity in Fascist Verona through the Lens of Hollywood's *Romeo and Juliet*". In *New Perspectives in Italian Cultural Studies*, vol. 2, edited by Graziella Parati, 223–43. Lanham, MD: Fairleigh Dickinson University Press with Rowman and Littlefield.
Della Corte, Girolamo. 1596. *L'istoria di Verona*, bk 10. Verona: Girolamo Discepolo.
Eco, Umberto. 1986. *Travels in Hyperreality. Essays*. San Diego, New York and London: Harcourt & Brace.
Fairclough, Norman. (1992) 2013. *Discourse and Social Change*. Cambridge and Malden, MA: Polity.
Foucault, Michel. 1981. *The Hisory of Sexuality*. Harmondsworth: Penguin
Friedman, Ceil, and Lise Friedman. 2006. *Letters to Juliet. Celebrating Shakespeare's Greatest Heroine, the Magical City of Verona, and the Power of Love*. New York: Stuart, Tabori and Chang.
Grimoldi, Alberto. 1994. "Restauri a Verona: cultura e pubblico 1866–1940". In *L'architettura a Verona dal periodo napoleonico all'età contemporanea*, edited by Pierpaolo Brugnoli and Arturo Sandrini, 121–93. Verona: Banca Popolare di Verona.
Guidorizzi, Mario. 2003. "Giulietta e Romeo da Verona a Hollywood". In *Medioevo ideale e medioevo reale nella cultura urbana. Antonio Avena e la Verona del primo Novecento*, edited by Paola Marini, 317–18. Verona: Cierre.
Hedrick, Donald, and Bryan Reynolds. 2000. *Shakespeare Without Class. Misappropriations of Cultural Capital*. Houndmills, Basingstoke: Palgrave.
Isenberg, Nancy. 2012. "'Caesar's word against the World': Caesarism and the Discourses of Empire". In *Shakespeare and The Second World War*, edited by Irena R. Makaryk and Marissa McHugh, 83–105. Toronto, Buffalo, London: University of Toronto Press.
Kottman, Paul A. 2012. "Defying the Stars: Tragic Love as the Struggle for Freedom in *Romeo and Juliet*". *Shakespeare Quarterly* 63 (1): 1–38.

Lefebvre, Henri. (1974) 1991. *The Production of Space*. Translated by Donald Nicholson-Smith. Oxford: Blackwell.
Llewellyn, Nigel. 1991. *The Art of Death*. London: Reaktion Books.
Martelletto, Maria Grazia. 2001. "Sulle trace del mito shakespeariano". In *Suggestioni del passato. Immagini della Verona scaligera*, edited by Maristella Vecchiato, 129–39. Ministero per i Beni e le Attività Culturali.
Murray, Thomas, ed. 1838. *Byron's Life, Letters and Journals*. London: John Murray.
Nigri, Lucia. 2014. "Review of Lindsay Kemp's *Perché sei tu?* (directed by Lindsay Kemp at Teatro Nuovo, Verona, 12 April 2013)". *Shakespeare* 10 (4): 443–4.
Reynolds, Bryan, and Janna Segal. 2005. "Fugitive Explorations in 'Romeo and Juliet': Transversal Travels through R&Jspace". *Journal for Early Modern Cultural Studies* 5 (2): 37–70.
Romano, Angelo, ed. 1993. *Le Storie di Romeo e Giulietta*, vol. 1. Roma: Salerno Editrice.
Rykwert, Joseph. (1963) 2013. *The Idea of a Town*. London: Faber.
Schechner, Richard. (2002) 2013. *Performance Studies: An Introduction*. London and New York: Routlegde.
Shakespeare, William. (1984) 2003. *Romeo and Juliet*. Edited by G. Blakemore Evans. Cambridge: Cambridge University Press.
Zagata, Pier e Jacopo Rizzoni. 1797. *Cronica della città di Verona ...* Verona: Ramanzini.
Zumiani, Daniela. 2003. "Giulietta e Verona: spazi e immagini del mito". In *Medioevo ideale e medioevo reale nella cultura urbana. Antonio Avena e la Verona del primo Novecento*, edited by Paola Marini, 203–21. Verona: Cierre.

13 *Perché sei tu?*

Lindsay Kemp's "gift of memory"

Jacquelyn Bessell

This chapter examines the contribution of text, practice, and memory to the reception of a one-off instance of civic performance, a dance-theatre adaptation of *Romeo and Juliet* staged by Lindsay Kemp in Verona in April 2013. In particular, it will interrogate the concept and function of the Prologue, and the role that training, technique, and repetition play in creating a civic instance "Shakespearean performativity" (Worthen 2003, 29), inflected by powerfully affective personal memories and collective associations.

PROLOGUE: ENTER THE CHORUS

The Prologue to *Romeo and Juliet* is packed with vivid antitheses, from the "ancient grudge" set against "new mutiny" in the third line, to the "miss" and "mend" of the final, fourteenth line. For the actor these antitheses are a category of 'operative' words or ideas; the actor must 'coin' these words or ideas, to give clarity and shape to the line overall. However, the prologue is more limited in the range of psychophysical actions (or, 'tactics') an actor can play, with the goal of affecting the addressee (in this instance the audience); in a section of dialogue the responses of the listener are either scripted or strongly implied, but as the prologue is a sonnet/soliloquy, most often the responses of the audience can only be imagined. Moreover, the narrative structure of the prologue suggests that the speaker will know at the beginning of the speech, what they are going to say at the end of it; so what is often called the 'need to speak' may be straightforward, but it can seldom sound spontaneous. As the ability to respond truthfully to changing external stimuli with a good range of psychologically motivated, psychophysical actions is widely considered one of the hallmarks of a 'good actor', and one of the building blocks of what is commonly associated with 'good' (read 'naturalistic') acting, I am quick to point out to the actors I train that such speeches do not make good audition pieces, and I counsel them to choose something else. This chapter will describe how a very specific instance of 'civic theatre' – Lindsay Kemp's *Perché sei tu?*, a dance-theatre workshop production of *Romeo and Juliet*, at the Teatro Nuovo, – caused me to question all of my assumptions about the function and theatrical value of prologues.

Before I begin, in the tradition of any good Shakespearean prologue, I will give away the ending: Kemp invents the most remarkable Prologue for this evening, in the form of an hour-long warm-up-cum-masterclass, which will acquaint his audience with key aspects of the practice he developed over the course of a very lived life in the theatre. This will prime the audience, making them conversant in a kind of physical rhetoric, that Kemp and his performers will use to coin a sequence of unique transactions with "the public" (as Kemp addresses us). This creates a sort of civic event, an instance of 'inductive theatre', in which the action of the play 'happens to' the audience.

PROLOGUE: ENTER THE WRITER, TEATRO NUOVO, VERONA, 12 APRIL 2013

Every theatre has a beauty of its own, but as I take my seat in the stalls in the unquestionably fair Teatro Nuovo in Verona (where we lay our scene) awaiting the start of *Perché sei tu?*, I think about the Prologue to *Romeo and Juliet*, and of Shakespeare's notion of a "fair" Verona, "[w]here civil blood makes civil hands unclean" (4). The Teatro Nuovo is plush and genteel, the audience tonight equally so. In my current surroundings I see only one half of that violent antithesis that Shakespeare yokes together in the Prologue, in the "fair" and "unclean" in Verona, of this binary-heavy story of "death-mark'd love" (9). Violent antitheses are the most Shakespearean of tropes, his last rhetorical stand, as well as the building blocks and most concise expression of the playwright's "mixed attitude of alternating praise and execration" (Locatelli 1993, 74) towards his adopted (or imagined) Italianate setting. John Barton goes so far as to claim that Shakespeare "*thought* antithetically" (2009, 56), and it is fair to say that antitheses most distinguish Shakespeare's writing as immediate and dramatic. And yet, as Stephen Purcell reminds us, a prologue is "something ambiguous and transitional" which "announces the start of a play while simultaneously marking itself out as before-the-start" (2013, 75), and being so, prologues are paradoxical, obstacles to immediacy. Tonight's prologue will be different, though, because tonight's prologue will be given by Lindsay Kemp.

BUT, BEFORE I START …

In April 2013 my grasp of Lindsay Kemp's practice extends little further than knowing he taught Kate Bush how to dance and David Bowie how to mime, but my expectations are (almost) boundless, and, as ambiguous and transitional figures go, I would expect him to be up there with the best. Lindsay Kemp is many things to many people: in addition to being the man who helped both David Bowie and Kate Bush to find their respective grooves, he is these things, too, and more (in no particular order): an acclaimed outsider with a taste for populist pantomime; a choreographer with equal and opposing concerns for form and anarchy; a mime artist and a punk; a self-proclaimed "song and dance man" and a devotee of Jean Genet. Lindsay Kemp is also (theatrically speaking) a thief.

Accolades and accusations of this kind are to Kemp just so much water off a duck's back, and in an interview with a panel of academics the morning after the performance, he confessed:

> I steal from the best! I think it was Picasso who said 'genius steals; the talented merely borrow' … all of my performances are made up of what I can gather, ideas from other people, other directors … what you see are not stolen goods, but a reinvention. It's a reinvention, my own version, because I don't have the gift of memory.
>
> (Kemp 2013, "Interview")

There is a powerful irony at work here, because, as I will argue in what follows, *Perché sei tu?* relies very much on memory, and on the idea of performance as a gift: one could read *Perché sei tu?* as precisely Kemp's "gift of memory" to his audience. This tension between appropriation and theft, between homage and robbery, makes Kemp's work at once central and marginal. One cannot discuss his work without reference to Peter Brook; equally, he will not discuss his work for very long without reference to Mr Punch. To try to separate or isolate these antithetical elements of high art and low comedy is perhaps as pointless as trying to separate ancient grudges from new mutinies, or indeed the Democratic and the Dionysian elements of theatre's very origins. So, perhaps all I need say is that Lindsay Kemp is, in most every kind of company, a quintessential man of the theatre.

PROLOGUE: ENTER KEMP

Meanwhile, back in this specific theatre in Verona, a prologue of sorts is about to start. I say *a* prologue because, in common with the bulk of Shakespeare's text, *the* famous Prologue will remain unspoken in tonight's performance; but in the gap left by this geographical name-check, a unique alternative prologue will present itself in the unorthodox rhetorical form of Lindsay Kemp himself. Miked-up like Madonna, cracking jokes with the audience like Groucho Marx, and capering with the energy of someone one third his age, Kemp is a perfect storm of visual and verbal contradictions and is ready for action. The action will – as is customary in both prologues and Shakespeare more generally – require our imaginary forces to be engaged, but like Artaud, Kemp must believe that "the masses think with their senses first and foremost" (Artaud 2010, 60), and appropriately his opening conversational gambit has a positively Dionysian feel:

> Time to get drunk! Time to get *intoxicated*. Time to release our *personal madness*. So, how do we get drunk? On music ... for the moment!
> (Kemp 2013, *Perché sei tu?*)

For the moment! Kemp's prologue is provocative and enticing, and, as all good prologues should, it leaves us wondering what could happen next, perhaps hoping (or fearing) that *anything* might happen next. As it turns out, the intoxication he has in mind involves no alcohol, but rather an hour-long masterclass, out of which will bleed a performance of *Romeo and Juliet*. The class, for nine (Romeos) and nine (Juliets) is underscored throughout by Kemp's verbal commentary via the radio mike. The play has not started yet, but the evening has definitely begun.

During the warm-up-cum-masterclass, Kemp uses the radio mike to prompt and urge the performers to "project this joy out to the public", ensuring, of course, that this is exactly what we, the public, see and feel. Kemp works both his actors and his public in a perfectly judged exercise in inductive theatre. Long before the actual performance proper gets underway, the play itself is *happening to us*. If Kemp's commentary occasionally seems direct to the point of being clunky – "everyone wants to join us in flight ... all experiences are *shared* experiences..." (2013, *Perché sei tu?*) – it is nonetheless undeniable and the means by which a contract is sealed. That contract, between Kemp and his public, defines the rules of engagement for this unique form of civic engagement between onstage and offstage citizens of Kemp's imagined Verona, enclosed within the walls of the 'real' Verona outside.

COMMENTARY, SPOKEN SUBTEXT, AND PERFORMATIVITY

The wording of the contract to which I refer above lies in present-tense prompts – "and we're flying ..." (Kemp 2013, *Perché sei tu?*) – which work like performative utterances (Austin 1976) because it feels for all the world as if the performers, as if *we*, are. Kemp's commentary via the wireless radio mike will simultaneously interpret and amplify the gestural language of the performers and is, therefore, central to our reading of everything that follows. In effect, Kemp's live commentary replaces Shakespeare's text in this part of the performance, and refreshes Worthen's concept of "Shakespearean performativity", by evoking "the pastness of the text and what the text represents ... in the present action of performance" (2003, 29). Kemp's commentary is a kind of spoken subtext that makes concrete connections between intention and action, as well as establishing the aesthetic conventions which will govern the performance to follow. The commentary primes the audience first to distill, and later to recall aural information (Kemp's prompts in the warm-up) when only the visual information (the specific gesture) is repeated, in performance. Kemp understands that, having experienced the connection between intention and form in the context of the class, the audience will experience subsequent repetitions or iterations of these forms as similarly performative.

THE POWER OF 'YOU'

I am suggesting that much of the success in this conceit lies in Kemp's mode of address for this running commentary. Like a successful songwriter composing a love ballad, Kemp understands the power of 'you': by addressing the performers over the mike using the second-person, Kemp trusts the audience to infer that it is being addressed too:

> You have to dance as if it might be your last dance. You've got to dance as though there is no tomorrow ... your most generous dance, your craziest dance, your most courageous dance, your most thrilling dance. (2013, *Perché sei tu?*)

Later, Kemp switches to first-person plural, the "we," which feels inclusive and inductive: again, the audience is encouraged to include itself in the collective "we": "we" are part of the experiential, kinaesthetic element of this event:

> For the first time, the arms lift: a miracle. We lift, and we fall ... falling ... falling from heaven ... falling into our lover's arms ... falling under the rose bushes ... falling under the sheets ... and we roll ... rolling ... and returning ... falling under the waves ... and up ... we are reborn ... seabirds... (Ibid.)

"For the first time" is a phrase Kemp returns to many times in this urging commentary. This ignores Schechner's "Performance means: never for the first time" (1982, 40) and instead chimes with Brook's preferred definition of performance: from the French *representation*, which he calls "a making present" (2008, 139). In this moment the performers, arms aloft, slowly and gently paddle through the heavy air:

> Walking! It's as if you are walking for the first time. It's a miracle! Courage. Preparation. The foot is kissing, caressing the earth. The earth releases a perfume: new mown grass – don't keep it to yourself. It is an experience that we make into a gift.
>
> (Kemp 2013, *Perché sei tu?*)

This commentary calls attention to somatic experience that is concrete, specific, and yet wildly imaginative. Kemp does not allow us to distance ourselves from the effort of the performers, nor does he allow us to give in to an illusion without embracing it as such.

This is what inducts me into Kemp's community for the evening. This is how he creates a civic experience out of this well-rehearsed play.

KEMP AND THE REVELATION OF SPACE

Kemp, like Brook, believes in the sacred space of performance, and he reminds his young actors not to take this for granted. Weimann's influential concepts of the *platea* (liminal space) and *locus* (space for central action) (Weimann 1978) are here aired in a refreshingly unfussy way. Over in the liminal space in the wings upstage right, he explains to his performers (and by dint of the mike, to all of us in the audience) that "over *here*, you can have a cigarette, or have a glass of gin ..." before moving to centre stage (the *locus*, in Weimann's view), where "my *god*, over *here* is something very special" (Kemp 2013, *Perché sei tu?*). Kemp's great gift is one of belief: he trusts his instincts, his skill, and his ability to inspire and engage his public, staging the absolute truth in Brook's equally confident opener to *The Empty Space*:

> I can take any empty space and call it a bare stage. A man walks across this empty space whilst someone else is watching him, and this is all that is needed for an act of theatre to be engaged. (2008, 11)

Sure that we (the audience) are watching him, Kemp needs to establish these spatial relationships between the *locus* and the *platea*, linked to the sacred and profane, in order to flout them; as if to test Brook's theory, he purposefully walks across the stage, then pauses centre, to coyly turn upstage and scratch his arse. He tells me the next day that he might be descended from Will Kemp, Shakespeare's unruly clown, and I believe him.

"... BETTER WITHOUT THOSE WORDS ..."

Brook, I assume, would see this kind of liberty-taking as quintessentially Shakespearean, "immediate" theatre, a bringing together of "the unreconciled opposition of Rough and Holy [theatre]" (2008, 86) in an evening of dance theatre which works "like the plague, by intoxication, by infection, by analogy, by magic; a theatre in which the play, the event itself, stands in place of a text" (ibid., 49). Indeed, taken in isolation, the text poses challenges in this production, and not just because the audience comprises both Italian and English speakers. The problem, Kemp argues, begins with his own troubled relationship with words in general:

> I have a great problem – especially for an actor – in that I don't remember words. My language is gesture. I've been deprived of the gift of words – mind you, I don't seem to be doing too badly! – but this has been replaced with this universal language, so when I remember the play, I remember it through movement, through the gesture of the lovers hands, which Zeffirelli reminds me of … that is where it started … when I began to remember the movie, I remembered the line 'Do you bite your thumb at me sir?', [sucks thumb] which appeals to my own childishness! There were places where I just felt that we needed a few words, musically, I wanted the public to understand the story. And later I regretted that decision, because I think the storytelling would have been better without those words.
>
> (Kemp 2013, "Interview")

The choice of word or text fragment, of course, is all. Kemp may be troubled by the text in a general sense, but his commentary alights on words and images, which not only help his performers connect the technical elements of the class to the text, but also form the audience's framework of reception for the performance that follows. The process is one of identification and repetition, in a nod – more than a nod perhaps – to Pina Bausch, and Samuel Beckett. Like Bausch, when Kemp uses repetitions of movement, shape and gestures "[i]ntellectual as well as emotional associations come tumbling to mind" (Confino 2013, 47). Like Beckett, Kemp uses live, amplified repetitions of words as "a central and necessary concept within all attempts to understand individual and social being and representation" (Connor 2007, 1). When these elements are combined as, for example, when the ensemble turn to face the audience in a slow and sustained choral *port des bras*, underscored by Kemp's words "for you" (2013, *Perché sei tu?*), the intention is clear, the moment is performative, and the emotional impact on the audience is frankly overwhelming.

Repetition in rhetorical writing works in just the same way, of course, and intentionally so. Simon Palfrey argues that: "Whatever the emotion – indeed, whatever the expected attitude to the emotion – repetition of word, phrase, and rhythm was able to underscore it" (2011, 58). Palfrey reads the play's central relationship through a "kind of ecstatic verse, full of hyperbolic repetitions and impatient exclamations" (ibid., 83) and would no doubt find the same "extravagant indecorum" (ibid., 58) in Kemp's masterclass-with-commentary, whereby the repetition of a series of somatic schema constantly reinforces and expands the effect of the original iteration.

IN DEFENCE OF PRACTICE

Kemp explained his rationale for including such personal intervention (the commentary and warmup) into the performance, in the interview the following day:

> I wanted the public to be moved by what they saw, to be lifted by what they saw, to be involved, and to be a bit liberated, to feel the joy and the pleasure that the dancers on stage were extending as an invitation to participate, from the very beginning. So what I endeavoured to show was simply the actors' preparation for the performance, and then a rehearsal of an imagined performance of a much shorter version of Shakespeare's play. (2013, "Interview")

All of this may well be true, but there is something that smacks of an apology in it, where none is necessary. The "preparation" is rigorous and physical, embodied and thrilling to watch, and Kemp's deference in his "imagined performance" is unwarranted.

Practitioners who allow their process onto the stage or the screen do so out of generosity; for those of us who can identify only the most basic shapes and choreographic gestures by name, the masterclass-with-commentary provides an empowering vocabulary and framework with which to read the performance that will follow. Further, I recognize in Kemp a pleasure in coaching, prompting, of repetition and of variation. Those familiar conventions used by so many acting, voice and movement teachers in the studio, are here deployed in an explicit and celebratory recognition of practice, which argues for itself. These conventions find support from other, more surprising quarters too, witness Worthen (again), this time with an excellent analysis of the 'ancient grudge' between literature and practice:

> ... acting classes tend to be very repetitive: the goal is to do that movement, that gesture, that sentence, over and over, until the implications of doing it one way or another are clear to the performers and to the audience (this sense of the purpose of repetition is shared by a wide range of acting regimes, from Noh to Viewpoints). What is sometimes discredited as merely technical training across the campus in Literature Hall explicitly resembles the teaching of old-fashioned rhetoric: its technical devices are the means for making something happen, happen significantly, in a practice in which style is precisely where meaning is construed. (2015, 283)

Worthen chooses the fifteenth century Japanese Noh tradition and late-twentieth-century American Viewpoints system to suggest the sheer range of methodologies for which repetition as a key concept, but of course these choices are neither random nor unrelated. The Viewpoints, as created by Bogart and Landau, adopt a key concept from Noh theatre, that of *jo-ha-kyu* (2005, 148), or (very) roughly translated, 'beginning, middle, and end'. Each key element of performance, be it on the macrocosmic structural level of a play, or the microcosmic level of action or gesture, has an introduction *(jo)*, development *(ha)* and conclusion *(kyu)*, and these elements are necessarily connected, part of a cycle of repetition and variance; describing effective composition strategies, Bogart and Landau argue that "every *kyu* (ending) contains the next *jo* (beginning) ... [o]nce you begin to recognize and experience *jo-ha-kyu* in action, you are instantly responsible to it" (ibid.). Brook takes this point of 'responsibility' further, arguing that "anyone who refuses the challenge of repetition knows that certain regions of expression are automatically barred to him" (2008, 138). For Brook the process of repetition is central to the concept of *representation,* which "takes yesterday's action and makes it live again in every one of its aspects – including its immediacy" (ibid., 139). The action is repeated, as Kemp would have it, "as if for the first time".

THE PAVANE

I have reached this point of the discussion without questioning the historic connection between Shakespeare's *Romeo and Juliet* and dance more generally. Danced interpretations and adaptations of *Romeo and Juliet* are of course numerous and well-known. Eusebio Luzzi created the first recorded choreographed response to the play in Venice, in 1785, and Prokofiev's famous score (1935–36) has received several different choreographic treatments, among which those by Kenneth Macmillan (1965) and Rudolf Nureyev (1976) are perhaps the most well-known, and it could be argued that the recent production history of this love story belongs as much to dance as to Shakespeare or to theatre. The centrality of dance to Shakespeare's *Romeo and Juliet* cannot, therefore, be disputed, but neither is it conventional. In *Romeo and Juliet,* Brissenden notes, dance "is not used as a disguise for evil", as it is in many of the Italianate tragedies popular at the time, "but is closely and ominously connected with it" (1981, 63). This is putting it mildly; Romeo's choice to ignore his instinct to avoid the dance at Capulet's house literally proves fatal. *Perché sei tu?* necessarily ignores this caution in its source material, and reconstructs the meeting of the lovers at the dance with more emphasis on memory than on foreshadowing. This sequence in Kemp's production owes much to Zeffirelli's 1968 film, a fact Kemp freely acknowledges in his *homage* to the choreography by Alberto Testa:

> I first began to think about the bits that I remembered from the play ... all the love bits, and all the dance bits and all the swashbuckling bits ... I have a great problem – especially for an actor – in that

I don't remember words. My language is gesture ... so when I remember the play, I remember it through movement, through the gesture of the lovers' hands, which Zeffirelli reminds me of. When I came here with my choreographer and my accomplice Daniela [Maccari] we had some of these half-remembered ideas ... and Daniela helped me reinvent the dances of Zeffirelli.

(Kemp 2013, "Interview")

Kemp memorializes Testa's choreography in a sequence in which nine other couples mirror the physical rhetoric of the central couple. Choosing to use Nino Rota's music from the original soundtrack for the film – "Did My Heart Love 'Til Now?" and "The Moresca" (Saltarello) – cements the connection between this live event and Zeffirelli's famous film, but important differences in the staging outline ways in which Kemp's version also challenges some conventions at work not just in Zeffirelli's film, but noticeable in other popular danced versions of the play. In Zeffirelli's film Juliet appears to Romeo flanked on either side by a man. Kemp alters this in his version, and while he is at it, reinvents aspects of Kenneth MacMillan's male-led choreographic score (to Prokofiev's *Dance of the Knights*) for the same scene. In a reversal of MacMillan's gender-ordering, it is Kemp's female dancers who dominate the opening section, and whereas MacMillan's female dancers "execute the codified steps of patriarchal ideology, thus embodying female containment and subordination" (Fiorato 2012, 82) Kemp's women take centre stage, the men lining up as onlookers only. Women, not men, define the steps of the *pavane* in Kemp's version, and it is the men who join them in a subsequent moment, not vice versa, as is the case in Macmillan's piece. Once the stage is filled with couples dancing palm to palm in a strong echo of Testa's choreography, Kemp follows a tradition of clearing space in the central *locus* for one pairing, in an attempt to move to a close-up on Romeo and Juliet themselves. In this way, nine Romeos and nine Juliets split off hierarchically and throw focus to a dominant pair, centre stage.

As I have already said, Shakespeare's text remembers things rather differently: Romeo, in fact, stands out in the company as "he ... that would not dance" (1.5.130), and this may be one of the reasons that Kemp's reworking of Testa's *pavane* seems to me to be governed by a different agenda to other aspects of the piece. With neither Shakespeare's text – the lovers' dialogue in the foreground – nor Kemp's invented commentary for background, the *pavane* stood out (for me) as 'a number'; I could not "see the intention behind the step" (Robbins 1957, 2), because Kemp had not primed me to do so. Kemp's strategy in following Testa's lead for the *pavane* resonated strongly with those who remembered the detail of Zeffirelli's film, but, not being part of this group, I had a nagging feeling that this sequence was not intended for me. That is the selfish aspect of memory, of course: had Kemp chosen to restage the same sequence from Baz Luhrmann's version instead, being more familiar with this source, I expect my response would have been more invested, and more generous.

DANCE AND MEMORY

I suggest above that memory can be collective, personal, embodied or inferred, evoked or merely glanced at, but that it is always useful in live performance that seeks to create a communal or civic experience of some kind. How then does this sit with the immediacy of the live experience? Though Kemp's memory of Zeffirelli's film might not have played a key role in my experience of *Perché sei tu?* that is not to say that my own memory was not actively engaged in other ways by Kemp's work. In the next section I want to map Kemp's "imagined performance" paradigm onto my vivid memory of another danced response to the heightened language of another poetic tragedy of forbidden love.

There are four reasons why I want to do this: the first is because of the obvious connection that exists between *Perché sei tu?* and Carlos Saura's film *Bodas de sangre* (1981) in the subject matter of the primary sources; the second is because both Kemp and Saura explicitly recognize the dramatic value of rehearsal practices, in prologue-commentaries which frame both pieces; the third reason is because both Kemp and Saura transcend their sources at the climax of their respective performances. The final reason is that Kemp's performance, by evocation of a past memory in the present moment, found a way of dancing with ghosts, a sense of which I would like this chapter also to capture.

BODAS DE SANGRE AND *PERCHÉ SEI TU?*

Saura's *Bodas de sangre* (*Blood Wedding*) records a dress rehearsal of the choreographer Antonio Gades' flamenco-ballet version of Lorca's famous tragedy of the same name. Gades first created the choreography for *Bodas de sangre* in 1974, the same year in which Kemp created his flagship piece, *Flowers,* an adaptation of Jean Genet's *Our Lady of the Flowers*. Like Kemp, Gades and Saura omit the source text for the most part, or rather make a somatic translation of the original, incorporating very short extracts of the play text on a handful of occasions only. Saura's film also anticipates Kemp's *Perché sei tu?* in blurring the distinction between rehearsal and performance, and suggesting

> an awareness that the world constituted in performance is not separate from the world outside ... the ballet itself is only reached after backstage scenes that establish the systematic sequence of events that is demanded by the performance: the arrival, the warm-up, the costuming and the rehearsal.
>
> (Stone 2002, 76)

Like Kemp, Saura provides a sort of prologue to the main action. Part of this is a voiceover spoken by Gades, which underscores a single close-up shot of his reflection in the dressing room mirror as he contemplates the work ahead. In the voiceover, Gades remembers his mentor Vincente Escudero, whom he is said to resemble physically, and with regard to dancing style. Gades claims Escudero came to see him dance and that when he met him "It was as if he were my grandfather, and I was the grandson he'd always wanted" (Gades 1981). Gades notes the extraordinary coincidence which led him to occupy exactly the same apartment in Paris that Escudero had once lived in for twenty years, as a young man. The viewer watches Gades regard his reflection in the mirror, as the identities of the two men merge, and Gades espouses the *credo* which he inherited from Escudero. Gades implies that while other flamenco dancers may have sacrificed the authenticity of their dance on the altar of populism:

> He was a man of great dignity throughout his whole career. He was very serious and would never fool around. He always did what he believed he had to do. He never sold himself, and he died with amazing dignity. (Ibid.)

In the interview the day after the performance, Kemp is just as forthcoming about his influences, and just as keen to merge his identity with those who have gone before him. His references are characteristically eclectic, but his intention is the same as that of Gades:

> I'm a song and dance man, I've always been an entertainer; I had to keep the public happy to survive in a horrible boarding school in England, to survive the blows of the bullies I *had* to entertain them, and certainly the Elizabethan actors had to entertain their public to survive … I read Stanislavsky much later, and then I lost my copy – when I was in between boxers and strippers [mimes both] – but I did find Antonin Artaud, and of course Antonin Artaud, and later Jean Genet said 'Right. You've got it *right* Lindsay!' … the theatre should be like the plague: it spreads, and it affects you all … hopefully with a happier effect! Jean Genet said a theatre should always be built next to a cemetery.
>
> (Kemp 2013, "Interview")

Lineal traces using either recorded voiceover (Gades) or unscripted commentary (Kemp) provide a touchstone for what follows (Gades) and what went before (Kemp). Both strategies promote a sympathetic and privileged relationship between audience and performer: Gades tells us he came to dance "out of necessity, from hunger" (1981), while Kemp needed it "to survive".

The section which immediately precedes the main action of *Blood Wedding* is a full-company warmup led by Gades. Here again, analogies may be drawn with *Perché sei tu?* as Gades takes his company through their paces, working on diagonals across the studio in much the same format as that used by Kemp onstage in the warmup-cum-masterclass. But whereas Kemp's accompanying commentary serves to take the audience through the same process as the performers, a switch in narrative modes at this juncture by Saura, from Gades' voiceover to filmed dialogue, reduces the status of the viewer, whose only remaining privilege by virtue of the camera point of view, is to be in the room. Gades uses only the counts and the shorthand he needs for his dancers, with no editorializing. Careful consideration of camera angles ensures that Saura's faith in the process being sufficiently interesting to carry the narrative for several minutes is well-placed. Gades, like Kemp, favours imperatives when addressing his dancers, but unlike Kemp he draws attention to the discipline, and effort involved in the dance:[1]

> Let your back hold it! Hold your back and stretch the fall, but suspend it here, don't just fall into it! The head goes side and then front. Lift up! Stretch everything! Your head! Hold it, hold it, and then draw out the fall. Don't look down! Don't raise your eyebrows! A little more. Lift up!
> (Gades 1981)

Both Gades and Kemp allow the audience a carefully managed view 'behind the scenes'. Both explicitly stake a claim to a formidable artistic heritage and emphasize the important contribution of physical rigor and risk to a performance; however, where Gades emphasizes the responsibility of the performer to certain strictures and forms, Kemp is inclined to emphasize a need to transcend those forms, to make big imaginative leaps as well as *grands jetés*.

Though most of the critical reception of Saura's film emphasizes the political implications of Saura's technical framework and filmmaking choices, Henrik Enckell's discussion of the film's psychoanalytic framework is perhaps most appropriate to consider here. Enckell notes:

> *Blood wedding* shows what happens when the distinction between reality and fiction becomes blurred. The structure of the film is very clear ... *Blood wedding* starts as reality (i.e. as documentation) and ends as fiction. There is a clear point where one modality gives way to the other. This could be seen as an ideal for psychoanalysis: we should move in the direction of fiction, and we should be clear on the difference between sharing in reality and sharing in fiction. In the real psychoanalytic world, the difference is not always clear. (2013, 125)

In the real experience of live theatre, the difference between the sharing in reality and sharing in fiction is similarly blurred, and in the case of *Perché sei tu?*, a complex of boundaries – between preparation and performance, between *locus* and *platea*, between real and imagined Veronas – is thrillingly drawn, breached, and finally blurred. Sitting in a theatre in Verona, we necessarily move toward the fiction Kemp presents us, in his revision of Shakespeare's tragic conclusion

CRISIS AND RECONCILIATION: "FOR THESE DEAD BIRDS SIGH A PRAYER"

Perché sei tu? and *Bodas de sangre* are separated by time and medium, but the thematic concerns are similar. In both source plays, no reconciliation of the civil crisis is possible by the union of the young lovers. Shakespeare's play promises something of this sort only by the deaths of the lovers, and Lorca's play contains no such resolution. Departing from Lorca's finale, Saura's film does not include the scene in which the Bride returns to the village to confront the Groom's Mother and Leonardo's Wife; instead, Saura chooses to conclude on a note of unresolved crisis, with a mid-shot of Cristina Hoya staring into the mirrored wall with blood on her hands and her breasts in which Michelle Heffner Hayes argues:

> [t]he doubled stain of blood echoes the traumatic image of the open wound ... she recognizes herself as castrated in the mirror, but the self-consciousness of her double marking suggests that she occupies strange space ... it exists on the margins. (2009, 107–8)

Kemp also changes the finale provided by his source material, finding an alternative resolution that needs no help from the generation the dead lovers leave behind. Kemp moves beyond the implications of Shakespeare's script, or rather, rises above them. Here is no "glooming peace" between two grieving households watched over by an audience of glum voyeurs, but rather a prismatic sequence suggesting a shared experience of the lovers' ascension after death.

Kemp's finale begins conventionally enough, except for the numbers involved. As the finale is imagined as an ensemble piece, so nine Romeos discover nine seeming-dead Juliets (to Henry Purcell's "When I Am Laid in Earth") and die by mime-drinking poison in slow, sustained choral movement. This being done, the nine Juliets rise simultaneously, and in a sequence underscored by a frenetic bowed cymbal, bury nine mimed happy daggers in their abdomens. The redemptive finale comes as the Romeos rise together in the same slow, sustained effort, and, in a sequence underscored by Händel's aria for counter-tenor from *Rinaldo*'s "Lascia ch'io pianga", the Romeos lift their Juliets heavenwards, paddling once more the heavy air in an astonishing moment that reminded one audience member of the closing line of *The Phoenix and the Turtle:* "for these dead birds sigh a prayer" (l. 67). The gliding effort of the music complements the light and sustained physical effort of this movement, and the company finish on a similarly slow and sustained ensemble bow which reprises the "for you" *port des bras* described above. At this point, the audience begin to breathe again.

Certainly those who know dance will argue that Prokofiev's *Romeo and Juliet: on motifs by Shakespeare* (1935) reimagines Shakespeare's ending to *Romeo and Juliet* even more radically than Kemp's *Perché sei tu?* (Prokofiev preferred an intervention by the Friar to prevent the deaths of the lovers altogether) but in choosing to cast the whole company at the end as the lovers in ascension, Kemp has a broader, more inclusive agenda:

> Even if I wanted to, I am not sure I could have done Shakespeare's play justice ... I am always obliged to do things 'my way'; I have no choice, you see ... the seabird represents ascent, bringing light ... the light that comes with freedom, with liberation. I prefer plays which have a happy ending! I thought, 'well, even though they're dead, there's also their rebirth', which is a constant theme in all my work and in the classes ... we are constantly falling and being reborn ... so the play ends with this hope ... and it was my way, my device, of lifting the spirits of the public. Artaud said that when the public leave the theatre, they should feel they have had an act of surgery performed on them ... so I gave them a pair of wings! (2013, "Interview")

Kemp's rationale for rewriting the ending betrays a slight anxiety; under the circumstances – these being a question-and-answer session in front of an assembly composed almost entirely of Shakespeare scholars and textual editors – this trepidation is perhaps understandable. However, the theatrical impact of this decision is far-reaching, effectively rewriting Shakespeare's ending, recasting not just the performers but also the role of the audience. In his finale to *Perché sei tu?* Kemp upholds Brook's argument for:

> a special arena in which each moment is lived more clearly and more tensely. The audience assists the actor, and at the same time for the audience itself assistance comes back from the stage. (2008, 140)

Kemp's "assistance" for his audience begins with his alternative prologue, which, *inter alia,* uses the performative potential of words to anticipate, elicit and amplify a series of profound kinaesthetic responses to music, wordless gesture and movement. The civic and celebratory aspects of Kemp's workshop production are significant, in that Kemp chooses to redeem not just the young lovers, but ultimately 'the public'; that is, the citizens of Kemp's imagined Verona, built for one night only, within the walls of the city's Teatro Nuovo. Kemp's final gift to us is not, as might have been expected, a ringside seat at the lovers' funeral; instead, Kemp gives us wings.

EPILOGUE: A SURPRISING ARTICLE IN TODAY'S *GUARDIAN* ...

> So how, when it comes down to it, has Brook changed modern theatre? He has, for a start, helped us to banish everything from the stage that is physically superfluous and to embrace the exciting provocation of an empty space. He has also taught us that the theatre of the future depends on cheap seats, a shared experience, a communal joy. He has radically influenced the way we look at Shakespeare ... [b]ut perhaps one of Brook's least acknowledged achievements has been to see theatre as a totally inclusive medium where vaudeville, audience-participation and even comedy are perfectly compatible with an exploration of neurological disorder. There are endless facets to Brook's multi-dimensional career. But, if we go on asking basic questions about what the medium is for and why it is worth preserving, we have this still-active 90-year-old human earthquake to thank for it.
> (Billington, 2015)

Scholarship is evaluated by the degree to which it engages with voices from the present, and looks for new territory to inhabit, new knowledge to contribute; it is risky, some would say, to argue for the present critical significance of either *Blood Wedding,* film made in 1981, or *The Empty Space* written nearly half a century ago. But it is equally fair to say that practice evolves in a rather different way to literary criticism or performance studies, as the date of the Billington quote illustrates. Although one can take for granted the 'newness' of live performance, it cannot choose but be of the present; ghosts, however, hold their theatrical value and tend to have a longer shelf life in the theatre than in the corridors of what Worthen calls "Literature Hall".

Kemp's unique prologue to *Perché sei tu?* reveals not just those aspects of his own practice upon which the performance is built; it also suggests a correlative framework of past practices evolved over the post-World War II period to which the present performance points, explicitly and implicitly. These correlative practices are associated with key figures from personal and collective past memory: Escudero's ghost haunts Gades in the dressing room mirror; Kemp comically credits "Pina Brook" as a major influence on his work, before chuckling over his coining of a "compound-icon" wondering "who would be the most slighted" (2013, "Interview"). Kemp is up-front (if inaccurate) in naming his sources, and Billington expects his remarks about the "90-year-old human earthquake" Brook to be taken seriously. Saura's *Bodas de sangre* has imprinted strongly on my memory, and these memories have inflected my reception of Kemp's *Perché sei tu?* in ways I could not have predicted, but should not deny, because of all the elements in a live theatre experience, resonance, association and memory are among those most affecting, and least easily contained. A series of affective past memories have shaped the form and content of Kemp's work, and something very similar enhanced my kinaesthetic and imaginative response to it; when this complex of elements converges in the present moment, one evening in Verona, it is "as if for the first time".

NOTE

1. Gades, "a man of high principles, great stubbornness and exceptional discipline and rigour in his work" distinguished himself within the international dance community by "his rigorous dedication to self-improvement" (Eude 2004).

WORKS CITED

Artaud, Antonin. 2010. *Theatre and Its Double*. Richmond: Oneworld Classics.
Austin, John L. (1962) 1975. *How to Do Things with Words: The William James Lectures delivered at Harvard University in 1955*. Edited by J.O. Urmson and Marina Sbisa. Oxford: Oxford University Press.
Barton, John. 2009. *Playing Shakespeare*. London: Methuen.
Billington, Michael. 2015. "Still Centre Stage at 90: Peter Brook, Human Earthquake of Modern Theatre". *The Guardian*, 19 March. Accessed 20 March 2015. http://www.theguardian.com/stage/2015/mar/19/peter-brook-theatre-director-at-90
Bodas de sangre. 1981. DVD. Directed by Carlos Saura. Choreography by Antonio Gades. Distributor.
Bogart, Anne, and Tina Landau. 2005. *The Viewpoints Book: A Practical Guide to Viewpoints and Composition*. New York: Theatre Communications Group.
Brissenden, Alan. 1981. *Shakespeare and the Dance*. London: Macmillan.
Brook, Peter. (1968) 2008. *The Empty Space*. London: Penguin.
Confino, Barbara. 2013. "The Theatre of Images: Pina Bausch and the Expressionist Temperament". In *The Pina Bausch Sourcebook*, edited by Royd Climenhaga, 45–8. Oxon: Routledge.
Connor, Steven. 2007. *Samuel Beckett: Repetition, Theory, and Text*. Oxford: Basil Blackwell.
Eude, Michael. 2004. "*The Guardian*: obituary for Antonio Gades, 22 July". Accessed March 8, 2015. http://www.theguardian.com/news/2004/jul/22/guardianobituaries.artsobituaries.
Enckell, Henrik. 2013. "Carlos Saura's Blood wedding". *The Scandinavian Psychoanalytic Review* 36 (2): 121–5.
Fiorato, Sidia. 2012. "Mise en scene and Subversion of Political Power Through Dance: Sir Kenneth MacMillan's *Romeo and Juliet*". In *Visualizing Law and Authority: Essays on Legal Aesthetics*, edited by Leif Dahlberg, Klaus Stierstorfer, and Daniela Carpi, 74–91. Berlin and Boston: Walter de Gruyter.
Heffner Hayes, Michelle. 2009. *Flamenco: Conflicting Histories of the Dance*. London: McFarland & Company.
Kemp, Lindsay. 2013. "Interview" by Jacquelyn Bessell, Silvia Bigliazzi, and Lisanna Calvi. Verona, April 13, 2013. Unpublished text.
Kemp, Lindsay. 2013. *Perché sei tu?* Unpublished text of the performance. Teatro Nuovo, Verona.

Locatelli, Angela. 1993. "The Fictional World of *Romeo and Juliet*". In *Shakespeare's Italy: Functions of Italian Locations in Renaissance Drama*, edited by Michele Marrapodi, A.J. Hoenselaars, Marcello Cappuzzo, and L. Falzon Santucci, 69–86. Manchester: Manchester University Press.

Palfrey, Simon. (2005) 2011. *Arden Student Guides: Doing Shakespeare*. Huntingdon: Arden Shakespeare.

Purcell, Stephen. 2013. *Shakespeare and Audience in Practice*. Houndmills, Basingstoke: Palgrave Macmillan.

Robbins, Jerome. 1957. "Choreographic Manual". *West Side Story*. New York: Josef Weinberger Ltd.

Schechner, Richard. 1982. "Collective Reflexivity: Restoration of Behavior". In *A Crack in the Mirror: Reflexive Perspectives in Anthropology*, edited by Jay Ruby, 39–81. Philadelphia: University of Pennsylvania Press.

Stone, Rob. 2002. *Spanish Cinema*. Harlow: Pearson Education.

Weimann, Robert. 1978. *Shakespeare and the Popular Tradition in the Theater: Studies in the Social Dimension of Dramatic Form and Function*. Edited by Robert Schwartz. Baltimore: Johns Hopkins University Press.

Worthen, W.B. 2003. *Shakespeare and the Force of Modern Performance*. Cambridge: Cambridge University Press.

Worthen, W.B. 2015. "The Shakespeare performance campus". In *Shakespeare on the University Stage*, edited by Andrew J. Hartley, 264–87. Cambridge: Cambridge University Press.

Zeffirelli, Franco. (1968) 2003. *Romeo and Juliet*. DVD. Paramount.

14 Stage(d) Reconciliations

Romeo and Juliet and the Politics of Bilingual Shakespeare Productions in Germany

Bettina Boecker

Romeo and Juliet is a play with a strong political agenda, demonstrating as it does the high personal price that has to be paid by the individual in a society torn by internal strife. The deaths of the two young lovers have been interpreted in a number of ways – as the ultimate step towards individuation and personal freedom (Kottman 2012, 1–38), as a version of *Liebestod* (Kamps 2000, 37–46), as a manifestation of the play's queerness (Freccero 2011, 302–8), and so on. On a rather more basic level, the death of the young lovers is, of course, a side effect, albeit unintended, of the feud between their parents, a feud that has detrimental effects on the entire community of Verona. A 'pacifist' reading of the play hence suggests itself, though this is an interpretation that has, somewhat surprisingly, received less attention from academic critics than it has in actual performance and in film versions of the play. Representative instances include a 1994 joint Israeli-Palestinian production of the play by the Khan and El-Qasaba theatres in Jerusalem, Clare Stopford's 2000 *Romeo and Juliet* set in gang-ravaged Cape Town and most recently, during the World Shakespeare Festival in 2012, *Romeo and Juliet in Baghdad*. The play's iconic status and the perceived ease with which its central conflict can be mapped onto the political situation of such diverse geopolitical regions as South Africa, Iraq or the West Bank have made *Romeo and Juliet* a firm favourite with directors seeking to make a political impact – so much of a favourite as to have spurred its own spoofs, such as the 2005 *West Bank Story*, a *Romeo and Juliet* set among rival falafel sellers in the West Bank (Fischlin 2007). The play's mapping of civic space and civic strife in "fair Verona" has thus proved supremely transferable to other locales. The crises that shape *Romeo and Juliet* have provided a vocabulary with which the conflicts and grievances of geographically and temporally distant societies may be articulated, as well as their longing for resolution and reconciliation. As a commentary on and intervention in the politics of their own day and age, such 'translated' *Romeo and Juliet*s are a supreme example of civic Shakespeare. They present an engagement with public issues, frequently in a contact zone and almost always in the context of a conflict between two opposing political and/or social groups.

This essay focuses on bilingual productions of *Romeo and Juliet*, arguably an intensified version of the 'translated', multicultural *Romeo and*

*Juliet*s mentioned earlier. It investigates the motives for staging such productions, their desired political effects, how individual productions handle the stumbling blocks that Shakespeare's text contains for a bilingual approach, and finally how bilingualism affects the conflict between the civic and the personal that is at the heart of the play. Most of the material under discussion comes from Germany (in one case, from Switzerland). However, the issues raised by bilingual *Romeo and Juliet*s are at least to some extent independent from the languages and cultural contexts involved, and the productions analyzed in this paper should yield some more general insights in this particular form of civic Shakespeare.

Outside Great Britain and increasingly even inside the UK, bi- or multilingual Shakespeare is a well-established way of 'doing' the Bard. This tradition has formed its own repertoire within the larger canon. *Romeo and Juliet* is a particular favourite, followed by *A Midsummer Night's Dream* and *The Tempest*. The reasons for this are rather obvious: all of these plays are highly popular and/or highly theatrical, which helps alleviate some of the problems that arise when a bilingual production faces what is often a not quite bilingual audience. It is hard (though certainly not impossible) to imagine a bilingual *Henry VI* Part 3. Still more importantly, all three plays pit two or more distinct groups against each other, inviting an approach that maps the oppositions inherent in the plot onto a linguistic opposition between two camps that, literally, do not speak the same language. More or less abstract cultural differences are thus translated into the very concrete reality of a language barrier, which lends additional poignancy to the political 'message' of the production – and of the three plays just mentioned, *Romeo and Juliet* is certainly the one that most easily lends itself to a 'message', all the more so given its popularity (or assumed popularity) with young people. The play is predestined for theatrical ventures that conceive of themselves as – in the widest possible sense – didactic.

As we have seen, the tale of the two young lovers tragically divided and ultimately killed by their parents' strife is easily mapped on the real-life political conflicts of the twentieth and twenty-first centuries. This mapping usually includes a broadly pacifist agenda, in which the lovers' deaths signal the futility of war and ultimately turn into a call for other, non-militant ways of solving conflicts and furthering peace among the nations. For obvious historical reasons, this agenda is particularly resonant in Germany. The country's ongoing concern with *Vergangenheitsbewältigung* (the process of coming to terms with the National Socialist past) makes it fertile terrain for the kind of *Romeo and Juliet* outlined above, not least because such productions can reasonably expect to raise considerable public funding. In what follows, I want to take a closer look at three bilingual productions in particular – one German-Polish, one German-Czech, and one German-Russian. Reconciliation with and making amends to these nations, all of them attacked and occupied by the Third Reich, has been high on Germany's political agenda ever since the 1950s, a fact which significantly sharpens the civic relevance or profile of the productions under discussion here. Not only do they, sometimes very explicitly, hope to reflect, even influence the relations between Germany and the respective nations as they exist today, they are also and often very tangibly supported, even instigated by state authorities, to a degree that is well above even the wonts of the heavily state-subsidised German theatre scene. This form of civic theatre would seem to resemble that of classical Greece, where, as the editors put it in their introduction to this volume, theatre was involved in "the construction of an ethical and political ideology"[1] for the *polis*.

The German-Polish *Romeo and Juliet* produced by the Uckermärkische Bühnen in Schwedt, a small provincial theatre on the Polish border, is a particularly good example of this. The production was commissioned to mark the 1,000-year-jubilee, in the year 2000, of the signing of the Peace of Gnesen by the German king Otto the Third, which is traditionally regarded as the inception of Polish national sovereignty. The Polish Foreign Office made a request to the Ministry of Education of the federal state of Brandenburg to the effect that Brandenburg "react to this event by artistic means" (*Märkische Allgemeine* 14 March 2000). Obviously, this did not mean re-running the long and varied history of German-Polish aggression and antipathy, but making an artistic contribution to reconciliation and understanding between the two nations. This took the form of a production of *Romeo and Juliet* that relied heavily on music and visual effects, and on a strategic use of bilingualism. But although it is virtually a constant in the marketing of bilingual *Romeo and Juliet*s, the connection between bilingualism and a conciliatory agenda is by no means logically imperative.[2] It is utterly dependent on a notion one might call the myth of Shakespeare's linguistic transcendence, i.e. the idea, familiar from intercultural productions of Shakespeare, that a Shakespeare play in performance "transcends, and is transmissible outside of, verbal communication". In this logic, Shakespeare's "dramatic value and power are [believed to be] intrinsic, and come into their own when divorced from colonial 'baggage' – including the English (colonial) language" (Lan 2005, 529–30). This hypothesis is not limited to colonial contexts. Implicitly or explicitly, it informs all manner of productions that start from the premise that Shakespeare can thrive not only without his original language, but without *any* form of successful linguistic communication, and that this is what permits his plays to travel, or even act as mediators, between different cultural contexts.

In his 1993 *Foreign Shakespeare*, Dennis Kennedy diagnosed that given the proliferation of non-English Shakespeares, one could no longer define the greatness of Shakespeare's art as resting on the words: outside Britain, Shakespeare obviously prospered without his language (1993, 1–18). As Peter Holland put it in his review of *Shakespeare in the New Europe* (Hattaway, Sokolova, and Roper 1994), there were obviously "world[s] elsewhere, the rich cultures in which Shakespeare speaks, in which, indeed, he is the uniquely necessary voice, often speaking with many times the eloquence he currently attains in English" (Holland 1997, 77). Now, twenty years later, that voice has left those foreign worlds and made its way back to Shakespeare's mother country. Even inside Britain, he now quite manifestly prospers without his language, witness for example the Globe to Globe Festival of 2012. These festivals, and especially their audiences, are complex cultural phenomena that have been analyzed elsewhere.[3] The productions they featured are relevant to my purposes because of their *difference* from the bilingual, sometimes multilingual ones that this essay explores. This difference seems to lie primarily in the fact that with a monolingual production, even if it is an Armenian production playing to a London audience, the assumption is that someone somewhere will understand everything being said. The production has a linguistic home, even if it has left that home to become an exotic spectacle elsewhere. A multilingual production, by contrast, has no such home, no defining point of origin in the sense that productions at the Globe to Globe festival had. As the importance of the spoken word diminishes or disappears altogether, other sensory channels such as music and particularly the performing body move to the centre of the theatrical experience.

The non-understanding or partial understanding that is intrinsic to intercultural performativity (Lan 2005, 533) becomes a particularly prominent part of the audience's experience when more than one language is spoken on stage. Hybrids between foreign and native, or – in a European context – naturalized Shakespeare, multilingual productions throw the myth of Shakespeare's linguistic transcendence into particularly sharp relief as spectators can settle neither into the familiarity of a text in their native language nor into the unfamiliarity of a foreign-language version of Shakespeare. Instead, they are confronted with the foreign and the familiar at the same time (or given, the linearity of theatrical performance, in very close temporal proximity). By thus alienating the audience from established dichotomies like self *vs* other or home *vs* abroad, bilingual productions arguably further thinking in commonalities rather than differences. This, in any case, is a point habitually made with regard to bilingual *Romeo and Juliet*s, and with particular aplomb by the PR material for my second example, a German/Russian *Romeo & Juliet* staged in the university town of Tübingen in 2010. This production grew out of a phenomenon that, at a grassroots level, is emblematic of Germany's post-war efforts at international, particularly European integration: town twinning. Every German town of more than 10,000 inhabitants has at least one twin town, often more, and the average citizen will not only be able to name his or her community's twin, but will often have visited in person since various form of exchange (of students, of football teams, of choirs) are one of the main manifestation of 'twinship'. The rationale is that two nations thus linked on a microlevel of personal connections will never go to war again. Tübingen, a town of around 85,000 inhabitants, has no less than eleven twins, among them the city of Petrosawodsk in Russia. The German-Russian *Romeo and Juliet* under discussion here was a cooperation between the municipal theatres of Tübingen and Petrosawodsk. As such, it was obviously meant to participate in the spirit of town twinning. The production's director made the point with due diligence:

> Thematically, what is at the centre of our production of this classic text is communication and understanding across linguistic and hence cultural barriers. Dialogue between hostile groups, fear of the other, aggression against the alien and the utopia of overcoming these barriers in loving intoxication are the salient points of this gripping love story. In this Babel of emotions, this polyphony of opinions, love is the only lingua franca. (my translation)[4]

By using two different on-stage languages, the production foregrounds precisely the "linguistic and cultural barriers," which it is its avowed intention to overcome. The desired conciliatory effect can hence be achieved only by positing a kind of meta-language that, while enabling communication between members of the two opposing camps, does not partake in the divisionary character that is attested to language in general. In a not entirely original move, love is declared to be that language. In this production, the actors playing Romeo and Juliet hence face the challenge not only of doing without or partly without what is arguably one of the most important tools of their trade – language in the form of a coherent dialogue – but also of demonstrating its effective dispensability. Superimposed on this is the additional difficulty of turning the tragedy of Romeo and Juliet into a theatre event with an ultimately comedic structure.[5] The cooperation of two theatre companies from different cultural and linguistic backgrounds is meant to succeed precisely where the Verona of Shakespeare's play fails: in overcoming fear of the other and aggression towards the alien. What the warring Montagues and Capulets learn only through the sacrifice of their children, contemporary actors and audiences are meant to learn through acting in, respectively watching, a bilingual performance.

This ultimately didactic objective is built into the very institutional framework of my third example, a Czech-German production of our play by the Youth Theatre of Bavaria. A venture designed to "raise enthusiasm for the theatre in young people who live outside the big cities",[6] the Youth Theatre of Bavaria is a travelling company playing to audiences in the smaller towns of Bavaria and its European neighbours. The company will typically involve local students in the production, both as actors and in creating an actual venue for playing in communities that have no theatre. Though state subsidized and staffed by a number of full-time employees, the Youth Theatre thus arguably constitutes a form of amateur drama. Traditionally, this would have barred it from any serious critical attention. But as Michael Dobson writes in his account of (anglophone) amateur Shakespeare, amateur performance is "one of the most widespread and significant ways in which the plays of William Shakespeare have participated in English-speaking culture over the four centuries since they were written. ... [T]he long history of how Shakespeare has been performed by amateurs is a story of how successive groups of people have committed themselves to incorporating these plays into their own lives and their own immediate societies ..." (2011, 1–2). This last point would seem to establish a kind of natural affinity between amateur Shakespeare on the one hand and civic Shakespeare on the other, and hence a rationale for looking for the civic in the kind of production I discuss in this paper, productions that are perhaps not incorrectly described as provincial – and I do not mean this in the pejorative sense. The federal structure of Germany is mirrored in the institutional structures of German theatre. There is no single 'centre' in the manner of London, for example – theatre afficionados look to more than one city for innovation, sophistication, and up-to-dateness.[7] Arguably, one of the biggest strengths of the German theatre is its sheer geographical presence. It is no great exaggeration to say that it is rarely more than half an hour's drive to the closest professional stage (though this probably truer for what used to be West Germany than it is for the East). Just how professional that stage will then be, and how it will rank for artistic ambition are other questions, but the mere existence of such non-metropolitan, perhaps peripheral theatres should not be discarded lightly in the context of civic Shakespeare, or indeed of a 'civic' theatre. If civic theatre is indeed involved in the creation of an ideology for the *polis,* or in this case, the nation, then this process cannot be limited to the big cities: it must spread to more rural areas and less than professional enterprises as well. The point Dobson makes about British amateur theatre holds true for German theatre outside the big cities as well. Amateur productions, Dobson states, over time "have been far more numerous [than professional ones], and at several important points in theatrical history the geographical scope and social inclusiveness of the amateur theatre have dwarfed those of the commercial and subsidized playhouses" (2011, 1). Similarly, German Shakespeare, and with it civic German Shakespeare is not limited to big houses like Munich's Residenztheater or the Thalia-Theater in Hamburg. In fact, the more peripheral settings tend to throw the rationale behind a civic theatre into particularly sharp relief, especially when it comes to the implicit or explicit didacticism that often informs the bilingual *Romeo and Juliet*s under discussion here.

As stated earlier in this chapter, these productions almost uniformly present the play as containing an irenic 'message'. But for this irenicism to appear convincing, what is a tragedy for the Veronese clans must be turned into an ultimately comedic event for the audience, at least if the ultimate aim of the production is to argue that "international understanding" is not just a necessity, but also, and more fundamentally, a real possibility. A commentator on the Youth Theatre of Bavaria's German-Czech *Romeo and Juliet* demonstrates how this can be done. He succinctly remarks: "Where the two warring dynasties fail – in finding some sort of common ground, in creating understanding despite the fact that they don't speak the same language – the team at the Youth Theatre of Bavaria succeeds impressively".[8] The production not only stages, but continues or even improves upon Shakespeare's tragedy, leading it to a different, happier ending. By doing so, it not only mirrors but ultimately solves or at least helps solve the conflicts of its own day and age. By reminding the audience of its duties and obligations in 'keeping the peace', the production secures the welfare of the commonwealth, here imagined as the community of (two neighbouring) nations. Arguably, these responsibilities are situated somewhere between the private and the public. Although it is the individual who is tasked with the recognition, acceptance, and cultivation of the commonalities between two different nations or cultures, it is the individual as *zoon politicon,* in his or her capacity as a citizen. (Romeo and Juliet would have lived happily ever after had their parents shown more community spirit). In appropriating the play as a kind of peacekeeping operation, bilingual *Romeo and Juliet*s can thus present themselves as a means of obliterating the sort of mindset that ultimately leads to armed conflict.

Or so the programmes, the interviews and, often, the reviewers say. The actual realities of creating understanding (in the many senses of the word) by means of a bilingual production are often more complicated than the marketing material would have one believe, not least because of the challenges of the text itself. Any production will have to decide on a language for the prologue, a language in which the lovers communicate, and a language (not necessarily the same one) for Friar Laurence and Duke Escalus, respectively. Because its choices regarding these features are particularly instructive, I want to look at a fourth production here, a German-French *Romeo and Juliet* staged in Fribourg (Switzerland) in 1989. In this production, the prologue was presented in both languages – "an important decision", Balz Engler writes in his analysis of the show, "as it indicated from the outset how the two languages would be juxtaposed with each other. The prologue suggested, at a level beyond the story presented in the play, that languages might co-exist in harmony, even though no longer in the one suggested by the poetic form of the sonnet in the English text" (2011). As a mediating figure, Friar Laurence also spoke French and German, as did the young lovers, though their linguistic competence differed from his. While he was simply competent in both languages, Romeo and Juliet mingled the two rather than keeping them tidily apart. That way, they effectively created a language of their own. (In the Tübingen production, the lovers were language learners, gradually acquiring a working knowledge of, respectively, German and Russian. Some productions also choose to let the lovers communicate entirely without language, reinforcing the point that love as the ultimate harmonizing force is (supposedly) a meta-linguistic phenomenon). As verbal communication recedes into the background, other sensory channels gain in importance. As one director put it,

> Above all, we were interested in playing out the topic of communication on a number of different levels, using every kind of non-verbal

language which humankind in general and the theatre more specifically has at its disposal. Music plays an important role. And every form of corporeality. Dancing, fencing, fighting ... kissing, to be sure, you can't do *Romeo and Juliet* without that.[9]

This professed trust in the medium of theatre is a staple feature of bilingual productions, and, more generally, the phenomenon that for lack of a better term I will call 'Shakespeare Without (All of) the Words'. This is not "foreign Shakespeare" in the sense of Dennis Kennedy's 1993 collection of essays. "Foreign Shakespeare" is assumed to play to an audience that actually understands the (foreign) text. With bilingual productions, like those that played at the Globe to Globe Festival, at least partial non-understanding is an accepted[10] feature of the theatre experience on offer – to be compensated for, at least theoretically, by particularly intense theatricality.

Two points are to be made about this: one, trust in the medium of theatre is greatly facilitated when, as in the case of our play, a majority of the audience can be assumed to be already familiar with the plot; and two (and here I return to bilingual *Romeo and Juliet*s), despite their professed trust in the theatre and its ability to transcend language, many productions tend not to rely on it altogether. Some productions provide translations on overhead screens. Another common and less mechanical version is the introduction of an epic element in the form of a conferencier or commentator figure. This figure will usually speak not two languages but one only, a subtle acknowledgement of the fact that many bilingual productions play to largely monolingual audiences. It seems safe to say that spectators are generally expected to have no fundamental problem with not understanding large parts of what is being said. Though one needs not have any principal objections to this, it is somewhat at odds with the professed political mission of these productions. Accepting that one does not understand a foreign language/culture is different from actively trying to comprehend it, and those in charge of public theatre funds would probably think the latter superior to the former. Not to put too fine a point on it, it is probably rather hard to get public money for a project demonstrating the utter or partial incomprehensibility of, say, the Poles.

The discrepancy between the conciliatory mission to which so many bilingual *Romeo and Juliet*s subscribe and the effect the production potentially has on an actual audience brings me to a figure that is perhaps the biggest challenge the play holds for a bilingual approach, and that is Escalus. Significantly, this is also the figure that most pointedly brings out the play's 'civic' dimension, i.e. the effect that a seemingly private feud and an apparently purely personal love story have on the community as a whole.

In 5.3 of Shakespeare's text, a few dozen lines before the end of the play, Escalus says:

> Where be these enemies? Capulet, Montague?
> See what a scourge is laid upon your hate

> That heaven finds means to kill your joys with love!
> And I for winking at your discords too
> Have lost a brace of kinsmen. All are punished. (5.3.291–5)

Upon this, Capulet and Montague shake hands, initiating the termination of their long-standing feud. It is significant that Escalus spurs rather than decrees this reconciliation, and that he includes himself among those responsible for the young lovers' deaths. If he stands above Old Capulet and Old Montague, it is only to a degree. While he was not part of their strife, he has allowed it to run out of control, to the detriment of the community for which he is responsible. This mixture of involvement and detachment is hard to map onto a bilingual approach. In the French-German production in Fribourg in 1989, the Montagues spoke German, the Capulets spoke French, and Escalus spoke the original English. This solves the problem of how to mediate between the two hostile camps without becoming a part of either, but as Engler points out, English is more than simply the language of authenticity here:

> In a world where English is the language of a world power that, no matter who is in government, has a tradition of intervening in other countries' affairs and, with various degrees of subtlety, to force its decisions on them, the choice of English for Duke Escalus must be problematic. (2011)

It is only fitting that the production modified the play's ending to suit this. Reconciliation between Montagues and Capulets is achieved not on the families' own initiative, but decreed by Escalus, making the play about the failure of two individual families rather than about the failure of the sovereign himself. Also, it turns the feuding families into passive recipients of orders instead of citizens, contributors to the public weal in their own right. The deaths of the young lovers thus do not quite achieve what they achieve in Shakespeare's play. The power to resolve an existing conflict is accorded to a force more or less from the outside rather than to the two warring camps themselves.

The German-Polish *Romeo and Juliet* mentioned earlier took a similar approach, though with a twist. This particular staging of Shakespeare's play is noteworthy for the way it handles the two languages, having the Polish actors involved in the project speak much of their text in German, while some of the German actors were made to speak with a Polish accent – surely a remarkable move in a production commissioned to mark the inception of Polish sovereignty, and a challenge for which, according to the reviews, not all of the actors were really prepared. But what the production lost in terms of an opposition of languages, it made up for in terms of visual oppositions. The Montagues wore the German national colours of black, red, and gold, while the Capulets were dressed in red and white, the colours of the Polish flag. Escalus spoke French, again a language used by no one else in the production, but was dressed in blue, the colour of the European Union – a particularly meaningful choice at a moment in time when Poland's entry into the Union was still being negotiated. This choice, though far from subtle, perhaps preserves more of Shakespeare's Escalus than the Fribourg production with its proto-American peacekeeper. At the very least this production seemed to have a pretty concrete idea of how to remedy the "ancient grudge" that was its subject.

A radical solution was developed by the 2010 German-Russian production referred to earlier, which left out the figure of Escalus altogether. Part of his final lines ("See what a scourge is laid upon your hate / That heaven finds means to kill your joys with love!") is given to Benvolio – and these are the lines on which the play ends. There is no reconciliation between Capulets and Montagues, and no reference made to the community at large. The deaths of Romeo and Juliet have no effect whatsoever on the political situation of Verona, they are a private misfortune resulting from what is ultimately a private choice. Interestingly, the rapprochement between Germans and Russians which is the express aim of the *production* apparently necessitates the deletion of the rapprochement between the Montagues and the Capulets as described by the *play*. This German-Russian co-production, the most consistently *bi*lingual endeavour of all the productions mentioned, was heavily subsidized by one of Germany's largest funding bodies, the Federal Foundation for the Arts. It conceived of itself as a quintessentially 'civic' art project in that it explicitly hoped to have an actual political effect. In a manner not entirely untypical of the productions analyzed in this paper, this civic 'mission' was undertaken on the basis of a text whose civic dimension had been severely curtailed if not cut altogether. In keeping with the production's emphasis on theatricality over text, its desired political impact was obviously believed to derive at least as much from the mere fact of playing bilingually as from the actual play thus staged.

In an even more explicit manner than other multicultural *Romeo and Juliet*s, bilingual productions of the play tend to subscribe to a broadly 'pacifist' political agenda. Often heavily subsidized, they provide a lens on theatre as a continuation of politics by other means. Even where the text's civic dimension is largely ignored, the production's political relevance is usually vigorously promoted. These efforts implicitly or explicitly rely on an opposition between the structure of the text and the structure of the theatrical event. In bilingual performance, *Romeo and Juliet* is believed to work like the love between the text's protagonists: as an agent of reconciliation between opposing camps. That way, bilingual productions pick up on what scholarship has long identified as a certain generic ambiguity of the play. When performed bilingually, it seems, the First Folio's "tragedie" becomes an agent in a comedy of universal peace and understanding, a play that by staging crisis eventually helps resolve it. *Romeo and Juliet* is the blue helmet in the Shakespeare canon.

NOTES

1. See above, p. 5.
2. Witness Jan Klata's notorious Polish-German *Titus Andronicus*, a cooperation between Teatr Polski in Wrocław and Staatsschauspiel Dresden (premiere in Wrocław on 15 September 2012 and in Dresden on 28 December 2012). Heavily drawing on national stereotypes, this production used bilingualism to put additional emphasis on the clash of cultures which, rather than a clash of individual characters, it presented as the focal point of the play. Though the linguistic barriers between 'Goths' (Germans) and 'Romans' (Poles) did produce comical effects in this production, bilingualism was patently not employed to hint at anything like the existence of a communal code shared by the two groups. As one reviewer concluded, the production seemed to be suggesting that "we need to find new ways of communicating between languages and cultures – not only in non-Anglophone performance of Shakespeare, but also in our increasingly globalised world" (Mancewicz 2013). Unlike the *Romeo and Juliets* analyzed in this paper, however, it offered no clues as to what these new ways of communicating might be.
3. See e.g. Huang 2013; Bennett and Carson 2013, 17.
4. "Thematisch steht die kulturelle Verständigung, die Kommunikation über sprachliche und somit kulturelle Grenzen hinaus im Zentrum der Inszenierung des klassischen Stoffes. Die Annäherung verfeindeter Gruppen, die Furcht vor dem Anderen, die Aggression dem Fremden gegenüber und die Utopie der Überwindung dieser Barrieren im Rauschgefühl der Liebe sind die thematischen Bezugspunkte dieser packenden Liebesgeschichte. Im Kauderwelsch der Gefühle, der Vielstimmigkeit der Meinungen, wird die Liebe zur einzig verständlichen Weltsprache". "*Romeo und Julia - Ромео и Джульетта*. Landestheater Tübingen. Accessed February 25, 2013. http://www.landestheater-tuebingen.de/spielplan/romeo-und-julia.
5. See, however, Rozett (1985, 153): "Shakespeare places Romeo and Juliet, and to a lesser extent Antony and Cleopatra, in typically comic situations: both set of lovers must overcome social and political obstacles to be united; both are surrounded by variations on comic character types who contribute to the complications in the love plot; and both entangle themselves in tragic renditions of the pattern of misunderstanding and confusion leading to clarification and reunion so prevalent in Shakespeare's romantic comedies".
6. Accessed November 26, 2014. http://www.jltb.de/zielsetzungen.aspx. My translation.
7. In fact, this may be a reason why amateur theatricals are less widespread in Germany than they are in Britain.
8. "Das was die beiden Geschlechter/die Nationen der Liebenden in Shakespeares Drama nicht schaffen, zu einander zu finden und trotz ungleicher Sprache Verständnis zu erzeugen, schafft das Team vom Jungen Landestheater Bayern". Cf. "Szenen einer eindrucksvollen Inszenierung". Charmer Zeitung. 2007. Accessed February 25, 2013. http://www.jltb.de/kloster-chotesov-pressestimmen.aspx. My translation.
9. "Uns kam es darauf an, das Thema Verständigung auf verschiedensten Ebenen durchzuspielen und sämtliche Sprachen, die der Mensch und die das Theater jenseits der Worte hat, aufzubieten. Musik spielt da eine wichtige Rolle. Und

jede Form der Körperlichkeit. Tanzen, Fechten, Kämpfen ... Küssen, klar, das bleibt bei Romeo und Julia nicht aus." – "Traurig, aber schön" – Interview with Ralf Siebelt zur *Romeo und Julia / Ромео и Джульетта* Inszenierung. Tübingen. 2010. Press material supplied by Landestheater Tübingen. My translation.

10. In fact, it seems that non-understanding was not just accepted, but even endorsed. In their introduction to *Shakespeare Beyond English*, Susan Bennett and Christie Carson recount that "[in] the early days of the festival, many of the companies opted for selected words in English to ensure moments of interaction with the entire audience. Often this provided a linguistic punchline that the actors could be sure everybody would understand. But, partway through the festival, the organizers asked companies to stop using English words ... [This] produced a particular artifice that insisted on the performances as 'other'" (2013, 7). How exactly this othering would have worked does not become entirely clear, though, for Bennett and Carson also mention that at virtually every production, a majority of the audience was fluent in the language in question, and that "over a six-week period, repeat customers simply got better at working with different languages and different performance styles" (ibid., 7–8). One wonders what "getting better at working with different languages" means – actually acquiring a basic level of competence in them, or simply coming to terms with their ongoing elusiveness?

WORKS CITED

Bennett, Susan, and Christie Carson. 2013. "Introduction: Shakespeare Beyond English". In *Shakespeare Beyond English: A Global Experiment*, edited by Susan Bennett and Christie Carson, 1–11. Cambridge: Cambridge University Press.

Dobson, Michael. 2011. *Shakespeare and amateur performance: a cultural history*. Cambridge: Cambridge University Press.

Engler, Balz. 2011. "Shakespeare's Languages". Accessed February 25, 2013. http://www.balzengler.ch/files/Iasi-Article.pdf.

Fischlin, Daniel. 2007. "A Note on Adaptations of *Romeo and Juliet*". *Canadian Adaptations of Shakespeare Project*. Accessed February 25, 2013. http://www.canadianshakespeares.ca.

Freccero, Carla. 2011. "Romeo and Juliet Love Death". In *Shakesqueer: A Queer Companion to the Complete Works of Shakespeare*, edited by Madhavi Menon, 302–8. Durham and London: Durham University Press.

Hattaway, Michael, Boika Sokolova, and Derek Roper, eds. 1994. *Shakespeare in the new Europe*. Sheffield: Sheffield Academic Press.

Holland, Peter. 1997. "Shakespeare in the New Europe". *The European English Messenger* 6 (2): 75–7.

Huang, Alexander C.Y. 2013. "What Country, Friends, Is This? Touring Shakespeares, Agency, and Efficacy in Theatre Historiography". In *Theatre Survey* 54.1 (*A Year of Shakespeare: Re-living the World Shakespeare Festival*) (The Arden Shakespeare), edited by Paul Edmondson, Paul Prescott, and Erin Sullivan, 51–85. London: Bloomsbury.

Kamps, Ivo. 2000. "'I Love You Madly, I Love You to Death': Erotomania and *Liebestod* in *Romeo and Juliet*". In *Approaches to Teaching Shakespeare's 'Romeo and Juliet'*, edited by Maurice Hunt, 37–46. New York: The Modern Language Association of America.

Kennedy, Dennis. 1993. "Introduction". In *Foreign Shakespeare: Contemporary Performance*, edited by Dennis Kennedy, 1–18. Cambridge: Cambridge University Press.

Kottman, Paul A. 2012. "Defying the Stars: Tragic Love as the Struggle for Freedom in *Romeo and Juliet*". *Shakespeare Quarterly* 63: 1–38.

Lan, Yong Li. 2005. "Shakespeare and the Fiction of the Intercultural". In *A Companion to Shakespeare and Performance*, edited by Barbara Hodgdon and W.B. Worthen, 527–49. Malden and Oxford: Blackwell.

Mancewicz, Aneta. 2013. "Review of *Titus Andronicus* directed by Jan Klata for Teatr Polski in Wrocław and Staatsschauspiel Dresden at Teatr Wybrzeże, Gdańsk Shakespeare Festival, Poland. 3 August 2013". Accessed November 26, 2014. http://bloggingshakespeare.com/reviewing-shakespeare/titus-andronicus-teatr-polski-teatr-wybrzeze-gdansk-shakespeare-festival-poland/.

Rozett, Martha Tuck. 1985. "The Comic Structures of Tragic Endings: The Suicide Scenes in *Romeo and Juliet* and *Anthony and Cleopatra*". *Shakespeare Quarterly* 36: 152–64.

Afterword
"What's past is prologue": Civic Shakespeare in *Romeo and Juliet* and Beyond

Ewan Fernie and Paul Edmondson

1. EWAN FERNIE

"What's past is prologue" (*The Tempest*, 2.1.249).[1] So says Shakespeare in another play, but I want to appropriate his phrase here in order to underline that the essays in this volume have opened or reopened the way to seeing *Romeo and Juliet* as even more than just a splendid work-of-art transcending our collective life. For this book at least, *Romeo and Juliet* is equally importantly at work in the ordinary social world of whatever culture performs or otherwise engages with it.

And so, with reference to this volume, what is past is prologue, I hope, to a more civic, more engaged view of Shakespeare's tragedy, and what it might mean and do in our society. In the wake of the essays you have read, I want to return to the play's own famous Prologue in order to affirm and initiate the play's further potential for a more civic reading after the intervention that this book represents.

Powerful recent interpretations of *Romeo and Juliet* by Simon Palfrey (2012) and Paul Kottman (2012) have argued in their different ways that the play, turns, with its lovers, emphatically away from the civic. That also is Wagner's reading in *Tristan und Isolde*, but Wagner had to excise the civic from Shakespeare and this volume has suggested that a central interest of *Romeo and Juliet* remains its exploration of free love in relation to ongoing civic crisis. Kottman's "new interpretation of the play", he says, "yields a deeper understanding of our struggle for freedom and self-realization as lovers". In this context, he argues that *Romeo and Juliet* "mutes" the "conflict between the individual desires and the reigning demands of family, civic and social norms shaping those desires" (2012, 5).[2] But in line with the tendency of some of the most influential films, productions and appropriations of the play – think of Baz Luhrmann's smash-hit, *William Shakespeare's Romeo + Juliet*, or for that matter of *West Side Story* – the essays in this book have productively turned the volume back up on such conflict. And, notwithstanding the fact that it is most famous for its notion of "star-cross'd lovers", returning to the Prologue confirms they were not wrong to do so.

For the Prologue to *Romeo and Juliet* firmly subordinates the idea of doomed love to civic crisis from the beginning:

> Two households, both alike in dignity,
> In fair Verona, where we lay our scene,
> From ancient grudge breaking to new mutiny
> Where civil blood makes civil hands unclean. (Prologue 1–4)[3]

These four lines lay the emphasis squarely on social conflict. And there is enough poetic compression in their language to suggest that in the play they introduce such conflict will be more than just 'muted' background. This opening passage imagines social strife as a dormant disease suddenly bursting into new virulence: the similarity of "two households both alike in dignity" phases into identical subjection to the same, shared "ancient grudge" and then into the "new mutiny" of its current conflagration. The elision, in the speech, of any actual fighting – a not untypical effect of Shakespeare's swiftness – helps encourage this impression of shared suffering, to the effect that I see, in my mind's eye, not so much a violent contention between enemies as a single figure looking down at hands that are wet with its own blood.

Soon enough this image of self-harm will take more explicit shape in the Prince's condemnation of the street fighting of the first scene: "What ho, you men, you beasts, / That quench the fire of your pernicious rage / With purple fountains issuing from your veins" (1.1.81–3). And the purple fountains here cannot but suggest the fountains so central to Italian public architecture grotesquely alienated from their proper function of establishing public order and pride.

The "star-cross'd lovers" come into the Prologue's next sentence:

> From forth the fatal loins of these two foes
> A pair of star-cross'd lovers take their life,
> Whose misadventur'd piteous overthrows
> Doth with their death bury their parents' strife. (4–7)

The lovers are, therefore, the second idea in the play, and even as such their doomed love is completely secondary to the crisis already established. Once again in these four lines the poetry is complex and challenging, not such as would simply and quickly establish mere 'muted' background. Shakespeare imagines his "star-crossed lovers" dredging their own being from the "fatal loins" – and it is worth stressing here that the "fatal loins" actually precede the far more famous malignant stars of *Romeo and Juliet*'s Prologue. But then, to some extent, such is the process of poetry, that first image is modified by the second, retroactively refashioning the fatal loins into a sublime constellation of the night sky. It is the malevolent aspect of this, presumably, which causes the "misadventur'd piteous otherthrows"; but because

Shakespeare's couplets are so fast-moving and suggestive, this phrase also works backwards, recalling the immediately preceding, comparable phrase: "take their life". The upshot is that we entertain the idea that the star-crossed lovers derive their lives from fatal loins at the same time as the idea of their "misadventur'd piteous overthrows" collapses back, in our minds, into "take their life", suggesting that they have committed suicide.

Now of course at this point *Romeo and Juliet* is a relatively abstract affair – we do not yet *know* Romeo and Juliet, and everything will change when we do – but the complex intensities of these few lines nonetheless powerfully prefigure the idea that the lovers' lives are not their own, and nor even is their rejection of them. "To be or not to be" may be the question, but the life the lovers take are tainted at source (see *Hamlet*, 3.1.58). That source is the life of a civil war wet with its own blood. And worse, the lovers' rejection of such a life – of such adverse conditions – is but an extreme expression or symptom of its self-destructive perversity.

Only now that we are hooked in to this disturbing, fledgling plot does the love story of Romeo and Juliet arguably edge into prominence over civic strife in the third sentence:

> The fearful passage of their death-marked love,
> And the continuance of their parents' rage,
> Which, but their children's end, nought could remove,
> Is now the two hours' traffic of our stage; (8–11)

But Romeo and Juliet hardly blaze into prominence even here. And these lines, also, are complexly ambivalent, and in such a way as again reduces rather than augments the lovers' importance. "Which, but their children's end, nought could remove" admittedly at first seems to mean that nothing other than the tragedy of Romeo and Juliet would have worked, would have been effective; and this keeps the focus on the kids, albeit only insofar as they redeem their parents. But there is another possibility. The line could mean, admittedly somewhat more obscurely, but also more positively and suggestively, that "nought" could do this redeeming work *even without Romeo and Juliet*. And this at least starts to make sense when we consider that what is valuable about the love of Romeo and Juliet, at least as the Prologue has painted it, is its rush (its "fearful passage") towards death, towards "their children's end". To put it another way, Romeo and Juliet bring their parents face-to-face with "nought". And the rub is that, for all the terrible beauty of this one, there are many ways to "nought" – in fact, even if you believe that there is another more absolute and eternal life on the other side, *every* way is the way there. Maybe, then, these lines partly suggest, the lovers *just* serve the purpose of giving their society the kind of deadly shock which alone will jerk it out of its habitual and violent disease?

All this functions with what we have already heard to keep social strife and crisis rather than doomed love firmly central to the Prologue's point, and to register such social crisis as not at all banal or bland but, to the contrary, as complexly, disturbingly engaging.

The very end of the Prologue introduces an intriguing note of self-doubt:

> The which, if you with patient ears attend,
> What here shall miss, our toil shall strive to mend. (13–14)

It cannot, it would seem, all be said in 14 lines, and this Prologue knows it. Big things are at stake, maybe things even bigger than love. Or maybe love *is* the main thing, as the history of the reception of – as the myth of – *Romeo and Juliet* would seem to suggest. But surely the Prologue has done enough to make plain, that even if it is, civil strife in the play is much more than nicely contrasting scenery? The Prologue suggests civic strife is dialectically involved with love. It may be its horizon and terminus. Insofar as Romeo and Juliet redeem this strife, they do so, according to what we have been told, not so much by their love as by their deaths, to which strife "where civil blood makes civil hands unclean" was in any case tending. The violence of Romeo and Juliet's love is, this suggests, just another version of the disease of violence afflicting the world of the play in general. They die, but then so does Mercutio. Still, it *is* true to say that Romeo and Juliet do more to discover the richly positive if terrifying potential of "nought" or total devastation...

I hope this admittedly discomfiting reading of the Prologue begins to exemplify the kind of complex and relatively neglected life in this much studied play which the more deliberately civic approach pioneered in this book might yet uncover. But of course a civic approach to literature has to go beyond close reading! That is why many of the essays here explore the uses and abuses of *Romeo and Juliet* within a range of social contexts. Such assessments give us the measure of civic Shakespeare to date; but I want to use the words remaining to me to salute the inspiring piece of programming by which the editors of this volume, Silvia Bigliazzi and Lisanna Calvi, took the cause of 'civic Shakespeare' one step further forward.

In Verona in April 2013, they laid on not just a conference on *Romeo and Juliet* but also several funded free events that were not just for conference delegates but were also for residents of and visitors to Verona in general. This was important, in my view, because it carried an academic consideration of civic Shakespeare out into the civic sphere itself.

I was very struck by one of these events, which took place in the courtyard of the historic Castelvecchio museum from 5pm on April the 11th. It was composed of various readings from, in the phrase of the conference literature, "novellas and other literary texts on 'the pair of star-cross'd lovers' authored by Luigi Da Porto, Matteo Maria Bandello, Pierre Boaistuau, Arthur Brooke, Alessandro Carli, Vittorio Betteloni, Berto Barbarani". As this eclectic list will suggest, a range of different European languages, therefore, merged and melded on what turned out to be a mercifully sunny April day in telling, in their different ways, the story of Romeo and Juliet. At the same time, music was playing; and an artist, too, improvised responses. And while all this was going on an identifiably Shakespearean Romeo and Juliet popped up in various places – on the battlements, down in the courtyard, and so on – with Shakespeare's words emerging, only to fade away again into other tongues and voices.

One effect was to suggest something of the richness and mobility (often inaccessible to me, owing to my own ignorance) of a common European culture, and to place Shakespeare within it; and even if you did not understand everything being said this was interesting, moving, and instructive. And I also found the free instantaneity of the artist's and musician's improvised responses exhilarating, particularly in the midst of a traditional academic conference. The painter covered a page with 'real-time', unmisgiving reactions, and then just began again, on a fresh page! It suggested something about the immediacy and experimental quality of direct aesthetic response which careful, expert academic treatments find it difficult to capture.

Many of the conference delegates were there, in the courtyard of the Castelvecchio, but many others stopped by to take it all in as well. And it was not presented to delegates as a leisure activity: as 'down time' and respite from more serious and demanding academic business. Instead, it was given equal prominence to the more scholarly offerings, as an alternative exploration of the civic potential of *Romeo and Juliet*. It was a memorable symbolic attempt to take academic life – source study, 'appropriation' and interpretation – *to the streets*. People were intrigued and drawn in as they would not have been by a traditional lecture. Of course, there *were* lectures at the conference and there remain many things you can say and teach at the lectern that were beyond the capacity of the Castelvecchio event to convey. But as well as suggesting something of the complex European credentials of *Romeo and Juliet*, and something of the urgent immediacy of aesthetic response, what happened at Castelvecchio also conveyed a further simple, consequential and easily forgotten fact: the fact that sources, appropriation, and interpretation – and, for that matter, literature and theatre themselves – are forms of *life,* and that as such they may, at least on occasion, benefit from being put back into connection with life more broadly. The literature of the past – all the more so in its civic aspect – has not always been just an academic affair. Silvia's and Lisanna's experiment in Verona 2013 in bringing civic Shakespeare into a civic space asked if it could play a more than academic part in the world again – and, crucially, it asked this not just theoretically but *actively*.

The other highlight for me of the series of events in Verona in April 2013 was the Lindsay Kemp Workshop which has already been written about in this volume by Jacquelyn Bessell. In Verona's Teatro Nuovo, Kemp presented to his audience some nine pairs of Romeo and Juliet, all of whom danced and died. This generalization of the star-crossed lovers and their fates was extremely moving, particularly in the context of the civic ambition of the conference as a whole. And after the multiple resurrection of his dancers, Kemp brought the evening home by gingerly stepping along the perimeter of the stage, repeating the same gracious gesture and the murmured phrase, "For you, for you".

Here the interplay native to *Romeo and Juliet* between individual passion, death and collective life was visibly plain, and strange and stirring. It was resonant with the urgently discomfiting quality I have tried to draw out of the play's Prologue. It encouraged us to ask the big question of what *Romeo and Juliet* really means for our collective life now. It very much manifested the promise for me of what in this book we have been calling civic Shakespeare.

2. PAUL EDMONDSON

> *Civic Shakespeare*
> Our cheering calls to mind the Jubilee
> In Stratford, England, 1769,
> When Garrick's civic pride set Shakespeare free
> From libraries, studies, stages – helped define
> A poet for the people in the streets
> (Who couldn't wear their costumes in the rain);
> That many-coloured spirit sings and greets
> Verona, time for Jubilee again.
> We long, like groundlings, for our Juliet,
> Can send her e-mails, letters. Though we know
> She isn't real, she answers; and we're met
> With echoes round her grave of Romeo.
> > Wave, wave your rainbow ribbon, reaching far:
> > A lover's kiss to bless Piazza Bra.

NOTES

1. Shakespeare references are, unless otherwise indicated, to Shakespeare 2008.
2. Some critics, of course, have argued that the civic plays an important part in the tragedy. Susan Snyder clearly defined the communal aspect of the play (1970, 400–1). And Hugh Grady has argued that "the play presents a civil space with density enough to provide a social context to a young couple's love and marriage" as well as that "[i]t is within this carefully sketched civic space – a representation of early modern European life that is capable of constant updating – that the legendary love of Romeo and Juliet is kindled, and it is precisely love that challenges the power of the social" (2009, 208, 210). Jonathan Goldberg observes that *Romeo and Juliet* has come to dominate American high-school curricula: "*Julius Cesar* has been usurped; the sexual revolution has replaced the civics lesson". But, like Grady, he insists that "love, from the start of the play, is implicated in the social not separate from it" (2001, 194, 199).
3. *Romeo and Juliet* references, unless otherwise indicated, are to Shakespeare 2012.

WORKS CITED

Goldberg, Jonathan. 2001. "*Romeo and Juliet*'s Open Rs". In *Romeo and Juliet*, edited by R.S. White, 194–212. London: Palgrave.

Grady, Hugh. 2009. *Shakespeare and Impure Aesthetics*. Cambridge: Cambridge University Press.

Kottman, Paul A. 2012. "Defying the Stars: Tragic Love as the Struggle for Freedom in *Romeo and Juliet*". *Shakespeare Quarterly*, 63 (1): 1–38.

Palfrey, Simon. 2012. *Romeo and Juliet*. Chippenham: Connell Guides.

Shakespeare, William. 2008. *The Norton Shakespeare*. Edited by Stephen Greenblatt. New York: Norton.

Shakespeare, William. 2012. *Romeo and Juliet*. Edited by René Weis. London: Bloomsbury (Arden Shakespeare Third Series).

Snyder, Susan. 1970. "*Romeo and Juliet*: Comedy into Tragedy". *Essays in Criticism* 20 (4): 391–402.

Contributors

Guido Avezzù is professor of Greek literature at Verona University. His major interests are in Greek theatre and its reception. His publications include the critical editions of Sophocles's *Oedipus at Colonus* and *Philoctetes* (2008 and 2003) and monographs on the relation between myth and tragedy (*Il mito sulla scena. La tragedia ad Atene*, 2003), and on the staging of the story of Philoctetes (*Il ferimento e il rito. La storia di Filottete sulla scena ateniese*, 1988). He also edited a selection of rewrites of Oedipus's myth (*Sofocle, Seneca, Dryden-Lee, Cocteau. Edipo. Variazioni sul mito*, 2008), and of Electra's myth (*Sofocle, Euripide, Hofmannsthal, Yourcenar. Elettra. Variazioni sul mito*, 2002). His latest works include essays on the same line of enquiry (on Sophocles, in Citti - Iannucci eds, *Edipo classico e contemporaneo*, 2012, and in Markantonatos ed., *Brill's Companion to Sophocles*, 2012; on the philology of Richard Porson, in Volpe Cacciatore ed., *Seminario di studi su Richard Porson*, 2011; on Euripides, in *Picturing Drama*, 2014; and on Aeschylus, in Jouanna - Montanari eds, *Eschyle à l'aube du théâtre occidental*, 2009).

Jacquelyn Bessell is a stage director and teacher of acting. She has directed productions of modern and early modern plays in New York and London, and in regional theatres across the United States and United Kingdom. Her research interests came into focus during her time as head of research at Shakespeare's Globe, during Mark Rylance's tenure as artistic director. Her recent print publications explore the impact of physical theatre and post-Stanislavksi actor training methodologies on Shakespeare's plays in performance. She is currently head of postgraduate studies at the Guildford School of Acting, University of Surrey, where she leads the MA acting programme.

Silvia Bigliazzi is professor of English literature at Verona University. She has worked on literature and the visual arts, publishing a volume on modernism (*Il colore del silenzio*, Marsilio 1998), and editing with Sharon Wood a collection of essays (*Collaboration in the Arts from the Middle Ages to the Present*, Ashgate 2006). Her more recent fields of interests are textual performance (*Sull'esecuzione testuale*, ETS 2002), Shakespeare

(*Oltre il genere. Amleto tra scena e racconto*, Edizioni dell'Orso 2001; *Nel prisma del nulla. L'esperienza del non-essere nella drammaturgia shakespeariana*, Liguori 2005), and John Donne's poetry. She has edited and translated into Italian John Donne's major poems (with A. Serpieri, *Poesie*, Rizzoli 2009^2), and *Romeo and Juliet* (Einaudi 2012). Her recent publications include the edition of a collection of essays on Renaissance literature on mental insanity (*Distraction Individualized*, Cierre 2012), of a volume on translation for the theatre (with P. Kofler and P. Ambrosi, *Theatre Translation in Performance*, Routledge 2013), and, with Lisanna Calvi, of a miscellany on *The Tempest* (Revisiting The Tempest. *The Capacity to Signify*, Palgrave 2014).

Bettina Boecker is a senior lecturer at the University of Munich, as well as executive officer and research librarian at the Munich Shakespeare Library. She has published on a variety of early modern topics, but is particularly interested in the popular culture of the period and Shakespeare's afterlives. Her current research focuses on the role of Shakespeare's Elizabethan audience in Shakespeare criticism (*Imagining Shakespeare's Original Audience, 1660–2000: Groundlings, Gallants, Grocers* will be published by Palgrave in 2016). Other interests include children and children's literature in the early modern period, Cold War Shakespeare, and Shakespeare in performance.

Lisanna Calvi is a lecturer of English literature at Verona University. Her main research interests have focused on Restoration and early modern drama and literary culture. She wrote a book on Restoration and early eighteenth-century tragedy (*Kingship and Tragedy*, QuiEdit 2005) and on James II's devotional papers and *Imago Regis* (*La corona e la Croce*, ETS 2009). She also authored articles on John Dryden (2000), Robert Browning (2002, 2010), Thomas Otway (2007), Edmund Gosse (2009), *The Tempest* and the *commedia dell'arte* (*Shakespeare*, Routledge 2012), and madness and autobiography in seventeenth-century England (2012 and 2013). She edited, with an Italian translation, the autobiographical writings of Dionys Fiztherbert and Hannah Allen (*Memoria, Maliconia e autobiografia dello spirito*, Pacini 2012) and, with Silvia Bigliazzi, a miscellany on *The Tempest* (Revisiting The Tempest. *The Capacity to Signify*, Palgrave 2014).

Michael Dobson is director of the Shakespeare Institute, Stratford-upon-Avon, and professor of Shakespeare studies at the University of Birmingham, having previously worked at institutions including Oxford, Harvard, the University of Illinois at Chicago, and the University of London. His publications include *Shakespeare and Amateur Performance* (Cambridge, 2011), *The Making of the National Poet* (Oxford, 1992), *The Oxford Companion to Shakespeare* (with Stanley Wells, 2001, about to reappear in its latest revision in 2016), *England's Elizabeth* (with Nicola Watson, Oxford, 2002), *Performing Shakespeare's Tragedies*

Today (Cambridge, 2006), articles in *Shakespeare Survey, The London Review of Books, Around the Globe, The Guardian* and elsewhere, and programme notes for companies including Shakespeare's Globe, the RSC, the Beijing People's Arts Theatre, Mokwha Repertory, Passion in Practice, and Sam Mendes' Bridge Project. He edited Thomas Middleton and William Rowley's *Wit at Several Weapons* for the *Complete Oxford Middleton* (2007) and introduced *Twelfth Night* for the New Penguin Shakespeare (2005). Never obviously casting for Romeo, he played Friar Laurence in a student production of *Romeo and Juliet* in the early 1980s.

Paul Edmondson is head of research and knowledge and director of the Stratford-upon-Avon Poetry Festival for The Shakespeare Birthplace Trust and an Honorary Fellow of The Shakespeare Institute, University of Birmingham. His publications include: *Twelfth Night: A Guide to the Text and Its Theatrical Life*, and (co-authored with Stanley Wells) *Shakespeare's Sonnets*. He has co-edited *Shakespeare Beyond Doubt: Evidence, Argument, Controversy* (with Stanley Wells) and *A Year of Shakespeare: Re-living the World Shakespeare Festiva* (with Paul Prescott and Erin Sullivan). He is co-series editor for Palgrave Macmillan's *Shakespeare Handbooks*, and co-supervisory editor of the Penguin Shakespeare (to which he contributed several introductions). His other publications include work on Shakespearian biography, Shakespeare and the Brontës, and the poetry of Shakespeare and Christopher Marlowe. His recent publications include *Shakespeare: Ideas in Profile* (Profile Books 2015), and (co-edited with Stanley Wells) *The Shakespeare Circle: An Alternative Biography* (Cambridge University Press 2016). He is an associate minister in the Church of England at St Andrew's Church, Shottery (near Stratford-upon-Avon).

Roy Eriksen is professor of English Renaissance studies at University of Agder (Norway) and publishes in English and Italian interdisciplinary Renaissance studies. He is Series Editor of EMMS (Serra) and co-edits EMCO with Professor Stuart Sillars. He has authored *The Forme of Faustus Fortunes* (Humanities 1987) and *The Building in the text. From Alberti to Shakespeare and Milton* (Penn 2001), and has edited e.g. *Form and the Arts* (Kappa 2003) and *Ashes to Ashes* (L'Ateneo 2006), *Imitation, Representation and Printing* (Serra 2009). He is currently preparing monographs on Marlowe, Alberti and Renaissance Urbanism, and Bruno and the Elizabethan Stage. The edited volume (with Peter Young), *Approaches to the Text: From Proto-Gospel to Post-Baroque* (Serra), and the monograph *L'Edificio testuale* appeared in 2014.

Ewan Fernie is chair, professor and fellow at the Shakespeare Institute, University of Birmingham, in Stratford-upon-Avon, where he co-convenes the pioneering MA in Shakespeare and creativity and helps run the collaboration with the RSC at The Other Place. He is general editor (with Simon Palfrey) of the *Shakespeare Now!* series, and his latest critical book is *The Demonic: Literature and Experience*. Fernie also writes creatively. He led the AHRC grant-winning project which culminated in *Redcrosse*: a new poetic liturgy for St George's Day that was performed in major UK cathedrals and by the RSC, and published in 2012. And he is currently preparing a *Macbeth* novel, written with Palfrey, for publication. In addition, he is seeing through the press a volume of essays edited with Tobias Döring on Shakespeare and Thomas Mann. His current critical project is a book provisionally entitled *Shakespeare for Freedom*.

Mera J. Flaumenhaft has, since 1977, been a tutor (tenured faculty) at St. John's College, Annapolis, Maryland, an integrated four–year curriculum based on the study of great western works of literature, philosophy, politics, mathematics, and science. She is the author of *The Civic Spectacle: Essays on Drama and Community* (1994), translator of Machiavelli's *Mandragola* (1981), and has published articles on Jonah, Homer, Aeschylus, Euripides, the Parthenon, and Twain, as well as Shakespeare's *Othello, As You Like It, Henry V*, and *Richard III*.

Robert Henke is professor of drama and comparative literature at Washington University in St. Louis. He is the author of *Pastoral Transformations: Italian Tragicomedy and Shakespeare's Late Plays* (Delaware), *Performance and Literature in the Commedia dell'Arte* (Cambridge), and *Poverty and Charity in Early Modern Theater and Performance* (Iowa). With Eric Nicholson, he has coedited two essay collections published by Ashgate and issuing from the "Theater Without Borders" research collective, of which he is a founding member: *Transnational Exchange in Early Modern Theater* and *Transnational Mobilities in Early Modern Theater*. He is presently editing the early modern volume of *A Cultural History of Western Theatre* (Bloomsbury Academic). In St. Louis, where he lives, he is the co-director of the Washington University Prison Education Project, a program that provides liberal arts college courses to a local prison.

Loretta Innocenti is professor of English literature at the University of Venice. Her main theoretical interest is on the relation between word and image and her works in this field range from English emblems to typographical devices in *Tristram Shandy* to visuality as a model of perception and representation, especially in seventeenth-century poetry. Since the 1980s she has also studied English theatre and published on the Elizabethan stage, on Restoration adaptations of Shakespeare's plays, and on contemporary drama. She is one of the founding members of Associazione Sigismondo Malatesta, for which she co-organized a cycle of International Seminars on "The Orient in Western Arts" and more recently a project on "The Pleasure of Evil". She is on the scientific board of the annual Malatesta Colloquia of Comparative Literature in Santarcangelo di Romagna.

Lucia Nigri is a lecturer in early modern English literature at the University of Salford-Manchester. She has published on intertextuality on stage

(2007 and 2014), maternal misrecognition in early modern tragedies (2010), the notion of self-knowledge and self-doubt in Shakespeare and his contemporaries (2011 and 2014), the question of authorship in *Arden of Faversham* (2012), the relation between dominant and marginal languages in translating for the theatre (2013), and performativity in the Victorian adaptations of *The Tempest* (2014). She has also extensively written on the figure of the malcontent (2012 and 2014). She is currently editing, with Dr Naya Tsentourou, a volume on *Forms of Hypocrisy in Early Modern England* (forthcoming).

Nicola Watson presently holds a chair in English literature at the Open University (UK), having worked previously at Oxford, Harvard, Northwestern, and Indiana. A specialist in Romanticism, she has published five books and many essays, most recently concentrating on the phenomenon of literary tourism in the eighteenth and nineteenth centuries. Recent publications concerning Shakespeare tourism have included *The Literary Tourist; Readers and Places in Romantic and Victorian Britain* (Palgrave 2006), "Shakespeare on the Tourist Trail" in *The Cambridge Companion to Shakespeare and Popular Culture* (CUP 2007), and "Dear Shakespeare-land': Investing in Stratford" in *Critical Survey*.

Stanley Wells, C.B. EW., F.R.S.L., is honorary president and former chairman of the Trustees of Shakespeare's Birthplace, emeritus professor of Shakespeare studies of the University of Birmingham, and honorary emeritus governor of the Royal Shakespeare Theatre. He holds honorary doctorates from Furman University, South Carolina, and from the Universities of Munich, Hull, Durham, Craiova, Marburg and Warwick. His books include *Literature and Drama; Royal Shakespeare: Studies of Four Major Productions at the Royal Shakespeare Theatre; Modernizing Shakespeare's spelling; Re-editing Shakespeare for the Modern Reader;* and *Shakespeare: the Poet and his Plays*. He edited *A Midsummer Night's Dream, Richard II,* and *The Comedy of Errors* for the New Penguin Shakespeare and *King Lear* for the Oxford Shakespeare. He writes for the *New York Review of Books* and many other publications. He has edited *The New Cambridge Companion to Shakespeare Studies* and is general editor (with Gary Taylor) of *The Complete Oxford Shakespeare* and co-author of *William Shakespeare: A Textual Companion*. His most recent books are *Shakespeare in the Theatre: An Anthology of Criticism; The Oxford Dictionary of Shakespeare; The Oxford Companion to Shakespeare* (edited with Michael Dobson); *Shakespeare For All Time; Looking for Sex in Shakespeare; Shakespeare's Sonnets* and *Coffee with Shakespeare,* both co-authored with Paul Edmondson, *Shakespeare & Co.; Is It True What They Say About Shakespeare?;' Shakespeare, Sex, and Love* appeared from OUP in 2010, and *Great Shakespeare Actors: Burbage to Branagh* and *Shakespeare: A Very Short Introduction* in 2015.

Index

Achilles Tatius 51, 58, 59
Achilles-Patroclos paradigm 123
Acton, William 227
Adams, John Cranford 29
Addison, Joseph 207
Aeschylus 59
Ainsworth, William Harrison 232
Albert, Emperor of Austria 69
Alberti, Leon Battista 94
Alighieri, Dante 68, 69, 189, 231, 255
Althusser, Louis 15, 140, 143
Altrocchi, Paul H. 39
Amaseo, Gregorio 68
Ambrosi, Paola 28
Amussen, Susan Dywer 128
Amyot, Jacques 47, 58
Anderson, Benedict 218, 222
Andrews, Richard 80
Anonymous *Consensus parentum* (1585–90?) 249
Anonymous *Pamphilus and Eurydike* (I century BC) 49, 52
Anonymous *Tell-Trothes New Yeares Gift* (1593) 149
Anonymous *The Office of Christian Parents* (1616) 166
Antonius Diogenes 50, 51
Appelbaum, Robert 120
Archer, Ian W. 172
Ariès, Philippe 157, 167
Aristotle 96, 141
Arne, Thomas 187
Artaud, Antonin 262, 263
Ascher, Barbara 248, 249
Ashley Cooper, Anthony, 1st Earl of Shaftesbury 204
Athens 4, 5, 48, 86
Atkinson, David 138, 139, 143
Augustine, Aurelius 188
Avena, Antonio 245, 246, 248
Averell, Richard 7
Avezzù, Guido 20, 21, 181

Babbitt, Frank Cole 60
Babylonia 50, 51, 54, 61
Bacon, Francis 118
Balfour, Andrew 227
Bandello, Matteo 21, 35, 39, 57, 66, 67, 68, 70, 71, 73, 74, 75, 76, 77, 78, 79, 121, 174, 183, 227, 239, 241, 242, 254, 255, 256, 294
Barbarani, Berto 243, 254, 294
Barchiesi, Alessandro 46
Barish, Jonas 5
Barry, Richard, 7th Earl of Barrymore 220
Barry, Spranger 219
Barston, John 84, 89, 90
Barton, John 261
Bate, Jonathan 59
Batt, Barthelemy 150, 154
Batzer, Hazel M. 205
Baudrillard, Jean 241
Bauman, Richard 9
Bausch, Pina 266
Bavaria Youth Theatre 27, 282, 283
Baxandall, Michael 96
Beckett, Samuel 266
Becon, Thomas 152, 153, 166
Bednarz, James P. 195
Bekker, Immanuel 61
Bellamy, George Anne 222
Belsey, Catherine 29, 140, 141
Beltramini, Gino 250
Bennett, Susan 288, 289
Bergeron, David M. 28
Bernstein, Leonard (*West Side Story*) 12, 79, 291
Bessell, Jacquelyn 26, 257, 295
Betteloni, Vittorio 243, 244, 254, 256, 294
Bible: *Ecclesiastes* 152; *Ecclesiasticus* 165; *Genesis* 204; *Job* 165; *Proverbs* 152; *Psalm* 127 147, 165; *Matthew* 108

Bigliazzi, Silvia 9, 22, 23, 25, 26, 28, 61, 136, 163, 182, 183, 204, 294, 295
Billings, Joshua 28
Billington, Michael 275
Blakes, Charles 222
Blaze de Bury, Marie Pauline Rose Stewart 233
Bloom, Harold 14
Blount, Edward 192
Boaistuau, Pierre 39, 83, 95, 182, 254, 294
Boccaccio, Giovanni 35, 68
Boecker, Bettina 26, 27
Bogart, Anne 268
Boitani, Piero 48
Boldieri, Gherardo ('Clizia') 241
Book of Common Prayer 166, 194
Borgogno, Alberto 61
Botero, Giovanni 93, 94
Bowie, David 261
Bowie, Ewen L. 51, 61
Bozzetto, Lino Vittorio 256
Bradley, Andrew Cecil 29
Breval, John 227, 228, 235
Brisman, Leslie 141
Bristol, Michael 28
Britten, Benjamin 199
Brognoligo, Gioachino 68, 244, 256
Brook, Peter 242, 262, 264, 268, 274, 275
Brooke, Arthur 20, 21, 25, 29, 39, 40, 41, 46, 52, 56, 57, 66, 72, 73, 78, 79, 80, 82, 83, 88, 93, 102, 110, 111, 113, 114, 123, 126, 127, 133, 141, 155, 166, 167, 179, 180, 202, 213, 214, 215, 216, 217, 222, 239, 254, 294
Browne, Thomas 118
Bruster, Douglas 127
Bryson, Anna 120
Bullough, Geoffrey 39, 62, 72, 95, 114
Burke, Kenneth 251
Burke, Peter 28
Burnet, Gilbert 227
Bury, Robert Gregg 59
Bush, Kate 261
Byblis 46
Byron, George Gordon, Lord 224, 230, 243

Cadell, William Archibald 228
Caesar, Gaius Julius 205
Calbi, Maurizio 12
Calderwood, James L. 29, 161, 163, 181
Callaghan, Dympna 15, 16, 83, 140, 143, 165
Callcott, Maria 230
Calvi, Lisanna 23, 25, 26, 205, 294, 295
Canfield, Douglas J. 206
Carli, Alessandro 254, 294
Carlson, Eric Joseph 149, 165, 166
Carlson, Marvin 8
Caro, Annibal 58, 59
Carrière, Jean-Claude 242
Carroll, William C. 40, 172, 181
Carson, Christie 288, 289
Carter, Mary 228
Castiglione, Baldassar 35
Catullus, Gaius Valerius 193, 224
Caunus 46
Čechov, Anton Pavlovič 188
Chapman, George 191, 192
Chariton 45, 50, 51, 53, 57, 58, 59
Charles II, King of England 204
Charlton, Henry B. 29
Chateaubriand, François-René de 230
Chaucer, Geoffrey 193
Chester, Robert 191, 193
Cibber, Susannah 219
Cibber, Theophilus 210
Cicero, Marcus Tullius 35
Cinyras 46
civic passim; and civil 2, 10, 18, 19, 22, 116, 120–6, 129, 132; and political 2, 4, 5, 20, 21, 28, 56, 66, 68, 69, 76, 79, 116, 154, 157, 159, 221; and popular 2
civic practices: celebrations 3, 9, 10, 13, 14, 20, 24, 25, 187, 213, 234, 241, 242, 243, 252, 253; tourist appropriation 13, 20, 25, 26, 224–34, 245–57; urban reconstruction 244–9
Clark, Glenn 18, 19, 120, 121, 125, 142
Claudianus, Claudius 224
Cleaver, Robert 151
Clizia *see* Boldieri
Cohen, Thomas Vance 12, 29, 157
Colie, Rosalie L. 29, 140, 172
Colley, Linda 222
Conder, Josiah 230
Confino, Barbara 266
Conforti Calcagni, Annamaria 255
Connor, Steven 266
Contarini, Gasparo 89, 96
Cook, Ann J. 166

Cooper, Nicholas 158
Costantini, Nereo 247
Costello, Louisa Stuart 232
Cotton, Charles 227
Cowen Orlin, Lena 11, 159, 160
Crane, Mary Thomas 160
Cremona 68
Cressy, David 151, 163, 165, 166, 167
Critias 47
Crowne, John 204
Csapo, Eric 28
Cukor, George 234, 245, 246, 256
Cunin, Muriel 84
Currie, Chris 167

D'Angelo, Michela 95
D'Anniballe, Maria 234, 256
Da Porto, Luigi 21, 45, 62, 66, 67, 68, 70, 71, 72, 73, 74, 75, 76, 77, 78, 79, 80, 174, 182, 231, 239, 241, 242, 246, 253, 254, 255, 256, 294
Dalmeyda, Georges 53
Daniel, Samuel 84
Dash, Irene G. 167
Davis, Lloyd 15
De Grazia, Margreta 165
De Vere, Edward, 17th Earl of Oxford 39
Dekker, Thomas 87
Delahoyde, Michael 39
Della Corte, Girolamo 227, 242, 255
Della Scala 79, 246, 247, 257; Bartolomeo 68, 79, 255; Cansignorio, 173, 255
Devereux, William Cope 232, 233
Dickens, Charles 231
Dickey, Stephen 182
Dicksee, Frank 233
Dillon, Janette 28
Dobson, Michael 25, 29, 203, 206, 282, 283
Dollimore, Jonathan 2, 28, 96
Donne, John 188, 195, 202, 211
Douce, Francis 45, 62
Dover Wilson, John 138
Dresden 288
Dressler, Alex 61
Dryden, John 204, 207, 227
Duncan-Jones, Katherine 196
Dunlop, John Colin 62
Dunn, Francis M. 54
Dunton, John 227
Duppa, Richard 230
Dwight, Theodore 228

Eagleton, Terry 129
Eco, Umberto 241
Edmondson, Paul 24, 27
Eliot, Thomas Stearns 189
Elizabeth I, Queen of England 8, 47, 183, 191, 196
Elizabeth of York, Queen consort of England 173
Enckell, Henrik 272
Engler, Balz 284, 286
Ephesus 50
Erasmus 147, 148, 149
Eriksen, Roy 21, 22, 84, 95, 142
Escudero, Vincente 271, 275
Eude, Michael 276
Euripides 48
Everett, Barbara 192
Ewbank, Inga-Stina 192

Fabbri, Patrizia 181
Fairclough, Norman 2, 29, 182, 251, 252
Fenton, Geoffrey 121
Fernie, Ewan 17, 27
Feud 3, 15, 18, 45, 57, 66, 67, 68, 71, 83, 100–14, 115, 116, 122, 123, 124, 127, 128, 129, 130, 132, 134, 136, 139, 143, 155, 160, 161, 163, 168, 178, 181, 202, 207, 208, 214, 217, 218, 226, 239, 240, 253, 278, 285, 286
Field, Richard 192
Finglass, Patrick J. 48
Fiorato, Sidia 269
Fitter, Chris 124, 126, 128, 142, 202
Flaumenhaft, Mera J. 22, 28, 160
Florio, John 35
Foakes, Reginald A. 29
Ford Madox Ford 238
Foucault, Michel 182, 251
Fowler, Alastair 95, 97
Fracci, Carla 257
Freccero, Carla 278
Freetown 22, 41, 82, 83, 89, 91, 92, 94, 96, 102, 126; *see also* Villafranca, Villefranche
Fribourg 27, 284, 286, 287
Friedman, Ceil 249, 250, 257
Friedman, Lise 249, 250, 257

Gades, Antonio 270, 271, 272, 275, 276
Galiffe, Augustin 229
García Lorca, Federico 270, 273
Garrick, David 13, 14, 25, 29, 187, 188, 199, 200, 210, 213, 218, 219, 220, 221

308 *Index*

Garrison, David Lee 59
Gascoigne, George 84, 95
Gasdia, Cecilia 257
Gaselee, Stephen 60
Genet, Jean 262, 270
Genette, Gérard 203
Gentleman, Francis 218
Gesner, Carol 57, 58
Ghosh, Jyotish C. 207
Gibbon, Charles 150, 151, 154
Gibbons, Brian 126, 138, 167
Gigola, Giovanni Battista 246
Gillespie, Stuart 2, 11, 27, 28, 29, 47
Giraldi Cinthio, Giovan Battista 36
Girard, René 127
Goffman, Erving 28
Goldberg, Jonathan 16, 296
Goldhill, Simon 28
Golding, William 35, 39, 46, 54, 55, 56, 59
Gorges, Arthur 205
Gould, John 28
Gounod, Charles 256
government: domestic 128, 141, 151; of the city 122, 141
Grady, Hugh 17, 18, 296, 297
Greek theatre 3–5; Greek tragedy 45–57
Greenblatt, Steven 28, 59
Greene, Robert 47
Gridley, Carl James 142
Grimoldi, Alberto 256, 257
Groto, Luigi 66
Guazzo, Stefano 125
Guettel Cole, Susan 4
Guidorizzi, Mario 245
Gurr, Andrew 10, 11, 28, 29, 37, 148, 175, 182

Habrich, Elmar 61
Halliwell, James Orchard 38
Hamburg 283
Händel, Georg Friedrich 273
Harrison, William 29
Harth, Philip 205
Harvie, Jen 9
Hattaway, Michael 280
Hayez, Francesco 246, 256
Hazlitt, William 14
Heath, Charles 230
Hedrick, Donald 1, 251
Heffner Hayes, Michelle 273
Hegel, Georg Wilhelm Friedrich 1, 27, 53
Heliodorus 59

Henderson, Jeffrey 59
Henke, Robert 21, 167
Henry VII, King of England 173, 181
Herbert, Henry, 2nd Earl of Pembroke 142
Herman, Peter C. 128, 141
Herodotus 60
Hieatt, Kent A. 84
Hill, Thomas 167
Hillard, George 231
Hobhouse, John Cam 224, 225, 231
Hogan, Charles Beecher 218, 222
Holland, Peter 280, 281
Holmer, Joan Ozark 142
Holzberg, Niklas 59
Homer 59
Horace (Quintus Horatius Flaccus) 245
Hoskins, William G. 158, 159, 167
Hosley, Richard 29, 168
Höttemann, Benedikt H. 95, 96
Houlbrooke, Ralph 166, 168, 183
household 12, 17, 19, 69, 100–14, 115, 120, 121, 122, 123, 126, 127, 128, 129, 132, 134, 136, 141, 142, 151, 157, 161, 167, 172, 173, 175, 176, 177, 178, 179, 208, 215, 273, 292
Howells, William Dean 231, 232
Hoya, Cristina 273
Huang, Alexander C.Y. 288
Hüls, Rudolf 59
Hunter, Lynette 18, 19, 116, 122, 130, 141, 142, 143, 148, 167, 168
Hutson, Lorna 96

Iamblichus 50, 51
Innocenti, Loretta 24, 29, 203
Ireland, Thomas James 233
Isenberg, Nancy 240

Jackson, Shannon 8
Jacobi, Derek 39
James, Duke of York 204
James I, King of England 7
Johnson, Mark 143
Johnson, Matthew H. 167
Johnson, Samuel 38
Jonson, Ben 84, 191, 192
Juliet Club 250, 257

Kahn, Coppélia 15, 166
Kamps, Ivo 278
Kantorowicz, Ernst H. 181
Kemp, Lindsay 26, 253, 260–77, 296
Kemp, William 10

Kennedy, Dennis 3, 280, 285
Kenney, Edward John 46
Kenyon, Lloyd 220
Kerényi, Karl 48
Kiernan, Ryan 14
Kilian, Ted 2, 12, 175, 240
Klata, Jan 288
Knight, G. Wilson 192
Knutson, Roslyn L. 165
Kofler, Peter 28
Kottman, Paul 12, 17, 27, 117, 119, 120, 254, 278, 291
Kristeva, Julia 29, 182

Laird, David 141
Laitinen, Riitta 12, 29, 157
Lakoff, George 143
Lan, Yong Li 280, 281
Landau, Tina 268
Lanier, Douglas 1, 13, 27
Laurana, Francesco 96
Laurents, Arthur (*West Side Story*) 12, 79, 291
Le Loyer, Pierre 52
Leahy, William 28, 39
Lee, Nathaniel 207
Lefebvre, Henri 2, 12, 249
Leigh, Nicholas 148
letters to Juliet 26, 187, 226, 249–51, 253, 257
Lev Kenaan, Vered 61
Levenson, Jill L. 11, 82, 128, 142
Levin, Harry 29
Lewis, Clive Staples 192, 194
Lewknor, Lewes 96
Lichtenfels, Peter 18, 19, 116, 122, 130, 141, 142, 143, 148, 167, 168
Lightfoot, Jane L. 60
Limon, Jerzy 142
Livorno 95
Llewellyn, Nigel 168, 171, 181, 249
Lloyd-Jones, Hugh 48, 60
Locatelli, Angela 261
Lodge, Thomas 87
Loehlin, James N. 11, 148
London 86, 87, 96, 125, 128, 202, 204, 219, 222, 226, 242, 281, 283
Longo, Oddone 4
Longus 58, 59
López Martínez, María Paz 60
Lord Chamberlain's Men 10
Lucan (Marcus Annaeus Lucanus) 205
Luhrmann, Baz (Mark Anthony L.) 66, 78, 79, 269, 291

Luzzi, Eusebio 268
Lynch Piozzi, Hester 227, 228

Maccari, Daniela 269
Macfarlane, Alan 165, 166
Machiavelli, Niccolò 142
Machin, Robert 167
MacMillan, Kenneth 26, 268, 269
Macready, William Charles 230
Madonna (Madonna Louise Veronica Ciccone) 262
Mancewicz, Aneta 288
Manciolino, Antonio 126
Mantua 40, 75, 76, 77, 78, 103, 107, 111, 112, 214, 215, 216, 217, 219
Manzini, Giovanni Battista 58
Maquerlot, Jean-Pierre 87
Marcus, Leah S. 28
Margherita, Queen consort of Italy 256
Marie Louise, Duchess of Parma 230, 231
Marius, Gaius 202–12
Marlowe, Christopher 84
Marozzo, Achille 126
marriage: novelistic motif 71, 73, 74, 75, 76, 77, 80, 88: civic function of m. 147–68
Marsden, Jean 203
Marshall, Cynthia 182
Marston, John 87, 192
Martelletto, Maria Grazia 255
Martial (Marcus Valerius Martialis) 58
Martin, John Jeffries 118
Martin, Selina 235
Martindale, Charles 59
Martindale, Michelle 59
Marx, Groucho 262
Masefield, John 197, 198
Massinger, Philip 6
Masuccio Salernitano (Tommaso Guardati) 51, 57, 58, 67, 68, 69, 79, 80
Mauro, Valerio 254
McGinn, Colin 28
McKernan, John 165
McLellan, Henry B. 234
Melchiori, Giorgio 10
Merini, Alda 257
Messeri Savorelli, Gabriella 60
Milan 37, 38, 39, 224
Miller, William 234
Milton, John 85
Misson, Maximilien 227
Mithridates 206

Montaigne, Michel de 188
Montfaucon, Bernard de 58
Montrose, Louis Adrian 159
Moore, Thomas 224, 255
Moretti, Franco 202
Moryson, Fynes 124
Muir, Kenneth 21, 46, 56
Mulcaster, Richard 8
Mullaney, Steven 3, 5, 7
Munday, Anthony 6
Munich 283
Munns, Jessica 206, 208
Munro, John James 20, 45, 62
Munro, Lucy 7, 45, 62
Murray, Barbara A. 204
Murray, John 230, 231, 233, 243
Myrrha 46, 59

Nagle, Betty Rose 59
Napoleon I Emperor of the French 228
Nashe, Thomas 35, 36
Neill, Michael 12, 171, 177
Nelthorpe, Frances 228
Nigri, Lucia 23, 61, 257
Ninus and Semiramis 54, 55, 56
Ninus see *Ninus and Semiramis*
Norman, Marc 213
North, Thomas 47
novella: Greek n. 45–57; Italian n. and its tradition 21, 23, 66–79, 82, 173, 179, 202, 227, 239, 241, 246, 253, 255, 294
Novy, Marianne 15
Nureyev, Rudolf 268

O'Neill, Eliza 221, 223
Oates, Titus 204
Orgel, Stephen 6, 28
Otto III, Holy Roman Emperor 280
Otway, Thomas 13, 14, 24, 29, 202–12
Ovid (Publius Ovidius Naso) 20, 21, 35, 39, 45, 46, 47, 48, 50, 52, 54, 55, 56, 59, 193

Padua 36, 37, 86, 227
Painter, William 40, 82, 83, 95, 126, 173, 174
Palfrey, Simon 17, 266, 291
Park, Honan 96
Parthenius, 47, 49, 50, 58, 60
Pasquin Valéry, Antoine Claude 230
Paster, Gail 85, 86
Patterson, Annabel 28
Payne, Nevil 209

Peck, Francis 235
Peele, Albert 165
Pellegrini, Federica 257
Peltonen, Markku 84, 90, 94, 120, 142
Pepys, Samuel 13
Perry, Reuben 230
Petrarch (Francesco Petrarca) 35, 193
Petrosawodsk 281, 282
Pfister, Manfred 228, 230
Phlegon Trallianus 52, 58
Photius 51, 61
Pienza 96
Piero della Francesca (Piero di Benedetto de' Franceschi) 96
Plato 61, 196
Platt, George P. 28
Plautus, Titus Maccius 35
Plutarch 47, 52, 58, 60, 205, 206, 207, 208
Pocock, John Greville Agard 94
Poliziano (Angelo Ambrogini) 58
Pollard, Tanya 6
Pollock, Frederick 230
Pompey (Gnaeus Pompeius Magnus), 205
Pope, Alexander 37, 138
Porter, Joseph A. 16
Powell, James 220
Power, Martin J. 128
private and public spaces 2, 3, 9, 10, 11, 12, 15, 16, 19, 21, 23, 24, 66, 67, 69–75, 79, 83, 85, 148, 154, 159–63, 165, 167, 172, 174–6, 179, 180, 208, 209, 284; and stagecraft 10–11, 177–8
Prokofiev, Sergej Sergeevič 268, 269, 274
Pugliatti, Paola 5, 28
Purcell, Henry 273
Purcell, Stephen 261
Puttenham, George 84
Pygmalion, 78
Pyramus and Thisbe 20, 45, 46, 48, 50, 53, 54, 55, 56, 57, 59, 60, 193, 202
Pyramus see *Pyramus and Thisbe*

Quasimodo, Salvatore 241

R&Jspace 240, 242, 253, 254; Juliet space/s 26, 241–2, 247, 251
Rabkin, Norman 29
Raine, Craig 189
Raleigh, Walter 47
Rankins, William 6

Renner, Theodor T. 60
Reynolds, Bryan 1, 115, 126, 132, 140, 142, 143, 172, 182, 239, 240, 251
Rhodes, Neil 2, 11, 27, 28, 29
Ribner, Irving 138, 139
Ricciarelli, Katia 257
Richard III, King of England 181
Richards, Ivor Armstrong 192
Richards, Jennifer 120
Richardson, Catherine 11
Righter, Anne 207
Rigino, Giovanni 181
Rizzoni, Jacopo 255
Roach, Joseph 9
Robbins, Jerome (*West Side Story*) 12, 79, 269, 291
Roberts, Sasha 15, 16, 168
Robortello, Francesco 97
Roe, Richard Paul 38, 40, 41
Rogers, Samuel 228, 230, 232, 233
romance 67, 68, 76, 79; Hellenistic r. 45–62; Shakespeare's r. 207
Romano, Angelo 174, 182, 256
Rome 2, 24, 28, 36, 96, 149, 205, 208, 210, 227, 256
Romeo and Juliet scenes: aubade 214; balcony 11, 16, 22, 67, 71, 109, 111, 134, 154, 213, 222, 223, 233, 234, 246; ball 104; tomb 11, 177, 178; wedding 110
Roper, Derek 280
Rosati, Gianpiero 54
Rose, Mark 83, 84, 87, 95, 96
Røstvig, Maren-Sofie 84
Rota, Nino 269
Rozett, Martha Tuck 288
Rudd, Niall 59, 60
Rykwert, Joseph 244

Sabbioneta 96
Salusbury, Sir John 24, 191, 192, 193
Sandy, Gerald N. 58
Saura, Carlos 26, 270, 272, 273, 275
Savorgnan, Antonio 68
Scala, Flaminio 66, 80
scapegoat(ing) 22, 23, 115, 116, 117, 127, 128, 129, 131, 134, 135, 136, 140, 239
Schechner, Richard 4, 8, 9, 12, 28, 247, 264
Schmitt-von Mühlenfels, Franz 59
Schwedt 27, 280
Scott, James, Duke of Monmouth 205
Scott, William 84

Segal, Janna 115, 126, 132, 140, 142, 143, 172, 182, 239, 240
Semiramis *see* Ninus and Semiramis
Seneca, Lucius Annaeus 35
Serpieri, Alessandro 28
Sextus Empiricus 47
Shakespace/s 1, 241
Shakespeare in Love see Norman; Stoppard
Shakespeare, William passim; works *All's Well That Ends Well* 194; *Antony and Cleopatra* 66, 189, 195, 242; *As You Like It* 194; *The Comedy of Errors* 41, 85, 195; *Coriolanus* 2, 28, 94, 96, 205; *Cymbeline* 193, 194, 200; *Hamlet* 14, 24, 138, 187, 188, 189, 194, 218, 293; 2 *Henry IV* 84, 96; 3 *Henry VI* 279; *Julius Caesar* 96, 139, 209; *King Lear* 194, 206; *Love's Labour's Lost* 188, 195; *Macbeth* 206; *The Merchant of Venice* 36, 141, 194; *Measure for Measure* 194; *The Merry Wives of Windsor* 85, 86, 194; *A Midsummer Night's Dream* 55, 60, 86, 193, 195, 202, 242, 279; *Much Ado about Nothing* 86, 141, 193; *Othello* 24, 36, 57, 194, 197; *The Phoenix and the Turtle* 24, 189, 190, 191, 192, 193, 194, 196, 197, 200, 273; *The Rape of Lucrece* 192; *Richard II* 24, 194, 206, 209, 242; *Romeo and Juliet* passim; *Sonnet 109* 195; *Sonnet 116* 195; *The Taming of the Shrew* 36, 125, 141; *The Tempest* 27, 95, 242, 279, 291; *Titus Andronicus* 60, 96, 288; *Troilus and Cressida* 193; *Twelfth Night, or What You Will* 194, 195; *The Two Gentlemen of Verona* 24, 37, 39, 40, 86, 95, 194, 195, 226; *Venus and Adonis* 192; *The Winter's Tale* 37, 200
Shaughnessy, Robert 2, 27
Shelley, Mary Wollstonecraft 231
Sherlock, Peter 164, 171, 172
Shrank, Cathy 28, 120, 141, 147, 148
Sidney, Philip 84, 95
Silk, Michael Stephen 28
Simeoni, Sara 257
Simoni, Renato 241
Sinfield, Alan 2, 28
Skelton, John 193
Slater, William J. 28, 29
Smith, Albert Richard 165, 231

Smith, Dudley 89
Smith, Henry 165
Smith, Thomas 29, 89
Snyder, Jon 85
Snyder, Susan 15, 17, 29, 83, 116, 129, 132, 134, 140, 143, 168, 296
Socrates 196
Soens, Adolph L. 142
Sokol, B. Jerry 149
Sokol, Mary 149
Sokolova, Bolka 280
Solimani, Ettore 249
Sondheim, Stephen (*West Side Story*) 12, 79, 291
Sophocles 48, 60
Spencer, Hazelton 203, 206
Spencer, Terence John Bew 59
Spenser, Edmund 84
stage and city 10, 11; Athens 5; London 5, 6, 7, 8, 28, 29, 87, 204, 205; public and/or private 213–23
statues (Romeo's and Juliet's) 56, 113, 114, 140, 162–3, 165, 168, 171–4, 181, 188, 200, 217, 222, 239, 240
Stephens, Susan A. 60
Stevens, Wallace 66
Stone, Lawrence 116, 126, 128, 142, 151, 157, 165
Stone, Rob 270
Stopford, Clare 278
Stoppard, Tom 213
Stow, John 87, 125
Stramaglia, Antonio 49, 60
Stratford-upon-Avon 25, 40, 86, 87, 187, 188, 196, 199, 213, 221, 222, 223, 225, 226, 233, 296
Strehler, Giorgio 241
Stubbes, Philip 5, 7, 152
suicide 15, 21, 24, 40, 45–57, 60, 76, 111, 112, 116, 120, 137, 138, 139, 143, 176, 180, 188, 189, 190, 206, 217, 255, 293
Sweet, Rosemary 228
Swinburne, Henry 154, 155, 166
Syracuse 50, 53, 85, 195

Tadpole, Christopher 231
Tamassia, Giovanna 257
Tamassia, Giulio 250
Tassinari, Lamberto 35
Tate, Nahum 204, 205, 207
Taylor, Gary 204
Terence (Publius Terentius Afro) 35
Tertullian (Quintus Septimius Florens Tertullianus) 5
Testa, Alberto 26, 268, 269
Theobald, Lewis 38, 227, 235
Thisbe *see* Pyramus and Thisbe
Thomas, Julia 226
Thomas, William 35
Thomson, Leslie 177, 178
Timbs, John 230
Tommasoli, Nicola 257
Torre, Roberta 12
Tübingen 27, 281, 282, 284, 288, 289
Turner, Victor 3, 6, 9, 28
Tylus, Jane 67

urban space 87–95, 101, 111–12

Valls-Russell, Janice 60
Van Caenegem, Raoul Charles 89
Vandersmissen, Marc 60
Vaughan, John, 3rd Earl of Carbery 204
Vaughan, William 153
Venice 36, 68, 89, 96, 205, 224, 228, 268
Vernant, Jean-Pierre 4
Verona passim; Arche 247, 255, 257; Cittadella 182, 183; Juliet's house (Capulets' house; [dal] Cappello house; *hospitium a Cappello*; via Cappello) 11, 18, 19, 25, 26, 41, 71, 86, 93, 104, 105, 106, 108, 109, 110, 112, 122, 131, 132, 136, 157, 158, 159, 167, 175, 177, 179, 180, 214, 226, 232, 233, 234, 241, 242–9, 250, 251, 253, 256, 257, 268; Castelvecchio 74, 246, 254, 294, 295; Juliet's (Capulets') tomb (crypt, vault) 11, 14, 15, 19, 23, 25, 26, 29, 40, 61, 67, 76, 77, 78, 79, 86, 105, 108, 111, 112, 113, 114, 139, 162, 163, 164, 168, 171–81, 182, 183, 188, 217, 218, 225–35, 239, 240, 241, 242–9, 250, 251, 253, 254, 255, 256, 257; Ponte Nuovo 255; Romeo's house (Montagues' house, Casa Nogarola) 104, 105, 255; St Francis church and monastery (San Francesco al Corso) 40, 41, 73, 102, 108, 157, 161, 179, 182, 183, 225, 247, 248, 255; St Peter church 41, 112, 142
Vidal-Naquet, Pierre 4
Villafranca 41, 82, 126; *see also* Freetwon, Villefranche
Villefranche 83, 95; *see also* Freetwon, Villafranca
Virgil (Publius Vergilius Maro) 35

Wagner, Richard 291
Waldie, Jane 228, 230
Wallace, John M. 206
Walsh, Jaquelyn W. 203
Ward, Adolphus William 206
Ward, Joseph P. 5
Warren, Roger 38
Watkins, Thomas 228
Watson, Nicola J. 25, 225, 226, 255
Watson, Robert N. 182
Weever, John 164, 165, 168
Wehrli, Fritz 48
Weimann, Robert 28, 127, 265
Weinberger, Jerry 16, 17, 123, 125, 140, 142, 161
Weis, René 114
Wells, Stanley 14, 20, 87, 167
West Side Story see Bernstein; Laurents; Robbins; Sondheim; Wise
Whetstone, George 151, 162
White, Robert S. 13
Whittier, Gayle 29
Wikander, Matthew H. 208
Wiles, David 28
Williams, Helen Maria 219, 220
Wills, Richard 84, 95
Wilshire, Bruce 28
Wilson, Benjamin 218, 222

Wilson, James 228
Wilson, Peter 28
Wilson, Thomas 141, 147
Winkler, John J. 60
Wise, Robert (*West Side Story*) 12, 79, 291
Withington, Philip 97
Wolff, Samuel Lee 58
Woods, Gillian 14
Worthen, William B. 260, 263, 267, 275
Woudhuysen, Henry R. 196
Wrocław 288
Wyatt, Thomas 47

Xenophon Ephesius 45, 50, 51, 54, 57, 58, 59, 61, 62
Xylander, Guilelmus (Wilhelm Holtzmann) 52

York, Michael 39

Zagata, Pier 255
Zanolli, Maurizio 254
Zeffirelli, Franco 26, 234, 266, 268, 269, 270
Zelnick, Stephen 18
Zumiani, Daniela 243, 245, 247, 255

For Product Safety Concerns and Information please contact our EU
representative GPSR@taylorandfrancis.com
Taylor & Francis Verlag GmbH, Kaufingerstraße 24, 80331 München, Germany

www.ingramcontent.com/pod-product-compliance
Lightning Source LLC
Chambersburg PA
CBHW070232230426
43664CB00014B/2278